Multinational Corporations in China

Yadong Luo

Multinational Corporations in China

Benefiting from Structural Transformation

Copenhagen Business School Press
HANDELSHØJSKOLENS FORLAG

Cover designed by Kontrapunkt
Book designed by Jørn Ekstrøm
Set in Plantin by ABK-Sats, Denmark
Printed by Reproset, Copenhagen, Denmark

ISBN 87-16-13490-7

Asia Business Development Series

Distribution

Scandinavia:
Munksgaard/DBK, Siljangade 2-8, P.O. Box 1731,
DK-2300 Copenhagen S, Denmark,
phone: +45 3269 7788, fax: +45 3269 7789

North America:
Copenhagen Business School Press
Books International Inc.
P.O. Box 605
Hendon, VA 20172-0605, USA
phone: +1 703 661 1500, fax: +1 703 661 1 1501
E-mail: intpubmkt@aol.com

Rest of the World:
Marston Book Services, P.O. Box 269,
Abingdon, Oxfordshire, OX14 4YN, UK
phone: +44 (0) 1235 465500, fax: +44 (0) 1235 465555
E-mail Direct Customers: direct.order@marston.co.uk
E-mail Booksellers: trade.order@marston.co.uk

Contents

List of Tables

Preface

This book addresses how multinational corporations (MNCs) can maximize economic benefits earned from structural transformation of various industries in the People's Republic of China, the largest emerging economy in the world. Most of Chinese industries are now undergoing structural transformation, which presents a great deal of new opportunities as well as a tremendous amount of uncertainty to MNCs interested or active in this market. In order to help MNCs best prepare to exploit the former and circumvent the latter, this book discusses structural dynamics of major industries, identifies opportunities and challenges of these industries appealing to MNCs, elaborates industrial policies stipulated by the Chinese government, analyzes various structural attributes of each industry, and provides guidelines to select an appropriate Chinese industry. Several case studies are also included to show how MNCs enter, invest, and operate in this promising yet complex market.

This book is written for international executives and business school students who have interest in doing business in China. Although dozens of books on doing business in this country are in the market, none of them, to the best of my knowledge, has systematically delineated insights of every major industry in which MNCs may participate. In addition to presenting industrial and structural dynamics, this book is intended to provide important managerial lessons and insightful practical guidance for international executives. It is my hope that this book, characterized by a strong combination of succinct analysis and managerial recommendations, will cast some new light on structural dynamics of Chinese industries.

In the course of writing this book, I have benefited from financial support by the Center for International Business Education and Research (CIBER) at the University of Hawaii. I am also indebted to a number of friends and former colleagues at the Ministry of Foreign Trade and Economic Cooperation (MOFTEC), China, for their help in obtaining the most recent information and policies. Lastly, this book is dedicated to my family in recognition of their patience and understanding throughout this project.

Yadong Luo, Ph.D
College of Business Administration
University of Hawaii

1. Multinational Corporations in China

Chapter Purpose

The past two decades have been the era of globalization, with rapid growth of international trade, financial flows, and foreign direct investment (FDI) increasingly affecting more and more.During this period, China has undergone an unprecedented structural transformation and has established about 320,000 foreign-invested enterprises, becoming the largest FDI recipient among developing countries. This chapter will describe the background of multinational corporations (MNCs) and FDI in China. The discussion is divided into four sections. While the first section provides an overview of major characteristics of MNCs and FDI in the country, the second section articulates major emerging problems concerning FDI in China at the turn of this century. The third section outlines a series of new FDI policies the Chinese government has adopted, which will have an enduring impact on investments and operations of MNCs as they proceed into the next century. Finally, the chapter highlights the Chinese macroeconomic environment, including its past achievements, present problems, and strategic outlook.

1.1 MNCs in China: An Overview

International production by MNCs has grown continuously in recent years, as shown in Table 1.1. All major indicators related to MNC activities demonstrated high rates of growth over the past years. Specifically, worldwide FDI stock, which constitutes the capital base for MNC corporations, rose by over 10% annually in the past decade. It is held by a minimum of 53,000 MNCs – large and small (*World Investment Report*, 1998). The regional distribution of outward FDI stock is heavily skewed towards developed countries, indicating the fact that in the past, most FDI originated and stayed in developed countries, although there are some noticeable recent increases in the stock of developing countries. The share of South,

East and South-east Asia in world inward FDI nearly doubled during the past decade. Table 1.2 lists the world's largest contributors and receivers of FDI. It shows that China is the second largest recipient in the world of FDI, surpassed only by the United States.

Table 1.1: Major Indicators of FDI during 1986-1997

Item	Annual Growth Rate (%)			
	1986-1990	1991 1995	1996	1997
FDI inflows	23.6	20.1	1.9	18.6
FDI outflows	27.1	15.1	-0.5	27.1
FDI inward stock	18.2	9.7	12.2	12.7
FDI outward stock	21.0	10.3	11.5	13.7
Cross-border M&A	21.0	30.2	15.5	45.2
Foreign affiliates sales	16.3	13.4	6.0	7.3
Foreign affiliates assets	18.3	24.4	12.0	13.0

Source: Adapted from UNCTAD: *World Investment Report* 1998, p.2

Table 1.2: The World's Top Contributors and Recipients of FDI, 1996

	FDI Inflows ($bil)		FDI Outflows ($bil)	
Rank	Economy	Value	Economy	Value
1	United States	76.5	United States	74.8
2	China	40.8	United Kingdom	34.1
3	United Kingdom	26.0	France	30.4
4	France	22.0	Germany	29.5
5	Belgium & Luxem.	14.1	Hong Kong, China	26.4
6	Brazil	11.1	Japan	23.4
7	Singapore	9.4	Netherlands	23.1
8	Mexico	8.2	Switzerland	11.6
9	Netherlands	7.8	Canada	8.5
10	Spain	6.5	Belgium & Luxem.	8.4

Source: Adapted from UNCTAD: *World Investment Report* 1998, p.11

China has been remarkably successful in attracting FDI and directing it to help promote the country's long-term development plans, despite economic ups and downs and FDI inflows along the way. From 1979 to the end of 1998, Chinese authorities approved the establishment of over 300,000 foreign-invested enterprises (FIEs) involving $522.4 billion in foreign capital. The actual value of FDI during this period reached $265.72 billion (see Table 1.3). In 1997, FDI in China accounted for over one-half of the flow into Asia and 11 percent of the world total. The country continues to maintain its position as the second largest FDI recipient in the world and the largest among developing countries. China's FDI boom (invested value) has now lasted for seven consecutive years since 1992.

Contractual FDI reached $52.13 billion in 1998, a 2.21 percent increase and first growth since 1996. Materialized FDI hit $45.58 billion, up 0.67 percent. Unlike some Asian nations, China has maintained economic stability and continues to be a fast-growing economy with a stable currency value. FDI from the European Union and the United States to China has surged since 1997, partially making up the decline from the Asian region. As of May 1999, China has utilized over U.S.$ 280 billion of FDI in the past 20 years; and investors from over 170 countries and regions have built over 320,000 FIEs in China.

FDI has undergone three phases in China. Phase 1 (1979-1985), the initial stage of foreign investment in China, started with the promulgation of the Joint Venture Law by the Chinese government in 1979, and the establishment of four Special Economic Zones (SEZs) in Guangdong and Fujian provinces where preferential economic policies were pursued. In 1984, 14 coastal cities were opened to foreign investment, resulting in a spread of FDI from the SEZs to other coastal regions and led to the first boom of FDI in 1984-85. However, the initial boom ended in late 1985 because of high inflation and a lack of legal clarity about FDI. During this stage, foreign investments were concentrated in small-sized assembling and processing for exports.

Phase 2 (1986-1989) proceeded with the Chinese government publication of the 'Provisions for the Encouragement of Foreign Investment' in October 1986 and was followed by a set of central regulations to implement them as well as a flurry of provincial and municipal-level regulations. These Provisions and regulations clari-

Table 1.3: Actual Value of FDI in China: 1979-1998 (U.S.$100 million)

Year	Materialized Value of FDI
1979-1983	1,802
1984	1,258
1985	1,661
1986	1,874
1987	2,314
1988	3,194
1989	3,392
1990	3,487
1991	4,366
1992	11,007
1993	27,515
1994	33,767
1995	37,521
1996	41,726
1997	45,260
1998	45,580
1979-1998	26572

Sources: *China Statistical Yearbook*, annual editions

fied the legal environment for FDI and provided solutions to some major problems facing foreign-invested enterprises such as foreign exchange balance requirement. To encourage foreign investment in high technology industries, all open coastal cities set up the Economic and Technical Development Zones (ETDZ) where extra tax breaks and other incentives were offered. The improved investment environment promoted a quick recovery of FDI after 1986. Over 70 percent of FDI projects were involved in manufacturing industries in this period. However, because of worsening economic and political conditions, the new investment boom ended in mid-1989.

Phase 3 (1990-Present) commenced upon recognition of the negative reaction of foreign investors to the worsening investment climate, with the Chinese government issuing the Amendments to the Joint Venture Law in April 1990. These amendments codified several rules designed to encourage investment. In 1991, the Income Tax Law for Enterprises with Foreign Capital and Foreign Enterprises was passed and standardized the income tax rates for different forms of FIEs. In 1992, the Chinese government adopted a 'socialist market economy' strategy and sped up market-oriented reforms. A set of commercial laws and regulations were passed to improve the legal framework and policy settings in which foreign business operated. As a result, foreign investment surged after 1992. As of 1994, foreign investment in China entered a new stage of adjustment and consolidation, resulting in some new features. The average capital size of foreign investment projects increased, with the main focus shifting to large infrastructure and manufacturing projects. The growth rate of FDI decreased to a sustainable level from an unusually high level.

FIEs have played a major role in the modernization of the Chinese economy. As shown in Table 1.4, total industrial output of FIEs reached 18.6 percent in 1997. Total national export volume of FIEs climbed to 41 percent in the same year, with a tax contribution to the nation's total of 13.2 percent. FDI already accounted for 17 percent of total gross domestic investment in 1996, and by the end of 1997, 17.5 million Chinese were employed in FIEs, 12.7 million more than six years before.

FDI can affect a local economy at both the macro and micro levels. At the micro level, FDI may influence the technological and managerial efficiency of joint ventures and local firms through technology transfer, labor training, and spill-over effects. At the macro level, FDI may affect both 'real' macroeconomic variables (e.g., domestic investment, economic growth, employment, exports, and imports) and 'financial' variables (e.g., interest rates, exchange rates, inflation). The macroeconomic impact of FDI in China is primarily reflected by its effect on 'real' economic variables, as opposed to 'financial' variables which are essentially controlled by the governmental administrative force.

Recently, several studies found that FDI significantly promoted the economic growth of China during the 1979-1996 period by contributing to domestic capital formation, increasing exports, and creating new employment. Moreover, FDI improved the productive efficiency and resource allocation efficiency of Chinese domestic sectors by transferring technology and facilitating inter-regional and inter-sector flows of labor and capital. While realizing these benefits, some side effects must be acknowledged as

Table 1.4: Contribution of FDI to China's Economy: 1991-1997

Item	91	92	93	94	95	96	97
FDI inflows ($bil)	4.4	11.2	27.5	33.8	35.8	40.8	45.3
Average amount per project ($mil)	0.9	1.2	1.3	1.8	2.5	n/a	n/a
FDI/gross domestic investment(%)	3.9	7.4	12.7	17.3	15.1	17.0	14.8
FDI stock/GDP (%)	5.6	7.1	10.2	17.6	18.8	24.7	n/a
FIE exports ($bil)	12.0	17.4	25.2	34.7	46.9	61.5	75.0
FIE exports/national exports (%)	17.0	20.4	27.5	28.7	31.3	41.0	41.0
FIE output/national output (%)	5.0	6.0	9.0	11.0	13.0	n/a	18.6
Number of employees (mil)	4.8	6.0	10.0	14.0	16.0	17.0	17.5
Tax contribution as share of total	n/a	4.1	n/a	n/a	10.0	n/a	13.2

Source: Adapted from UNCTAD: *World Investment Report*, 1996, p. 198; 1998, p. 204

well. These include worsening environmental pollution as a result of shifting polluting industries to China, and income losses for the host state and firms as a result of using transfer pricing among foreign affiliates by MNCs.

FIEs have diverse foreign sources. Tables 1.5 lists the top ten countries or regions that directly invested in China in 1995 and 1996. The top ten sources together constitute 92.61 percent of China's total FDI in 1996. Amongst them, Hong Kong and Macau took the lead in direct investment in the mainland, contributing $21.46 billion, or 51.43 percent of the national total in 1996. They were followed in order by Japan (8.85 percent), Taiwan (8.34 percent), the United States (8.25 percent), Singapore (5.39 percent), South Korea (3.60 percent), and the United Kingdom (3.12 percent).

Interestingly, of the top ten foreign sources, five come from Asian developing countries or regions. They collectively contributed about 70 percent of the total actual FDI in China in 1996, whereas their counterparts from Japan, the U.S., the U.K., and Germany accounted for only 21.46 percent (Table 1.6). The accumulated number of FDI by the end of 1996 also suggests that FDI contributed by developing countries has been more than three times that contributed by developed countries over the last seventeen years.

Although Hong Kong and Taiwan are the top two investment sources, in a broad sense, they simply move relatively labor-intensive activities into China in order to escape rising labor costs and space constraints at home. Moreover, the average size of investment from these two sources is relatively small. For instance, the average equity pledged by U.S. investors is nearly twice as high as that put forth by investors from Hong Kong and about 50 percent higher than those from Taiwan and Southeast Asia.

Table 1.5: Foreign Direct Investment in China from Top 10 Countries or Regions in 1995-1997 (in U.S.$ million)

Rank	Country/Region	1995	1996	1997	% in 1997
1	Hong Kong/Macao	20,625	21,458	21,954	41.91
2	Japan	3,212	3,692	4,390	8.38
3	United States	3,084	3,444	3,461	6.61
4	Taiwan	3,165	3,482	3,342	6.38
5	Singapore	1,861	2,247	2,607	4.98
6	Republic of Korea	1,047	1,504	2,228	4.25
7	United Kingdom	915	1,302	1,860	3.55
8	Virgin Islands	304	539	1,717	3.28
9	Germany	391	519	1,009	1.93
10	France	287	425	476	0.91

Source: China Statistical Yearbook, 1997 (p.606-607) and 1998 (p.603-604)

While Hong Kong and Taiwan investors emphasize labor-intensive and simple industrial processing for light industrial and textile goods aimed at the international market, the U.S. and European firms tend to place emphasis on capital or technologically intensive manufacturing sectors in an effort to gain access to the growing Chinese domestic market. Japanese investors, while also interested in China's domestic market, have placed less emphasis than their U.S. counterparts on manufacturing and have instead become more involved in various forms of property development.

FDI in China has been active in a variety of industries. Table 1.6 presents industrial patterns of foreign direct investment in China in 1996, with the industrial sector accounting for 68.90 percent of total FDI and leading all other sectors in influence on the economy. The real estate and utility sector follows, involving $12,85 billion in investments or 17.54 percent of the total. Commercial and food services, construction, transportation and telecommunication services, and agriculture are also important sectors, ranking from third to sixth, respectively.

Table 1.6: Approved FDI in China By Sectors (1996)

Sector	# of Projects	Value ($mil)
Agriculture	812	1,139
Industry	18,280	50,486
Construction	387	2,001
Transportation & telecommunication	196	1,599
Commerce & food service	1,655	2,347
Real estate & utility	1,961	12,851
(Tourist hotels)	(81)	(291)
Health care & sports	128	354
Education, culture & arts	63	171
Scientific research	124	175
Others	950	2,154
Total	24,556	73,277

Source: *China Statistical Yearbook*, 1997, p. 611

The different sectors have idiosyncratic patterns of FDI growth. FDI in agriculture, industry, transportation and telecommunication services, and health care and social welfare services has boomed over the past years, growing from 12 percent to 75 percent between 1993 and 1995. FDI in other sectors, especially real estate and construction have slowed down. For instance, foreign investment in hotel and construction sectors decreased by 55.35 percent and 10.2 percent, respectively, during the same period. This reflects structural changes in Chinese FDI policies over the past few years.

Foreign investors are generally free to choose their mode of entry into the deregulated Chinese industries. Table 1.7 depicts the recent pattern of foreign investment, including both FDI and foreign loans. FDI dominated in foreign capital inflows, representing about 90 percent of the nation's total (in 1996). Among FDI in 1997, equity joint ventures accounted for 40.64 percent, wholly foreign-owned enterprise represented 34.62 percent, and contractual joint ventures the remaining 23.66 percent. Longitudinally, the ratio of wholly foreign-owned ventures has grown in recent years, having been only 7 percent prior to 1990. Nevertheless, the equity joint venture remains the primary entry mode used by MNCs to expand to the Chinese market.

Table 1.7: Approved Foreign Investment in China by Forms (U.S.$mil)

Investment Forms	1995	1996	1997
Foreign Direct Investment	91,282	73,276	51,003
Equity JVs	39,741	31,876	20,726
Contractual JVs	17,825	14,297	12,066
Wholly foreign-owned	33,658	26,810	17,658
Joint exploration	57	293	402
Share enterprise			151
Other Foreign Investment	635	371	4,183
International lease	42	33	289
Compensation trade	404	129	124
Processing & assembling	189	209	1,696
Stock/bond issuance			2,074
Foreign Loans	11,288	7,962	5,872
Government loans	4,754	4,203	754
Loans from int'l organizations	3,680	1,682	3,732
Commercial/export loans	2,854	2,077	1,386
Total	103,205	81,610	61,058

Sources: *China Statistical Yearbook*, 1997 (p.605) and 1998 (p.602)

In closing, China has experienced an unprecedented boom in FDI inflows over the past two decades. The boom has been fueled by various factors, including the country's large and continuously growing domestic market, its export-oriented strategy and successful penetration of world markets, the liberalization of its internal-industrial upgrading to neighboring economies, as well as the low level of FDI stock relative to the size of the economy until recently. The latest survey from Kang Management Adviser Company indicated that China has replaced Brazil, becoming the second most popular region among foreign investors after the U.S.. This rank reflects the confidence index of FDI, as perceived by presidents, finance chiefs, and other senior staff from the world's top 1,000 companies. By now, 400 of the 500 most famous MNCs have invested in China. From 1999 to 2005, China will import equipments, technologies and products totaling U.S.$ 1500 billion. At the same time, tariffs on industrial products will be reduced to 10 percent. MNCs, therefore, face opportunities in both investment and export.

1.2 Emerging Problems at the Turn of the Century

On the negative side, China is presently faced with difficulties in attracting foreign investment. Both China's exports and inward foreign investment dropped in the first half of 1999 due to the adverse effect of the Asian financial crisis (a large proportion of FDI originated from Asian countries) and a deflated national economy (especially, stagnant consumption). China registered a decline in FDI in terms of both contractual volume (-19.87 percent) and paid-in volume (-9.21 percent) in the first half of 1999. Another sign that FDI inflows may be slowing is a drop of 20-30 percent in each of the past two years of the total value of newly pledged foreign investment contracts, indicating that growth in future actual foreign investment inflows will soon likely drop as well. As China tries to move upstream and encourage high value-added, high-technology investments, newer investments have not yet caught up with its program, nor with declines in labor-intensive, low-cost joint ventures.

This slowdown raises the question of whether the FDI boom in China is nearing its end. The relevance of this question is twofold. First, considering the position of FDI in both gross fixed capital formation and GDP in China (among the highest in the world), a major change in FDI inflows may have wide-ranging consequences for the Chinese economy. Second, developments with respect to FDI in China will have a sizable impact on FDI trends in Asia and the developing world generally, since China has become the single largest FDI recipient among developing countries and the second largest recipient worldwide.

To the extent that FDI approvals are indicative, they do suggest that actual flows may decline in the coming years. Approvals have been declining for some years, falling from $111 billion in 1993 to $52 billion in 1997. Experience suggests that decreased or increased approvals that occur prior to a given period of approvals will affect the inflows to follow, meaning that the decline in approvals by 20 percent in 1996 and 30 percent in 1997 may be followed by a decline in actual inflows in the short-to-medium term. Various developments in pull and push factors of FDI in China suggest that such a prediction is plausible.

FDI tends to be positively correlated with GDP growth. Hence, reduced economic growth in China can be expected to have a negative impact on FDI inflows. Although GDP growth has remained high in China (at 7.8 percent in 1998), it is below the double-digit growth of earlier years. More importantly, GDP projections point to a further slowdown, to about 7 percent in 1999. Weak demand in China would in particular depress inflow of market-seeking FDI.

FDI to China's industrial sector will be the first affected by worsening demand. It may turn out that the massive foreign and domestic investment of the recent past resulted in excess capacity in a number of industries, such as some consumer electrical and electronics products, textiles and clothing, and other light industrial products. The capacity of such industries to absorb further FDI inflows may thus be limited in the next few years. This is true especially of industries in the coastal area, in which FDI has been concentrated. Competition in the coastal area for sales in the domestic market is becoming more intense and, in addition to foreign enterprises, a few domestic firms are emerging as strong competitors. This suggests that the "golden rush" of investors into certain manufacturing industries of China may be coming to an end. The pressure on profit rates stemming from excess capacity and increased competition could reduce the incentive for the latecomers among MNCs to undertake new FDI. At the same time, established

MNCs are likely to postpone sequential FDI unless a reasonable balance between demand and supply is restored.

A high percentage of FDI inflow, particularly from small international companies, went into labor-intensive export processing operations. Several factors have played a role in creating a new set of conditions: (1) wage increases, particularly in China's coastal areas where FDI is concentrated, are eroding incentives for MNCs to establish labor-intensive export processing operations; (2) despite special efforts by the government, MNCs' relocation of investment from China's coastal regions to the interior has not been significant. MNCs have preferred, rather, to move to other low-income countries where transportation costs are lower and infrastructure more advanced than in China's interior provinces; (3) for certain labor-intensive products, even though they remain internationally competitive, the potential of exporting from China is constrained by trade barriers in major export markets (import quotas, anti-dumping provisions, etc.). In addition, the demand for labor-intensive products in these markets is likely to decline if expectations of an economic slowdown in the world economy turn out to be correct. The recession in Japan is of particular relevance here; and (4) China's price competitiveness in international markets has been reduced vis-à-vis that of a number of South-east Asian countries which recently devalued their currencies. This could break the flying-geese pattern of industrialization in Asia, from which labor-intensive industries in China have benefited in the past.

These problems could not only discourage profit-driven FDI in China but also affect the country's impressive export performance. In the short run, exports will indeed likely slow down, especially to South-east Asian countries currently affected by the financial crisis. With regard to total exports, a decline in annual growth from 20 per cent in 1997 to 3 per cent in 1998 and 1999 has been forecast.

FDI in China has mainly come from within the Asian region. Hong Kong, Taiwan, Singapore, Japan, the Republic of Korea, Thailand, and Malaysia rank among the top investors, accounting for 80 percent of China's inward FDI stock. The share of these countries in approved FDI in China in recent years is also high. It is questionable, however, to what extent these approvals will be realized, given the current constraints on outward investment facing some of these countries. A significant decline of flow from other Asian economies to China can thus be expected in coming years. In 1998, for instance, contracted FDI was up only 2.5 percent through the third quarter over the same period last year, to $53.58 billion. Utilized investment for the period was down 0.6 percent to $31.4 billion.

The composition of FDI in China is also changing. Though Asian investment still constitutes the majority of FDI, its share slipped in the first three quarters of 1998, accounting for 74 percent of projects (down 3 percent from 1997), 53 percent of contracted investment (down 9 percent), and 70 percent of utilized investment (down 4 percent). Despite a 36 percent increase in investment from Singapore over the period, utilized investment from Asia dropped over 10 percent. Investment from Hong Kong, which constituted 43 percent of utilized FDI, fell almost 11 percent. As capital flows from other parts of Asia slow, the share of FDI from the United States and Europe is growing. Utilized investment from the United States and Europe was up 45 and 20 percent, respectively, over the same period in 1997. The most dramatic increase in FDI came from the Virgin Islands, which rose 198 percent.

To sum up, FDI in China will probably decline in the short run. Although the financial crisis in Asia has not directly affected China, its indirect repercussions are as yet unclear. If they are serious, and if the country's economic growth slows down considerably, various structural weaknesses may come to the surface and erode investors' confidence in the short and medium term. It should be noted, however, that FDI flows are an incremental measure, representing additions to a stock of assets for production; it cannot be expected that they will grow forever at the same rate, even if a host country continues to have a relatively high rate of economic growth. As long as flows fluctuate around a relatively high level, they contribute, other things being equal, to the increase in stocks and play an important role in the host economy.

However, China's attractiveness to most foreign investors remains strong. The liberalization of FDI policies is still under way. Some industries that had been off limits to foreign investors, including air transport, general aviation, retail trade, foreign trade, banking, insurance, accounting, auditing, legal services, the mining and smelting of precious metals, and the prospecting, extracting and processing of diamonds and other precious non-metal minerals, are gradually being opened. Moreover, there is a significant potential for FDI participation in infrastructure. Several build-operate-transfer (BOT) schemes have already been concluded. Foreign investors are now allowed to acquire state-owned enterprises. Finally, according to the Ministry of Foreign Trade and Economic Cooperation (MOFTEC), the following tax policies will guide FDI in the future: (1) General preferential tax rate: For manufacturing businesses, a preferential income tax rate of 33 percent will apply; (2) Reduced tax rate extended to special areas: For FIEs located in the SEZs or manufacturing businesses in the economic and technological development zones (ETDZs), a 15 percent income tax will apply. The income tax rate of 24 percent will apply to foreign-invested manufacturing enterprises located in the old town of a city located in the coastal economic open areas, SEZs, or ETDZs; (3) Reduced tax rate extended to special sectors: For Sino-foreign joint ventures which meet certain qualifications and engage in energy, transportation, port or pier construction, a 15 percent income tax rate will apply; (4) Preferential tax rate extended to special businesses: The flow of FDI to high-tech businesses or export-oriented businesses will continuously be encouraged. Once confirmed as these two types of businesses, they will be granted special tax incentives; (5) Manufacturing FIEs with a term of operation over 10 years will continue to be granted tax exemption for two years starting from the profit-making year and given a half rate the three years thereafter; (6) If foreign investors make additional investments by profits made from the FIEs, they shall get a refund of 40 percent of the income tax they have already paid.

As a result of the above, the great importance of FDI to China's economy will remain. Thus, while FDI inflows to China will likely fall in the next few years, there is reason to believe that this will be a temporary adjustment rather than a response to a change in general economic factors. One strong piece of evidence supporting this speculation is that the top 12 MNCs from the United States that already have the biggest stakes in China are maintaining their commitment through ongoing construction and investment. In conclusion, China will remain one of the top FDI destinations in the world marketplace.

1.3 New Policies in the Turn of the Century

Although China has more than 150 major laws and regulations that apply to foreign investment, the legal and regulatory system in general lacks transparency and consistent enforcement. As an institutional response to the Asian financial crisis, dwindling foreign investments, and falling exports, the State Council and its ministerial organs enacted a series of new laws, regulations, and policies during 1998 and 1999. Both existing or new MNCs will have to deal with these policies which constitute an FDI-related institutional framework that will have a sustaining influence on both investments and operations well beyond the Year 2000.

Investment Guidelines

Some new measures have been introduced to simplify procedures for foreign investors, but ambiguities still abound. New investment guidelines were contained in two documents issued in June of 1995, the Provisional Regulations Guiding Foreign Investment and the Catalog of Industries Open to Foreign Investment. These guidelines clarified existing practices and for the first time, detailed the sectors in which foreign investment was encouraged and those in which it was restricted or completely prohibited. The government's stated intention in promulgating the guidelines was to channel foreign investment into infrastructure building and basic industries. In the case of the latter, it especially encouraged involvement in advanced technologies and high value-added, export-oriented products. In December of 1997, the Catalog of Industries was reissued in revised form, with a number of additions and deletions in all three categories of foreign investment-encouraged, restricted, and prohibited areas.

The Chinese central government has introduced measures very recently to prevent speculative investment (e.g., in real estate) and has forced some 'phantom' foreign affiliates to terminate operations. It has also strengthened monitoring by setting up 'administrative procedures for appraising foreign invested property' in early 1994. The appraisals aim at preventing speculative investments or using inferior capital equipment. China has also become more selective in screening FDI projects to ensure compliance with economic development objectives. This is reflected in the government's newly adopted FDI guidelines that are in line with the national development plan and the country's industrial policies. Moreover, the nation is targeting large MNC investments. This is reflected in the incentives aimed at attracting large MNCs to technologically advanced or capital intensive projects.

China is making efforts to level the playing field for domestic and foreign firms in order to facilitate its entry into the World Trade Organization (WTO). Policy measures since 1994 have been adopted to eliminate preferences for foreign investors. These preferences have distorted markets and have led to a bias against domestic firms. Such measures include the unification of the tax system and the elimination of exemption of import duties granted to FIEs.

China continues to firmly back its policy to open the economic and technological development zones (ETDZs) and hopes to increase their use of overseas investment. ETDZ is a pioneering part of China's reforms and open door policy. In a decade and a half of exploration and construction, they have even expanded to central and western China, which now has 32 state-level such zones. They account for much of China's overseas investment and still have many preferential policies.

Foreign companies continue to prefer strong management control and have taken advantage of China's 1996 policy to allow greater flexibility in establishing wholly foreign-owned enterprises (WFOEs). WFOEs have become the favored investment vehicle for FDI, making up almost 50 percent of all projects in 1999. While 7,395 WFOEs were approved, a 9 percent rise over the previous year, only 5,841 equity joint ventures were approved, a decrease of almost 11 percent. Most contracted FDI went into WFOEs, which accounted for roughly 43 percent of total FDI. EJVs accounted for only 34 percent of total FDI; nevertheless, they still make up the lion's share of utilized investment, perhaps reflecting past commitments. Only about a third of utilized investment went into WFOEs.

The decline in foreign investment appears to have attracted the Chinese government's attention. Recent moves, including the reinstatement of certain capital equipment duty exemptions, accelerated approval procedures, and attempts to abolish illicit fees, are aimed at increasing FDI. The government is now planning for the opening of China's service industries to foreign investment, promoting investment in central and western China, and increasing investment incentives for multinational corporations. Problems for foreign investors persist, however. New administrative procedures for obtaining foreign exchange are complicating bilateral trade, causing costly delays for current-account transactions and restricting capital-account transactions. The government moves to re-evaluate both locally approved retail ventures and the so-called "Chinese-Chinese-Foreign" telecom investment structure as well as to ban direct selling has called into question the security of investments in China. Though overall investment flows for 1998 are likely to approximate the previous year's total of $45 billion, they could drop in 1999 unless China takes concrete measures to improve a deteriorating investment environment.

Recent policy changes are expected to have certain impacts on FDI over the next few years. The movement towards national treatment will discourage 'round-tripping' (that is, capital outflows that are repatriated back in China disguised as FDI, taking advantage of tax and regulatory incentives to FIEs) and 'phantom' foreign ventures. Tighter screening and monitoring of FDI projects may significantly reduce the overvaluation of FDI that takes place through incorrect invoicing of imported equipment.

Industrial Structure

The Chinese government now puts greater emphasis on ensuring that new foreign investments in China are in industries and in geographic locations that the government wants to encourage. Over the past three years, China has implemented policies introducing further incentives for investment in high-tech industries and in the inland parts of the country. Incentives currently available include priority treatment in obtaining basic infrastructure services and significant reductions in national and local income taxes, land fees, and import and export duties. Special preferences have also been established for projects involving high-technology and export-oriented investments. Foreign investors also receive benefits by reinvesting profits. They obtain a refund of 40 percent of the tax paid on their share of income if the profit is reinvested in China for at least five years, and a full refund if the reinvestment is in high-technology or export-oriented enterprises. Many foreign companies have adopted a strategic plan for China that requires reinvestment of profits for growth and expansion.

Policies on restricting and prohibiting foreign investment have for the most part been designed to protect domestic industries for political, economic or national security reasons. For example, in April of 1996, China eliminated duty and value-added tax exemptions for equipment imported as part of a foreign investment, thereby significantly increasing the costs of foreign investment in joint venture and wholly foreign-owned manufacturing. Not only did the government receive complaints about the elimination of these incentives, but it also noted a drop in foreign investment in some of the industries it wanted to encourage. So in January of 1998, it reintroduced the duty and VAT exemptions. In addition, the exemptions were extended retroactively to cover many investments made during the period in which the incentive had been eliminated.

In part to prepare for the increased competition that will come when it eventually accedes to the World Trade Organization, China has been gradually relaxing some restrictions on foreign ownership and establishment of businesses. Since 1992, for example, new service sectors such as retail, insurance, and tourism have been opened to foreign investment on an experimental basis. These experiments in the service sector are limited by number and location, although China recently announced plans to expand both the numbers and locations allowed. In late 1996, three years after authorities announced they would allow a few joint-venture chain stores, two were approved, one involving a Dutch company and the other a Japanese consortium. Each of the two reportedly plans initially to open three retail locations in Beijing. Foreign investment in such joint ventures is limited to a minority stake, and it is still prohibited in wholesaling and distribution. Although eight foreign insurance companies have been approved to do limited business in China, all but one are restricted to operations in Shanghai (one U.S. company is allowed to operate in Guangzhou). All are also limited in the products they can offer and the customers they can solicit.

Foreign investment in other previously closed sectors is being encouraged on a limited basis. Since August 1993, when plans to allow foreign investment in roads and harbors were announced, there have been a number of minority-stake foreign investments in toll roads and port facilities, such as container handling terminals. China announced in May of 1994 that it would allow foreign investors to take up to a 35-percent stake in Chinese airlines (with the percentage of voting shares limited to 25 percent), and the first such investment was made in late 1995, when an investment consortium led by an American investor purchased a 25-percent stake in Hainan Airlines. Also in mid-1994, foreign investment was allowed in selected gold mines. The Pudong area in Shanghai is currently particularly worth watching as most experiments in FDI deregulation are tried out there.

Taxation

China's taxation system was overhauled in 1994, unifying most policies concerning domestic and foreign-funded enterprises, except for enterprise income tax. Under the new unified law, tax breaks go towards industries which the government wishes to encourage, regardless of whether the firm is local or foreign.

The government recently reversed the course regarding value-added tax (VAT) rebates to exporters, which it had reduced in July of 1995 and again in January of 1996. The reductions cut into what had already been fairly thin profit margins for many exporters (115 percent) and significantly affected the operations of both foreign-invested and domestic enterprises that exported goods produced with domestic inputs. As the financial crisis in Asia threatened to negatively effect Chinese exports, the government moved to increase the VAT rebates for exports of certain products, such as textiles, beginning January of 1998.

To be more specific, in the tax reform undertaken in 1994, the turn-over tax regime and individual income tax regime were unified. As a result, both domestic and foreign firms are now governed by a unified set of rules on value-added, consumption, business operations and individual income taxation. A notable exception, however, is the corporate income tax regime, under which foreign investors still enjoy preferential treatment.

In April of 1996, China substantially reduced the average general tariff level from 35.9 percent to 23 percent, covering nearly 5000 tariff lines with an average reduction margin of 36 percent. At the 1996 APEC meeting, China again announced that it would reduce the average general tariff level to 15 percent by the year 2000. China is phasing out the non-tariff measures and has submitted a timetable for the gradual elimination of the remaining non-tariff measures applied to around 400 tariff lines. FIEs face the same duties and import-related taxes as domestic firms on all imported equipment, materials, and all other items since April of 1996. Although overall tariff rates had already been lowered considerably at the beginning of 1996, the abolition of the preferential import duties awarded to FIEs is important, given that nearly 70 percent of China's FDI is in the form of imported capital equipment or raw materials.

The State Administration of Taxation has launched a crackdown on thousands of companies which enjoy preferential tax rates by falsely claiming themselves as foreign ventures. Under newly issued regulations, the taxation authorities will strip "foreign" tax status from any venture with less than 25 percent of its paid-in capital originating from overseas. Since the early 1980s, national and local governments have lured foreign investment by offering tax rates lower than those applied to domestic firms, particularly in designated economic zones (SEZs). But the growing difference between the amount of contracted and actual foreign investment in recent years has revealed widespread abuses of the system. In one typical scenario, a domestic company seeking tax breaks arranges a false marriage with a foreign partner, which in fact injects little or no capital. Because joint ventures also get preferential access to land, overseas companies have also set up under-capitalised firms to speculate on Chinese real-estate prices. The new policy – expected to hit thousands of companies hard – leaves open the door for ventures to re-gain their tax breaks by absorbing enough foreign capital to cross the 25 percent margin.

Foreign Exchange

There have also been changes in the area of foreign exchange controls. China announced full convertibility of its currency under the current account on December 1, 1996, and instituted new and more liberal regulations allowing foreign-invested and domestic enterprises to freely convert currencies for current account transactions (for example, trade transactions and profit repatriation). While all FIEs are entitled to open and maintain a foreign exchange account for current account transactions, they must first apply to the State Administration of Foreign Exchange (SAFE) for permission. SAFE grants permission for the account and also sets a limit on the amount the account may hold, based on an enterprise's anticipated foreign exchange operational needs. In the fall of 1996, the government began approving foreign bank branches in the Pudong area of Shanghai to engage in local currency business, though mainly limited to providing services for FIEs.

In 1996, China incorporated FIEs into the system of buying and selling foreign exchange through banks and realized the convertibility of the Renminbi (RMB) under current accounts in December of the same year. At the same time, China keeps the foreign exchange swap center as a source of procurement and settlement of foreign exchanges. Nevertheless, more and more FIEs are likely to choose designated banks to buy or sell foreign exchanges because the new scheme offers much greater benefits. RMB convertibility under current accounts will help improve the investment and operating environment for foreigners. It provides a more adequate institutional guarantee of the legitimate revenues of foreign investors, minimizes the risks involved in the remittance of profits and gives a stronger sense of security to foreign investors. Meanwhile, the removal of restrictions on payment and transfer of foreign exchanges helps streamline the procedures for examination and approval, which will in turn increase the turnover rate of capital, thus improving business performance.

FIEs are also allowed to use funds in their foreign exchange clearing account as time deposits, a practice that had been banned up to now. This will allow them to receive interest and have more freedom in using these funds. The move will enable foreign-funded companies to employ their capital in a more productive manner. In addition, deregulation of local currency loans is expected to improve the financing capacity of foreign-funded companies by increasing their fund raising channels. The procedure applicable to foreign-funded companies for buying and selling foreign exchange used to import technology will also be streamlined.

Finance

China has eased restrictions on FIEs by making local currency loans more accessible. As of July 1999, FIEs no longer need to provide information about their debts or security for the loans obtained from authorized local foreign exchange banks. The maximum tenure of such loans has also been extended to five years. Under the new policy, the debtor is freer to spend the renminbi loans because the only thing not permitted is purchasing foreign exchange with the money.

Under regulations promulgated in March 1987, the government restricts the debt-to-equity ratio of foreign-funded firms and sets minimum equity requirements. The report lists these requirements as follows: for investments under $3 million, debt cannot exceed 30 percent of the total investment; for investments of $3 million to $10 million, $10 million to $30 million, and over $30 million, the debt/capital ratios cannot exceed, respectively, 50 percent, 60 percent, and 70 percent. For investments over $60 million, debt is limited to two thirds of the total value of the investment. Although it is legal for FIEs to raise funds in China through the sale of bonds, only a few have tried to do so.

Employment and Union

FIEs are free to recruit employees directly or through agencies, but representative offices of foreign firms must hire all local employees under contract with approved labor services companies. These companies pay contracted local employees only a portion of the amount the foreign companies pay for their services, and the employees are technically employed by the labor services companies.

To obtain local employees, FIEs can take over a joint venture partner's work force, hire workers through a local labor bureau or job fair, advertise in newspapers, or rely on word of mouth. Skilled workers are often in short supply, though many companies report that they have found plenty of talented and highly motivated workers among recent university graduates. Shortages can be acute in southern China, where there are fewer higher education institutions than there are in the north. While finding engineers and technicians can sometimes be difficult, the real difficulty is in finding and keeping managers and anyone with marketing skills. Foreign ventures report that workers often move rapidly from job to job among foreign-invested companies and in the growing private sector. Employers pay workers a salary or hourly wages, or piece-work wages. The practice of providing subsidized services, such as housing and medical care, is widespread, and compensation beyond basic wages makes up a large portion of a venture's labor expenses. Recently, however, employer-provided housing has been decreasing, as the government has stepped up efforts to reform the country's housing system and promote home purchase through a mortgage system.

Local governments also tax enterprises and workers to support social security and unemployment insurance funds. In general, foreign ventures are free to pay whatever wage rates they wish, above a locally designated minimum wage. The national labor law specifies rates of compensation for overtime under various circumstances. Under Chinese income tax laws, it may be more advantageous for a venture to provide greater subsidies and services rather than higher wage rates, but taxes are not the only consideration; such decisions are often made after observing local practice. A firm's ability to terminate workers varies widely, depending on its location, type and size. Terminating individual workers for cause is legally possible, but it may require prior notification and consultation with the local union. In general, it is easier to fire employees in southern China than in the north, and in smaller enterprises than in larger ones. The Labor Law and collective labor contracts can be used to specify wage levels, working hours, working conditions, and insurance and welfare benefits. In recent years, most of the coastal provinces have gone beyond the national regulations, requiring unions in all FIEs. The All-China Federation of Trade Unions (ACFTU) began a drive in 1996 to conduct collective negotiations in at least 90 percent of the FIEs, and this goal seems to has been reached.

Service Sector

China is now experimenting by allowing Sino-foreign joint venture international trading companies in Pudong, Shanghai. A pilot registration system for granting trading rights to production enterprises in the five Special Economic Zones (SEZs) has been introduced. Foreign banks have begun to do local currency business in Pudong on a trial basis.

Foreign retail and wholesale giants are now allowed to set up joint venture outlets in dozens of large inland cities which were formerly restricted areas. Qualified foreign investors may now establish outlets in virtually all the country's main urban centers, including the 30 capitals of China's provinces and autonomous regions. Chinese authorities had previously restricted such foreign-invested retail business to 11 major cities and special economic zones along the coast. Nevertheless, the reform still limits access to big foreign names and sets tough local equity minimums. Retailers must have recorded average worldwide sales of $2 billion annually in the three years prior to application and assets of $200 million. The figures are set at $2.5 billion and $300 million, respectively, for wholesalers. Chinese partners must hold at least a 51-per cent stake and the foreign investors must already have a heavy presence in China, although the regulations say the State Council can grant exceptions to companies that sell large amounts of Chinese-made goods overseas.

Property Rights Protection

China has made continued progress is the protection of intellectual property rights (IPR). Since the conclusion of the 1992 U.S.-China memorandum of understanding on the protection of intellectual property rights, China has followed through on its commitments to join relevant international conventions and enact or amend IPR legislation. China is now a member of the World Intellectual Property Organization (WIPO), the Paris Convention for the Protection of Industrial Property, the Berne Convention, the Madrid Trademark Convention, the Universal Copyright Convention, and the Geneva Phonograph Convention. In the extension of the Memorandum of Understanding (MOU) in March 1995, China confirmed that it would not impose nontariff restrictions on the importation of audiovisual or published products, and it made a commitment to allow joint ventures with Chinese entities in audiovisual products and computer software. China also agreed to allow U.S. individuals and companies to enter film products into revenue-sharing arrangements in China. However, there are still unwritten quotas for both foreign films and foreign music in China, as well as persisting trademark violations of many name-brand consumer products. Nevertheless, illegal importation of CD and VCD products, end-user piracy of business software, continuing retail piracy, growing trademark counterfeiting, and problems in obtaining administrative protection for pharmaceuticals still abound. Moreover, China's trademark registration process is inconsistent, and the problem is exacerbated by the lack of judicial review of decisions made by the trademark office.

China has responded to the growing importance of resolving IPR disputes by establishing special IPR courts in several cities and provinces, including Beijing, Shanghai, Guangzhou, Fujian and Hainan. However, the effectiveness of these courts has been limited because many of the trial court judges lack legal training. To address this problem, Chinese authorities have established IPR law centers at Beijing University and People's University and are studying the training of IPR professionals in foreign countries.

Research & Development

A significant amount of research and development funding in China is allocated through the "Torch" program of the State Science and Technology Commission, a government initiative aimed at promoting the commercial application of science and technology research. The government encourages foreign joint ventures, but not wholly foreign-owned companies, to participate in Torch programs as a means to introduce high technology. During the 1994 meeting of the U.S.-China Joint Commission on Science and Technology, both the U.S. private sector and Chinese enterprises were invited to participate in and collaborate on U.S. and Chinese government-sponsored R&D efforts in new pharmaceuticals, advanced materials, environmental technologies, and energy production. China is currently considering the role foreign companies play in joint research and development activities with Chinese partners.

Dispute Settlement

China is a member of the International Center for the Settlement of Investment Disputes (ICSID) and has ratified the New York Convention on the Enforcement of Foreign Arbitral Awards. Nevertheless, the government puts strong emphasis on resolving disputes through informal conciliation and consultation between the parties. And if it becomes necessary to employ a formal dispute resolution mechanism, Chinese authorities greatly prefer arbitration through Chinese agencies. Litigation is considered only reluctantly and as a last option. Investment contracts often stipulate arbitration in Stockholm, as the setting is considered neutral. Most Chinese contracts stipulate arbitration by the China International Economic and Trade Arbitration Commission (CIETAC). Another forum for resolving investment and trade disputes is the Beijing

Conciliation Center (BCC), an organization affiliated with the China Council for the Promotion of International Trade (CCPIT). In 1992, BCC and the American Arbitration Association (AAA) agreed to work together in joint conciliation to resolve trade and investment disputes between U.S. and Chinese parties.

Legal System

The supreme legislative authority in China is the National People's Congress (NPC) and its Standing Committee which works primarily through the Legislative Affairs Committee. Under the 1982 Constitution, the State Council and the People's Congresses at the provincial and municipal level have the authority to formulate administrative regulations and local legislation that are not inconsistent with national law. The formal legal system consists of the People's courts, the People's Procuratorate, and the Public Security Bureau. In cooperation with the NPC, the Supreme Court interprets new laws and passes guidance down to lower courts. The system is a mixture of common law and continental legal systems, but it places relatively less emphasis on legal precedents. The establishment of economic courts at the Supreme Court and three levels of provincial courts was authorized by the 1979 Organic Law of the People's Courts of the People's Republic of China. The economic courts have jurisdiction over contract and commercial disputes between Chinese entities; trade, maritime, insurance, and intellectual property rights; other business disputes involving foreign parties; and various economic crimes, including theft, bribery, and tax evasion. In 1994, the lowest level of provincial courts started to try economic cases involving foreign parties. Foreign lawyers cannot act as attorneys in Chinese courts, but they may be present informally. During the past year, the U.S. and China have been working on projects related to commercial and economic law under the U.S.-China Joint Committee on Commerce and Trade.

1.4 Macroeconomic Environment in the Turn of the Century

In the last 20 years, China has undergone its own industrial revolution and structural transformation. Between 1978 and 1997, China's industries grew by an average of 12 percent a year. Assets of industrial enterprises totalled 11.6 trillion yuan (U.S.$1.39 trillion) by the end of 1997, 26.6 times the figure 20 years ago. Tax and profits stood at 760.2 billion yuan (U.S.$91.5 billion), a 700 percent increase. Since 1978, deregulation of the rigid mechanism of the planned economy has enabled Chinese enterprises to exploit their potential productivity better. Enterprises affiliated to the government 20 years ago have been able to source raw materials freely and alter production to meet market demand. Management now has rights over price setting, employment, salaries and the use of capital. More liberal tax rules have allowed enterprises to invest heavily in research and development and to expand their market. Employees, freed from the "cradle-to-grave" egalitarian mindset, earn wages and bonuses based on performance.

China is in the throes of two transitions today: from a command economy to a market-based one and from a rural, agricultural society to an urban, industrial one. So far both transitions have been spectacularly successful. China is the fastest growing economy in the world, with per capita incomes more than quadruple since 1978. Economic reforms have advanced China's integration with the world economy, maintained a strong external payments position, essentially privatized farming, liberalized markets for many goods and services, intensified competition in industry, and introduced modern macroeconomic management. In two generations it has achieved what probably took centuries for other countries. This has been a most remarkable development for a country whose population exceeds that of Sub-Saharan Africa and Latin American combined. By the year 2000, China's consumer market will be larger than the United States or Western Europe.

China's record growth started in 1978 when it officially opened the door to the outside world. Between 1978 and 95, annual per capita real GDP growth in China averaged 8 percent while it was only 1.5 percent in the United States. This growth makes China the fastest growing economy in the world over the past two decades. Starting from a position of near-autarky, China has been catching up rapidly with other developing countries in integrating with the global economy. Increased integration and openness have paid rich dividends in the way of faster growth, despite much room for progress. China's economic growth accelerated after reforms started in 1979. Remarkably, the improvement was achieved entirely by an improvement in total factor productivity growth – of between 3.6 and 4.1

percentage points. Market-based transactions now dominate the Chinese economy, with over 90 percent of retail prices and 80 percent of producer and agricultural prices determined by the market.

Table 1.8: Major Economic Indicators of Chinese Economy (1966-1998)

	1991-97		1997		1998	
	China	World	China	World	China	World
Real GDP growth	11.8	2.3	9.1	3.2	7.2	1.8
GDP/capita growth	10.6	0.8	8.1	1.8	6.2	0.3
Inflation	11.2	4.4	2.3	2.8	1.7	2.9
Current acct. balance (% of GDP)	1.0	-0.1	2.1	0.2	2.6	0.0

Source: World Bank, *Global Economic Prospects 1998/99*, p.194-197

China's effort to engineer industrial growth has included measures designed to gradually introduce market competition, encourage mergers and acquisitions, and foster the expansion of collective enterprises. As a result of industrial reform, firms have had increasing autonomy over determining how and with whom they will conduct business. From methods of production to decisions about hiring and firing workers, Chinese business organizations are becoming less and less dependent on central authority. Managers have more responsibility for finding productive inputs, determining appropriate production and inventory levels, and locating markets for their products. Bankruptcy and unemployment, unheard of in the past, have also increased in recent years, demonstrating that poor firm performance may result in failure for the firm and unemployment for the firm's managers.

The introduction of the contract responsibility system has proved to be a significant success. The policy, initiated in the mid-1980s, has inspired the enthusiasm and creativity of small State-owned and collective enterprises. The productivity and profitability of the industrial sector was twice as high in 1992 as the year the policy was introduced. Conglomerates like the Haier, Shougang and Changhong groups have also evolved rapidly and begun to acquire an international reputation.

By localizing the processing of products for export from China, foreign-funded enterprises have brought advanced technologies and management expertise to their domestic partners, thus promoting the technical upgrade of national industries. Exports of electronic products in 1997 were 110 times those of 1978, while textile exports were up tenfold. These sectors now account for 9.8 percent and 25.4 percent of China's export earnings. Aerospace, aviation and shipbuilding have made considerable progress over the past 20 years and have become increasingly competitive on the global market. The days of supply shortages are a thing of the past. Most Chinese households now own TV sets, refrigerators and washing machines. More of the new rich display their wealth by commuting to work by car. Personal computers have become a common feature in urban households. Microelectronics, telecommunications equipment, new materials, and automobile manufacturing have been designated among the nation's pillar industries. Manufacturing products currently make up about 86 per cent of total exports in value terms.

Three features of China's rapid growth since 1978 are especially noteworthy. First, the benefits of growth have been widely shared among China's country-size provincial economies. Although the coastal provinces grew faster than average at 9.7 percent a year, the other provinces also fared well. In fact, if China's thirty provinces were counted as individual economies, the twenty fastest-growing economies in the world would have been Chinese. Second, Chinese economic development has been coupled with the sharp cyclical pattern of economic growth. The growth cycles have been accompanied by similar fluctuations in the rate of inflation, revealing fault lines in macroeconomic management stemming from partially completed reforms in the fiscal, enterprise, and banking systems. Third, China's growth has been less dependent on volume increase in inputs of capital and labor than on productivity growth, relative to other emerging economies. This suggests that factors other than capital accumulation have been important determinants of China's GDP growth.

China's remarkably rapid growth since 1978 has been driven by the following factors: The first is a high savings rate, which has supported vigorous rates of investment and capital accumulation. China's savings rate averaged 37 percent of GDP between 1978 and 1995, in sharp contrast to the collapse of savings in the transition economies of Eastern Europe and the former Soviet Union. Contributing to half of total savings, household savings exploded from about 1 percent as a share of income before reforms to 21 percent since then. Second, structural change has been both a cause and an effect of growth. This change has given a significant boost to China's growth over the past two decades. Since a large portion of the agricultural labor force was underemployed, productivity leaped as workers moved from low-productivity agriculture to more productive employment in industry and services. This process contributes about 1 percentage point a year to GDP growth. The changing pattern of ownership also contributes about 0.5 percentage point a year to growth, as employment shifted to the collective and private sectors, where productivity is higher. Third, pragmatic reforms were well suited to China's unusual circumstances and enjoyed broad support. China's economic reform in 1978 was triggered by neither economic crisis nor ideological epiphany. Reform measures were introduced incrementally and involved decentralizing authority over capital spending. A favored approach of central authorities was to experiment with new policies in selected provinces, prefectures, counties, and even firms. If the experiments worked, they were quickly replicated. This approach, or what is called 'crossing the river by groping for stepping-stones', has been a systematic component of Chinese reforms. Pragmatism and incrementalism were also behind the government's evolving objectives. Lastly, economic conditions in 1978 were especially receptive to reform. Contrary to popular perception, planning was less entrenched in China than in other transition economies. China's economy could be described as a dry prairie, parched by years of planning, awaiting the first sprinklings of market reform.

The Chinese economy is still only about halfway through its transition from a centrally planned to a market economy. Reforms that are difficult to implement are still on-going, in particular the development of the legal, administrative, and regulatory framework which supports a modern economy. As reform rolls ahead, a seemingly endless array of gaps, obstacles, shortcomings, and problems comes to the surface. Swift growth and structural change, while resolving many problems, have created new challenges: employment insecurity, growing inequality, stubborn poverty, mounting environmental pressures, and periods of macroeconomic instability stemming from incomplete reforms.

Lack of progress in reforming SOEs is a major bottleneck hampering deepening reform in China. The delay in SOE reform is largely responsible for delays in fiscal, financial, and trading system reform. A bankruptcy law introduced in the late 1980s has had minimal effect, as until recently it has rarely been used because of fear of the social consequences. State banks still cannot refuse to extend loans to loss-making SOEs if the authorities so request. Liberalization of bank interest rates and trade protection has been slowed because of fear of the impact on cash strapped SOEs. Wage pressures sometimes divert earnings away from much-needed long-term investment. Government supervisory agencies continue to interfere with shareholding firms' management. It is still too early for shareholders to gauge firm performance through the two stock markets, which have had their share of insider trading and stock manipulation. Moreover, most SOEs will be restructured, at least in the medium term, into limited liability companies rather than limited liability stock companies. Therefore, bank credit, rather than share issuance, likely will be the dominant source of financing for most SOEs. However, the deeply troubled state banking sector is not yet capable of imposing financial discipline on SOEs. The most daunting challenge that has remained to be solved for years is how to manage state assets efficiently and by whom. Currently, the State Asset Management Commission and various sub-commissions are the major authority to manage these assets of the state. It is well recognized that asset management by these commissions is ineffective due to lack of professional knowledge, organizational responsibility, and managerial incentive. It is easy to change SOE ownership structure, but it is difficult, if not impossible, to manage state assets effectively and maximize their value when the government still controls the ownership of these assets. As loss-making SOEs continue to demand soft loans, the success of banking reform, taxation reforms, and social welfare reforms are all affected by the pace and pattern of SOE reforms in productive sectors.

Since 1999, China's economy has started to sputter as the large sources of its economic strength all show signs of fatigue. Foreign investment is slowing because cash-starved Asian companies can no longer afford to build in China. Exporters are seeing business shift to cheaper factories in Thailand and Malaysia. The real estate boom in the rich coastal provinces is turning into a bust. Bad loans keep piling up in the state-owned banks, threatening the health of the entire economy. Consumer demand is dropping fast, and many retailers are desperate for shoppers. At Beijing's new Cofco Plaza shopping center, for example, the top two floors are empty of shops. And the designer clothes and bedding sold in the largest third-floor shop come from boutiques elsewhere in the building in order to fill up otherwise unoccupied space. Such signs are alarming. If growth slips below 7 percent, the economy will not generate nearly enough jobs to soak up the 6 million Chinese entering the workforce each year, as well as the 12 million laid off by restructured state enterprises. Unemployment is expected to jump by an additional 10 million through 2001. The steel industry will dismiss a half-million workers – 38% of its workforce – by 2000. The country's textile machine shops will probably lose 600,000 jobs in the next few years.

Given the continued drop in exports, pressure to devalue the Renminbi is increasing. The government still reckons that the gains would outweigh the costs of devaluation – political loss of face, more expensive imports for swathes of export-oriented and import-intensive companies, the risk of higher inflation at a time of economic stimulus, more expensive debt-service costs for some shaky Chinese borrowers, and a generally heightened sense of instability as a result of the government's reversal of policy on an issue on which it had previously been adamant. The gains would include an enhanced ability to compete on price without denting margins or being accused of dumping as well as deterring cheap imports. And many export markets, especially in Asia, are regarded as being too severely depressed to respond to a devaluation of the renminbi on any scale that has occurred previously.

In closing, over the past twenty-five years, China's GDP growth averaged 10 percent a year and its share of world trade tripled to about 3 percent. The strength of the Chinese economy over the past two decades, however, does not guarantee that China will continue to grow rapidly in the future. Nevertheless, China has some real advantages that can bolster its economy. Its high saving rate, large domestic market, and record of reform bode well for future growth. China's Five-Year Plan for 1996-2000 targets GDP growth of 8 percent a year.

Even so, the future will be an increasing challenge, probably increasingly so. Rapid economic growth is not the government's sole objective nor should it be. It is very likely that the pace of reforms will slow down if social instability intensifies as a result of income disparity, bureaucratic corruption, and hyper-underemployment. Hurdles over future growth also include incomplete foundations of reforms. China is midstream in its transition to a market economy. The government's role in laying the institutional, social, physical, and legal foundations for market development will be crucial in completing the transition. Although China is now restructuring and downsizing its governments at various levels, it remains to be seen as to what extent and about how long it can fulfil its goal to establish an efficient and clean governmental system.

Whether or not China can meet these challenges and sustain rapid growth depends largely on continuous reforms into the future. First, the spread of market forces must be encouraged, especially through reforms of state enterprises, the financial system, grain and labor markets, and pricing of natural resources. Second, the government must begin serving markets by building the legal, social, physical, and institutional infrastructure needed for their rapid growth. Finally, integration with the world economy must be deepened by lowering import barriers, increasing the transparency and predictability of the trade regime, and gradually integrating with international financial markets.

2. Industrial Structure and Policies

Chapter Purpose

This chapter describes the industry structure in China and its influence on foreign direct investment. An introduction of Chinese industry structure and its changes in recent years is followed by a presentation of current industrial policies toward foreign direct investment. The next section highlights structural attributes of industry that have to be analyzed before making FDI decisions. Some important recent findings and results concerning Chinese industry are then presented. The following section discusses the implications for international investors active in China. China's entry into WTO and its impact on structural transformation are elaborated in the last section.

2.1 Overview

Deregulatory Effects

In the past twenty years, China has undergone its own industrial evolution and structural transformation, passing from a traditional rural economy to a more modern, industrialized society. Between 1978 and 1997, China's industries grew by 12 percent a year on average. Consider the following growth that has taken place within the last two decades:

1. Assets of Chinese industrial enterprises grew 26.6 times to 11.6 trillion yuan (U.S.$1.39 trillion).
2. Tax and profits have increased 700 percent to 760.2 billion yuan (U.S.$91.5 billion).

Since 1978, deregulation of the rigid mechanism of the planned economy has enabled Chinese enterprises to exploit their potential productivity better. Enterprises affiliated to the government 20 years ago have been able to source raw materials freely and alter production to meet market demand. Management now has rights over price setting, employment, salaries and the use of capital. Tax reforms have allowed enterprises to invest heavily in research and development and expanding their market. Employees, freed from the "cradle-to-grave" egalitarianism mindset, earn wages and bonuses based on performance.

The widespread use of the contract responsibility system in most sectors has proved to be a significant success. The policy, initiated in the mid-1980s, has inspired the enthusiasm and creativity of small State-owned and collective enterprises. The productivity and profitability of the industrial sector was twice as high in 1992 as it was in the mid-1980's.

Most industries are in transition. Exports of electronic products in 1997 were 110 times those of 1978, while textile exports were up 10-fold. These sectors now respectively account for 9.8% and 25.4% of China's export earnings. Aerospace, aviation and shipbuilding have made considerable progress over the past 20 years and become increasingly competitive on the global market. Most Chinese households now own TV sets, refrigerators and washing machines. More of the new rich are displaying their wealth by commuting to work by car. Personal computers have become a common feature in urban households. Microelectronics, telecommunications equipment, new materials, and automobile manufacturing have been designated among the nation's pillar industries. Manufacturing products currently make up about 86 per cent of total exports in value terms.

Structural transformation has even proceeded under strong interference by the central government. For example, public sector investment in energy, transportation, and telecommunications has soared in recent years.

Consider the following recent shifts in capital investment toward infrastructure and technology:

I. Energy industry shot up to 357.5 billion yuan (U.S.$43.07 billion) in 1997.
II. Transportation and telecommunications industry investment also dramatically up to 328.8 billion yuan (U.S.$38.65 billion) in 1997.
III. In contrast, significant reductions in textile production. (Reductions of 4.5 million spindles of cotton thread with 500,000 less workers. Reductions of 1 million spindles of wool thread will be cut within three years.)

IV. 25,800 coal mines will be closed and coal output reduced by 250 million tons in 1999.
V. And, to enhance industry-specific advantages, no additional or new steel and iron-producing plants will be established until the year 2000.

The reform of State-owned enterprises remains a challenging task, however. By the end of 1997, about 2,000 enterprises had gone bankrupt, and another 5,000 had been acquired by larger ones. The country's 1,600 largest industrial conglomerates contribute 70 percent of industrial output and 80 per cent of taxes. Moreover, the internal structure among industrial sectors is not fully rational. Repetitive investments also exist in many regions. Additionally, the existing ownership structure does not fit the industrial structure in many ways. To solve these problems, the central government continues to adopt a series of measures to provide systematic guarantees for optimization of the industry structure, create more industrial competition, and better distribute social resources.

China's economic growth mainly comes from three sources: 1) exports, 2) domestic consumer market, and 3) government investment in infrastructure and industries. Because of the Asian financial crisis, the export contribution to economic growth has decreased in recent years. Domestic consumption is also weak, mainly because of the growing unemployment problem, which not only reduces many people's purchasing power but also shakes consumer confidence. Therefore, government investments become the major source supporting economic growth, e.g. the government plans to invest about 3 trillion yuan (more than U.S.$300 billion) in infrastructure projects such as water supply, ports, airports, and power generation and distribution. In fact, the World Bank estimates that from 1995 to 2004, China will require over $280 billion for infrastructure and public facilities investments/projects.

The Chinese government has decided to develop modern and strategically important industries, such as electronics, information technology, software, automobile, pollution control and raw material industries. China wants to develop these sectors not only to modernize its industries, but also to create new economic growth sources. To develop these sectors, the government will invest heavily and try to attract more foreign capital and technologies within these sectors.

Structural transformation of traditional industries such as textile and light industries will produce more mergers and acquisitions. Instead of increasing production capacity, the government encourages organizational restructuring of existing firms. Many of them are now too small to enjoy economies of scale. Further, the government has restricted additional investments, nationwide, for projects that have low market potential or in which China already has excessive manufacturing capacity. The main objective for reforming these industries is to use advanced technologies to renovate and upgrade existing facilities and help companies develop new products, thus increasing overall industrial competitiveness on a global scale.

2.2 Industrial Structure

China's transition from socialist central planning to a market-oriented economy is historically unprecedented. With neither a benchmark in past experience nor a well-formulated theoretical framework, China has proceeded in a trial-and-error manner. Since China's initial reform efforts began as experimental changes aimed at improving performance rather than, as in Eastern Europe, establishing a Western-style market system, it is not surprising that institutional change has been gradual and uneven, with many features of the pre-reform system surviving even today. Rather than attempting a 'big bang,' China's reform path is more akin to 'growing out of the plan'.

Industry, which by Chinese convention includes mining and utilities as well as manufacturing, is the largest sector of China's economy, accounting for 50 percent of total output, 80 percent of exports, and employing 102 million workers in 1992. Its robust growth, amounting to well over 10 percent annually in the past years, underscores China's standing as the world's fastest-growing economy. Industry also stands at the core of China's reform problem. Efforts to revitalize and restructure domestic industry are closely linked to reforms in pricing, banking, public finance, ownership, social welfare, and research and development. If China's recent accomplishments carry distinctive implications for policy design, it is industry, where reform has side-stepped privatization and other standard remedies, that is the most likely source of these lessons.

Reform has meant an expansion not only of markets, but also of industrial competition. Market forces tend to equalize financial returns to production factors employed in different lines of business. Naughton (1992) observes sharp reductions in the dispersion of profitability across all Chinese industrial sectors. There is also evidence of convergence in financial returns on capital, labor and materials across ownership types. These tendencies are attributable to the decline and convergence of profit rates due to the continuing erosion of barriers that formerly protected state enterprises against competition from collective firms, imported products, and foreign invested enterprises (FIEs). As a result of past efforts to build 'complete sets' of industries in every province, market concentration by leading state enterprises tends to fall considerably below comparable figures for the United States and Japan. With military industries converting to civilian production, declining barriers to internal trade, FIEs' market expansion on the rise, and the prospect of sweeping reductions in import restrictions if China joins WTO, we see the competitive market a well-entrenched fixture in China's industrial economy. This emerging structural environment will influence not only the market and financial performance of FDI but also how investment strategy will be formulated.

The growing irrelevance of traditional planning mechanisms not only contributes to macroeconomic instability, but also unleashes opportunistic investment behavior that results in an undesirable industrial structure. The continuing fall in profit rates throughout industry, coupled with the expansion of enterprise claims on profit flows, has also caused the government to suffer a crushing revenue decline. Fear of inflation has left the state with little choice but to restrict the growth of subsidies and push an ever-growing list of industries into the hurly-burly of the marketplace. In addition, the central government has expanded the role of market transactions in coal, petroleum, steel, and other sectors formerly regarded as bastions of mandatory planning. By 1993, central planning controlled only 7 percent of industrial output. Even these mandatory commodity allocations often depend on market prices. These initiatives have contributed to the continued outward shift of industry's efficiency frontier.

A continuing inflow of foreign direct investment has played a pivotal role in this shift. Among economic sectors, the manufacturing sector leads with 54.94 percent of total FDI in 1994. These investments have infused local enterprises with both technological and organizational skills. These skills, combined with China's readiness to assimilate them, have helped push the economy into a higher orbit. Indeed, the contribution of foreign direct investment to the transformation of China's industry structure is substantial. However, the impact of FDI on China's industrial structure is idiosyncratic according to the type of industry. This can be seen from the following details. First, the structural influence of FDI on heavy industry, chemical industry, and raw materials industry is very limited. For instance, there have not yet been any FIEs established in the steel and aviation transportation industries. The output share of FDI in oil refining, petroleum chemicals, cement, and electric power generation industries is all less than 5 percent of an industry's total (see Table 2.1). Second, FDI tends to dominate 'import-substitution' industries (e.g., elevator and car manufacturing) where it has early-mover advantages in the country. As shown in Table 2.1, the FIE shares within the listed industries exceed 50 percent of China's total output. In addition, there are very few competitive local rivals due in large part to the shortage of technology or capital. Instead, the major competitors are other FIEs and foreign exporters. For instance, despite the dominance of FIEs in the elevator industry (60 percent), China imported more than 5,000 elevators in 1995. Third, structural influence of FDI in light industry, electronics products, machinery, and pharmaceutical industries is enormous. The vigor of competition between FIEs and Chinese domestic firms is intense. The market shares possessed by all FIEs range from 13 percent (pharmaceutical) to 72 percent (color TV display tube). The majority of FDI in China, in terms of both the number of projects and the contributed capital, was launched in these categories of industry.

As indicated in Table 2.2, 68.33 percent of the total FIEs in China are investing and operating in various light industries, with the rest in heavy industries. Among light industries, 66 percent of FIEs use farm products as raw materials (Table 2.2). In heavy industries, most of the FIEs (78 percent) focus on manufacturing sectors. The number of FIEs in the excavation and raw materials sectors and their role in contributing to these sectors' GDP, sales, profits and taxes are extremely limited. The major reason lies in the vigorous controls maintained by the central government over those industries that are 'strategically vital' to the Chinese economy.

Table 2.1 Structural Pattern of FDI in China in 1995

Industry	FDI's Output Share* (% of nation's total)	Investment#
Steel, Aviation	0.00%	none
Oil Refining	<1.00%	2 FIEs
Petroleum Chemicals	<5.00%	NA
Electric Power Generation	<1.00%	$1.9 bil. 18 FIEs
Cement	2.90%	18 FIEs
Elevator	60.00%	5 FIEs
Car	70.00%	296 FIEs
Wash and Cleanse Products		$0.2 billion
Detergent	32.00%	NA
Soap	27.20%	NA
Soft Drink	39.70%	$0.7 billion
Beer	20.00%	$0.5 billion
Electronic Products	33.33%	$8.0 billion
Glass	17.00%	NA
Pharmaceutical	13.00%	1,500 FIEs
Color TV Display Tube	72.00%	NA

* FDI projects in these industries are generally oriented on local markets, thus output share can be regarded as proxy of market share.
# All FIEs in the table refer to large and medium sized foreign-funded enterprises.
Source: Adopted from Luo and Tan (1997).

Although more FIEs have invested in light industries rather than in heavy sectors, these two types of industries each have an equal impact on shaping the Chinese economy. Table 2.2 suggests that these two categories are proportioned similarly in gross output, added industrial value, total sales revenue, total profit before tax, and total contributed value added tax (VAT). In addition, the differences in total assets, liabilities, and owners' equity between the two broad sectors are fairly minimal.

The financial and output performances of FIEs (total population) in every industry in 1995 are presented in Table 2.3. 12 percent of FIEs invested in garment and fiber products industries, 8.5

percent in textiles, 6.13 percent in plastic products, and 5.85 percent in electronics and telecommunications. These are followed by investments in raw chemical materials and chemical products (5.30%), nonmetal mineral products (5.14%), leather, furs, down and related products (5.07%), metal products (4.78%), food manufacturing (3.85%) and food processing (3.82%).

The following factors may contribute to the distribution of FIE investment described above. First, under the incremental reform approach, the central government still maintains control restricting or prohibiting FIEs from entering and operating within certain industries. FDI is therefore more actively involved in light industries or industries in their maturity stage of life cycle. Second, Great China multinationals, especially those from Hong Kong, Macau and Taiwan, often seek cost minimization and export benefits by focusing on less technology-intensive or less capital-intensive industries. This strategy not only fits their organizational capabilities, orientations, and strengths, but also enables them to enjoy preferential treatment by the Chinese government, which aims at encouraging export.

As far as economic contributions are concerned, however, FDI has had a significant impact on industrial development. Table 2.3 shows the importance of such industries like electric power, electric equipment and machinery, machine building, and transportation equipment manufacturing in contributing added industrial value and value added taxes to the country. It has been reported that an increasing number of Western MNCs have commenced operations in these technology- and capital-intensive sectors. Their asset size and economies of scale are substantially greater than those of Great China MNCs. As a result, despite smaller numbers of FIEs in these sectors, the industrial value they add is greater. This pattern is likely to be reinforced in the future because Western MNCs in China are more long-term oriented than their counterparts from Asian countries.

2.3 Industrial Policies

The Chinese government has determined the industrial sectors appropriate for FDI in order to comply with the State plan for national economic growth and social development, with gradual advan-

Table 2.2 Major Economic Indicators of FIEs in 1995 (¥100,000,000)

	# of FIEs	Gross Output	Added Value	Total Assets	Total Liability	Total Equity	Total Sales	Total Profit*	Total VAT
National Total	49559	10714	2586	13348	7908	5441	10116	792	306
By Ownership									
FIEs from foreign countries	20190	5326	1354	6486	3588	2898	5051	470	169
Equity joint ventures	15078	4088	1017	5257	2901	2356	3897	410	151
Cooperative joint ventures	1848	414	131	489	253	236	354	29	9
Wholly foreign owned	3264	824	206	740	434	306	800	31	9
FIEs from HK, Macau & Taiwan	29369	5388	1233	6862	4320	2543	5066	322	138
Equity joint ventures	18927	3891	911	5168	3323	1845	3665	274	114
Cooperative joint ventures	3497	549	116	652	418	234	522	18	11
Wholly foreign owned	6945	948	206	1043	579	464	878	30	13
By Light/Heavy Industry									
Light industry	33863	6283	1374	6935	4166	2769	5902	374	153
Using farm products as materials	22365	3876	879	4241	2548	1692	3631	228	96
Using nonfarm products as materials	11498	2407	495	2694	1617	1077	2271	146	57
Heavy industry	15696	4431	1212	6414	3742	2672	4214	419	153
Excavation	340	75	52	101	13	88	40	10	1
Raw materials	3155	1131	317	2321	1394	927	1086	123	52
Manufacturing	12201	3225	843	3991	2335	1656	3088	285	100

* Profit before tax.
Source: China Statistical Yearbook (1996): 424-425.

Table 2.3 Performance of FIEs Across Different Industries in 1995 (¥100,000,000)*

	# of FIEs	Gross Output	Added Value	Total Assets	Total Liability	Total Equity	Total Sales	Total Profit*	Total VAT
National Total	49559	10714	2586	13348	7908	5441	10116	792	306
Coal mining & processing	29	3	0.5	4	2	1	2	0.2	0.1
Petroleum & gas extraction	5	58	47	75	0.5	75	24	9	0
Ferrous metals mining & processing	12	0.2	0.1	0.6	0.2	0.4	0.2	0.1	0
Nonferrous metals mining & processing	40	2	0.6	3	2	1	2	0.1	0.1
Nonmetal mineral mining & processing	250	12	3	19	9	10	11	0.6	0.4
Other mineral mining & processing	2	0.1	0	0	0	0	0.1	0	0
Logging & transport of timber & bamboo	3	0	0	0.1	0	0.1	0	0	0
Food processing	1893	623	102	548	364	184	606	27	10
Food manufacturing	1909	301	68	395	215	180	283	27	13
Beverage manufacturing	1202	271	75	440	222	219	285	42	15
Tobacco processing	10	6	3	12	7	6	6	3	0.4
Textiles	4218	824	182	1035	651	384	761	27	16
Garments & other fiber products	5965	737	174	604	376	227	684	28	12
Leather, furs, down & related products	2513	523	103	403	278	125	483	11	6
Timber processing, bamboo, cane, palm fiber products	1270	115	23	156	97	60	100	3	3
Furniture manufacturing	741	68	16	92	62	31	62	4	2
Papermaking and paper products	1079	173	37	266	149	118	164	12	6
Printing and record pressing	860	74	20	137	65	72	71	6	3
Stationery, educational and sports goods	1188	186	37	160	94	66	178	5	2

Continued from the previous page	# of FIEs	Gross Output	Added Value	Total Assets	Total Liability	Total Equity	Total Sales	Total Profit*	Total VAT
Petroleum processing & coking products	133	29	4	31	23	8	29	1	10.4
Raw chemical materials and chemical products	2625	503	129	648	394	254	453	53	21
Medical and Pharmaceutical products	868	188	68	276	144	133	165	31	10
Chemical fibers	363	111	20	190	126	64	99	3	3
Rubber products	470	155	32	192	117	75	147	12	5
Plastic products	3038	376	70	490	279	210	346	10	8
Nonmetal mineral products	2548	353	105	789	428	362	316	27	16
Smelting and pressing of ferrous metals	380	230	50	305	191	114	235	13	6
Smelting and pressing of nonferrous metals	459	173	30	194	125	70	161	9	3
Metal products	2371	439	91	575	344	231	404	21	9
Ordinary machinery manufacture	1450	336	96	486	261	225	319	42	14
Special purpose equipment manufacture	1303	156	45	213	114	99	147	13	5
Transportation equipment manufacture	1409	813	189	918	541	377	803	101	35
Electric equipment and machinery	2230	631	139	729	438	290	599	42	16
Electronics and telecommunications	2900	1518	374	1360	860	500	1474	112	30
Instruments, meters, cultural & office machinery	999	169	45	172	97	75	162	12	4
Other manufacturing	2559	218	55	233	127	106	200	9	4
Electric power, steam & hot water production	229	337	150	1185	699	486	329	74	27
Gas production and supply	17	3	1	7	4	4	5	0.2	0.2
Tap water production and supply	17	0.3	0.1	3	1	2	0.2	-0.1	0

* Average exchange rate in 1995: US$1=¥8.3507

Source: China Statistical Yearbook (1996): 424-425.

ces in step with world economic development. FDI guidance is usually maintained through laws and regulations relevant to specific sectors and through periodically compiling and updating the *Orientation Directory of Industries for FDI*, with specific implementation by various levels of related government departments in charge of FDI projects.

Industries Encouraging FDI

According to regulations stipulated by the Chinese government, FDI is sought for infrastructure facilities, basic industries and technological renovation of enterprises, as well as funding of technology-intensive industries.

The following are the target industries for which the Chinese government encourages FDI:

(1) New agricultural technologies, comprehensive agricultural development, and energy or communications and key raw materials industries urgently needed for development;

(2) New, high, or advanced technologies urgently needed by the State or new equipment or materials that can improve product performance, conserve energy and raw materials, upgrade enterprises' technological level, or result in manufacturing import-substitution products that meet market needs;

(3) Projects generating more foreign exchange revenues in satisfying international market demands, which improve product quality, open new markets, or increase product export volume;

(4) New technologies or equipment projects that comprehensively utilize resources, recycle resources, or reduce environmental pollution;

(5) Other projects stipulated in state laws, decrees, or regulations.

FDI-Restricted Industries

Following are the areas restricted from foreign direct investment:

(1) Sectors in which China has already developed or introduced advanced technologies and where the production capacity is already satisfying domestic needs;

(2) Sectors in which China is implementing a trial introduction of foreign investment, or businesses monopolized by the state in selling, transacting, or operating;

(3) Exploration or mining of rare natural resources;

(4) Other projects stipulated in state laws, decrees, or regulations, such as those with quota or permit restrictions.

Projects restricted from obtaining FDI are classified into the Restricted Category A (e.g., wristwatch chips or assembly, refrigeration boxes, cans, aluminum materials, photocopiers, one-time syringes, cassette recorders, ordinary antibiotics, luxury office buildings) and Category B (e.g., offshore or inland fishing, table salt, cigarettes, cotton or woolen textiles, chemical fibers, film, sedan cars, air-conditioners, color television sets, video recorders, arterial railways, aviation and water transportation, foreign trade, luxury hotels, banks, insurance, publishing, printing). A complete list is regularly compiled, modified, announced, and implemented, by government departments.

FDI-Prohibited Industries

FDI is prohibited in the following sectors:

1. Projects that do not contribute to China's national security, national economy, social development, or social or public interest;
2. Projects that pollute the environment, destroy natural resources, or endanger human health;
3. Projects that manufacture products using technologies uniquely owned by China;
4. Other projects stipulated in state laws, decrees, or regulations.

All industries, apart from those specifically encouraged, restricted or prohibited, allow foreign direct investment. Foreign investors thus have great flexibility in selecting industries for investment.

Sectors Newly Opened to FDI

The following sectors have been opened to FDI since 1992:

(1) *Energy*: inland petroleum prospecting and mining, power generation, and energy recycling;

(2) *Communication and telecommunications*: highways, harbors, railways, civil aviation, and telecommunication facilities;

(3) *Natural resources*: exploration and mining of low-grade gold;

(4) *Forestry*: Forest planting on barren hills or wasteland to develop forestry, in the form of either equity or cooperative joint ventures with Chinese partners;

(5) *Merchandising and foreign trade*: commodity retail business in some major central cities, in the form of either Sino-foreign joint ventures or wholly foreign-owned ventures, and foreign trade business in designated development zones;

(6) *Financing and banking*: banks in some open coastal cities, in the form of either joint ventures or wholly foreign-owned businesses;

(7) *Tertiary sector*: real estate development and management of urban renovation projects in large or medium-sized cities.

As China does not have much experience pertaining to FDI in these industries, the opening up of these areas is on a trial basis and will be only gradually expanded over time.

Measures Promoting FDI

The Chinese government has adopted a series of preferential steps to boost FDI in those industries they wish to encourage. Major steps include:

(1) Regardless of where it is located, a project exceeding U.S.$30 million, upon approval by the state tax authorities, is entitled to enjoy the same preferential taxation treatment applied in economic and technological development zones;

(2) FIEs engaged in the building and operations of energy or communication infrastructure facilities (coal, electric power, local railway, highway, or harbor), with a large investment and a long projected time for return on investment, may expand their business scope in relation to their business, subject to approval;

(3) FIEs introducing new, high, or advanced technologies urgently needed by China, or new equipment or materials to manufacture import-substitution products, with the capability of balancing their own foreign exchange, may be free from the requirement to export;

(4) When the total investment amount exceeds U.S.$100 million, the percentage of the registered capital against the total investment may be made lower than stipulated by the regulations, subject to approval;

(5) Priority will be given to FIEs requesting export quotas when their products involve such quotas.

Measures Confining FDI in Restricted Industries

These restrictive measures include:

(1) The length of operations of Sino-foreign joint ventures must be specified in the joint venture contract;

(2) For projects falling within the Restricted Category A, 100 percent of the total investment is to be the registered capital if the total investment is below U.S.$10 million; 70 percent if the investment is between U.S.$10 and U.S.$30 million; and 60 percent if the investment is above U.S.$30 million. Further, a Chinese partner in the project must use his own funds for investment in fixed assets. Project approval is confined by quota limitations set by the State Council;

(3) For projects within quota limitations and Restricted Category B, project proposals are to be reviewed and approved by the government department in charge directly under the State Council and filed with the State Planning Commission or the State Economic and Trade Commission.

(4) Projects falling within Restricted Category A, upon approval, may be treated as though in allowed areas and thus free from restrictions, should either of the following specified conditions be satisfied: (i) the export value takes up over 70 percent of their total production; (ii) the existing manufacturing capabilities are used to improve the level of their products, so that the export value is increased by over 30 percent annually.

2.4 Industrial Structural Attributes

Despite great improvements in recent years, the industrial structure of China remains one of the bottlenecks hampering economic development. Inter-industry variance in after-tax profitability still abounds during transition, due primarily to long-rooted industry structure imperfections, the gradual approach of economic reforms, and a cumbersome consolidation tax system. Similarly, there is also an immense difference in sales growth across industries, attributable mainly to a government industrial policy which does not allow all sectors to be decentralized and privatized at the same time. In addition, one major structural 'headache' lies in the central government's need to control the ownership of state firms' assets while allowing them to be acquired by or merged with domestic or foreign investors. The higher asset intensity industries thus are subject to greater government interference.

In other words, inter-industry variations in asset intensity can lead to differential treatment for firms in different industries. Moreover, the growth in the number of firms in an industry is enormously idiosyncratic across industries. Controlling the number of new firms established in the industry is a predominant means for the government to monitor structural development. This entry barrier consequently leads to the heterogeneity of the degree of competition in different industries. Furthermore, industry structure is highly dynamic and uncertain, arising mainly from the transitional nature of the national economy and the experimental nature of an array of new industrial policies.

These structural characteristics lead to the following structural attributes that are important in China: (i) industry profitability, (ii) industry sales growth, (iii) industry asset intensity, (iv) the growth in the number of firms in an industry, and (v) industry structural uncertainty. Table 2.4 shows the major structural characteristics of Chinese industries in recent years.

Industry Profitability

Inter-industry variance in terms of profitability has long been an enduring characteristic of mixed and centrally-directed economies due in major part to governmental control and intervention. As Table 2.4 shows, standard deviations of profitability growth rates were extremely high. They were even higher in a late period (90-93) than an early period (88-91), suggesting increasing variations as structural transformation evolves. Table 2.4 also exhibits that the variance of after-tax profit growth across industries is significantly higher than that of before-tax profit growth. This implies that the turbid, industry-specific Industrial and Commercial Consolidation Tax (ICCT) system further compounds profit discrepancies across industries.

One dominant characteristic of governmental policy in China is that the width and depth of the removal of government-induced asymmetries in an industry depend upon the industry's profit level. Competitive entry by more efficient rivals as a result of economic decentralization and privatization usually takes place first in low-profitability industries. Hence lower-profitability industries move more quickly toward the position of market equilibrium in the transitional phase. On the other hand, however, the pursuit of social stability during economic transition necessitates state control over industries that are strategically vital to national security and economic development. The level of before- and after-tax net income in these industries is usually higher than that in other industries. As a consequence, continued government hinderance, particularly in the area of business entry, remains in high-return industries. This interference results in appreciable barriers to new entry and enables existing local firms and foreign investors in the industry to keep their market power, advantageous competitive position and favorable profitability.

Whenever a particular industry displays high profitability over the years, FIEs are likely to concentrate on exploring abnormal efficiency from a monopolistically competitive local industry, rather than on exporting to home or international markets. Furthermore, when operating in high-profitability industries, FIEs are likely to confront more government hinderance in material supply and products distribution, high latent competition pressure from new rivals and great market fluctuations, since the objective of the economic transition in formerly planned economies is to orient the industry structure toward less disequilibrium and greater market force determination.

Industry Sales Growth

A fundamental difference in sales growth across industries abounds in China, due mainly to the government industrial policy which allows only some sectors to be decentralized and privatized. Industry sales growth represents a key component of market attractiveness.

Table 2.4 The Calculation of Growth Rate (GR) for Chinese Industry Structure Attributes (Part I)

Industrial Sector	(1) GR(%) of # of Enterprises		(2) GR (%) of Net Output		(3) GR(%) of Sales		(4) GR (%) of Net Fixed Assets	
	88-91	90-93	88-91	90-93	88-91	90-93	88-91	90-93
Coal Mining & Dressing	0.78	1.76	20.35	34.65	12.39	24.25	16.26	10.21
Petroleum/Natural Gas Extraction	6.47	30.89	9.75	40.56	26.46	48.04	27.03	23.14
Ferrous Metal Mining & Dressing	4.49	21.23	22.08	42.63	30.81	36.57	13.39	9.28
Nonferrous Metal Mining & Dressing	7.48	5.07	21.87	28.4	12.33	24.89	14.99	17.91
Building Materials & Other Nonmetal Mineral Mining	-0.67	4.23	22.51	59.80	14.66	44.22	11.92	40.20
Salt Mining	3.35	-1.25	16.25	16.89	14.89	11.13	20.49	18.63
Other Minerals & Dressing	6.26	45.86	32.63	100.00	13.33	130.62	25.99	73.05
Logging & Transport of Timber & Bamboo	-7.59	1.58	5.07	17.56	19.80	21.21	7.74	5.50
Purification & Supply of Tap Water	7.13	6.44	35.42	56.46	44.49	36.50	22.35	18.93
Food Processing	-3.43	-12.41	23.71	35.18	13.50	11.49	17.21	7.73
Grain Processing	-4.07	-6.01	21.48	26.01	12.24	15.89	18.54	17.14
Beverage Processing	-3.39	-1.18	30.37	33.98	21.79	16.93	18.97	22.23
Tobacco Processing	2.67	7.24	22.81	12.35	8.86	14.75	34.77	30.53
Forage Industry	3.37	-1.31	43.52	29.49	26.42	29.31	32.30	24.45
Textile Industry	2.22	0.04	16.03	24.51	13.59	16.99	19.38	17.88
Cotton Textiles	6.34	-1.63	15.48	6.20	12.14	9.67	22.10	14.78
Woolen Textiles	4.66	-0.40	12.30	20.78	18.94	17.69	15.21	11.29
Silk Textiles	-1.76	-0.62	28.00	11.59	10.12	11.89	16.96	21.46
Sewing Industry	-2.70	1.30	25.93	47.74	27.28	33.43	24.17	35.70
Leather, Furs & Related Products	1.31	5.28	22.51	49.80	30.20	44.29	22.06	32.15
Timber, Bamboo, Cane, Palm & Straw Products	-0.63	5.26	8.17	58.31	25.10	41.78	17.58	24.12
Furniture Manufacture	-6.68	-6.20	9.60	30.48	17.37	26.42	12.93	17.26

Continued from the previous page

Industrial Sector	(1) GR(%) of # of Enterprises		(2) GR (%) of Net Output		(3) GR(%) of Sales		(4) GR (%) of Net Fixed Assets	
	88-91	90-93	88-91	90-93	88-91	90-93	88-91	90-93
Paper Making & Paper Products	3.66	3.97	16.29	17.45	16.49	24.07	16.39	22.71
Printing	2.25	6.21	19.58	35.70	20.96	26.54	13.05	26.43
Cultural, Educational & Sports Goods	3.39	5.41	19.40	36.58	30.99	32.88	21.79	30.89
Arts & Crafts	1.64	0.28	22.74	17.96	19.83	23.50	22.08	22.39
Power Generation, Stream & Hot Water Supply	-2.10	-67.61	21.70	37.25	20.94	32.13	18.17	28.62
Petroleumeum Processing	8.11	34.57	9.11	38.63	44.70	43.50	24.55	24.89
Coking, Gas & Coal Related Products	4.22	-2.69	26.10	0.05	23.86	23.31	28.42	27.65
Chemicals & Allied Products	7.09	6.83	21.78	20.02	12.18	19.62	20.89	20.24
Basic Raw Chemical Materials	7.40	0.93	23.95	5.46	12.91	15.51	27.28	20.24
Organic Chemical Products	8.51	5.78	16.13	10.36	6.17	12.68	24.78	7.37
Daily Use Chemical Products	7.96	2.83	37.13	16.61	15.18	13.60	23.76	15.62
Medical & Pharmaceutical Products	7.46	10.67	31.38	34.59	28.88	28.73	27.59	31.97
Chemical Fibers	12.29	24.78	33.10	23.88	19.46	16.82	14.36	30.99
Rubber Products	2.10	3.46	21.31	17.89	20.29	21.32	14.76	20.09
Plastic Products	3.22	4.56	23.84	33.86	30.39	27.96	20.37	24.90
Building Materials & Other Non-Metal Mineral Products	-2.23	0.88	16.76	48.37	24.60	39.83	13.25	21.01
Cement Manufacturing	0.49	-0.44	22.44	47.95	28.35	35.41	15.37	13.97
Smelting & Pressing Ferrous Metals	7.45	19.86	10.58	59.90	27.35	44.78	14.61	23.97
Smelting & Pressing Non-Ferrous Metals	8.38	12.76	20.46	39.00	22.16	29.71	14.87	24.31
Metal Products	-2.12	-0.48	16.74	41.41	21.94	34.82	15.39	25.93

Continued from the previous page

Industrial Sector	(1) GR(%) of # of Enterprises		(2) GR (%) of Net Output		(3) GR(%) of Sales		(4) GR (%) of Net Fixed Assets	
	88-91	90-93	88-91	90-93	88-91	90-93	88-91	90-93
Machine Building Industry	0.07	1.49	13.28	29.42	28.52	8.84	9.16	-7.62
Industry Equipment	2.14	0.29	12.65	23.56	25.15	29.49	8.37	11.28
Daily Use Machinery	3.74	-0.18	-1.32	10.52	31.20	26.46	10.97	13.19
Transportation Equipment	3.09	12.22	7.15	55.01	49.91	57.73	12.91	28.99
Electric Equipment & Machinery	1.76	5.81	21.10	36.22	22.80	37.17	17.23	27.23
Daily Use Electric Equipment	-0.03	-0.82	24.37	33.17	27.80	27.14	20.14	26.08
Electronic & Telecommunication Equipment	6.75	10.83	27.46	34.22	36.28	37.05	23.80	29.70
Daily Use Electronics Apparatus	4.19	-2.49	23.26	14.51	30.87	18.46	23.83	21.96
Instruments, Metals & Other Measuring Equipment	-0.19	12.35	16.00	44.72	29.50	52.64	10.42	30.54
Mean (%)	**2.48**	**5.64**	**20.63**	**36.44**	**23.73**	**32.80**	**18.81**	**24.16**
Standard Deviation	**4.31**	**16.28**	**8.20**	**17.14**	**9.19**	**19.69**	**6.15**	**11.87**

Table 2.4 The Calculation of Growth Rate (GR) for Chinese Industry Structure Attributes (Part II)

Industrial Sector	(5) GR(%) of After Tax Profit		(6) GR (%) of Pre-Tax Profit		Comprehensive Growth Index			
	88-91	90-93	88-91	90-93	88-91 Mean(%)	90-93 St.D	88-91 Mean(%)	90-93 St.D
Coal Mining & Dressing	62.17	29.90	167.97	63.40	46.65	57.52	27.36	19.65
Petroleum/Natural Gas Extraction	-17.34	-23.24	-17.53	126.71	5.81	18.14	41.03	44.62
Ferrous Metals Mining & Dressing	8.13	31.07	11.09	33.65	15.00	8.90	29.07	10.94
Nonferrous Metals Mining & Dressing	-2.24	-0.03	1.19	4.50	9.27	8.18	13.46	10.86
Building Materials & Other Nonmetal Minerals Mining & Dressing	2.31	29.80	7.98	35.23	9.78	7.73	35.58	16.83
Salt Mining	-2.66	-5.98	3.29	-0.96	9.27	8.36	6.41	9.56
Other Minerals & Dressing	26.00	25.99	44.22	51.83	24.74	12.36	71.23	35.18
Logging & Transport of Timber & Bamboo	72.28	71.25	-18.87	28.56	13.07	29.13	24.28	22.90
Purification & Supply of Tap Water	26.10	64.53	25.19	58.59	26.78	11.53	40.24	21.60
Food Processing	-13.45	-4.45	-2.75	-0.95	5.80	13.16	6.10	15.17
Grain Processing	1.04	3.60	1.96	6.66	8.53	9.48	10.55	10.40
Beverage Processing	-11.42	114.83	8.51	32.08	10.81	14.55	36.48	36.90
Tobacco Processing	-499.9	-3177.1	11.79	10.52	-69.83	192.61	-516.91	1189.70
Forage Industry	4.90	38.96	14.98	24.85	20.92	14.55	24.29	12.40
Textile Industry	-20.73	-546.19	-0.51	-8.64	5.00	13.55	-82.57	207.65
Cotton Textiles	-140.80	-16.73	-16.91	-14.71	-16.95	56.73	-0.40	11.89
Woolen Textiles	-29.57	511.12	-18.22	32.84	0.55	18.11	98.89	184.63
Silk Textiles	-14.60	-18.37	4.05	-5.84	7.13	13.55	3.35	13.17
Sewing Industry	-3.42	32.26	4.79	25.81	12.68	13.41	29.37	14.16
Leather, Furs & Related Products	-33.17	128.17	-9.12	50.41	5.63	21.99	51.68	37.52
Timber Processing, Bamboo, Cane, Palm Fiber & Straw Products	-56.35	158.18	-31.54	84.64	-6.28	28.69	62.05	194.43

Industrial Sector	(5) GR(%) of After Tax Profit		(6) GR (%) of Pre-Tax Profit		Comprehensive Growth Index			
	88-91	90-93	88-91	90-93	88-91 Mean(%)	90-93 St.D	88-91 Mean(%)	90-93 St.D
Furniture Manufacturing	-35.17	106.55	-14.09	41.25	-2.67	18.25	35.96	34.78
Paper Making & Paper Products	-33.22	-8.47	-11.98	9.35	1.27	18.51	11.51	11.40
Printing	0.82	8.77	4.92	13.72	10.26	8.07	19.56	10.69
Cultural, Educational & Sports Goods	-2.27	26.60	1.84	22.76	12.52	12.18	25.85	10.15
Arts & Crafts Articles	-12.10	14.19	1.44	13.88	9.27	13.12	15.37	7.67
Power Generation, Stream & Hot Water Production & Supply	17.08	23.34	15.69	19.85	15.24	8.05	12.26	36.16
Petroleum Processing	-13.43	57.16	3.75	20.67	12.80	18.08	36.57	12.04
Coking, Gas & Coal Related Products	-52.02	-106.07	-25.29	-148.79	0.88	30.05	-34.42	67.82
Chemicals & Allied Products	-15.45	-19.83	-0.10	0.25	7.73	12.91	7.42	14.18
Basic Raw Chemical Materials	-21.99	-23.15	-3.91	-1.00	7.61	16.79	3.00	13.93
Organic Chemical Products	-14.77	3.26	-4.16	0.56	6.11	12.89	6.67	4.08
Daily Use Chemical Products	-2.56	-6.40	9.46	3.75	15.16	12.62	7.67	8.32
Medical & Pharmaceutical Products	-4.65	29.14	2.61	27.25	15.55	14.23	27.06	7.71
Chemical Fibers	6.45	5.58	14.08	7.20	16.62	11.33	18.21	9.32
Rubber Products	-8.73	14.02	2.60	15.94	8.72	10.91	15.59	5.89
Plastic Products	-18.94	13.72	-7.08	18.46	8.63	17.70	20.58	9.64
Building Materials & Other Non-Metal Mineral Products	-19.80	121.24	-1.72	61.39	5.14	14.74	48.79	37.76
Cement Manufacturing	-16.71	246.56	1.91	78.76	8.64	15.16	70.37	82.70
Smelting & Pressing Ferrous Metals	-14.12	66.05	2.20	51.12	8.01	12.57	44.28	17.19
Smelting & Pressing Non-Ferrous Metals	-16.38	10.18	-3.43	17.97	7.68	13.17	22.32	9.95
Metal Products	-15.38	32.62	-3.51	29.66	5.51	13.55	27.93	13.71

Continued from the previous page

Industrial Sector	(5) GR(%) of After Tax Profit		(6) GR (%) of Pre-Tax Profit		Comprehensive Growth Index			
	88-91	90-93	88-91	90-93	88-91 Mean(%)	90-93 St.D	88-91 Mean(%)	90-93 St.D
Machine Building Industry	-25.41	26.66	-11.99	13.56	2.27	17.47	12.06	13.08
Industry Equipment	-23.61	26.25	-10.97	23.68	2.29	15.88	19.09	10.12
Daily Use Machinery	-41.23	458.67	33.40	31.62	6.13	24.83	91.71	164.42
Transportation Equipment	1.50	58.79	6.90	57.14	13.58	16.64	44.98	17.94
Electric Equipment & Machinery	-22.49	39.14	-7.11	31.17	5.55	16.52	29.46	11.30
Daily Use Electric Equipment	6.36	100.86	7.05	35.38	14.28	10.32	36.97	30.94
Electronic & Telecommunication Equip.	-17.55	39.26	-9.15	34.24	11.27	19.63	30.92	9.45
Daily Use Electronics Apparatus	-34.54	17.45	-19.98	8.95	4.61	24.30	13.14	8.05
Instruments, Metals & Other Measuring Equip.	-13.92	34.17	-5.40	36.40	6.07	14.36	35.14	12.52
Mean (%)	**-19.85**	**-62.55**	**4.51**	**26.02**	**8.38**		**10.42**	
Standard Deviation	**81.58**	**515.60**	**29.67**	**38.15**	**15.38**		**89.05**	

Source: The author's own calculation based on the China Statistical Yearbook.

Growth has served as an indicator of disequilibrium, a condition favorably associated with entry, and as an indicator of industry evolution. Porter (1980) argues that rapid industry growth ensures that incumbents can maintain a strong financial performance even though new entrants take some market share. When a sector is undergoing transition or has been privatized, thus freeing from government control over market supply, a rapid initial development will usually ensue. This take-off is reflected in a surge in industry sales growth, which in turn provides foreign companies preemptive opportunities to capitalize on. Nevertheless, when the local market for a particular industry appears to grow dramatically, foreign investors will face more competition from local incumbents, foreign rivals, and new entrants. Thus, selecting an industry with high sales growth does not ensure the ultimate success for MNCs. Instead, foreign companies need to have operational strategies that align properly with both environment and objectives and maintain a sustained competitive edge in the industry chosen.

Industry Asset Intensity

Asset intensity varies greatly across different Chinese industries, differentially impacting a company's ability to enter a target industry and subsequent performance. As a plausible indicator for capital requirements, industry asset intensity constitutes a proxy for entry barriers. A high level of asset intensity in an industry has also been viewed as reflecting exit barriers created by substantial resource commitments that may not be fully recoverable. Indeed sunk investment represents a risk that is assumed by firms only when profitability is also high. Following the lifting of state-instituted price controls, entry barriers due to high capital requirements may increase industry concentration and facilitate collusive pricing behavior even in the absence of any formal collusion among firms. As a result, MNCs in a high-asset-intensity industry are likely to maintain a high level of financial return.

In the course of economic transition, one major dilemma faced by the Chinese government lies in the control of the ownership of state firms' assets while allowing firms to be acquired or merged by domestic or foreign investors. Thus the higher asset intensity industries are subject to greater government interference. In other words, inter-industry variations in asset intensity can lead to treatment variations for firms in different industries. However, oligopolistic rivalry in transitional economies is played out in an uncertain, ever-changing environment. While the evolution of this environment permits managers to learn about market conditions and competitors' intentions, it also presents the constant danger that a rival will undercut the existing pricing structure in search of competitive advantage.

Growth in the Number of Firms in an Industry

China's industry structure before economic transition was characterized by high concentration (relatively small numbers of enterprises) and by the limited freedom of action permitted to these enterprises. This system causes widespread poor performance in many industries. During the transitional stage, particularly in recent years, the performance has been remarkably improved. This is the result of increased competition and growing financial pressures that have accompanied a gradual and still incomplete shift from a planned economy to a market economy. In industry, the transition from planned to market environment starts with commodities and has now begun to penetrate the allocation of land, labor, and capital. Few firms remain immune from competition. For instance, the share of industrial products sold through markets now exceeds 85 percent. MNCs have played an important role in enhancing nationwide competition and pushing the economy forward to the market orientation. The degree of concentration is low and declining, and the barriers to domestic trade are increasingly porous.

Having decentralized many industry sectors which had been unable to meet market demand, the number of firms in these now-more-competitive industries has drastically grown and this growth constitutes a good proxy for competitive vigor in the transitional phase. Wherever the vigor of competition is not reflected in the increase in the number of firms (i.e., government-controlled state firms still dominate the industry), MNCs are generally not permitted to enter. Economic theory recognizes that other things (such as the height of entry barriers) being equal, competitive intensity is positively related to the number of firms in the industry. As a result of the decentralization and privatization of many sectors during structural transformation, entry barriers to these industries are markedly reduced, and the number of firms including both local enterprises and FIEs increases. These developments boost competition in the industry, lessen the difference of firm's profitability between industries, and slow down the average growth rate of local sales for individual firms.

2.5 Statistical Analysis and Implications

Based on the cross-sectional data for 186 FIEs covering the years 1988 through 1991 obtained from the Jiangsu Provincial Commission of Foreign Economic Relations and Trade, together with the industrial data as calculated in Table 2.4, I examined a relationship between major structural attributes and performance of FIEs in Jiangsu (see Luo, *JBR*, 1999). The following results were found:

First, industry profitability is found to have a significant impact on overall performance of a FIE and a strong positive effect on its efficiency and local market expansion, but a negative effect on its export and risk reduction. This evidence suggests that industry profitability in China vigorously affects all the major dimensions of FIE performance, but is heterogeneous according to the dimension considered. The trade-off between efficiency and risk reduction and between local market expansion and export performance supports the notion in FDI literature that FIE performance is multidimensional and its evaluation should correspond to the roles of the venture stipulated by the parent firms. Additionally, asset size is found to mediate the positive function of industry profitability on a firm's efficiency.

Second, industry sales growth is significantly related to FIE's overall performance and positively linked with firm profitability and domestic sales growth. However, FIE's export growth is an inverse function of industry's sales growth. This finding demonstrates that FIEs in China attain economic rents from local industry sales growth, participating in local expansion at the expense of exports. When domestic industry conditions are unfavorable, FIE's strategic aim necessitates cost-minimization and is reflected in the high performance of exports.

Third, industry asset intensity has no significant effect on FIE's overall performance, but has a modest positive influence on a firm's profitability and a negative influence on the firm's export and risk reduction. This finding, based on the Chinese context, is consistent with observations by Bettis (1981) of firms in developed market economies. Bettis found that capital requirement is positively associated with a firm's profit level at the expense of risk reduction. Also consistent with our earlier prediction, the results demonstrate that FIEs investing in high asset intensity industries appear to manifest a long-term commitment to local production rather than to export expansion. In addition, an FIE's type of project is also found to moderate the form of the relationship between industry asset intensity and firm efficiency.

Fourth, the growth in the number of firms in an industry is positively associated with FIE's profitability and local market expansion in a significant way. Unlike advanced market economies, high growth in the number of firms in an industry in China does not simply represent increased competition. Rather, it mirrors industry growth when government-instituted control over market supply is lifted during the economic transition.

Finally, it is observed that industry structural uncertainty has a significant effect on FIE's overall performance. Specifically, FIE's operational risk is an increasing function of industry's uncertainty. Nevertheless, the form of this univariate relationship is moderated by FIE's operation length. A greater length of operations in China lessens the unfavorable impact of structural uncertainty on the operational stability of FIEs in this context.

Overall, these results reveal some similarities in the structure-performance relationship for international production between China and a developed market economy on which early studies are often based. The similarities reside in performance implications of such structural variables as industry profitability, sales growth, and asset intensity. Nevertheless, in two areas the relationships diverge according to context. First, whereas market economy-based studies find that the growth in the number of firms in an industry is negatively related to a firm's accounting return and market growth, the studies based in China observe a positive relationship. Indeed, when government-instituted controls over industry supply are lifted during a transitional phase, high growth in the number of firms in an industry signals industry growth, rather than, simply increased competition. In other words, it seems that 'an emerging economy' is aptly named, since the explosion in the number of participants in newly competitive industries does not exhaust its potential. Second, while market economy-based studies demonstrate that there is not necessarily a causality between industry structural uncertainty and operational risks facing firms, the studies based in China show a positive relationship between the two, implying that macro environmental factors outweigh micro firm characteristics in China. This may derive from the nature of industry structural uncertainty. If, as is very probable, uncertainty is attributable mostly to government policies, then no single firm can escape the risks of changing rules and their consequences.

The above findings may have some managerial implications for MNC managers. First, industry profitability and its sales growth are important for FIE's overall performance and both have a profoundly favorable influence on FIE's economic efficiency and market growth in the country. Nevertheless, they are negatively associated with either risk reduction or export growth. Second, industry asset intensity, a proxy for an industry's economy of scale and capital requirement, has a positive effect on FIE's profitability, although it is not significant for FIE's overall performance. Third, the growth in the number of firms in an industry is positively, rather than negatively, linked with FIE's market growth and accounting return. High growth in this number seems to be not a representation of increased competition, but rather a signal of more business potential once the various government-instituted interventions are gradually eliminated. Fourth, industry structural instability is significantly and positively related to FIE's operational risk. It is difficult for FIEs to avoid the risks derived from the uncertainty of Chinese industrial policies. Finally, the relationship between industry structural variables and firm performance is modified by such firm-level attributes as length of local operations, type of project, and FIE size.

These results suggest that industry structural attributes in the Chinese economy are not only important to the overall performance of international expansion of foreign businesses, but also crucial to several aspects of FIE performance taken separately. It is found that the relationship between an industry's profitability, sales growth, and asset intensity and FIE performance in the Chinese context is similar to that in developed market economies, but the effects of structural uncertainty and growth in the number of firms are different. Moreover, the results indicate enormous differences in the effect that different variables have on FIE's overall and unidimensional performance. In addition, each individual structural variable affects differently the various dimensions of FIE performance. Overall, evidence from China suggests that industry attractiveness in a host country constitutes a significant source for explaining variations of MNC performance.

Industry structural characteristics constitute an important driver of international investment performance in China. As a critical investment strategy element for foreign investors, industry selection in the host country influences not only economic efficiency and local market expansion but also operational risk and export growth. In the process of industry selection, foreign investors should assess all the important structural attributes of the industry they opt for, including sales growth, profitability, asset intensity, growth in the number of firms in the industry, and structural uncertainty. Foreign investors seeking profitability should enter those industries which reveal high profitability, high sales growth, or high asset intensity. For foreign investors seeking market growth in China, it is advisable to enter those industries which exhibit high growth in the number of firms or high sales growth. Alternatively, foreign investors pursuing risk diversification are warned not to enter high structural uncertainty or high profitability industries. Dynamically, length of operations in China can facilitate the positive influence, or mitigate the negative effect of related structural attributes on foreign investment performance.

During the past seventeen years, China's industrial economy has achieved important progress toward building a market system. The accumulation of market experience and the confidence inspired by a large increase in living standards have created a consensus favoring a market-based economy with a limited role for state ownership, government planning, and bureaucratic regulation of economic activity. Today, competition is emerging as a powerful force for beneficial change in all segments of China's semi-market industrial system. As a result, this episode of partial reform raises the level of industrial output and enhances economic welfare while creating the foundation for a market system. The steady decline in entry and trade barriers in the new system opens up the Chinese market to MNCs. Indeed, the potential benefits for China from FDI are enormous, and it would be a rational choice for the government to maintain a policy of welcoming transnational investors. In late June 1994, the State Planning Commission (SPC) released its industrial development outline for the remainder of the decade. The SPC's blueprint gives special attention to FDI in 'pillar' industries such as petrochemicals, autos, construction, electronics, and machinery, and infrastructure industries such as transportation, telecommunications, oil drilling, and power generation. Indeed, given the country's population of 1.2 billion, the consumer and investment market will be practically impossible to saturate if the economy stays on a reasonably healthy and stable path. The government has planned that in the next ten years China will invest $500 billion in its infrastructure alone, and a sizable portion of that amount needs to come from the international capital markets. The energy industry, for example, will need to raise $20 billion in foreign capital before the year 2000.

Although extremely promising, the Chinese market can present daunting challenges to unwary investors. The Chinese government has taken a series of measures to make FDI in important industries consistent with its planned priorities. For example, the government requires all new projects in the auto industry: i) to produce autos with 80-90 percent local content within a few years of operation, ii) to hold no more than 50 percent share of equity in any new joint venture, iii) to establish R&D facilities within ventures, and iv) to balance foreign exchange through export of vehicles or components. In the aircraft manufacturing industry, Boeing was required to successively assist the main Chinese aircraft manufacturer in Xian in establishing the capacity to produce spare parts, to manufacture whole sections of aircraft, and to assist in establishing a capacity to produce complete aircraft within China.

In plunging into the Chinese market, MNCs should keep a wary eye on the dynamics of structural transformation and on government policies during this process. Today, the globalization of markets and products has intensified competitive rivalry in industry after industry, where a large number of companies battle each other for market share in more and more countries. This rivalry has driven down profit rates and made it all the more critical for companies to maximize their efficiency, quality, customer responsiveness, and innovative ability. China and other formerly centrally-planned economies are now no longer totally new territory for most MNCs. In fact, many of them have established second generation ventures there. Only those who pioneer new industries, markets, products, ways of doing business, and government relations are able to gain a competitive edge over local or foreign rivals.

2.6 WTO Entry and Its Influence

Overview

For more than thirteen years, China has sought entry into the WTO. Intense negotiations with both the WTO body and with individual members of said organization are currently taking place and will eventually determine China's fate within this realm. However, all parties involved have much to lose if China is not admitted to the organization.

Let's consider the following important elements and motives involved in the complex negotiations:

1. *WTO Motivation:* The WTO's motive is to act as the main, undisputed authority in regulation and mediation of global trade. Shameless in its self promotion, the organization views stabilization of world markets and global peace as its core ideology. China's importance within the global economy cannot be ignored and is growing in strength. How can the WTO achieve its mission without having one of the globally most significant economies, with a population and market to match, included? The answer is that the WTO cannot achieve its mission without China on board and thus the position of the WTO can be determined.
2. *U.S. Motivation:* Different political administrations can have a profound influence on the overt motivation of the U.S. Currently the overt position has been "engagement" with China. Nevertheless, as overt administration messages can change, the main U.S. motivation remains the same – freer access to the enormous potential that China's market represents. China is a growing economy with an unprecedented population base. U.S. business views this as the "golden egg" of the east, where future growth depends on access to China's market. The U.S. also has more political motives involved. The U.S. can, for reasons it de-

cides alone, block China's entry into the WTO. Knowing that China is officially looking for entry, the U.S. views China's entry as a great bargaining chip with which to manipulate China into making socio-political reforms which may or may not have much to do with actual economic issues. However, one senses a growing restlessness on the part of U.S. business groups for an expedited approval of China's entry into the WTO. In fact, Thomas Donohue, president of the U.S. Chamber of Commerce urged the Clinton administration to strike a WTO pact with China without delay.
3. *China's Motivation:* China's burgeoning industries would benefit greatly from export access and most favored nation trading status in trading its good with other nations. It is also argued that entry into the WTO would also "legitimize" China's standing as a global power. However, in negotiating entry, China is understandably apprehensive to make sweeping reforms that would place the country in a less favorable trading position. Examples include: 1) the debate over China's classification as a "developed" or "developing" nation; 2) trading rights; 3) regulation of intellectual property rights; and 4) reduction of tariffs. Similar to the U.S., China also has its own political motivations to enter into the WTO – Taiwan. Taiwan is also seeking membership into the WTO and, some would argue, is further along the process than China. Taiwan's acceptance into the WTO before China would be viewed as a political "loss of face" to powerful China. This extra element places a time-sensitive motivation on China for her application.

One cannot blame nations for acting in their own self interests. This is exactly what is happening with China's entry into the WTO. And, it is not a matter of if China will be allowed membership into the WTO. Barring any unusual or unforeseen circumstances, it is almost inevitable and only a question of when. For as outlined above, it is in all the major players' best interest to allow China entry. It is now that all the players are jockeying for the best position prior to the inevitable.

The WTO Director-General at that time, Renato Ruggiero, summed it up well during a recent speech at Beijing University – "The reality that China is already a leading power in an ever more interdependent global economy is apparent. China increasingly needs the opportunities and security of the WTO system to fulfill its huge potential for growth and development. And the WTO [and its member states] increasingly needs China as a full and active member to be a truly universal system."

Advantages

As a member, China would be entitled to take advantage of the free trade commitments made by the 135 members of the WTO – covering over 90% of the world's trade. This would result in a substantial benefit to China's export trade – particularly its low- to mid-technology labor-intensive industries, such as clothing, footwear, textiles, toys and consumer electronics. For example, following the Uruguay round, average tariff levels among the WTO's developed countries dropped from 6.3 percent to 3.8 percent. According to former WTO Director-General Renato Ruggiero, this benefit, together with the two outlined below, make up the three main reasons why China should join the WTO.

A key principle underlying the WTO is the Most Favoured Nation principle. This means that a WTO member must ensure that its commitments apply equally to all WTO members, without discrimination or exception. If a member grants a new concession to one of its trading partners in the WTO, it must extend the concession to all members. This assurance of non-discrimination would increase the certainty and stability of the export environment for China's exporters and also free the government from the threat that a trading partner might use economic sanctions against China in order to further a political goal. The prime example of this is the U.S. linkage of MFN status with its evaluation of China's human rights policy.

As mentioned previously, China would have the power to help draft the most important trading rules in the world if it became a member. As an outsider, China would only be able to accept or reject the trading arena created by the WTO members. This addresses the motivation of China's application for WTO membership to further legitimize her position as a true global power – for a true global power is not only subject to regulations which dictate global conduct but is an actual part of the apparatus making said decisions, regulations and policy.

A significant improvement over GATT, the WTO incorporates a

mechanism for the settling of disputes between its members. This reduces the chances that a larger country will rely on its economic might rather than its legal right to impose its will on smaller nations. For example, Venezuela won a trade dispute against the U.S. in 1996 regarding the U.S.' imposition of discriminatory standards on imported gasoline. While it is an economic power in its own right, China too could benefit from an orderly means of resolving trade disputes.

On an internal, political front, WTO membership could give Premier Zhu Rongji the necessary ammunition to carry out his fundamental reforms of the Chinese economy. He faces conservative forces and powerful opponents defending their vested interests against his plans to reform China's state-owned enterprises and banking and finance sector, and to introduce competition to spur the development of China's industries. For example, the Ministry of Information Industries' powerful leader, Wu Jichuan, strongly opposes efforts to increase competition in China's telecommunications industry. But if Premier Zhu can point to a binding requirement on China to liberalize market access, in a package of concessions negotiated as part of WTO accession, resistance will be greatly reduced. In short, WTO membership will help spur further market reform and prevent back-sliding. It is interesting to speculate whether this is in fact the main reason behind Premier Zhu's strong advocacy of WTO membership in 1999.

Disadvantages

The main disadvantage of membership is the potential effect of China's trade liberalization commitments on its burgeoning local industries, many of which are in the infancy stage and clearly uncompetitive on the global stage. The price China must pay for membership is a broad array of tariff, market access and other trade concessions. One of the key principles underlying the WTO is that of national treatment. This means that once a WTO member's goods or services have entered another WTO member country, they must be accorded the same treatment as the destination country's domestic goods and services. While it is generally considered a benefit of WTO membership, the principle of national treatment would work, overall, to the disadvantage of China. It would prohibit the giving of special advantages to local firms and requirements to "buy local." Such measures to boost local industry are commonly employed by the Chinese government at present.

China would be required to substantially lower its tariffs and reduce non-tariff measures for a broad range of agricultural and industrial products. And, China has already made progress to comply in this area:

1. In April of 1996, China announced a massive cut in import tariffs, bringing the average from 35.3% to 23%.
2. China has pledged to further lower the overall average tariff to 15% within the year 2000.

The immediate effect of these concessions would be [and is] a reduction of China's tax revenues; the longer term effect may be a loss of market share or even market exit by China's farmers and domestic enterprises in the face of more competitive foreign imports. This effect is compounded by the fact that China will also remove long-standing prohibitions on foreign firms against engaging in the import-export business and the distribution of goods within China.

Opinions are mixed as to whether the increase in competition will be beneficial in the long-run or will cause so much short-term pain as to cripple the development of Chinese industries. As a general rule, the threat of foreign competition is considered to be a healthy influence spurring domestic enterprises to improve their performance. On the other hand, infant industries may need a degree of protection before being exposed to highly-competitive foreign firms.

The effects of increased competition will vary from industry to industry. The reduction of tariffs on imported automobiles from 80-100% to 25% by 2005 will have a great impact on the market share of China's domestic automobile industry. Domestic companies such as Haier, Guangdong Kelon and Legend have learned from the competition and achieved dominant positions in their respective industries. The computer manufacturer Legend even seized a 5.4% share of the Asia-Pacific market (excluding Japan) in 1998.

It should also be noted that Chinese companies' exposure to competition may not be as great as it first appears. At the very least, they will enjoy a considerable period of adjustment. This is because foreign importers would need to overcome a large number of barriers which are not addressed by WTO requirements, such as labyrinthine distribution networks and the use of *guanxi* to govern business relationships. China's access concessions will only provide foreign firms with the key to open the first of many doors.

As services have been included in the WTO's jurisdiction since the Uruguay Round, China would also be required to make market access concessions in its services sectors, including telecommunications, banking, insurance and perhaps also securities. Generally speaking, China's services sector is weaker than its industrial sector and the impact of foreign competition may be most greatly felt in this sector.

Foreign banking and insurance firms are presently subject to many restrictions in terms of numbers of branches, permitted locations and scope of business. China may be required to greatly reduce these restrictions over a period of years. For example, foreign banks may be permitted to engage in renminbi retail banking by 2005, and foreign insurance companies may be allowed to issue types of insurance amounting to 85% of the insurance market. In my opinion, foreign competition would have a devastating impact on local Chinese banks and insurance firms. The modern conception of these industries is extremely new to China, and local firms would lack the sophisticated array of services, in-depth expertise and advanced information technology possessed by their highly-competitive Western counterparts. In addition, local banks are weighed down by a historical burden of non-performing loans to state-owned enterprises.

In the telecommunications sector, China has traditionally allowed Western firms to supply equipment, but has barred them from involvement in service provision. According to a U.S. statement, China proposes to allow 49% foreign participation in all services upon accession and 50% foreign ownership in value-added paging services within two years of accession. But foreign firms may still face significant difficulties in penetrating China's market, because the powerful incumbent provider (China Telecom) and its parent and industry regulator (the MII) can create informal barriers to competition. One might observe that since its inception in 1994, China Telecom's competitor China Unicom has only achieved a 1% market share overall (4% in mobile services), despite its backing by the former Ministry of Electronic Industries.

Implications

Despite the occasional muttering about the U.S.-China trade deficit, the U.S. and other Western nations are in favour of China joining the WTO, as far as the economic aspects of the issue are concerned (of course, the anti-Chinese sentiment of the U.S. Congress is a different story.) It is said that there can be no real "world" trade organization without the world's third largest economy. Western nations seem to have done their calculations and concluded that freer access to one of the world's largest markets will provide greater benefits than the detriment suffered from extending access to Chinese exporters. On the Chinese side, a director of Goldman Sachs considers that WTO entry could spur China's economic growth rate by 0.5 percentage points annually by 2005, but does not give his reasons for this projection.

In fact, one could present a strong case that the WTO needs China more than China needs the WTO. China's exports have done remarkably well in the 13 years during which it has waited for membership, save for the last year. China has arranged many bilateral trade agreements with, and concessions from, its major trading partners, which act as a partial substitute for WTO membership. Chief among these is the Most Favored Nation status (now known as Normal Trade Relations) accorded by the U.S., which extends WTO-level tariffs to China's imports to the U.S.. MFN is nominally subject to cancellation each year, but has been renewed for 8 consecutive years despite periods of strong anti-China feeling in the U.S. Congress. The granting of MFN has now been de-linked from China's human rights record. On June 3, 1999, President Clinton announced that MFN would be renewed once again.

China could fairly claim that the concessions asked of it are high relative to its current economic position. The general approach of the U.S., in particular, is to base its demands on what China is likely to be in the early 21st century, rather than what it currently is. This is illustrated by the heated debate over whether China should be classified as a developed or developing nation. A developing nation is subject to lower free trade commitments, and is given more time to phase them in. It is ludicrous that this debate is taking place at all. While the size of China's economy is immense – it is the third largest economy in the world – the nature of its economy is undoubtedly that of a developing nation.

To state matters more boldly, it seems that the U.S. regards China's WTO accession as a one-time opportunity to extract the largest number of concessions from China, so as to prepare itself for future economic rivalry with China. From its experiences with Japan, the U.S. has learned that it is difficult to use the WTO's multilateral trading rules to penetrate the opaque markets of a WTO fellow member. In view of its already huge trade deficit with China, the U.S. seems to be trying to achieve a better position vis-a-vis China.

The danger for China is that, in an attempt to quickly rectify its recent poor trade performance, it may have created too much pressure on itself to offer overly generous trade concessions. These concessions may have a detrimental effect on the development of China's local industries in the long term. China's poor export growth in 1998 and early this year is quite probably due to the economic crisis still plaguing many of its export markets in Asia. China's entry into the WTO will not stimulate demand in those markets – only an economic recovery will have that effect.

If China is not in an undue hurry for WTO accession, as a means to deliver a quick boost to exports, China can probably negotiate better terms than the ones currently on offer. The best course of action for the long-term health of China's economy may be to reject entry into the WTO on the current terms and to negotiate further to close the gap between the level of trade liberalization demanded by its major trading partners and the level of foreign competition which Chinese firms can benefit from or at least cope with, particularly in the areas of banking and insurance.

The current climate of economic reform and other political considerations in China may make the government more inclined to accept a package of extensive market-opening reforms. The massive reform task facing the government as it attempts to shift China's moribund socialist system to a modern, efficient market economy is beyond imagination. As mentioned previously, Premier Zhu is opposed by deep-seated and powerful forces on all sides. If reform attempts have reached an impassable bottleneck, the one solution may be to let in an irreversible wave of foreign firms and allow fierce market competition to force reforms that no amount of central government edicts can currently implement, despite the intense short-term pain that this will cause to local firms. In such a situation, China would not have the luxury of engaging in a lengthy negotiation and fine-tuning of an accession package in the manner described in the preceding paragraph. If this is indeed China's situation, the protests of the Chinese negotiators at the size of the concessions requested by the U.S. will be mostly for show, and we will see China join the WTO before the end of this year.

Future Impact

1) Service Trade Deficit

In terms of service trade, the U.S. has competitive advantages with a trade surplus of $0.9 billion in 1995, which will grow as China gradually opens its market to foreign partners. The service industry of China is still in the introductory or growth stage compared to its U.S. counterpart, which is at its maturity stage. For the sake of China's development toward a service-oriented economy, simply allowing liberal foreign competition entry may not be appropriate.

However, China will not be able to depend on protection of domestic service industry by keeping foreigners out. China should rather prepare for competition with foreign counterparts. One solution might be to form an alliance with foreign counterparts, as the Industrial and Commercial Bank of China (ICBC) did with Tokyo Mitsubishi Bank. Through such alliances, the Chinese side may learn the competencies they need to compete with foreign counterparts.

2) Position of state-owned enterprises (SOEs)

Participation in the WTO will make Chinese SOEs more competitive due to the pressure of competition not only with domestic non-SOEs but also with foreign enterprises. This sounds good for China but reform of SOEs is not so easy. The most important task for China now is how to keep social stability while introducing competition to increase the nation's competitiveness. Though obtaining membership in WTO might promote a certain level of SOE reform, the Chinese government will find a way to prevent too much social instability caused by closing loss-making SOEs or laying-off more workers.

3) Special Economic Zones

Some Western economists such as Jack Perkowski, the president of the U.S. direct-investment firm Asimco, predicts that China's expected entry into the WTO will eliminate the policy attraction of special economic zones (SEZ). This is due to the "National Treatment" clause, a key WTO principle which restricts member countries from treating foreign and domestic companies differently. This rule will take away SEZ core attractions, which are preferential tax rates and other exemptions for foreigners. A similar example is Ireland's Shannon Free Zone. Its primary role is facilitating industriel development and free trade for Ireland based industries after Ireland's integration with the EU common market.

However, even after these policy incentives disappear, systemic incentives such as superior power supply, telecommunications, and other advanced infrastructure will remain a key attraction. This will be obvious especially with SEZs built by central government or richer provinces in the coastal areas, thanks to its higher infrastructure investment per square foot ($96-120 million in Pudong) compared to SEZs set up by provinces and major cities (average $24 million) or lower-level zones (average $1.2 million). Considering these infrastructure incentives together with higher quality of workforce and adoption of more international standards, some of the major SEZs will remain a leading economic power, while other minor SEZs will gradually fade away if they do not have much systemic incentives other than policy incentives.

4) Industries

China's WTO entry will bring changes to almost all the industries in the country, especially the following areas:

(i) Direct selling: It was a shocking incident not only for companies like Amway or Avon but also for China watchers when China banned direct selling in April, 1998 for fear of economic disorder by their controversial selling system. The ban caused millions of dollars in losses for these companies. However, China has agreed to lift the ban by year 2003, if they enter WTO. China also agreed to make rules for direct sales based on the code of conduct of the World Federation of Direct Selling Associations. Some direct sales companies are still less optimistic compared to Avon, who is already in the market. However, more foreign firms will operate in China, which will help domestic direct selling industry to emerge and stimulate distribution industry as well. Direct selling will also help firms to extend their sales to rural areas, where infrastructure for retail operations is not so well developed.

(ii) Computer: There are more than 200 PC manufacturers in China, ten of which occupy nearly 60% of the market. In addition, more than 150 new manufacturers have already obtained production permits excluding numerous others that are applying for the license. If China is forced to open the PC market completely and repeal the requirement of manufacturing licenses, there will be more firms coming into the market.

Suppose the market share for the top ten companies remains around 60% and the annual growth of PC sales remains about 50%, the sales volume in 1999 will therefore be 1,837,500. If we simply allocate this volume equally to 340 existing non-top-ten companies, it turns out that each manufacturer produces only 5,400 PCs annually. This is too low to achieve economies of scale. Therefore, deregulation of industry following WTO entry might bring in new manufacturers and in the short-term the smaller firms will gradually disappear due to production inefficiencies. In long run, there will be a few domestic manufacturers and a couple of huge MNCs.

(iii) Telecommunication: Currently, Chinese telecommunication is open only in terms of manufacturing of equipment. However, after WTO entry, China will have to deregulate the prohibited area of telecom services. In the manufacturing sector, there are some domestic companies growing and gaining market share over foreign-invested firms. Therefore, there will be less impact on the domestic firms in this sector. However, in the service sector, China Telecom, who enjoyed monopoly status for a long time, just began to face its first competitor, China Unicom. Therefore, they are not ready for real competition with experienced foreign telecom service providers like AT&T. In addition, the telecom service industry is a sensitive industry, closely connected to national defense issues. It is expected that China will strongly resist the immediate opening of this market. However, in case of deregulation, both China Telecom and China Unicom would face severe challenges. They will be required to lower costs while improving quality of service, but this will benefit both the Chinese telecom industry and consumers in the long run.

The global economic system is both a system of dramatic change and of dramatic possibilities. It is estimated that the global economy could double by the year 2020 – unprecedented growth. This potential is generated by increased technology, communication and social progress which makes all nations more interdependent. What is at stake is not simply China's formal entry into a global trading arena. What is at stake is the future global economic condition. Without China as part of the formal, global economic trading apparatus, the greatest potential for economic advancement of all nations is not attainable. With the conclusion of the Cold War we are now standing at the "treshold" of a new era of possible global cooperation. Issues surrounding China's entry into the WTO seem to exemplify this circumstance and possibility in a real, concrete and observable manner. As frontrunner of the Cold War conclusion, the West, and particularly the U.S., holds an obligation to build relations with nations like China through an agenda of inclusive engagement. This means allowing said nations the opportunity to reach their full potential, as legitimate trading partners, by providing every reasonable means for reaching said potential.

Latest Development: U.S. – China WTO Agreement

On November 15, 1999, U.S. Trade Representative Charlene Barshefsky and China's MOFTEC minister Guangsheng Shi signed the U.S.-China Bilateral WTO Agreement in Beijing. This agreement, named as the 'Deal of the Century' by some critics, had been a full 13 years in the making. The U.S. seems to have secured most of the concessions that were on the table in April 1999 when Chinese Premier Rongji Zhu visited Washington. Both U.S. and Chinese negotiators want the agreement to be seen as a "win-win" proposition. Indeed, more than half of China's exports to the U.S. and the European Union are subject to non-tariff barriers. WTO membership is therefore vital to China's export sector, as it will ensure these markets stay open. In the short term, the benefits of China's accession are primarily psychological, especially as economic growth and foreign investment continue to slow in 1999. By opening previously closed sectors to foreign investment, and by promising established investors easier operating conditions, China should see a revival of foreign investor interest.

What follows is a highlight of the Sino-U.S. WTO Agreement. A detailed description of this agreement which was recently released by Public Liaison Office of the White House is attached (see this chapter's appendix):

(1) *Overall tariff and non-tariff reductions*: The overall tariff will fall to 17 percent with most quotas and other non-tariff barriers to be eliminated within five years; some to be phased out in two to three years; Tariffs on all industrial products will fall to an average of 9.4 percent (compared to 24.6 percent in 1997) by 2005.

(2) *Agriculture*: Tariffs on "U.S. Priority" products will be reduced from the current 31.5 percent to 14.5 percent by January 2004. China will not provide subsidies on crops including cotton and rice. However, China will restructure the import of wheat, rice, and cotton using quota systems of varying proportions.

(3) *Industry*: (i) Import tariffs on automobiles will be gradually reduced from about 90 percent at present to 25 percent by July 1, 2006. Foreign banks and non-bank financial institutions will be allowed to finance automobile purchases upon China's accession to the WTO; (ii) Tariffs on *IT equipment* will be eliminated by 2005. An average tariff on IT equipment is 13.3 percent; (iii) Tariffs on U.S. listed priority industrial products such as wool, paper, and medical equipment will fall to an average of 7.1 percent by the year 2003. Tariffs on chemicals will be reduced to 6.5 percent.

(4) *Services*: (i) Banking: Foreign banks will be allowed to conduct renminbi business with Chinese companies two years after China's accession to the WTO and with Chinese individuals, five years after accession. All geographic restrictions on foreign banks' operations will be lifted five years after accession; (ii) Securities: Upon China's accession to the WTO, foreign companies will be able to invest in joint venture fund management companies. The ceiling on foreign ownership will be 33 percent initially, rising to 49 percent three years after accession. Foreign-invested joint ventures in this sector will be allowed to underwrite domestic securities issues, and foreign currency-denominated securities (debt and equity). The ceiling on foreign ownership will be held at 33 percent; (iii) Insurance: China will permit foreign property and casualty firms to insure large-scale risks nationwide immediately upon accession, and expand the scope of activities for foreign insurers to include group, health and pension lines of insurance, which represent about 85% of total premiums, phased in over 5 years, and allow 50 percent ownership for life insurance. Life insurers may now choose their own joint venture partners; (iv) Telecommunication: China will allow 49 percent foreign ownership in all services, including the internet sector, upon accession; 50 percent ownership

in value-added paging services two years after accession; 50 percent foreign ownership in mobile telecoms in five years; 49 percent foreign ownership of international and domestic services in six years.

Other provisions will benefit all foreign companies, regardless of country of origin and whether they export or are already invested there. Trading and local distribution rights will be extended to foreign firms three years after accession. Requirements in local content, foreign exchange balance, and technology transfer will be eliminated upon accession. Foreign exporters will benefit from a reduction in China's overall tariff level to 17 percent and the abolishment of all quotas and other non-tariff barriers by 2005.

China's deal with the U.S. is of course a big step towards WTO membership. Since the U.S. has so much clout, this deal will spur China's negotiations with those WTO members yet to clinch bilaterial deals. Nevertheless, several obstacles remain. At least 24 of the WTO's 135 members, notably the European Union (among the other countries are Canada, Brazil and India), have yet to agree to entry terms with China, and the U.S.'s Congress has to endorse the deal. Before China can be guaranteed the benefits of WTO membership, Congress will have to grant it permanent Normal Trade Relations (NTR). Passage of permanent NTR for China, however, will face fierce opposition on Capitol Hill from the labor and human rights lobbies. These bilateral market-access deals then have to be stitched together into a multilateral agreement at the WTO. The WTO also has to assess whether China complies with its rules in areas such as intellectual property and health standards, and China will need to amend its laws where necessary.

Chapter Appendix

SUMMARY OF U.S. – CHINA BILATERAL WTO AGREEMENT*

I. Agreement Highlights

The U.S.-China WTO agreement covers all agricultural products, all industrial goods, and all service areas.

Industrial Tariffs

(1) China's industrial tariffs will fall from an overall average of 24.6% in 1997 to an overall average of 9.4% by 2005;
(2) On U.S. priority industrial products, tariffs will fall to 7.1% with the majority of tariff cuts fully implemented by 2003. Tariffs will fall on a range of products including: wood, paper, chemicals, capital and medical equipment;
(3) In information technology, tariffs on products such as computers, semiconductors, and all internet-related equipment, will fall from an average of 13.3% to 0% by 2005.

Agriculture

(1) On U.S. priority agriculture products, tariffs will be reduced from an overall average of 31.5% to 14.5% by January 2004, at the latest.
(2) China will expand access to bulk agriculture commodities, including corn, cotton, wheat, rice, barely, soybean oil;
(3) China will eliminate export subsidies – this is especially critical for U.S. cotton and rice producers;
(4) China will for the first time ever permit private trade (trade between private parties) in agriculture.

* *Source:* The White House Office of Public Liason. November 17, 1999

Priority Products	Tariffs Pre-Agreement	Tariffs Post-Agreement
Beef	45%	12%
Grapes	40%	13%
Wine	65%	20%
Cheese	50%	12%
Poultry	20%	10%
Pork	20%	12%
Overall Average	31.5%	14.5%

Services
(1) On industrial goods, China will for the first time permit the right to import and export without middle-men – so-called trading rights – as well as full rights of distribution including wholesale and retail and aftersale service, repair, maintenance, and transport;
(2) The telecommunications, insurance, banking, securities, audio visual, and professional service sectors, to name a few, will all have expanded market access under the agreement.

II. Resolution of key unresolved issues

(1) Import Surge Mechanism. China has agreed to a special safeguard mechanism that will remain in place for 12 years following accession and that can be used to address rapid increases in imports from China that cause or threaten market disruption.
(2) Anti-Dumping. The agreement ensures that the United States can continue to apply its current non-market economy approach in antidumping cases involving imports from China for 15 years. China can, of course, request review under U.S. law of specific sectors or the economy as a whole to determine if it is market-oriented and no longer subject to the special methodology.
(3) Motion Pictures. A previously unresolved issue had been the degree to which China restricted imports of films. Prior to the agreement, China permitted a maximum of 10 foreign films. Under

the agreement, China will quadruple imports to 40 films after accession, growing to 50 films in three Years, of which 20 will be on a revenue-sharing basis, in each of the three Years.

(4) Internet Access. Because of the enormous projected growth in internet access in China over the coming decade, a key priority of the U.S. was to ensure that China's telecom service commitment clearly included all aspects of internet service. The agreement ensures that Internet services will be liberalized at the same rate as other key telecommunications services.

(5) Satellites. China has clarified that it will permit provision of telecommunications services via satellite.

(6) Auto Financing. China has now made commitments for non-bank foreign financial institutions to be able to provide auto financing upon China's accession. This in combination with commitments regarding importation, distribution, sale, financing, and maintenance and repair of automobiles will help open up this key sector for U.S. industry.

(7) Accelerated Auto Tariff Reduction. As part of the efforts to find "win-win" solutions to sensitive areas, China agreed to accelerated tariff reduction in exchange for a slightly longer phase-in period. This provides earlier market access with auto tariffs still being reduced from the current 100-80 percent to 25 percent by July 1, 2006.

(8) Telecommunications. While the United States agreed to China's request to limit foreign equity participation in value-added and paging services to 50 percent, China agreed to both accelerate significantly the percentage of equity participation in the first two years and eliminate geographic restrictions on an accelerated basis. China had indicated it would allow 35 percent foreign ownership for value-added and paging services two years after accession and 51 percent four years after accession. China will now allow 49 percent foreign ownership in the first year of accession and 50 percent foreign ownership in the second year.

(9) Life Insurance. While the United States agreed to China's request to limit foreign equity participation in life insurance to 50 percent, China agreed to significantly accelerate the elimination of geographic restrictions and the percentage of equity participation in the first few years.

III: Summary of U.S. – CHINA bilateral WTO agreement

1. Agriculture

(1) The Agreement provides increased access for U.S. exports across a broad range of commodities and elimination of barriers. Commitments include:

a. Significant cuts in tariffs that will be completed by January 2004. Overall average for agricultural products will be 17 percent and for U.S. priority products 14.5 percent.

b. Establishment of a tariff-rate quota system for imports of bulk commodities, e.g., wheat, corn, cotton, barley, and rice, that provides a share of the TRQ for private traders. Specific rules on how the TRQ will operate and increased transparency in the process will help ensure that imports occur. Significant and growing quota quantities subject to tariffs that average between 1-3 percent.

c. The right to import and distribute products without going through state-trading enterprise or middle-man.

d. China has also agreed to the elimination of SPS barriers that are not based on scientific evidence and export subsidies on agricultural products.

2. Industrial Products

China's commitments will eliminate broad systemic barriers to U.S. exports, such as limits on who can import goods and distribute them in China as well as barriers such as quotas and licenses that restrict imports of U.S. products.

3. Tariffs

a. Tariffs cut to an average of 9.4 percent overall and 7.1 percent on U.S. priority products.

b. China will participate in the Information Technology Agreement (ITA), eliminating all tariffs on products such as computers, telecommunications equipment, semiconductors, computer equipment and other high technology products.

c. In the auto sector, China will cut tariffs from the current 100% or 80% level to 25% by 2006, with the largest cuts in the first years after accession.

d. Auto parts tariffs will be cut to an average of 10% by 2006.

e. Significant cuts will also be made in the wood and paper sectors,

going from present levels of 12-18% on wood and 15-25% on paper down to levels generally between 5 and 7.5%.
f. China will also be implementing the vast majority of the chemical harmonization initiative. Under that initiative, tariffs will be at 0, 5.5 and 6.5 percent for products in each category.

4. Elimination of Quotas and Licenses
WTO rules bar quotas and other quantitative restrictions. China has agreed to eliminate these restrictions with phase-ins limited to five years.

a. Quotas: Upon accession China will eliminate existing quotas the top U.S. priorities (e.g. optic fiber cable). It will phase-out remaining quotas, generally by 2002, but no later than 2005.
b. Quotas will grow from the current trade level at a 15% annual rate in order to ensure that market access increases progressively, and reduces the effect of quantitative restrictions.
c. Auto quotas will be phased out by 2005. In the interim, the base level quota will be $6 billion (the level prior to China's industrial auto policy) and this will grow by 15% annually until elimination.

5. Right to Import and Distribute
Trading rights and distribution are the major priority of the manufacturing sector. At present, China severely restricts trading rights (the right to import and export) and distribution (wholesaling, retailing, maintenance and repair, transportation, etc.). Under the Agreement, China will provide, for the first time, trading rights and distribution rights to U.S. firms. Trading rights will be progressively phased in over three years. Distribution rights will be provided even for China's most restricted distribution sectors such as wholesale, transportation, maintenance and repair. China will provide for trading rights and distribution.

6. Services
China has made commitments in all major service categories with reasonable transitions to eliminate most foreign equity restrictions (especially in sectors where the U.S. has a strong commercial interest), agreeing to accede to the Basic Telecommunications and Financial Services Agreements, and "grandfathering" of current market access for U.S. service providers.

7. Grandfathering

China will grandfather all existing current market access and activities in all services sectors. This will protect existing American distribution services, financial services, professional and other service providers in China, including those operating under contractual or shareholder agreements or a license, from restrictions as Chinese commitments phase in.

8. Distribution

In China today, foreign firms have no right to distribute products other than those they make in China, or to own or manage distribution networks, wholesaling outlets or warehouses. China also now frequently issues businesses licenses which limit the ability of American firms to conduct marketing, after-sales service, maintenance and repair and customer support. As the section on industrial goods noted, this is a severe barrier to goods exports as well as to service exports.

China's commitments address all these issues. They reflect a comprehensive commitment on distribution – including wholesaling, sales away from a fixed location, retailing, maintenance and repair, and transportation. Thus, Americans will be able to distribute imported products as well as those made in China, offering significant opportunity to expand U.S. exports of goods.
As noted above, China will phase out all restrictions on distribution services for most products within three years.

9. Services Auxiliary to Distribution

Chinese commitments in services auxiliary to distribution include rental and leasing, air courier, freight forwarding, storage and warehousing, advertising, technical testing and analysis, and packaging services. All restrictions will be phased-out in 3 to 4 years, at which time U.S. service suppliers will be able to establish 100% wholly-owned subsidiaries.

10. Telecommunications

China now severely restricts sales of telecommunications services and bars foreign investment. China's commitments mark its first agreement to open its telecommunications sector, both to the scope of services and to direct investment in telecommunications businesses. Through these commitments, China will become a member of the Basic Telecommunications Agreement. Specific commitments include:

a. Regulatory Principles: China has agreed to implement the pro-competitive regulatory principles embodied in the Basic Telecommunications Agreement (including cost-based pricing, interconnection rights and independent regulatory authority), and agreed to technology-neutral scheduling, which means foreign suppliers can use any technology they choose to provide telecommunications services.
b. Scope of services: China will phase out all geographic restrictions for paging and value-added services in 2 years, mobile/cellular in 5 years and domestic wireline services in 6 years. China's key telecommunications services corridor in Beijing, Shanghai, and Guangzhou, which represents approximately 75% of all domestic traffic, will open immediately on accession in all telecommunications services.
c. Investment: Under present circumstances, China allows no foreign investment in telecommunications services. With this agreement, China will allow 49% foreign investment in all services, and will allow 50% foreign ownership for value added paging services in two years, for mobile services, 49 percent in 5 years; and for international and domestic services, 49% in 6 years.

11. Insurance
For insurance, China now restricts foreign companies to operating in Shanghai and Guangzhou. Under the agreement:

a. Geographic Limitations: China will permit foreign property and casualty firms to insure large-scale risks nationwide immediately upon accession, and will eliminate all geographic limitations in 3 years.
b. Scope: China will expand the scope of activities for foreign insurers to include group, health and pension lines of insurance, which represent about 85% of total premiums, phased in over 5 years.
c. Prudential Criteria: China agrees to award licenses solely on the basis of prudential criteria, with no economic needs test or quantitative limits on the number of licenses issued.
d. Investment: China agreed to allow 50 percent ownership for life insurance. Life insurers may now choose their own joint venture part-

ners. for non-life, china will allow branching or 51% ownership on accession and form wholly owned subsidiaries in 2 years. Reinsurance is completely open upon accession (100 percent, no restrictions).

12. Banking

Currently foreign banks are not permitted to do local currency business with Chinese clients (a few can engage in local currency business with their foreign clients). China imposes severe geographic restrictions on the establishment of foreign banks.

a. China has committed to full market access in five years for U.S. banks.
b. Foreign banks will be able to conduct local currency business with Chinese enterprises starting 2 years after accession.
c. Foreign banks will be able to conduct local currency business with Chinese individuals from 5 years after accession.
d. Foreign banks will have the same rights (national treatment) as Chinese banks within designated geographic areas.
e. Both geographic and customer restrictions will be removed in five years.
f. Non-bank financial companies can offer auto financing upon accession.

13. Securities

China will permit minority foreign owned joint ventures to engage in fund management on the same terms as Chinese firms. As the scope of business expands for Chinese firms, foreign joint venture securities companies will enjoy the same expansion in scope of business. Minority joint ventures will be allowed to underwrite domestic securities issues and underwrite and trade in foreign currency denominated securities (debt and equity).

14. Professional Services

In the professional services, China currently tightly restricts operation of foreign law firms and accounting firms. In the Agreement, China has provided a broad range of commitments, including on legal, accountancy, taxation, management consultancy, architecture, engineering, urban planning, medical and dental, and computer and related services. China will permit foreign majority control except for practicing Chinese law (an exception common to many WTO members.) For accountancy, China has agreed to eliminate a mandatory localization requirement and will now allow unrestricted access to its market to professionals licensed and follow transparent procedures.

15. Audiovisual

China's commitments cover the right to distribute video and sound recordings and cinema ownership and operation. For video and sound recordings, China will allow 49% foreign participation in joint ventures engaged in the distribution of these products. China has also agreed to import 40 films after accession growing to 50 films in three years, of which 20 films will be revenue sharing in each of the three years.

16. Travel and Tourism

Hotels: China will allow unrestricted access to the Chinese market for hotel operators with the ability to set up 100% foreign owned hotels in 3 years, with majority ownership allowed upon accession.

Travel Services: Foreign travel operators can provide the full range of travel agency services. For travel agency services, China will allow access to government resorts as well as Beijing, Shanghai, Guangzhou and Xian.

17. Protocol Provisions

Commitments in China's WTO Protocol and Working Party Report establish rights and obligations enforceable through WTO dispute settlement procedures. China has agreed on key provisions relating to antidumping and subsidies, protection against import surges, technology transfer requirements and offsets as well as practices of state-owned and state-invested enterprises. These rules are of special importance to U.S. workers and business.
China had agreed to implement the TRIMs Agreement upon accession, to eliminate and cease enforcing trade and foreign exchange balancing requirements, to eliminate and cease enforcing local content requirements, to refuse to enforce contracts imposing these requirements; and only to impose or enforce laws or other provisions relating to the transfer of technology or other know-how, if they are in accordance with the WTO agreements on protection of intellectual property rights and trade-related investment measures.

These provisions will also help protect American firms against forced technology transfers, as China has also agreed that, upon accession, it will not condition investment approvals, import licenses, or any other import approval process on performance requirements of any kind, including: local content requirements, offsets, transfer of technology, or requirements to conduct research and development in China.

18. Antidumping and Subsidies Methodology
The agreed protocol provisions ensure that American firms and workers will have strong protection against unfair trade practices including dumping and subsidies. The U.S. and China have agreed to maintain the current antidumping methodology (treating China as a non-market economy) in future anti-dumping cases. This provision will remain in force for 15 years after China's accession to the WTO. Moreover, when the U.S. apply its countervailing duty law to China it will take the special characteristics of China's economy into account when identifying and measuring any subsidy benefit that may exist.

19. Product Specific Safeguard
The agreed provisions for the protocol package also ensure that American domestic firms and workers will have strong protection against rapid increases of imports.

To do this, the Product-Specific Safeguard provision sets up a special mechanism to address increased imports that cause or threaten to cause market disruption to a U.S. industry. China is a major exporting country that enjoys open access to U.S. markets. This mechanism, which is in addition to other WTO Safeguards provisions, differs from traditional safeguards measures. It permits the United States to address imports solely from China, rather than from the whole world, that are a significant cause of material injury through measures such as import restrictions. Moreover, the United States will be able to apply restraints unilaterally based on legal standards that differ from those in the WTO Safeguards Agreement and could permit action in more cases. This provision will remain in force for 12 years after China accedes to the WTO.

20. State-Owned and State-Invested Enterprises

The Protocol addresses important issues related to the Chinese government's involvement in the economy. China has agreed that it will ensure that state-owned and state-invested enterprises will make purchases and sales based solely on commercial considerations, such as price, quality, availability and marketability, provide U.S. firms with the opportunity to compete for sales and purchases on non-discriminatory terms and conditions.

China has also agreed that it will not influence these commercial decisions (either directly or indirectly) except in a WTO consistent manner. With respect to applying WTO rules to state-owned and state-invested enterprises, the U.S. side clarified in several ways that these firms are subject to WTO disciplines. Purchases of goods or services by these state-owned and state-invested enterprises do not constitute "government procurement" and thus are subject to WTO rules.

21. Textiles

China's protocol package will include a provision drawn from our 1997 bilateral textiles agreement, which permits U.S. companies and workers to respond to increased imports of textile and apparel products. This textile safeguard will be in effect until December 31, 2008 which is after the WTO Agreement on Textiles and Clothing expires.

3. Opportunities and Challenges in Technologically Intensive Industries

Chapter Abstract

This chapter describes opportunities and challenges for MNCs operating in technologically-intensive industries in China. As China continues its structural transformation to a market economy, technologically intensive industries present a large array of opportunities that can be preempted by MNCs. Despite the existence of institutional barriers and market complexities in these industries, foreign companies generally have competitive advantages over local rivals in capitalizing on business potential. This chapter begins with an overview of China's technologically-intensive industries. It is followed by a discussion of the major technologically sectors which appeal most to foreign investors, including the automobile industry, the computer industry, pharmaceuticals, telecommunications, electronics, machinery, and the chemical industry.

3.1 Overview

Since China's economy 'soft-landed' in 1996, it has entered a period of slower growth. GDP growth fell from 9.6 percent in 1996 to 8.8 percent in 1997 and 7.8 percent in 1998. This sluggish growth has worsened problems resulting from the stagnation of state-owned enterprises and growing worker lay-offs. The Chinese government has tried to mitigate these problems by placing emphasis on high-tech industries as a target for investment, along with the infrastructure. Lack of technological development in many sectors is seen as a bottleneck for further development of the entire economy. The government has recently set its sights on building up its knowledge-driven economy and becoming the second largest center for science and technology in the world.

Despite rapid growth over the past 20 years, China's high-tech industries need further technological innovation and development. Some high-tech industries, such as new materials and biological technology, are still in their infancy. Major problems hindering the country's scientific and technological development include: (1) slow technological transfer into production; (2) low yield of scientific research; (3) lack of technological innovation; (4) poor commercialization of high-tech products; and (5) an underdeveloped property rights system.

Nevertheless, progress within specific high-tech development zones has been made. Since 1991, the total output from 53 high-tech zones nationwide has increased by an annual average of 93.6 percent. Exports have risen by 99.6 percent. The per-capita output from high-tech zones has reached 170,000 yuan (U.S.$20,500) annually, much higher than found in traditional industries. Encouraged to absorb young talent, these 53 zones employ 1.2 million people with higher educational backgrounds.

The Chinese government has initiated a series of measures to attract FDI and develop high-tech industries such as information technology, biology, pharmaceuticals, new materials, electronics, and electrical appliances. Banks owned by the government provide more support to high-tech industries as part of a risk investment system. The government is working on finance, tax, and trade regulations to support the development of private firms and foreign MNCs in technologically intensive industries. It recognizes that world-famous companies such as Microsoft, Siemens, and Philips all emerged from cottage industries. Recent high-tech joint ventures such as Beijing Lucent Technologies Fiber Optic Cable Co. Ltd., Shougang NEC Electronics Co. Ltd., Beijing Ericsson Communication Systems Co. Ltd., and Novo Nordisk (China) Investment Co. Ltd. have begun operating in fields such as electronic information, biological engineering, new medicines, new materials, and energy.

Various local governments, especially in municipal and coastal cities, are actively attracting more foreign investment to technologically intensive industries. Beijing, for instance, will produce added-value high-tech products worth U.S.$19 billion by 2000, accounting for 27 percent of the city's industrial output. The Chinese central government and Beijing municipal government have kicked off a massive project to turn the city's northwestern Zhongguanchun area into a demonstration zone for high-tech industry, expected to match California's 'Silicon Valley' in the United States. Zhongguanchun is home to nearly 5,000 private high-tech businesses and hundreds of academies and research institutes, including the prestigious Beijing University and Qinghua University and the Chinese Academy of Sciences. Roughly 1,100 of the world's top computer companies, including IBM, Microsoft, Compaq, Hewlett-Packard, and Mitsubishi, have set up ventures in this area. Licences for high-tech enterprises can be obtained within five days of application in Beijing.

In Shanghai, high-tech output reached 54 billion yuan (U.S.$6.5 billion) in 1997, accounting for more than 15 percent of the city's total industrial output. The majority came from three new industries, namely information (computers), bio-medicine, and new materials, hitting 52 billion yuan (U.S.$6.3 billion), up 30 percent over 1996. Computer hardware and software led the way with output value worth 28 billion yuan (U.S.$3.4 billion). Shanghai's Pudong New Area also introduced a series of initiatives to boost development in a bid to form an energetic industrial base. The Zhangjiang High-Tech Industrial Park, one of the area's major zones, is being given priority in the development plan. Pudong has stepped up its efforts to attract high-tech projects and technological talent by offering strong financial support to build Zhangjiang into China's "pharmaceutical valley" as well as a major software development center.

In Shenzhen, the government has provided high-risk investment funding for foreign companies setting up profitable technological projects. Loans from local banks have become easier to get as Shenzhen works to stimulate domestic investment and high-tech growth. Its tax rebate rate has been increased to 17 percent for the export of high-tech products such as high-precision machinery and electronic equipment. Shenzhen's high-tech sector generated 65 billion yuan (U.S.$7.8 billion) in 1998, nearly half of the city's total industrial output.

Dalian, a port city in northeast China's Liaoning Province, is giving high-tech foreign ventures a wide range of preferential treatment, including tax rebates on added value if they market their own commodities, and exemption from tax levies on business earnings generated by services such as technological transfer and consultancy. To support industrialization, the development zone has also earmarked 20 million yuan ($2.4 million) annually for a scientific and technological progress fund. One percent of its revenue each year will also go to a scientific and technological risk investment fund.

High-tech industries are also encouraged in some smaller cities. For instance, Suzhou, famous for its gardens, canals, and silk production, has been successful in directing overseas investment into new, high-tech industries. Over the past six years, six emerging industries, namely electronics and information, machine manufacture, biological pharmaceuticals, chemicals, home appliances, and new materials, have become major pillars of the city's economy, generating about half of its GDP. Since 1992, Suzhou has approved over $4 billion a year in contractual overseas investment. More than 5,200 overseas-funded enterprises are now operational. The bulk of overseas capital has been injected into emerging areas, constituting 60 percent of the city's total investment in more than 100 key projects. The majority of these funds have been used to transform several traditional industries through the use of advanced technology and equipment.

Foreign firms should realize that domestic Chinese firms, especially collectively-owned businesses, can quickly become major rivals in some conventional high-tech industries. Local firms are well versed in entrepreneurial skills, absorptive capabilities, operational flexibility, and customer responsiveness. For instance, over the past two years, Huawei (in Shenzhen) and a handful of equally obscure Chinese firms such as Datang and Great Dragon, have taken nearly half the huge Chinese telecommunication equipment market from big foreign companies such as Ericsson and NEC, which have invested billions in China. In the mid-1990s, Western PC makers mounted an assault on the Chinese computer market and quickly grabbed more than half of it, but Chinese firms such as Legend, Founder, and Great Wall have fought back by cutting costs, improving technology, and outmarketing the foreigners to recapture the lead. Domestic firms now hold over 55 percent of the computer market share and Legend is the fastest-growing PC maker in Asia. The same is true in medical technology. Chinese firms are beating foreigners in sales of CAT scanners and radiation therapy machines. In power generation, state companies no longer need to buy generators below 600MW from foreigners. They now make these generators. Even Chinese car manufacturers are improving. Sales of the Alto are growing more rapidly than those of any other car in China; it was designed by Suzuki, but is made more efficiently by the all-Chinese company, Norinco.

3.2 Automobile Industry

By world standards, China's auto industry is relatively small. The country is fast on its way to becoming a major auto market, however. Prior to 1979, China produced only about 160,000 vehicles each year, and trucks and buses accounted for over 90 percent of total vehicle output. In 1992, for the first time, China produced 1 million vehicles, including sedans and minivans. Industry officials have set a target of over 3 million vehicles to be produced annually by the year 2000.

With the ultimate goal of producing passenger cars entirely designed and manufactured in China, the government named the automotive sector a 'pillar' industry in its Eighth Five-Year Plan (1991-1996), along with electronics, machinery, and petrochemicals. Over the next few years, China will attempt to consolidate the industry by bolstering passenger car production, improving the quality of vehicles and services, and increasing the percentage of local content used in manufacture.

Protecting China's infant auto industry remains a priority for the central government. Domestic assemblers and parts suppliers enjoy considerable government support. The original six major passenger car producers in China – Shanghai Volkswagen, First Autoworks, Second Autoworks, Beijing Jeep, Tianjin Daihatsu, and Guangzhou Peugeot – together with Shenyang Jinbei Automotive Corp., Nanjing IRECO, and Jinan Heavy Truck Corp., are the largest vehicle producers in China. By 1992, these companies produced 75 percent of China's total vehicle output.

During upcoming years, the Chinese government will continue its efforts to consolidate the industry though expansion of major production bases such as the First and Second Autoworks. Meanwhile, Chinese officials intend to improve research and development capabilities. China is also counting on the development of the domestic auto industry to stimulate growth in supporting industries such as steel, plastics, and glass.

New foreign entrants will find themselves joining European,

American, and Japanese companies producing a wide range of vehicles including minivans, sedans, pickups, vans, buses, and heavy trucks. The early foreign movers in the industry were grouped into a 'Big Three, Little Three' policy (see below) designed to consolidate auto manufacturing and develop economies of scale. To succeed in China's auto industry, foreign companies need to offer the right technology and gain access to the right players. Facing restrictions in the assembly of passenger autos, foreign investors should start with technologically advanced auto part production, then move into equity or cooperative joint ventures for producing complete units. In the non-passenger sector, a foreign investor faces no official restrictions on approval of new projects. Opportunities to produce buses, motorcycles, trucks, and the like remain abundant.

The major players in the Chinese automobile industry include "Big Seven" and "Big Three, Little Three, and Mini Two". "Big Seven" includes (1) First Automobile Group Corp.(FAW); (2) Donfang Motor Corp. (DMC); (3) Shanghai Automotive Industry Corp. (SAIC); (4) Tianjin Automotive Industry Group Corp. (TAIC); (5) Beijing Automotive Group Corp. (BAIC); (6) Yuejin Automotive Group Corp. (YAGC); (7) China National Heavy-Duty Truck Corp. (CNHTC). These manufacturers produce all varieties of automobiles.

"Big Three, Little Three, and Mini Two" refers to leading manufacturers of passenger cars. "Big Three" are SAIC (Santana); FAW (Red Flag, Audi, Jetta, Golf); DMC (Fookang). "Little Three" include TAIC (Charade), BAIC (Cherokee), and Guangzhou-Honda (Accord) (i.e., formerly Guangzhou-Peugeot). "Mini Two" includes Chang'an Automobile Co., Ltd (Alto) and Guizhou Aviation Industry Corp. (Skylark). GM has just begun production in Shanghai but within the next three years their production will be high enough to be included in the Big Three, changing the Big Three to the Big Four. Currently, the outputs of the 13 largest automobile corporations produce 93 percent of the nation's total output. The following table highlights production units of automobiles over the past several years.

The Chinese automobile industry is fragmented. China produces more than 100 models in 125 factories, although their aggregate output is less than the U.S.'s 'Big Three' auto manufacturers. These factories produce 1.6 million units annually, while the rest

Table 3.1: Automotive Production (millions of units)

	1986	1990	1991	1992	1993	1994	1995	1996	1997
Total	0.37	0.51	0.71	1.06	1.29	1.35	1.45	1.54	1.58
(cars)	0.01	0.04	0.08	0.16	0.23	0.25	0.32	0.39	0.48

Source: China Automotive Industry Yearbook, 1999

of the world's 18 manufacturers each produce an average of one million units annually.

The State Council published the Automobile Industry Policy (AIP) in 1994, stating that the automobile industry would be considered one of China's pillar industries. Pillar industries receive special privileges in financing, stock issuance, and business acquisitions. The government is seeking to consolidate automobile manufacturers in order to achieve greater efficiency. During the first stage, from 1996 to 2000, the goal is to have only 3 or 4 large manufacturers producing 300,000 to 500,000 vehicles, 6 to 7 key vehicle manufacturers, 8 to 10 international competitive motorcycle manufacturers, and 300 parts and component manufacturers.

During the second stage, from the years 2000 to 2010, the goals are to have 3 to 4 corporations that are internationally competitive, with a 1 million unit capacity at each firm. Four million vehicles will thus be produced annually. There will be 5 to 10 international component manufacturers. FAW, DMC, and SAIC are likely to become China's "Big Three" in the future. In the Ninth Five Year Plan, engine parts, chassis and related parts, electric automobile appliances, and other parts were identified as priorities for foreign direct investment.

In the early 1990s, the Chinese government announced that only a limited number of firms would be allowed to enter the Chinese market for an extended period of time. This created a fierce competition between car manufacturers in China. China was in strong bargaining position and could demand practically anything from foreign car manufacturers.

China's joining WTO will have a major impact on the automobile industry, however. China considers its automobile industry to be an infant industry. Although it would like to allow more time to protect its development, five years after joining the WTO, currently high tariffs of 80 to 100 percent will fall to 50 percent and in eight years to 30 percent. Imported cars will then be able to compete with domestically made cars; the high number of smuggled cars demonstrates that there is a demand for these imported vehicles. Foreign firms will then have demands of their own because they will have the option of importing cars or parts for their vehicles.

This will not only hurt domestic companies but also foreign joint ventures, however. Currently, China generally requires foreign joint ventures to have 40 percent local content when they start production and 60 percent within three years. When China joins the WTO, this will be phased out. In general, foreign firms strive to use domestically made parts because they are less expensive than importing them. On the other hand, China's joining WTO makes financial services open to foreign banks. This will help Chinese consumers finance car loans. The pressure to export will be reduced as domestic demand increases.

Table 3.2: Local Content of Passenger Cars Models (%)

Company	1996
Shanghai, VW Santana	90.45
Tianjin Charade	93.84
Beijing Jeep Cherokee CX-1	85.00
Guizhou Skylark	46.50
Chang'an Suzuki Alto	89.00
FAW, VW Jetta	80.00
Dongfeng-Citroen Fookang	42.44

Source: China Automotive Industry Yearbook, 1998

Currently, car manufactures must use Chinese distribution systems to sell their vehicles. The Chinese system is not very efficient. The Chinese do not have strong incentives to sell cars. Cars are not shipped to customers, they are driven. So when a consumer buys a supposedly new vehicle, it may already have a few thousand kilometers on the odometer. After China joins the WTO, foreign car manufacturers have more freedom to sell their vehicles. They could even set up their own distribution systems.

In Beijing, seven new laws have been passed that will control exhaust emissions. After April 1, cars that fail to meet the new standards will not be allowed within the third ring (cycle) road. These new laws affect foreign car makers like Shanghai Volkswagen and will cost car owners up to $485 when they buy a new car. This will only delay the time when the Chinese can buy private car in great numbers. BJC has laid off 1,000 workers because of the new restrictions.

Dongfeng Automobile Co. and Tianjin Auto Charade Co. plan to go public. In doing so they hope to prepare for the opening of the market. Both have begun offering 'A share' stock. The money they raise will be used to upgrade their facilities so they will be prepared to compete against imported vehicles. Since China hopes to improve safety and reduce pollution, the best opportunities for foreign firms is helping China develop components such as air bags, ABS breaks, and more efficient engines. Even foreign firms planning to import cars and parts will also need to set up body shops employing and training mechanics to work on their cars.

3.3 Computer Industry

Overview

The Chinese information technology (IT) industry began to grow in earnest in the early 1990s with the arrival of foreign companies. Until then, China's technological development hardly had a home market, capital, or any exchange of information technology. When China lowered its import tariffs on IT products in 1990, the domestic industry had to react. Today, conservative Chinese companies continue to fear that the World Trade Organisation will crush poorly developed domestic industries. China's IT companies have shown that this is unlikely, however. Original designs, falling prices on the world market, and arrangements with leading software producers have enabled the domestic IT industry to develop a previously non-existent market. Nevertheless, 90 percent of the administrative work is still done by hand in Chinese companies and governmental agencies.

China's computer industry, although suffering from the gloomy domestic economic situation, continued to enjoy sales growth in recent years. The computer sector secured a sales gain of 13.9 percent, reaching 148 billion yuan (U.S.$17.8 billion) in 1998, but this was much less growth than the 41.3 percent gained in 1997. China's computer market has maintained a rapid growth of more than 40 percent a year since 1994.

China's computer production capacity has grown seventeen-fold since the beginning of the 1990s, reaching 8.5 million units. This was caused by surging demand of more than 40 percent a year for the past seven or eight years. The customs, education, public health, and finance sectors are the leading institutional computer consumers.

The Chinese Government nurtures the local computer industry with low-interest loans and tax breaks and by pressuring foreign software companies to set up joint ventures. Since illegal software is so prevalent in China, Microsoft is most likely to make a profit by licensing its software to local PC manufacturers. As the bargaining power of local manufacturers increases, however, it might become more of a challenge to realize profits from pre-installed software.

Chinese computer manufacturers will face tougher competition in the future. This is because many large Chinese enterprises involved in the manufacture and retail of electrical appliances have also elbowed into the PC market. This increases both China's computer production capacity and market supply. Computer manufacturers need to improve their technology and after-sales services in order to consolidate their market position.

It has become a new trend for computer manufacturers to operate in accordance with the specific needs of customers rather than at their own whims. China's software and information service industries will maintain a strong momentum over the coming years. The advancement of the sector helps push forward development of China's PC market as telecommunication costs are cut and Internet services grow rapidly. The invention of more multi-media software for educational programs and family entertainment purposes will drive growth of PC sales in China.

Personal Computers (PCs)

China is the largest market for PCs outside of North America. The PC market sustained rapid growth in recent years. A total of 4.25 million PCs, worth 160 billion yuan (U.S.$19.28 billion), were sold in 1998 in China, representing growth of 40 percent over

1997. Domestic brands hit even higher growth rates, while computers made overseas suffered from negative growth for the first time. PC sales reached 5.1 million in China in 1999, up 20 percent from 1998. PC demand in China is expected to reach 10 million units by the year 2000.

After a slow start in the early 1990s, the home PC market has swelled significantly. Annual sales growth has been over 50 per cent since 1995. Beijing and Shanghai lead the country in home PC penetration, with 6 percent of households possessing a computer. This still leaves a huge market for family PCs. Domestic home PC makers dominate the Chinese market, claiming around 60 percent of the market share. Chinese companies lead the market by offering new concepts and applications to consumers. A balanced market network is taking shape in China, with sales centers expanding from Beijing, Shanghai, Guangzhou, and Shenzhen to inland cities like Wuhan, Xian, and Chengdu.

Almost all computer vendors in China, with Legend as the prime example, use traditional distribution channels by selling through dealers and retail outlets. Legend, China's No.1 brand, boasts 1,800 distributors throught China. It has not succeeded by selling cheap, although the company claims a 15 percent cost advantage over foreign brands in China. Its main strategy has been to focus on producing high-quality computers that provide the latest technology and are tailored for users with specific software packages, such as the Happy Family Home PC or My Office Commercial PC. Legend Holdings has chosen its name aptly, since the company's meteoric rise in the past years is the stuff of legend. Its market share in China grew to more than 17 percent at the end of 1998, double that of the next biggest seller, U.S. manufacturer IBM. Legend continues to trounce its competitors, whether domestic or foreign.

Founder is another competitive local company. It is run by the prestigious Beijing University, which provides the company with some of its top graduates. Since diversifying from Chinese-language software into PCs in late 1995, Founder has zoomed to the No. 8 spot in China. It plans to build 100,000 computer units annually. Recently, Founder adopted Computer Associates (CA)'s control information technology as its standard long-range control management tool in its 'Yuanming' servers. As a result, users can make full use of software and hardware resources. The two companies aim to create for a safe, healthy and effective IT environment for users. China Great Wall Computer, the third most competitive local firm, has three joint PC ventures with IBM and another in videoconferencing with Intel.

Before 1996, foreign PC makers took the lead in market share over local rivals. Major local competitors such as the Legend Computer Company and the Great Wall Corporation together held only about 12 percent of the total market share in 1994 (Table 3.3). Foreign competitors were stronger, with over 60 percent held by companies such as Compaq, AST, Hewlett-Packard, and DEC. AST is IBM's strongest overall foreign competitor, with 25 percent of the market share.

Table 3.3: Market Shares of Major PC Suppliers in China (1994)

Company	Market Share
AST	25%
Compaq	16%
IBM	8%
DEC	7%
Great Wall	6%
Legend	6%
Acer	4%
Langchao	3%
Changjiang	2%
Other imported	4%
Other producers	19%

Foreigner PC makers have been steadily losing market share since then. For instance, local firms enjoyed sales growth of 65 percent in the first three quarters of 1998, far outpacing the meager 14 percent of the major foreign players, Compaq, Hewlett-Packard, and IBM. Indeed, the top four foreign PC makers command just 19 percent of the market, down from 21 percent in 1997. That compares with 23 percent for the top four local players. This situation has forced foreign PC makers to recognize a need for change. For example, the Japanese giant, Toshiba Corp., like Compaq, is expanding ties with local partners. It recently announced a new joint venture with Chinese PC maker Tontru Information Industry Group Co., which is tied with Compaq for fourth place in the Chinese PC market. Meanwhile, IBM has expanded its joint venture with the Great Wall Group in Shenzhen, increasing its stake to 70 percent from an original 51 percent.

Foreign companies are also trying to break through one of China's biggest barriers, the distribution system. Given China's notoriously inefficient transportation network, companies rely on a vast number of local distributors to get their computers to customers. Customers in turn tend to often rely on distributors for other computer services. Dell Computer Corp. is planning to use its trademark direct-sales model to overcome this disadvantage, although the Chinese market may not yet be sophisticated enough to accommodate this approach. Dell has decided not to target retail buyers, who account for only about 10 percent of Dell's China sales. That way, Dell avoids going head-to-head against entrenched local market leaders like Legend. Established American PC makers in China, such as Hewlett-Packard, IBM, and Compaq, depend largely on resellers. Because of the cost savings derived from cutting out the middleman, Dell believes it can sell computers at lower prices than its competitors and thus steal market share. It recently opened a manufacturing plant in the southern city of Xiamen and already has 300 people working in China. By manufacturing locally, rather than importing machines from its factory in Malaysia, Dell is better able to compete with Legend and other Chinese companies. Before Dell opened its Xiamen plant, it had to pay 17 percent import duty on all the computers it sold in the country. To overcome the notion that foreigners cannot provide as complete services as local firms, Dell has also set up toll-free hot lines offering technical support. The company has even begun selling computers over the Internet in China. Already these gambits seem to be working: Dell's market share tripled to 1.2 percent at the end of 1998, while Compaq's fell from 3.5 percent to 2.7 percent. Dell is ranked eighth in PC shipments in China now. For beleaguered foreign PC makers, moves like this may turn out to be key in penetrating the China market.

Other foreign PC makers are also working closely with Chinese partners to improve their distribution systems and decrease reliance on imports. Toshiba has long relied on Legend to distribute its notebooks, while Hewlett-Packard has managed to become the leading printer brand in China by making use of the distribution network of seven Chinese firms, including Legend.

The dilemma for the dominant global players is thus not simply one of price. It is true that domestic PC manufacturers offer their products at a 10-20 percent discount over most foreign brands, but price is no longer the most powerful sales tool in China. Chinese consumers are now looking for the best deal on service and software options. None of the world's major PC brands can rival the service networks of Legend, China Great Wall, or Founder. Foreign firms realise they are missing out on a sizeable slice of revenue by not selling directly to China, but the cost of establishing a presence in the vast nation has forced their hand.

IBM has already invested in at least six joint ventures with Chinese partners and two information technology centers in Beijing and Guangzhou. IBM has also developed a branch office and three factories in China. The company donated $570,000 last year to build a computer-aided software engineering laboratory at Shenzen University. IBM focuses on reaching Chinese customers through service centers, often set up near busy railway terminals. In addition, 300 computer engineers around the country provide technological support to customers. This investment in service has been so successful that IBM sales in China have risen by 50 percent annually for the past three years, now reaching more than U.S.$500 million.

NEC in Shanghai recently released advanced business computer Powermates, a new computer different from both desktops and notebooks. It is very thin, light, and has an environmentally friendly, 14-inch, radiation-free, digital crystal display. Its size, weight, and energy costs are only a third of an ordinary PC, but it functions as well as a desktop. NEC's strategy therefore seems to focus on state-of-the-art technology.

Software

Foreign and Chinese software firms are both competing and cooperating to build a dynamic sector. As China's reliance on computers has grown in recent years, it is no surprise that the country's demand for software has kept pace. Software sales in China totaled 9.2 billion yuan ($1.1 billion) in 1996, a 35 percent jump over

1995. Computer hardware sales reached similar heights, with an estimated 71.5 billion yuan ($8.6 billion) sold in 1996, a 50 percent jump over 1995. Because most analysts expect such high growth to continue, foreign software companies, which together already claim a 60 percent market share in China, are braving the country's fragile intellectual property rights (IPR) regime to establish themselves for future expansion. In the process, these companies are bringing to China the strategies and practices that have proven successful worldwide.

The flurry of strategic alliances that have sprung up among competitors, both foreign and domestic, is just one example of the tactics that are laying the groundwork for a modern software industry in China. Companies are cooperating with one another to produce mutually compatible software and are pairing up to develop new products for China and the international market. Though industrial giants like IBM, Microsoft, and Oracle currently dominate software sales in China, domestic companies such as User Friend Software and Beijing Founder Electronics have also been successful. The relatively undeveloped market means that, perhaps more than in other industries, cooperation between foreign and Chinese software companies can benefit all participants.

Growth in the software market depends in large part on growth in the market for hardware. China had a total installed base of PCs of roughly 5 million by the end of 1996 and will have up to 5 million PCs a year by 2000 for the domestic market. Each of these computers will require its own set of software programs, including an operating system such as Microsoft's Windows 95 or IBM's OS/2 and applications that perform specific tasks from accounting to desktop publishing to word processing. Similar software requirements hold true for higher-end machines such as workstations, servers, and routers that power business and communications networks, management information systems, and advanced manufacturing and design systems.

At present, foreign companies control about 95 percent of the PC market for operating systems. The simplified Chinese version of Windows 95 is Microsoft's biggest seller in China, thanks in part to the large number of copies sold to original equipment manufacturers who load the operating system onto the PC at the factory. Microsoft has wholly foreign-owned operations in Beijing, Guangzhou, and Shanghai, and manufactures in-country most of the products sold in China. Foreign-language products are its main exports to the PRC. The Beijing office, in particular, conducts research and development activities. The China subsidiary is the company's fastest-growing division.

With China revenue growing an average of 50 percent each year, and eight joint ventures and one wholly foreign-owned enterprise, IBM also has a foothold in the Chinese software sector. Its OS/2 operating system has a sizable share of the China market, in part because OS/2 preceded Microsoft's large-scale 1994 entry into China. Meanwhile, U.S. database firms Oracle, Informix, and Sybase, together claim most of China's database market, although Microsoft appears to be gaining market share at the lower end. Oracle's products currently make up the bulk of this market. Through its operations in Beijing, Guangzhou, Shanghai, and Shenzhen, Oracle provides a full range of database and database development tools; packaged accounting, management systems, and decision support products; and full-service technical support, training, and consulting. Other foreign companies involved in the PRC software market include Long Island, NY-based Computer Associates Inc. (CA), which has signed a number of deals to provide its mainframe business software systems to PRC organizations.

A number of leading non-U.S. software firms are also developing their presence in China, most notably the German company SAP (Systems, Applications, and Products in Data Processing), the world's leading producer of client/server application software. As early as 1994, SAP was supplying its business process system SAP R/3 to Siemens AG's optical fiber joint venture in Chengdu, Sichuan Province. Japanese computer giant NEC announced its plan to start up software development operations in China and India because of these countries' ready supply of skilled programmers.

Foreign software firms face tough competition from local rivals. There are more than 13,000 software development firms in China, employing half a million people. Generally, Chinese software manufacturers are stronger in applications than operating systems. China's User Friend, a financial software company, has an accounting package that currently claims 40 percent of that market. Founder, meanwhile, has a popular desktop publishing program that Business Week reports has been sold to 80 percent of China's print media and publishing firms and is also popular in Southeast Asia. Founder reportedly also just released its own Email software, which recognizes all types of Chinese characters. The educational software developer Beijing Kelihua Co. currently holds a 30 percent market share in that subsector. Other successful Chinese software firms include: Stone Rich Sight Information Tech. Co., Ltd., a division of the Stone Group, which produces the RichWin line of software products including a Chinese language operating system and add-ons such as World Wide Web browsers that allow English-language systems to display Chinese characters; and Beijing-based SunTendy, which has developed Chinese Star, a supplement to English-language operating systems that enables viewing and entering of Chinese characters.

The competition has become strongly fiercer in recent years as the market matures. China's local software companies have made great efforts to enlarge their businesses by borrowing from foreign capital markets. Many companies such as Jinchen, Kelihua, Mingtai, and Jindie received investment from such markets. After Stone Rich Sight successfully obtained international venture capital in late 1997, many domestic software developers began eyeing this new financing strategy which has proved effective abroad in starting successful high-tech companies. Foreign companies made the competition even fiercer as they increased their efforts to tap the Chinese market. Apart from consolidating their advantage in operating systems, office software, and computer language software, these companies made significant headway in exploring the enterprise market, through promotion of electronic commerce and small and medium enterprise solution concepts. Commercial software, usually consisting of a large system which handles management, accounting, sales, and personnel applications is beyond the present development capabilities of most Chinese software companies. Foreign companies have thus met little competition in this sector from their Chinese counterparts.

Almost every software company inevitably faces intellectual property rights headaches. Some estimate that 96 percent of software in use has been pirated (compared to piracy in the U.S. at 27 percent). Foreign software companies lost about U.S.$704 million to Chinese pirates in 1996. China is the third largest source of software piracy losses in the world, but software companies are somewhat silent on the subject rather than offend the Chinese government. They also credit the Chinese government for closing down illegal CD-ROM plants and for raising the fines imposed on sellers of pirated products. Microsoft's deal with Legend to pre-install Windows on Legend's PCs was hailed by industry participants as a beneficial precedent, not just for Microsoft and foreign software makers, but for Chinese software firms and endusers as well. China's rampant piracy has threatened the survival of domestic software companies perhaps more than foreign firms. Meanwhile, chinese customers end up with inferior products. Foreign support for governmental anti-piracy efforts thus aids domestic competitors. Software piracy control should also improve with the establishment of the title verification office called for in the 1995 U.S.-China IPR (intellectual property rights) agreement. Meanwhile, Chinese consumers of high-end products are increasingly purchasing full-service support contracts to accompany their software, but lower-end and PC-based products remain vulnerable to piracy.

3.4 Pharmaceuticals and Bio-Medicine

Pharmaceuticals

When China catches a cold, pharmaceuticals companies pay attention. According to a recent survey, 90 percent of more than 100 urban consumers interviewed stated they had used cold medication in the previous six months; 50 percent said they had taken painkillers. China's overall pharmaceuticals market reached U.S.$ 7.5 billion in retail sales in 1992 and generated an annual industrial output of $14.45 billion in 1996, tripling that of 1978. Total output value of the sector topped $22.4 billion in 1999.

China, the world's second largest pharmaceuticals producer, annually produces 1,350 varieties of chemical medicines and 4,000 Chinese herbal medicines. Imported medicines and products manufactured by foreign- funded enterprises currently occupy nearly 60 percent of the market in some large Chinese cities. With the exception of herbal medicine, more than 97 percent of chemical drugs are imitations of foreign products. Over the past five years, foreign drug companies such as SmithKline Beecham and Schering-Plough have invested nearly $500 million in almost 1,500 joint ventures in China. Foreign and joint-venture sales account for up to 80 percent of the market in some of China's larger cities. In some sub-sectors, foreign drugs have dominated the market. SmithKline Beecham's cold medicine Contac, which is manufactured at the company's Tianjin joint venture, is one of the market leaders in China. Up to now, no Chinese chemical drug has been patented in a foreign country.

The Chinese pharmaceuticals market is over-supplied. Competition has become especially severe recently because of the Asian financial crisis which has forced products planned for export to be offered on the domestic market. Profits dropped by 250 million yuan ($30 million) in 1999. About 30 percent of more than 600 state-owned pharmaceuticals enterprises suffered from serious deficits in late 1990s. The governmental department administering the pharmaceuticals industry in China has halted redundant production, tightened control of imports, and speeded up bankruptcy of ailing firms in a bid to improve efficiency. Establishment of new factories has been put under strict control in order to reduce production. Imports are not allowed if domestic enterprises are able to provide sufficient quantities. About 40 to 50 percent of production lines are now unused.

The Chinese State Development Planning Commission announced price caps on pharmaceuticals in late 1998 that have had an unfavorable impact on foreign investors. Price controls are part of a much needed health care reform effort. For years, free medical treatment was something the government threw into the "iron rice bowl" of every citizen's basic entitlement. Free health care has now come to an end. As the population has grown and aged, the state has cut subsidies to hospitals and trimmed health insurance for workers. Only 50 percent of urban Chinese now have health insurance. Drugs are an obvious target for cutting costs. More than 50 percent of Chinese health care spending goes to pharmaceuticals, four to five times the share in most OECD countries. Overprescription is routine. Antibiotics are issued for practically any complaint and account for 40 percent of all spending on conventional (as opposed to traditional Chinese) medicines in some provinces, compared with only 10 percent in the West. Patients leave the dispensary with bags, rather than bottles, full of pills. Although drug prices are in theory controlled by the state, in practice they are artificially inflated by those who dole out the drugs. About 85 percent of drugs in China are dispensed by hospital pharmacies, which demand steep discounts from drug companies and then use the difference between their purchase prices and state reimbursement rates to subsidize hospital operations. Thus, the more drugs they sell, the more money they gain.

In proposing new regulations, the government hopes to get a grip on healthcare inflation and stem corruption, while devoting more of hospital budgets to patient services. The rules limit which drugs are approved for reimbursement. Instead of fixing prices, the new caps specify profit margins. Pharmaceuticals companies must open their books to the government. They will be allowed margins ranging from 8 percent for ordinary drugs to as much as 25 percent for new products that cannot be made in China. The margins are based on production costs, ignoring research spending and other shared overheads. This is not a problem for most Chinese pharmaceuticals companies since they concentrate on low-tech products such as vitamins or copy foreign drugs rather than doing their own research. It is, however, a threat to innovative western firms. Moreover, the new regulations fix a 25 percent marketing overhead rate for all drugs, whether a generic aspirin or the latest biotech wonder. This may seem generous, but it hampers companies trying to create a new market for drugs which address specific diseases of which doctors or patients are uninformed. To make matters worse, the percentage is calculated on each company's historic sales, which hurts firms trying to increase their business. If hospitals still demand discounts, Western firms will no longer be able to compensate by raising prices.

Another challenge facing foreign investors is difficulty protecting their technology and intellectual property (IP). A weakness in the nation's IP protection regime allows Chinese drug companies to legally copy drugs that have foreign patents. Many foreign pharmaceuticals firms apply to the State Drug Administration for administrative protection of patented drugs that the companies wish to introduce in China. While these applications are pending, the drug information is made available to Chinese companies during a lengthy public comment period meant to ensure that there is no overlap with existing drugs in China. Several drug companies with operations in China are feeling the effects of these regulations. For instance, Eli Lilly and Co. is competing against two local copies of its antidepressant's Prozac. Novartis is faced with local copies of its fungicide Lamisil and its immunosuppresent Neoral. Pfizer Inc. is expecting a local copy of its antidepressant Zoloft. Many foreign drug companies are hesitant to fight this controversial Chinese policy, fearing a backlash from China's drug regulators, who may withhold future new drug approvals. Most of these companies have limited their responses to meeting with U.S. Trade Representative officials.

Despite these regulations and increased competition, opportunities still abound. Foreign drug companies continue to enjoy an advantage because their products work better and consumers are willing to pay a premium for the cachet of a foreign brand. As most domestic manufacturers are small and medium grade enterprises with average assets well below 6 million yuan (U.S.$720,000), they do not have as much of a competitive edge as foreign firms. The growing population of seniors in China means more money for the pharmaceutical industry. China has more than 110 million senior citizens. By the year 2000, that figure is expected to reach 130 million, accounting for 10.6 percent of the country's total population. The nation's 864 million rural residents are becoming another valuable source of income as they become more aware of healthcare options. At present, China's rural population accounts for 80 percent of the nation's total, yet, rural medicine consumption accounts for only 20 percent of the country's total.

There is also hope that regulations will relax again. The National Planning Committee recently declared it will loosen limitations on the profit rates of medicine sales. This would enable foreign investors to obtain higher profits. Health insurance reform to date has several implications for foreign investors. First, it should moderate health expenditures over the next few years, diminishing the demand for imported drugs. Second, pharmaceutical consumption by uninsured urban residents could grow. Many of these uninsured are owners and employees of private and small businesses with high incomes. As their numbers rise together with disposable incomes, the consumption of pharmaceuticals by this group is expected to increase. Third, there will be higher spending in rural areas on pharmaceuticals and other health care as disposable income increases, especially along China's southeastern coast.

Fourth, joint venture products will become more popular. Patients eligible for reimbursement have opted for imported, high quality drugs regardless of price because their work units pay their medical care expenses. Though it remains difficult for imported products to be included on national or local drug reimbursement lists because of their high prices, joint venture products tend to be less expensive and thus more apt to fall within State imposed price ceilings. Furthermore, because of the Chinese preference for foreign medications, physicians and patients may choose joint venture products, even if they are not on the reimbursement drug lists.

Lastly, retail pharmacies could become a new battleground among foreign, joint venture, and local companies. The number of retail pharmacies, roughly 60,000 in 1996, is growing rapidly. Retail pharmacies mainly serve the uninsured. As many imported drugs are now left out of the State reimbursement system, insured patients are also turning to retail pharmacies. Under the capitation or average payment mechanisms, hospitals now have a financial incentive to sell fewer drugs. The sales of over-the-counter (OTC), imported, and expensive drugs will therefore shift from hospitals to retail pharmacies. The emergence of the OTC market and the expansion of retail pharmacies will create new opportunities for drug firms. The Ministry of Health began establishing OTC regulations in 1995, classifying pharmaceuticals as either OTC or prescription drugs, and plans to implement a separate OTC system by the year 2000. The Chinese Pharmaceutical Association also has begun to select drugs for the OTC market. The establishment of OTC regulations together with retail pharmacy networks should facilitate expansion of the OTC market.

Bio-Medicine

The central government is strongly encouraging foreign investment in the bio-medical industry. Foreign investors are expected to face less competition in this pharmaceutical sector, as well as less interference from the government. Currently, the bio-medical industry has been concentrated in a few major cities such as Shanghai and Beijing. The total output value of the industry reached 18 billion yuan (U.S.$ 2.16 billion) in Shanghai in 1998. During the first half of 1998, 30 bio-medical research projects were launched, involving a total investment of 20 million yuan (U.S.$ 2.4 million). Among the world's top 20 pharmaceutical giants, seven have invested in Shanghai's bio-medical industry, including Bristol-Myers

Squibb, Johnson & Johnson, and Schering-Plough from the United States, Roche of Switzerland, and Nycomed of Norway.

Similarly, the Beijing Economic and Technological Development Zone is building a valley for medical and biological companies whose annual output value is expected to reach 2 billion yuan (U.S.$240 million) by 2000 and 40 billion yuan (U.S.$480 million) by 2010. The ambitious blue print includes facilities for at least 10 giant enterprises in the valley, each of which could have an output value of 1 billion yuan (U.S.$120 million). Covering 3.3 hectares of land, the green house alone is 38,000 square metres in size. To attract investors, the center will provide comprehensive services, including funding, market information, and intellectual property rights protection. High-tech biological medical projects of strategic importance will have priority for getting loans. The zone offers them rent discounts or delayed collection of rent. Both domestic and foreign enterprises in the zone will be exempt from taxes for the first two years after they start making a profit. Taxation is cut by half for the following three years.

3.5 Telecommunications Equipment

China's telecommunications industry has been thriving. Production of major equipment has grown by a large margin in recent years. Production of optical communication equipment surged 62.9 percent annually, reaching 50,153 units in 1998. Carrier communication equipment increased by 25 percent to 7,026 units. Program-controlled switchboards hit 37 million, up 53.2 percent over 1997. China produced close to 16 million sets of mobile communications equipment, 49.3 percent more than in 1996.

The Chinese government has invested aggressively in its telecommunications infrastructure. Total spending on the telecom infrastructure has compounded at 62 percent annually over the past decade. It spent 124.5 billion yuan (15 billion dollars), or five percent of its total spending, on the telecommunication infrastructure sector in 1997, out of which six billion dollars was used to import electronics and telecommunications equipment. In 1998, China spent more than 150 billion yuan, while the revenue for operators grew 28 percent over 1997.

China's market for cell phones is exploding. Almost overnight,

China has become the second-largest market in the world after the U.S. for mobile phones and equipment. As recently as 1994 there were only 1.6 million cellular subscribers in China. Now demand races ahead at a rate of more than 1 million new subscribers a month. By the end of year 2000, China will have in excess of 50 million cellular subscribers. This compares favorably with the U.S. at 75 million. The handset market is dominated by the "three horses," as the Chinese call Ericsson, Motorola, and Nokia. Last year China became the largest market in the world for Ericsson; the country ranks number two after the U.S. for Motorola and Nokia.

It's not all gravy for foreign equipment suppliers. As a price of admission to the Chinese market they often have to agree to do most of their manufacturing locally through joint ventures with Chinese partners. Competition is keen. Still, this huge market appears to be strengthening their bottom lines. China probably accounted for at least 10 percent of Ericsson's 1998 net income.

Handset prices have been halved in two years, to an average of $250 at retail. The connection fee for new subscribers has fallen by more than 50 percent, to $125 to $200, in two years. That's still plenty of yuan in a country where the average pay in major cities is under $80 a week. But talk time of a nickel a minute is one of the cheapest in the world. On average, Chinese subscribers spend 400 minutes a month on their cell phones, three times as much as Americans.

Some of the credit for this explosion must go to aggressive marketing by handset vendors. Motorola, for instance, operates a fleet of 26 vans that hit the road 365 days a year, visiting 600 second-tier and smaller cities for some grassroots marketing. Motorola advertisements hammer home the message that cell phones create business breakthroughs and consumer peace of mind. Status and fashion also figure in the appeal, especially to teenagers and women. Since 1996 the government has permitted the sale of handsets through independent distributors and retailers. Motorola phones are now available in 10,000 outlets; Nokia will open 500 franchised shops within 18 months.

Foreign investors still are barred from operating cellular networks. Meanwhile, Beijing has injected some competition into the market by allowing a second state-owned operator, China Unicom, to compete with China Telecom. This represents competition between two different cellular standards. Over the past several years, competition has focused on the GSM (Global Systems for Mobile Communications) technology developed in Europe. China is already the world's largest market for GSM equipment. The Chinese government has awarded China Unicom a license to build a wireless network based on the CDMA (Code Division Multiple Access) standard used in the U.S.. CDMA proponents, such as Qualcomm, argue that its more efficient use of the spectrum makes it ideal for China's densely populated urban areas. China Unicom recently announced an ambitious plan to construct a CDMA network with a capacity to carry 10 million subscribers by the end of next year, rising to 40 million by 2003. Unicom has selected Lucent, Motorola, Samsung, and Nortel to build trial CDMA systems in four cities. China's Ministry of Information Industry (MII) projects that by the year 2010 there will be 200 million cell phone subscribers in the country. This would still represent a penetration rate of only 15 percent. Third generation mobile communications systems will be widely used in China in the coming years. The ongoing expo features various types of small GSM base stations. Major international telecom equipment companies such as Siemens, Ericsson and Nokia are also introducting third generation CDMA technology to upgrade GSM base stations.

Finnish-based Nokia opened an industrial complex in Beijing as part of an effort to expand both research and production of telecommunications equipment. Nokia's latest handset, smaller than a cigarette pack, features Chinese input functions. Heated competition has also emerged for various other products such as switchboards, data exchange equipment, and optical transmission facilities. Local rivals such as Huawei Technology Co. Ltd. have conducted extensive trials of its GSM equipment in Shanghai and several provinces and plan to start full-scale production within the next few years. A small group of companies, including Shanghai Bell Telephone Equipment Manufacturing Co. Ltd., currently dominate the Chinese market for program-controlled exchange equipment.

The market, although vast, is still restricted. Foreign companies must localize their operations and transfer technology. At the beginning of 1999, MII issued the first batch of special licenses for 18 Chinese and foreign telecommunications equipment manufacturers in a bid to combat smuggling and the marketing of inferior goods and to encourage foreign companies to transfer technology to China. China restructured the licensing system for telecommunications equipment, previously controlled by several authorities, by putting all the power into the hands of MII. Under the new system, telecommunications equipment made by both Chinese and foreign companies for the domestic market will be tagged. Products without the tag cannot be sold or used in China.

In order to guarantee service quality to license applicants, MII has set up two administration centers in Beijing. It has also abolished the practice of issuing licenses on the quota basis. Instead, various models can be sold in unlimited amounts. Among the first companies that have obtained licenses are Shanghai Bell, Motorola, and Nokia. Thirty-eight types of telecommunications equipment made by enterprises such as TCL in Guangdong, Motorola in Beijing, and Siemens in Shanghai have so far passed the examination of the State Bureau for Quality and Technical Supervision.

Almost every major player in the world telecom equipment market is now actively competing in China. About ten percent of Motorola's global sales are from China. Germany's Siemens is expected to have annual sales of 1.5 billion Marks in China by the year 2000. Siemens launched its sixth Chinese joint venture in 1999 in Chengdu, in the Sichuan Province. This new project involves a total investment of U.S.$28 million. It focuses on systems using fibre-optics and radio technology.

French telecommunications equipment maker Alcatel has already invested a total of 300 million dollars in 17 joint ventures in China, manufacturing products such as switching equipment, optical fibre lines, microwave transmission systems, fixed-wire and wireless access systems, and mobile radio infrastructure equipment. Alcatel is planning to invest another 300 million dollars in China over the next five years, including funding to make mobile telephone sets and satellites. Alcatel, a latecomer in mobile telecommunications after the major leaders such as Ericsson, Nokia, and Motorola, sold 2.5 million mobile phone terminals worldwide in 1997.

Lucent Technologies, another leading foreign telecom equipment supplier in China, is expected to strengthen its presence through a farsighted development strategy. The company focuses on cooperating with local partners and enhancing the research and development capabilities of its Bell Laboratories in China. Lucent became the first company to bring synchronous digital hierarchy (SDH) technology to China when the 2.5GB/s backbone transmission network between Hong Kong and Guangzhou became fully operational in 1994. In the past three years, the company has won more than 300 contracts for optical networking equipment, representing nearly U.S.$650 million worth of business.

Finland's Nokia has increased its exposure in both northern and southern China by securing new contracts and expanding its Guangdong joint venture. It set up a landmark contract recently with the mobile communications arm of Tianjin Telecom in Tianjin, a port city in northern China. The contract calls for Nokia to supply fiber optical transmission equipment to the city's global mobile telephone network. The agreement marked Nokia's first order for related equipment from China's telecommunications sector and its entry into new business areas in China. Its synchronous digital hierarchy (SDH) technology enables mobile communications centers to operate even during the installation stage. In another development, Nokia expanded the production capacity of its joint venture in Dongguan, in south China's Guangdong Province, in June 1998. The project enables the Dongguan Nokia Mobile Telephone Co. Ltd. to increase poduction of peripherals including mobile telephone sets. The joint venture is currently producing Nokia's most cutting-edge mobile telephone sets. As the world's leading cellular telephone supplier, Nokia has introduced new technology to China that was initiated worldwide. Nokia is also a leading supplier of mobile phones and network equipment to China's telecommunications market. It has established seven manufacturing centers and a global research and development unit in China. It employs more than 3,000 local people nationwide.

As the world's telecommunications giants compete for prime product markets in China, other firms are seeking market or technological niches. For instance, Ascom Corp. from Switzerland is seeking a niche in sub-telecom equipment and systems. Ascom had already offered a range of handy products to China, including base-band modems, payphones, and toll collection and mailing systems. The company has taken more than 40 percent of the country's payphone market. In an effort to meet increasing demand, Ascom established a joint venture last year in Guangzhou to produce 600,000 payphones a year. Similarly, British telecom equipment manufacturer GPT clinched its first commercial deal with Beijing Telecommunications Administration (BTA) to set up the core technology for a major expansion of the voice and data transmission network in Beijing. GPT will supply BTA with its latest versions of SDH (synchronous digital hierarchy) equipment and a network management system for the launch of Beijing's second local trunk telephone network. In addition, GPT supplies training, installation, and support services through its joint ventures in Shanghai and customer support center in Beijing.

3.6 Electronics and Machinery

Electronics

The electronics industry is among the fastest growing sectors in China. It is largely concentrated in the coastal provinces of Guangdong, Shanghai, Jiangsu, Beijing, and Tianjin. The restructuring of state-owned companies in this industry has proceeded rapidly. Over 260 firms under the Ministry of Machinery and Electronics Industries have been decentralized.

China's electronics industry produces a wide range of household appliances, from refrigerators, air conditioning, cleaning, ventilating and heating appliances to kitchen, cosmetic and health care utensils and a variety of accessories. There are several reasons for the boom in this highly competitive industry. First, export aspirations has made producers spend more on R&D and quality control to meet international standards. Second, localization of parts and components has greatly driven down the cost of production, which enhances global cost leadership. Third, Great China MNEs from Hong Kong, Taiwan, and Singapore have brought in many innovative ideas, technological skills, capital resources, international channels, and managerial expertise, further facilitating the competitive edge of the Chinese electronics industry in the global market. Today, IBM, Hewlett Packard, Hitachi, Siemens, Philips, Olivetti, Toshiba, NEC, Samsung, among other firms, have all made dramatic investments in China.

The electronics industry has grown by an average of 25 percent annually over the last few years. In 1997, production value amounted to 380 billion yuan (U.S.$45.8 billion) with profits and taxes reaching 18.5 billion yuan (U.S.$2.2 billion). Despite this rapid growth, many structural problems remain to be resolved in China's electronics industry. The supply of many products far exceeds demand. Only some high-tech goods are beating this trend. Intense competition has persuaded enterprises to accelerate restructuring and produced a series of mergers. As a result, production is now concentrated in a number of large industrial electronics groups.

Although the household electronic appliance sector is plagued by overcapacity, a huge market for high-tech products is yet to be tapped in China. At present, China's TV production lines have a total capacity of more than 45 million color TV sets every year, but only 46.1 percent of capacity is being used. Only 50.1 percent of the refrigerator production lines are working. The rate is even lower for factories making air-conditioners, range hoods, vacuum cleaners and washing machines. The government has adopted a policy of letting market competition regulate the electronics industry, but has not adopted effective measures for preventing overlapping investments in similar projects. For example, since the beginning of the 1990s, cities and regions such as Tianjin, Shandong, Jiangsu, and Guangdong have set up color TV production bases capable of turning out millions of sets every year. A joint venture in Shanghai alone has a production capacity of 3 million sets a year. By comparison, the high-tech sector of the country's electronics industry lacks such large enterprises. China now produces less than one-fourth of the 8 billion integrated circuits that it uses every year. About 80 percent of those made in China are from plants wholly or partially owned by foreign investors. Market competition has already forced a number of local electronics giants to readjust development strategies. Major TV manufacturers such as Changhong, Hai'er, and TCL have diversified into information technology. They have developed new products such as digital TV sets and multimedia computer terminals. There is a rising trend in the industry for computer and electronic appliance manufacturers to mix businesses.

China represents the world's biggest potential market for multimedia and consumer electronics. In fact, not only is China the fastest-growing market for multimedia products, it is in a position to set the standard for a renaissance of the disc-based video format that could ignite the global market. China has the largest Video CD (VCD) market in the world, with yearly sales increasing from 2 million VCD players in 1995 to approximately 15 million in 1997. In China, where VCRs and other consumer electronics arrived in the market more or less concurrently with VCD, a Video CD comprises the heart of every home entertainment system, combining a CD Audio player, Karaoke machine, and video player in one. More than 300 Chinese companies now manufacture VCD players; they have perfected the art of making and selling them cheaply. A Video CD player costs only about $100 and that price is on its way down.

In the relative absence of other sources of entertainment, VCDs are highly welcomed by Chinese consumers. With this kind of market clout, it's no wonder that the Chinese government's Ministry of Electronics Industry is becoming involved in defining China-specific extensions to the Video CD 2.0 White Book specification, owned by Philips, Sony, Matsushita, and JVC. It's also not surprising that these companies are planning to sell Chinese Video CD players to the rest of the world. The market, in other words, is going to become the marketer.

The most promising market for digital videodisks (DVD) is not the U.S., but China. There are nearly 300 million TV sets in China, but broadcast programming is limited and the average household does not have a VCR. China is a video *tabula rasa*, ready and willing to go digital with the latest hardware. It shouldn't be surprising that China can leapfrog over wealthy countries like the U.S. to become the largest market for DVD. At least ten million video CD players were sold in China in 1997. Chinese families that are still without the means of playing videos are likely to adopt a better technology, DVD. DVD players can serve as all-in-one entertainment machines that play both video and audio CDs. A huge variety of digital movies and karaoke selections is already available in China. Disks are often sold on street markets alongside farm produce and live chickens, going for under $2.50 each. More than 15,000 movie and karaoke titles are legally in print. Estimates of the number of pirated titles vary widely, but may be as high as 65,000. Matsushita, Samsung, and other Asian companies have already started shipping DVD players to China, where they sell in stores and open-air markets such as the huge electronics bazaar in Panyu. A U.S. company, Digital Video Systems, has set up shop in Panyu as well. A player typically costs $650, or about half the average annual income of a Chinese household, but prices are falling rapidly.

China's demand for digital cameras is expected to hit one million units in the year 2000, and account for approximately 11 percent of total camera sales worldwide. 11 million cameras were sold in China during 1998. The market is far from saturated, with only 30 cameras for every 100 urban families, and fewer than 3 cameras for every 100 rural households. Continuous improvement of living standards and the purchase of computers by more Chinese will increase the popularity of digital cameras. The current cost of digital cameras ranges from 2,000 yuan ($240) to 10,000 yuan ($1204), with highly sophisticated cameras costing as much as one million yuan ($120,000). The latter cameras are mainly used by journalists, passport offices, advertisers, insurance companies, and healthcare units.

Machinery

China's machinery industry consists of 12 major sectors: (1) automotive, (2) electrical equipment, (3) heavy and mining machinery, (4) petrochemical and general machinery, (5) agricultural machinery, (6) construction machinery, (7) internal combustion engines, (8) machine tools, (9) instruments and meters, (10) basic machinery parts, (11) food processing and packaging machinery, and (12) environmental protection machinery. Made up of 120,000 enterprises and 122 scientific research institutes, colleges, and universities, the industry employs 20 million people. In 1996, the value of its output reached about $65 billion. From 1990 to 1995 the industry grew at an average annual rate of 24 percent, up from the 16 percent rate achieved during the previous five years. By 1996, the machinery industry included nearly 5,300 officially approved foreign funded enterprises, with foreign direct investment totaling approximately $55 billion.

In order to revitalize the machinery industry, the government gives priority to specific areas seeking foreign expertise, technology, and cooperation:

(1) Power Generation: (a) hydropower generation, including development of huge hydropower units and large pump-storage units, auxiliary equipment for hydropower units such as speed governors and excitation systems, and computer monitoring devices for power stations; (b) thermal power generation, including development of new technologies such as recirculating fluidized beds, dust removal and desulfurization techniques, air cooling and heat dissipation techniques; (c) power transmission and transformation, including improvement of ultrahigh-voltage AC and DC transmission and transformation equipment.

(2) Instruments and Meters: development of automation control instruments and systems used in major technological equipment, quality inspection and control equipment needed by basic and pillar industries, environmental monitoring and analytical instruments for measuring air and water quality and pollution sources, and clinical analytical and medical instruments.

(3) Metallurgical Equipment: development of continuous thin-slab casting and rolling equipment, large coking ovens, and ladle cars to meet the needs of continuous casting and continuous rolling equipment mills and steel works capable of an annual output of about six million tons.

(4) Mining Equipment: development of large self-dumping trucks, rotary drilling rigs, excavators, electric shovels, and elevators as part of the effort to produce complete sets of equipment needed for open-pit mining with an annual output of 20 million tons, and underground mining with an annual output of five million tons.

(5) Agricultural Machinery: development of medium-sized tractors and associated farm implements, small and medium-sized self-propelled and knapsack harvesters, drainage and irrigation machinery, and processing and transportation machinery.

(6) Construction Machinery: development of large excavators, bulldozers, wheeled loaders, construction cranes, rock drilling machinery, surfacing machines, and compacting machines.

(7) Internal Combustion Engines, Fittings, and Accessories: development of new multicylinder diesel engines, as well as fittings and accessories that support large and medium-sized construction and agricultural machinery.

It is worth noting that packaging machinery is perhaps the most promising segment in this industry. It began to develop at the end of the 1970s and continued growing through the 1980s, with development speeding up significantly in the 1990s. As one of the few industries which is prospering in China's machinery sector, the packaging industry presents a huge market potential for foreign exporters. Currently, there are 1,500 enterprises involved in the packaging machinery industry, producing over 2,700 different products, among which 400 enterprises are large state-owned enterprises. With an average increase rate of total output of 20.45 percent, packaging machinery has far surpassed the machine tools industry and other machinery industries in the past ten years. China has a strong demand for packaging machinery in the following areas: high-tech, continuous, and automatic processing, energy conservation, and construction. Local firms are seeking to improve the technology level of products with high speed operations, develop varieties of packaging specifications, increase the reliability and durability of packaging machinery, produce aseptic packaging machines for the medical and food industries, develop advanced packaging machinery, combine packaging technology with electronic-mechanical technology, develop computer-controlled machinery, and design new products with advanced technology and computer assistance.

China is now the second largest packaging machinery importer in the world. It mainly imports from Japan, Italy, the United States, Germany, France, the United Kingdom, Switzerland, Korea, and Taiwan. Presently, many western countries consider China the most promising market for their packaging products. American packaging machinery exporters are witnessing a steadily increasing market share.

3.7 Chemical Industry

Total chemical industry production in 1997 was about 8 percent of GDP. Production has grown about 9 percent annually over the last decade. Forty seven chemical companies are among 500 enterprises the government is promoting on a priority basis. Until the end of 1996, total investment from overseas reached more than $10.1 billion, with the establishment of 7,141 joint ventures. Petrochemical revenues alone were U.S.$73 billion in 1997.

The country's petroleum and chemical industries recorded 10.3 billion yuan (U.S.$1.24 billion) in profits in 1998, more than one-quarter of the entire profits of state-owned enterprises. In 1998, the total industrial output of China's petroleum and chemical sectors was 499 billion yuan (U.S.$60 billion). The sector's total sales revenue reached 779.6 billion yuan (U.S.$94 billion).

The chemical industry is at the vanguard of China's effort to separate government and business, reflecting the sector's importance in the eyes of China's economic leadership. The new regulatory authority, the State Bureau of Petroleum and Chemical Industry (SBPCI) falls under the State Economic and Trade Commission. With the abolition of the Ministry of Chemical Industry (MCI) and the separation of governmental functions from petrochemical enterprises, the industry is now more decentralized. The government is cutting redundant production capacity while speeding up adjustment of products for the market. Technical innovation is especially encouraged and more research institutes are being merged into enterprises to boost technical development. Small refineries are being closed and the refined oil circulation system is being reformed to create a more orderly market. Other steps include increasing the capital utilization ratio and investment efficiency, diversifying property rights, improving capital structure, and reducing debts of state firms.

During the restructuring of the Ministry of the Chemicals Industry, two national level business groups, the China National Petroleum Corporation (CNPC) and the China Petrochemical Corporation (Sinopec), were given control of all state-owned onshore oil and gas exploration, refining, and petrochemical production. The country was divided between the two, giving CNPC control of the north and west and Sinopec control of the south and east. The goal is to make these two industrial behemoths competitive with global chemical companies. The existence of two parallel monopolies has created a difficult environment for global competitors. For example, Sinopec and CNPC set prices for all retail oil and finished petrochemical products.

China is encouraging foreign investment in the chemical industry in order to improve domestic production and bring financial relief to some of its state-owned enterprises. The Asian financial crisis has caused the government to scale back on some of its ambitious plans, however. Because of Asian imports flooding the market and uneven domestic demand, the Chinese government appears to be taking a more protectionist stance towards its existing chemical operations.

Shanghai and the surrounding East China region is a principal center for the chemical industry in China. Foreign investors are flocking there to take advantage of its economic strength and production resources. The U.S. is already an important player in China's overall chemical industry. U.S. companies supplied $2.43 billion in chemical products to China in 1998, a 13.6 percent share of total imports. Market opportunities abound in organic and inorganic chemicals, synthetic materials, and chemical fertilizers in Shanghai, Jiangsu, Zhejiang, and Anhui. Imports of synthetic resins and rubbers, specialized polymer materials, and sophisticated fine chemicals are high because China's domestic production can not meet demand in terms of quantity or quality.

China mirrors the world market in that inorganic and organic chemicals are both oversupplied and undersupplied. Inorganic chemicals such as caustic soda and soda ash are abundantly available whereas ethylene, propylene, butadiene and styrene are not being produced enough.

The domestic production of chemical fertilizers still cannot meet agricultural demands. The application of chemical fertilizer per hectare of cultivation is very low, despite the huge demand for food. Currently, China's annual production capacity of pure chemical fertilizer is 36.24 million tons, while the annual output level is only 27 million tons. In 1998, China imported $1.78 billion in chemical fertilizer.

China is the world's second largest producer of pesticides, but still lags a long way behind developed countries in product structure, use of technology, scale of operations, and basic knowledge of crop protection, especially among those at the working end. Thirty percent of China's grain growth has been attributed to the introduction of new technology. This compares unfavorably to the 60 percent advantage enjoyed by nations using advanced agricultural techniques. Recently, fifteen major international agro-chemical companies have formed an alliance to assist China to produce a better, safer food supply. The Crop Protection Association of China (CPAC), which was recently set up in Beijing, will work with Chinese organizations such as the State Bureau of Petroleum and Chemical Industries, the Ministry of Agriculture, and the CPA to introduce advanced crop protection technologies to China. The members of CPAC are AgroEvo, American Cyanamid, BASF, Bayer, Dow, DuPont, Elf Atochem, FMC, Monsanto, Novartis, Rhone-Poulenc, Rhom and Haas, Sumitomo, Uniroyal, and Zeneca, all of which have invested in China.

China is a large net importer of synthetic resin. Since 1993, the combined total import volume of five general types of synthetic resins – PE, PS, PVC, PP and ABS – has increased by around one million tons each year. In 1997, the import volume of these five synthetic resins reached 7.37 million tons. The automotive sector is an area of opportunity for synthetic resin sales. Currently, plastics only account for 5 to 6 percent of the weight of automobiles made in China, whereas they account for 15 percent of the weight of automobiles made in the U.S..

Despite heavy investing by both domestic and foreign chemical firms, the Chinese government continues to seek new investment in areas of continued weakness. For example, China is seeking investment for ethylene production facilities exceeding 600,000 tons, basic raw materials such as benzene, methylbenzene, and dimethylbenzene, fine chemicals, PVC Resin and PVC alloy, engineering plastics, and plastic alloys.

Japan, South Korea, and Taiwan are strong competitors of the U.S., especially in plastics and rubber. In 1997, South Korea exported 766,000 tons of PE and 551,000 tons of PP to China. In 1997, Japan exported 478,000 tons of PVC to China. Taiwan accounted for 32.7 percent of the import market of PS and 46.1 percent of ABS. Non-Asian exporters include Australia, which supplied 25.6 percent of China's imported inorganic chemicals in 1998, and Germany, which supplied 5.05 percent of China's imports of organic chemicals in the same year. Since late 1997, the Chinese petrochemical market has been flooded by cheap imports from other Asian countries suffering the effects of the Asian financial crisis. Additional price pressure comes from goods entering China through gray channels often emanating from Hong Kong.

China's fine chemical industry is developing rapidly and has become an economic growth point. The output value of the fine chemical industry already accounts for one third of the total output of the chemical industry and is expected to account for 45 percent in future. Fine chemical products have been widely used in various areas, playing an increasingly important role. The rapid development of other industries makes higher demands on fine chemical products, promoting the development of the industry. Its annual output value exceeds 100 billion yuan. There are 20,000 varieties of products. China boasts more than 5,000 fine chemical manufacturing enterprises. It plans to build 15 more fine chemical products bases in medium and small cities.

The biological industry is still in its infancy. China has listed it as a focus for development and plans to achieve the following before 2010: actively developing pollution-free biological pesticides for industry; upgrading the production of existing biological chemical products using modern biological chemical technology; developing new products using microbiological methods; treating pollution produced in the process of chemical industrial production with biological chemical technology; developing regenerated resources as raw materials for the organic chemical industry; and seeking new raw materials.

More opportunities are expected when China joins the World Trade Organization. During recent negotiations with the U.S., the Chinese made a commitment to address the principal barriers to American imports. Should China be allowed to join the WTO, the U.S. would gain full market access for distribution throughout China, tariffs for imported chemical products would be reduced, and quantitative restrictions on imports would be eliminated. Trading and distribution rights would be progressively phased in over three years, including in principle, sensitive, and protected industries such as chemical fertilizers, crude oil, and processed petroleum. China would phase out remaining quotas, generally by 2002, but no later than 2005. Specifically for the chemical sector, China has also agreed that if it joins the WTO it will reduce its tariffs to match those of other WTO members for 70 percent of chemicals. Tariffs would generally be reduced to 5.5 or 6.5 percent. Tariff on soda ash would be reduced to 5.5 percent. Tariffs on cosmetics, pharmaceuticals, film, and certain plastics will also be cut substantially below current levels.

4. Opportunities and Challenges in the Service Industries

Chapter Purpose

China will not become an economic giant unless it further liberalizes its service sector. With a view to speeding up the economic growth, cracking down on the high unemployment, and joining the World Trade Organization, China has been taking measures to stimulate this sector and open it up to foreign companies. This chapter profiles the major service industries in China that are particularly appealing to foreign businesses. The chapter begins with an overview of the Chinese service sector, followed by a detailed presentation of the insurance industry. The third section articulates the characteristics, opportunities, and challenges of the finance and banking service. The fourth section describes features of the retail service industry. The next two sections illustrate institutional and structural traits of first, the tourist, hotel, and civil aviation industries and second, accounting, consulting, and legal services. The last two sections introduce the advertising and telecommunications service industries. Suggestions for MNCs are addressed throughout the chapter.

4.1 Overview

China will not become an economic giant until it opens up its service sector and speeds foreign service trade. The service sector includes a host of industries such as finance, insurance, tourism, real estate, retail and wholesale, advertising, and telecommunications. Because many manufacturing industries in China are currently grappling with oversupply, the service sector has great potential for development. The growth would boost the nation's economy and ease the unemployment pressure incurred from reforming the State-owned business sector.

As the service sector develops, China needs to gradually open it to the outside world. At 30 percent of GDP, China's service sector still lags behind that of developed countries, where this sector often accounts for as much as 70 per cent of GDP. As international trade in the services industry plays an increasingly important global role and China comes closer to joining the World Trade Organization (WTO), more opening of the service sector becomes inevitable.

China has already taken a series of prudent measures to stimulate this sector. The service sector's sales hit a record high of more than 500 billion yuan ($60.3 billion) in 1998, a growth of 15 percent from 1997. Its export volume ranked sixteenth in the world in 1997, compared with the twenty-seventh in 1992. Total earnings from tourism was $12 billion in 1997, 27 times that of 1979. By the end of 1997, the country had approved 73,658 foreign-funded programs in the service sector, involving nearly $208 billion in foreign investment.

China's long-closed retail market has been open to overseas investors since 1992. Foreign companies have reacted quickly by setting up branches of international retail enterprises in China. Initially, rigid restrictions were placed on foreign banking activities, but these have gradually been loosened. Currently, 191 foreign financial organizations operate in China. The People's Bank of China now allows 19 foreign banks in Shanghai's Pudong area and 6 in Shenzhen to engage in renminbi exchange. The scale of overseas investment in the service sector is still too small, however. This is most obvious in such sectors as finance, insurance, retail, foreign trade, and telecommunications. Their low level of development means they still need some State protection. It would be impossible to open these sectors completely within a short period of time. In the global economy, however, these sectors are becoming the most dynamic areas for absorbing overseas funds since other countries have eased or lifted restrictions on foreign participation. In recent years, buying shares or merging enterprises have become important forms of investment. Recognizing this shift, some State-owned enterprises have sold shares to overseas investors in order to raise funds to upgrade technology and expand production.

Liberalization involves challenges and potential risk and various other adverse factors. The financial crisis in Mexico and the recent economic chaos engulfing Asia may provide some lessons to China. China needs to fully consider the under-development of its fledgling service industry and gradually proceed in line with the capacity of the national economy to withstand strains. It is already encountering pressure from several sources asking for more active liberalization policies. Countries negotiating for China's membership in the World Trade Organization (WTO) have urged the nation to immediately open up most of its service industries. Deflation of the national economy and stagnant market consumption also necessitate greater decentralization of the service sector to stimulate domestic consumption and thus promote economic growth. The private sector can also absorb a large pool of relatively uneducated people in a quick manner. Finally, China needs to open more service sectors in order to halt the trend in decreasing foreign direct investment.

Given this context, it is safe to predict that China will open its service trade sector wide to the outside, but on a gradual basis. China has already vowed to use more overseas capital in such service sectors as commerce, foreign trade, civil aviation, and engineering project contracts. Besides Shanghai and Shenzhen, many more cities will be approved for trading joint ventures, especially in central and western China. More airlines will be able to attract overseas investment and the ratio limit on overseas shares will be relaxed. More joint ventures in intermediary services, including accounting, commodities and quality inspection, will be allowed. The government will also encourage qualified Chinese companies to establish joint ventures with big international companies for contracting engineering projects overseas, especially in developed countries. China will also allow joint-venture travel agencies, making tourism one of the latest sectors to open up. In the long run, China is likely to grant equal status to domestic and foreign enterprises with regard to preferential policies, eliminate disparities between sectors, ensure balanced regional development, and moderate protective measures.

The major service sectors presently allowing foreign investment on an experimental basis are expected to become liberalized soon which will provide tremendous market opportunities and business potential for foreign companies. These sectors include: (1) financial and insurance services: Up to now, 191 foreign financial institutions and insurance companies have been licensed to operate in China. Most of these institutions are confined to Shanghai and the Guangdong Province. Further market access for foreign financial institutions will depend on the development of China's legislation and improvement of supervision and management; (2) retail sector: China has accumulated experience in the retail sector through experimenting with China-foreign retail joint ventures in over a dozen cities in the past several years. China is now prepared to allow foreign retailers to form joint ventures with Chinese retailers in major cities in all provinces, autonomous regions, and cities that enjoy provincial status; (3) foreign trade sector: China will allow foreign companies to set up foreign trade joint ventures with Chinese companies in major cities of economically developed inland provinces, following the success of experiments in Shanghai's Pudong Area and Shenzhen Special Economic Zone; (4) travel service: experiments in China-foreign joint travel agencies will be carried out in major tourist cities; and (5) telecommunications service: China will also open its telecommunications service market to international companies, but only after it improves its legislation in this sector. Once there is access, there will, as usual, be an experimental period before full liberalization. Each of these sectors will be detailed in the next sections.

4.2 Insurance Services

Background

Following the end of the Civil War in 1949, the sole surviving insurance company, People's Insurance Company of China (PICC), was nationalized and maintained a monopoly until 1978. The PICC became the market and the regulator all in one. In 1978, there were only about 3,000 employees in the PICC, which had a premium income of approximately U.S.D$ 200 million – remarkably small for a country of 1.2 billion people. Since then, the insurance market has grown rapidly, at a compound growth rate of almost 40 percent per annum. In 1995, the industry employed some 130,000 people along with nearly as many part time agents. They generate approximately U.S.$8 billion in premiums. However, China still has one of the world lowest per capita spending on insurance, at about U.S.$7 per annum.

By the end of 1998, there were 25 insurance companies in China, including 4 state-owned companies, 9 joint stock companies, 3 Sino-foreign joint ventures and 9 foreign companies. Over time, this competitive market has been more and more open to foreign participation. By the end of 1998, a total of 14 branches of foreign insurance companies and Sino-foreign joint ventures had started business or planned to start business in China. A total of 113 insurance institutions from 17 countries and regions were approved to set up 202 representative offices. Meanwhile, China's domestic insurance companies have established 33 branches and 8 representative offices in Hong Kong, Macao, Southeast Asia, and Europe, and North America.

China established the China Insurance Regulatory Committee (CIRC) on November 18, 1998. The Committee independently takes responsibility for the supervision and regulation of the country's insurance market.

Premium revenues for the top 7 insurance companies are shown in Table 4.1.

Table 4.1: Top Seven Insurance Companies in China in 1998

Company Name	Premium Revenue	
	RMB (billion)	U.S.$ (billion)
China People's Life Insurance	53,000	6,409
China People's Insurance Corp.	40,160	4,856
Ping An Insurance	16,100	1,947
China Pacific Insurance	12,417	1,508
Xin Hua Life Insurance	1,182	143
Tai Kang Life Insurance	490	59
Hua Tai Property Insurance	247	30

Source: http://www.chinaonline.com

Operations

China's insurance industry has four strong areas of growth: insurance brokers, life insurance, reinsurance sector, and flood insurance. On February 14, 1998, the People's Bank of China published industrial guidelines entitled, "Regulations on the Administration of Insurance Brokers," signifying the entrance of insurance brokers into the domestic market.

Life insurance is one of the fastest growing segments of the insurance market. The number of life insurance policies undertaken by the Guangdong Branch of China People's Life Insurance Company with insured values greater than RMB 1 million (U.S.$ 121,000) exceeded 200 in 1998, including four single policies whose insured value was each over RMB 10 million (U.S.$ 1,200,000).

Reinsurance is insurance on an insurance policy. The market for re-insurance, formerly the exclusive domain of foreign providers, is increasingly being handled by China's domestic insurers. In 1998, China implemented "Legal Cede Insurance," also called "Priority Cede Insurance", a regulation that requires an insurance company to insure 30 percent of its total business with one of the reinsurance companies of the People's Insurance Company (Group). The policy has already proven effective. During the first half of 1998, when the insurance market was severely affected by the financial crisis in Southeast Asia, reinsurance companies received RMB 3.35 billion (U.S.$405 million) in premiums, an increase of 3.38 percent over the same period a year earlier.

The number of flood insurance policies saw a significant increase in 1998 when the Changjiang, Songhuajiang, and Nenjiang river valleys experienced the most severe floods in a hundred years. Property losses amounted to RMB 166.6 billion (U.S.$20 billion). Losses in the Jiangxi, Hubei, and Hunan Provinces alone reached RMB 54 billion (U.S.$ 6.5 billion). However, claims only reached RMB 1.8 billion (U.S.$217 million), 30 times less than expected. Throughout China, the variance between claimed property losses and actual direct losses due to floods was equally large. The 1998 floods greatly raised the need and awareness of flood insurance. Rural insurance in general also rose significantly.

Other categories of insurance available in the Chinese market are, for example, military service insurance, disability insurance, and athletic insurance. The military service insurance system for officers and soldiers of the People's Liberation Army was implemented on August 1, 1998. Military service personnel are now offered two forms of insurance: disability insurance and life insurance. Athletic insurance also came into shape in 1998. Recently, the State Sports General Bureau concluded an agreement with China People's Life Insurance Company to cover 1,400 athletes in the State Sports Training Teams.

Premium breakdown by insurance type is revealed in Table 4.2.

Table 4.2 Insurance Premiums Breakdown in 1998

Source	Amount (RMB billion)	%
Property Insurance	49	39%
Life Insurance	68	55%
Health Insurance	6.5	5%
Others	1.23	1%
Total	124.73	100%

Source: http://www.chinaonline.com

Decentralization

Foreign companies should be aware of the Chinese Insurance Law, first promulgated on June 30, 1995 at the Fourteenth Session of the Standing Committee of the eighth National People's Congress of China, and revised on October 1, 1995. The law reflects significant changes in the increased knowledge of regulators and a shift in industrial control from PICC to the People's Bank of China (PBC), the country's central bank. The three major goals of these regulations are as follows: (1) to follow international standards of managerial accountability; (2) balance protection of both insured and insurer rights; and (3) define the role of the regulator. The 1995 Insurance Law contains 152 articles divided into 8 sections as follows: (1) general provisions; (2) insurance contracts; (3) insurance company; (4) insurance operation rules; (5) insurance supervision and regulation; (6) insurance agents and brokers; (7) legal liability; and (8) supplementary provisions. Overall, the Law focuses on two prime areas: 'Contract Law', which involves the rights and privileges of the consumer (insurer or policy holder), insurer, and agent or broker, and 'Regulatory Control,' which outlines the responsibilities, accountability and power of the management of insurers as well as regulators.

Some decentralization occured in 1998, when the China People's Property Insurance Company, the China People's Life Insurance Company, and the China People's Reinsurance Company were separated from the China People's Insurance Corporation. The China Pacific (Taipingyang) Insurance Company was also separated from the Ministry of Communications. The Ping'an Insurance Company transformed its six subsidiaries into branches directly under its administration. Several regional joint-stock insurance companies came into existence, such as Dazhong, Ping'an, Huatai, Yong'an, Hua'an, Taikang, and Xinhua.

Foreign Participation

Since China's insurance industry has not yet matured and is unable to compete with fully developed foreign companies, the government opened the insurance market gradually. Opening up the market to foreign companies will bring in advanced technology and management expertise, however. The government should encourage foreigners to form joint ventures with local partners, but the list of Chinese companies eligible to be joint venture partners is very limited. CIRC currently restricts local partners to Chinese insurance companies, but MOFTEC recently announced that soon all non-bank financial institutions will be able to act as local partners as well. This would allow foreign insurance companies far greater selection in their choice of partner.

By the end of 1998, 14 foreign and joint venture insurance companies had received approval to operate in China or were preparing to open branches. Representative offices in China were established by 113 insurance companies from 17 countries and regions. Examples of foreign participants in the Chinese market follow.

(i) Chubb China Operations: Chubb entered China in 1994. It is involved in many activities in China, including setting up the Chubb School of Insurance at the Shanghai University of Finance and Economics (SUFE), sponsoring a radio program, helping translate the new Insurance Law into English, and assisting set up of the Foreign Insurance Club in China.

(ii) American International Group, Inc. (AIG): As the leading U.S. based international insurance organization with a network throughout approximately 130 countries, AIG has used its long history and competitive strength to promote itself in China. Its office is in Beijing.

(iii) CMG: CMG has operated representative offices in Beijing since 1994 and in Shanghai since 1995. It has developed positive relationships with key ministries, become involved in a number of financial service projects, and shown its commitment to China by continuously increasing its investments both in Hong Kong and on the mainland.

(iv) Thomas Miller & Co: Its two offices are in Beijing and Shanghai. The Shanghai office is intended as the main point of contact for non-Chinese businesses, while the Beijing office builds and maintains strong relationships with Chinese authorities and business partners. Its U.K. parents claim a presence in China of more than 20 years.

(v) Allstate: It emphasizes building agencies that capitalize on technology and well-trained support staff to serve customer needs. It has an office in Beijing.

(vi) Aetna: Aetna entered China in 1992 with a representative office in Beijing. In October 1998, it launched a joint venture with a very strong local partner, China Pacific Insurance. The venture, called 'Pacific Aetna', is located in Shanghai. It offers life insurance to individual Chinese and foreign nationals.

Other foreign insurance firms that had been approved recently by the Ministry of Foreign Trade and Economic Cooperation (MOFTEC) are the John Hancock Mutual Life Insurance Company, the Sun Life Assurance Company (Canada), and the Prudential Corporation (U.K.). A major concern of these foreign companies is that China's very large population mostly lives in rural areas and is unlikely to be in the market for life insurance. Moreover, under current regulations, a new insurance company is restricted to doing business in a single Chinese city at first. Only after it has proved itself to the government's satisfaction is it allowed to expand into other cities. Mr. Derek Chilvers, chairman and CEO of John Hancock International Holdings, said that it wouldn't be worth it if the company only has access to one city. The potential revenue from Chinese operations is therefore expected to be miniscule for some time compared to these companies' overall sales. However, MOFTEC said that it will shortly announce new regulations for the cities where foreign companies are allowed to operate. The regulations will also cover the types of Chinese companies that are eligible to be joint venture partners and define the ownership percentage that foreign companies can maintain. These regulations may present new opportunities for foreign investors.

To sum up, despite rapid growth and restructuring over the past several decades, China's insurance sector is still in a preliminary stage of development. First of all, it is an oligopoly. At present, the

PICC Property Insurance, the PICC Life Insurance, the China Pingan Insurance and the China Pacific Insurance hold 96 percent of market share. Of these companies, the state-owned PICC Property Insurance and PICC Life Insurance together hold 70 percent of the market share. The PICC Life Insurance alone holds 77 percent of the life insurance market. The PICC Property Insurance alone holds 78 percent of the property insurance market and 82 percent of the motor vehicle insurance market. It is clear that although a competitive situation is taking shape, the insurance market remains divided among a very few state-owned insurance companies.

Second, as noted earlier, the insurance sector is still at a low level of development. Premium revenues should in general account for 3 to 5 percent of a country's GDP. In Western developed countries, annual premium revenues make up 8 to 10 percent of the GDP. By contrast, China's premium revenues in 1998 only accounted for 1.5 percent of its GDP, ranking about the seventieth in the world. The per capita premium was only RMB 100 or U.S.$12, ranking about the eightieth in the world.

The insurance market still has an uneven structure. Currently, all 25 Chinese and foreign insurance companies are headquartered in Beijing and coastal cities. Although there are branches across the mainland, most are concentrated in densely populated and economically developed areas and cities. In particular, all foreign companies and Sino-foreign joint ventures are located in coastal developed cities. Although these insurance firms make up 48 percent of the total number of firms in China, their market share is less than 1 percent. In particular, all foreign companies and Sino-foreign joint ventures are located in coastal developed cities. From a long-term point of view, this uneven distribution will be harmful to the Chinese economy as well as the insurance sector as a whole.

Another problem is that the industry lacks skilled human resources. Professionalism is at a low level. Most personnel have been transferred from the government or financial institutions. Less than 30 percent have received formal education about insurance. Actuaries and computer experts who have a profound understanding of the international insurance market are extreme rarities. Consequently, automatic management is at a low level and risk control is weak.

Furthermore, there is as yet no complete insurance system. While insurance markets are growing rapidly, intermediary institutions are developing quite slowly. There are no professional insurance agents that operate according to stipulated procedures or institutions providing intermediary services. The Insurance Regulatory Committee that exercises supervisory control over the insurance industry has only recently been established. China has an Insurance Law, but still needs to enact strict laws and regulations governing investment, tax rates and risk control.

Finally, complementary industries which support and stimulate the operational activities of the insurance industry have not been developed. The most obvious lack is a financial market. Since insurance operations must manage and invest available funds effectively, their performance relies tremendously on a developed financial market consisting of a money market and a capital market. Although the Shanghai Stock Exchange and the Shenzhen Stock Exchange have seen considerable progress over the past decade, their market mechanisms are still confined and do not have the confidence of both domestic and overseas investors. Lack of confidence in the financial market is due to several factors, such as the untrustworthiness of information disclosed by listed firms, poor accounting standards and unskilled auditors, and even doubt in the future of the Chinese economy.

4.3 Financial Services

For international banks, the modernization of China presents abundant opportunities to finance large infrastructure projects and engage in the potentially lucrative domestic Renminbi business. Hoping to capitalize on such opportunities, many foreign banks have strategically positioned themselves in the Chinese market, aggressively setting up representative offices, joint venture banks, and bank branches, particularly in the Pudong New Area in Shanghai.

The entry of international banks will introduce large amounts of foreign capital to China. The investment environment will improve, promoting development of an export-oriented economy. Domestic banks will acquire advanced management expertise and methods from their foreign counterparts. Thus, foreign banks have the potential to invigorate the domestic financial market, strengthen competition, and encourage domestic banks to commercialize.

Because China has made infrastructure development a national priority, international banks could play a key role in financing construction of China's roads, highways, power plants, bridges, airports, dams, ports, and telecommunications facilities. Between now and the year 2004, China will spend around U.S.$750 billion on infrastructure development. According to some estimates, it will need to raise U.S.$6 billion overseas to finance planned highway projects alone. If China is going to succeed in raising such large sums, it must further liberalize its economy, particularly in the areas of banking and foreign exchange control.

China began to allow overseas financial institutions to enter its market in 1979. By the end of 1998, there were 199 foreign financial institutions operating in China with assets totalling U.S.$36 billion. An enticing area of business attracting the attention of foreign banks is the possibility that some day they will be permitted to offer retail banking services to individual Chinese consumers. Foreign banks find the domestic Renminbi market alluring for two reasons: the extraordinarily high savings rates of individual Chinese depositors with relatively few alternative investment channels and the poor service at present offered by domestic Chinese banks. But for current governmental restrictions, foreign banks would dominate the domestic retail Renminbi market.

The Chinese Renminbi market is opening up, albeit guardedly. In 1998, China allowed limited foreign participation in Renminbi transactions. At present, the People's Bank of China (PBOC) has granted 19 foreign banks in Shanghai and 6 in Shenzhen the right to engage in limited Renminbi business with foreign individuals and foreign investment enterprises (FIEs). While foreign banks are prohibited from accepting deposits from Chinese individuals, the pressures of economic development and WTO accession will eventually push China towards even greater liberalization in this area. Meanwhile, China has also broadened the scope of yuan business that foreign banks can conduct. Initially, they were allowed to grant renminbi loans only to foreign-funded firms. Now they can also participate in syndicated lending to Chinese enterprises.

The six foreign banks offering renminbi services in Shenzhen are Britain's Standard Chartered Bank and the Hong Kong & Shanghai Banking Corp., Hong Kong-based Nanyang Commercial Bank and the Bank of East Asia, Citibank of the United States, and Japan's Bank of Tokyo-Mitsubishi. Citibank and the Bank of Tokyo-Mitsubishi are the most recent two banks given licences to conduct local currency business in Shenzhen. Citibank is thus the only U.Ss bank to conduct such business in Shenzhen. The bank's first local currency customers in Shenzhen include Philips Consumer Communications, SED Co. Ltd. and Shenzhen Samsung Display Devices Co Ltd. Renminbi services which foreign banks are allowed to handle include deposits, loans, clearing and settlements, issuance of guarantees, and investment in treasury bills and bonds.

In Pudong, Shanghai, three European banks, namely France's Exterior Trade Bank, Spain's International Bank, and Germany's Dresden Bank, recently established branches. This brings the number of overseas-funded banks in Pudong to 37. The three banks have combined assets of $12.9 billion. Other foreign banks which have been recently approved to start Renminbi business in Pudong include Credit Lyonnais, Sumitomo Bank Ltd., Bank of America, Sakura Bank Ltd., Credit Suisse First Boston, Bank of East Asia Ltd., Overseas Chinese Banking Corporation Ltd., Holland Bank, and the Development Bank of Singapore Ltd. The overseas-funded banks in Pudong have $1.63 billion in deposits and $9.71 billion in loans. In recent years, they have been more active in the yuan business. Pudong has maintained rapid economic growth since it was set up in 1990 and, despite the worsening effects of the Asian financial crisis, it had a GDP of 71 billion yuan ($8.52 billion) in 1998, an increase of 16.8 percent over 1997.

Foreign banks, however, do not operate without difficulty. Coupled with the financial crisis in Asia, restrictions limiting them to business dealings with foreign customers and a heavy tax burden have made it more difficult for some banks to operate in China. The business tax imposed on the entire turnover at the bank. This difficult environment caused Japan's Daiwa Bank to downgrade its branch in Shanghai to a representative office, while the Royal Bank of Canada has decided to close its Shanghai branch.

In order to solve some of its current problems, China is lifting the geographical limits to foreign financial institutions. As of 1999, foreign banks can apply to operate in any Chinese city in which they are interested, mostly in the form of branches or representative offices. Previously, only 23 major Chinese cities and the Hainan Province were open to foreign banks. The local currency business will also be expanded from Shanghai and Shenzhen to other cities. Given the huge potential of the Chinese financial services market (especially as a response to the WTO's requirement) and the often lengthy wait for permission to engage in some business activities, a foreign bank should seriously consider establishing a presence in China as soon as possible if it has not done so already.

4.4 Retail and Foreign Trade Services

Retail Service

Given the increase of purchasing power, the retail sector seems to have a good outlook. Disposable income and consumption per capita increased 45 percent and 43 percent respectively, between 1990 to 1995. Based on the 10 percent annual growth rates achieved over the past three years, it is likely that retail sales growth will continue to range 10 to 15 percent annually over the next decade. While Chinese consumers are spending more than ever, it is not at department stores and shopping malls that carry high-priced products. Instead, they shop for bargains at less glamorous supermarkets, convenience stores, and discount warehouses. As a result, sales at the country's large department stores increased by only 1.9 percent in 1998, while sales for the retail sector as a whole registered a robust 12.5 percent growth rate. Crowds are lined up at discount stores like Makro (based in the Netherlands), Wal-Mart (U.S.), and local warehouse-style grocery stores. But many newly opened upscale malls are struggling to attract customer traffic and some have closed off entire floors because they do not have enough tenants. Chain stores, with about 15,000 outlets as of 1997, are likely to replace the department store as the key retail outlet in the next century. Shanghai Hualian Supermarket and Shanghai Lianhua Supermarket are the two largest chains in China, with 248 and 230 outlets, respectively. Currently, chain stores account for 12 percent of total retail sales, while the top 249 department stores attract 29 percent. At the same time, supermarkets are expanding dramatically. For instance, Carrefour, currently operating in Beijing, decided to open three stores in Shanghai. Metro of Germany and Ekchor Lotus of Thailand also have plans for new stores in China.

China began opening up its retail sector back in 1992, when the government decided to allow pilot commercial joint ventures in 12 cities. The major rules include: (1) retail joint ventures must be approved by the State Council; (2) Chinese partners should hold at least 50 percent of the shares; (3) the shareholding requirement can be as low as 40 percent in the country's central and western regions; (4) in chain or warehouse stores, Chinese partners must hold a majority of the joint venture shares; (5) the Sino-foreign partnership can be for as long as 30 years in coastal regions and 40 years in the central and western regions; (6) those engaged in mail-order selling that do not have their own stores must open retail outlets. Joint venture retailers are banned from carrying out any wholesale activities or acting as import and export agents; (7) ventures have to balance their foreign exchange through exports; (8) ventures can import goods for up to 30 percent of their total annual sales; and (9) foreign partners must be well-established commercial multinationals. Firms that have bad management and fail their annual inspection will be closed down.

The Chinese retail market is increasingly more attractive to foreign investors as the standard of living rises. Meanwhile, six of the world's top 100 chain store groups have already entered China's market, including U.S.-based Wal-Mart. Foreign retailers share 1.3 percent of China's total retail sales. One hundred and ninety-one foreign-invested retail businesses from Hong Kong, Macao, and Taiwan account for 68.7 percent of the total. Of foreign-funded retail businesses, 225 are department stores, accounting for 81 percent of the total. The rest operate as chain stores, supermarkets, and distribution centers. The State Council has approved 20 foreign-funded retail businesses to date.

More recently, Germany's OBI Group is negotiating with the Chinese government to set up 30 retail stores in the country by 2005. Starbucks Coffee signed a licensing agreement with Beijing Mei Da Coffee to open retail locations in Beijing in 1999. IBM and JDA Software, an international provider of enterprise retail solutions, launched a partnership to deliver the most integrated suite of store and corporate office retail solutions in the Greater China region. In addition, U.S. direct-selling companies Avon, Mary Kay, and Amway, which had made a combined investment of $120 million in China, but were then banned by the State Council because of an uncontrollable rise of fraud and bad publicity, are restarting their businesses as retail stores.

The country has gained experience in the retail sector from experiments with China-foreign retail joint ventures in over a dozen cities during the past several years. Now the government is ready to allow foreign retailers to form joint ventures with local retailers in major cities in all provinces, autonomous regions, and cities that have provincial status. China will relax control over the establishment of joint-venture retail sales enterprises. It plans to open more cities for trial Sino-foreign retail joint ventures, and permit more such ventures in major cities where they are already allowed. Presently, only six coastal cities (Beijing, Dalian, Guangzhou, Qingdao, Shanghai, and Tianjin) and five special economic zones (Hainan, Shantou, Shenzhen, Xiamen, and Zhuhai) are open to foreign operation of retail businesses. This number will expand to 30. Initially, each foreign company was allowed to operate one or two retail chain stores in each city. Authorities will also relax those restrictions. China has discussed opening retail and wholesale areas during its talks on joining the WTO, but plans to move cautiously.

China still needs foreign investment in the retail sector even though this places great pressure on domestic retailers. Foreign retailers introduce capital and effective management, both of which are currently deficient. China's retail sector, already suffering from the effects of the planned economy, has been held back from development by its relatively small scale and the continued use of outmoded management systems. The Shanghai No. One Department Store, the country's largest store, had only 5.52 billion yuan ($665 million) in total sales in 1998, while Shanghai Hualian Supermarket Co., the country's largest chain store group, achieved only 2.04 billion yuan ($246 million). In contrast, the world's top 100 retailers achieve annual average sales ranging from $4.4 billion to $93.6 billion.

Earlier, 277 Sino-foreign retail joint ventures that never went through the required procedure for State Council approval were approved by local officials who overstepped their authority. Under central government regulations, only the State Council has the power to approve commercial joint ventures. Reorganization of these ventures was conducted during 1998 and 1999 by the State Development and Planning Commission (SDPC), the Ministry of Foreign Trade and Economic Cooperation, the State International Trade Bureau, and the State Administration for Industry and Commerce. Firms subject to reorganization will be allowed to continue operations if they can prove that foreign investment has materialized, their management is sound, they can pass annual inspections by the State Council, and they do not engage in any wholesale business.

Rather than facing the daunting approval process for retail equity joint ventures, many foreign firms choose to sell goods in China through indirect means such as management contracts, factory outlet stores, direct sales, television and mail order sales, and counter rentals and consignment sales. Under a management contract, for instance, a store may be a foreign joint venture in which the foreign retailer holds no equity or it can be an entirely domestic company managed by a foreign retailer. Forming a contractual relationship limits the retailer's exposure and allows a relatively inexperienced foreign company to take advantage of the network of connections possessed by the Chinese investor. Foreign retail partners who hold equity typically are involved in contractual rather than equity joint ventures beause the former is generally more flexible. Management contracts typically grant the foreign partner complete managerial control in return for a fee which might be a percentage of sales.

As Chinese law allows retailing of products that a foreign company manufactures in China, companies with joint venture factories that have broad product lines can open their own outlets, typically as branches of the manufacturing joint venture. An outlet store, however, is permitted to sell only products made by the parent joint venture. In the case of direct sales, a joint venture or wholly foreign-owned manufacturing plant sets up branches to serve as distribution centers. The manufacturing joint venture commissions and trains Chinese sales people, who purchase products from the distribution centers at wholesale prices and sell them at retail prices.

Direct sales have been under bureaucratic attack in China since 1995, however. The government now mandates a minimum investment of $5 million, and restricts certain types of employees from engaging in direct sales. Other forms of direct sales, including television and mail-order sales, are not prohibited from selling imported goods, however, which makes them popular retail avenues. Currently, 29 television stations in China have direct sales programs supported by 58 sales centers.

Counter rentals and consignments in department stores are appropriate choices for those considering quick access to Chinese consumers. In fact, most department stores derive at least half of their revenue from counter rentals and consignment sales. In a typical counter rental arrangement, a foreign vendor sets a sales counter, provides the product, and staffs the counter. Sales revenues are collected by the store, which keeps a commission of 20 to 30 percent. Alternatively, in a consignment sales agreement, a store sells a foreign company's products in return for a percentage of sales. This method gives the firm less managerial control than renting a counter does.

Foreign Trade Service

Shenzhen and Shanghai are the only two cities in China that have opened the export-import trade sector to foreign firms on an experimental basis. The central government has only approved the establishment of two joint ventures entitled to handle import and export business in Shenzhen. They are the Shenzhen Liang Mian International Trade Co. Ltd. and the Sino-American OCT International Trading Co. Ltd. The former was co-established by China National Cereals, Oils & Foodstuffs Import & Export Corp and Nichimen Corp., one of the top trading firms in Japan with total assets of $19.9 billion and annual sales of $50 billion. The latter was jointly established by the Shenzhen OCT Petroleum Trading Group and Dow Chemical Co of the United States. Founded in 1897, Dow Chemical Co. is one of the world's leading chemical makers. In Shanghai, three similar joint ventures have been licensed for import-export activities.

The above move is an important event in the country's efforts to promote reform and open its foreign trade system. It helps the foreign trade sector become more integrated into the world market system and will help these cities gain more experience in trading through agencies and upgrade their services trade. Since the emergence of foreign-funded trade firms increases competition in the foreign trade sector, it prompts domestic firms to improve their performance.

Foreign companies can consider Chinese private firms as local partners for foreign trade joint ventures. Private firms are making low-key progress in the foreign trade sector, which has been closed to them for almost half a century. A number of private firms (e.g., Stone) have been allowed to set up joint trading ventures with foreign partners. Under the Foreign Trade Law, private firms cannot engage in export or import, but a joint venture can. Private firms are mushrooming across China, in sharp contrast to large and medium-sized State enterprises, whose businesses continue to contract due to poor management as well as debts inherited from the planned economy. Many private firms have circumvented government prohibition on export business via personal connections with large State trade companies. State companies usually transfer part of their export business to private firms, which in turn hand back a certain amount of profit as commission. This practice has become common in many places, especially in coastal areas where the market economy has taken root.

4.5 Tourism and Hotel Services

Tourism Services

As one of the pioneer sectors in China's reform and opening to the outside world, the tourism industry has had great achievements. In 1998, 63.47 million overseas travellers visited China. There were also 694 million domestic tourists, an increase of 10.23 per cent and 7.8 percent, respectively over 1997. Tourism revenue in 1998 increased by 10.5 percent to 343.8 billion yuan (U.S.$41.4 billion). Of this total, foreign currency income from overseas tourists accounted for U.S.$12.6 billion. The country's tourism earnings from overseas visitors in 1998 was 48 times the 1978 figure. This puts China eighth in the world for foreign exchange earnings from overseas visitors, a remarkable leap from forty-first place in 1978. Earnings from domestic tourists are growing even faster than those from overseas visitors.

China is opening up its tourism sector to the world's major players by allowing joint ventures between local and international travel agents. These companies will only be permitted to arrange inbound and domestic travel tours. A ban has been placed on joint ventures arranging outbound travel itineraries. The China National Tourism Administration and the Ministry of Foreign Trade and Economic Cooperation drafted eligibility regulations: (1) Chinese tour operators must organize tours for 30,000 people annually and make RMB50 million (U.S.$6 million) from their tour operation business for three successive years; (2) To obtain a permit to do business in China, the foreign partner must be licensed to engage in the international travel trade or be an enterprise under a travel operator with "strong capitalization" that is a member of relevant trade associations; (3) The foreign partner must have annual sales of U.S.$50 million from the tour business and be linked to an international or at least its own computer reservations system.

Overall, establishing Sino-foreign travel service joint ventures remains experimental, although China intends to encourage selected domestic travel operators to cooperate with their foreign counterparts on inbound tourism operations. Pilot joint venture operations were launched in 1998. Travel operators based in China's 12 national holiday resorts were authorized to initiate cooperation with competitive overseas agencies. The first joint venture travel agency in China is Diethelm Travel Yunnan, established by the China International Travel Service (CITS), Yunnan Tourism Co. Ltd., and the Diethem Company of Switzerland. The Swiss company, which covers such business as trade, manufacturing, pharmaceuticals, and cosmetics, serves as a general agent in Southeast Asia for more than 30 European tourism companies. CITS is China's biggest tourist agency, reporting 1.5 billion yuan ($180 million) in business volume and receiving 400,000 tourists annually, while the Yunnan company is the leading tourist service in that province. In addition, five overseas travel agencies from Germany, the U.S., Japan, and Hong Kong have applied to form joint ventures in Shanghai or Beijing. These partnerships are expected to help restructuring the outdated management mechanisms in China's tourism industry, improve the quality of travel services, and promote the growth of China's tourism sector.

Hotel Services

China has more than 4,400 hotels with licences for accommodating foreign tourists. Of these, 2,600 are star-rated, including 55 five-star and more than 140 four-star operations. Turnover at the hotels totalled 73 billion yuan (U.S.$8.8 billion) in 1996.

Built during the real estate "bubbles" in the early 1990s, there is now an oversupply of hotels. An excessive number of office towers have been developed, which attract many clients who previously rented hotel rooms as offices. Many developers who found prospects bleak for office towers changed their projects into hotels.

Moreover, many so-called training centers that act as de facto hotels have been built by government departments and big companies, further exacerbating the over-supply in some cities such as Beijing. Over-supply of star-rated hotels is a problem mainly in the eastern regions. Hotel accommodations still lag behind demand in central and western regions, leaving space for further development of the hotel industry.

Financial turmoil has resulted in shrinking numbers of tourists coming to China from Southeast Asian countries, which formerly contributed 17 percent of all visitors. Falling prices resulting from devalued currencies in these countries have sharpened their edge in competing with China for tourists from other parts of the world. As a result, the average occupancy rate of China's hotels dropped from 57.5 percent in 1996 to 55 percent in 1997. The international rule of thumb is that hotels need occupancy rates of above 60 percent to be profitable. An unfavorable market has prompted some hotels to cut prices irrationally in their fight for market share.

The saturation of five-star hotels in major cities, together with projected increases in domestic travel, suggest that China's hotel market appears to be heading into a second stage of development aimed at cultivating business in secondary cities. Many international and management executives have been travelling around China, scouting out new locations for hotels. Whereas previously foreign visitors to China could choose between a lavish four- or five-star joint venture hotel and an inexpensive, domestic Chinese establishment with few, if any, Western-style amenities, many hotel chains are now attempting to fill this yawning gap by opening two- and three-star facilities. In addition to expanding geographically, hotel companies are also broadening their Chinese product lines by developing economy-class accommodations to serve both foreign and domestic Chinese travelers.

While international hotel investors expand their Chinese portfolios, many existing five-star hotels in major cities have been adding new attractions for deep-pocketed travelers. The China World, the Palace Hotel, the Great Wall Sheraton, and many others have developed "theme" package parties. At the Great Wall Sheraton, for example, a group of guests can have "Dinner with the Emperor", complete with waiters dressed in Qing dynasty costumes, tables set with period silver and porcelain, a traditional eight-piece ensemble, and a banquet menu featuring food fit for an emperor.

Civil Aviation Service

The Chinese civil aviation service sector is becoming open to the outside world, with increasing use of foreign investment and greater economic and technological cooperation with international enterprises. The industry has used U.S.$16.2 billion in foreign funds since the 1980s, including leasing 267 transport aircraft with U.S.$13.9 billion. Sixty-two joint ventures and cooperative enterprises have been established with the use of foreign funds totaling U.S.$500 million.

Facing a merger trend in the international air industry, China is continuing to reorganize a number of air companies and groups. Most of the 34 air companies in China with legal status are fairly small, but it is estimated that several big companies and groups will be formed over time with total assets of 40 billion yuan (U.S.$4.82 billion) and annual sales of 30 billion yuan (U.S.$3.61 billion). The industry has maintained a growth rate of 10 percent over the last decade. Recently, China's State Council approved conditional investment in the civil aviation service industry by foreign businesses.

Major regulations include:

1. Foreign investors are allowed to invest in the civil aviation industry in the form of either equity or cooperative joint ventures;
2. Foreign investors are allowed to invest in the construction of airport flight areas (including runways, sliding ways, aircraft parking areas, etc.) or construction of airport facilities such as terminals, cargo warehouses, land services, aircraft maintenance, catering, airport hotels and restaurants, and aircraft fueling or establish air transportation or aviation enterprises in the service of agriculture or forestry;
3. Foreign investors engaging in the construction of airports may expand their scope of business, with approval, to include managing airport facilities, as listed above;
4. Foreign investors, especially foreign air cargo shipment enterprises, are allowed to purchase shares of Chinese air cargo shipment enterprises or exchange shares with their Chinese counterparts or set up air cargo shipment enterprises;
5. Stipulations have been made with regard to foreign shares in investment in the civil aviation industry and nomination of the board chairperson and the general manager.

4.6 Accounting and Legal Services

Accounting Services

By the end of 1998 China allowed the Big Six accountancy firms to open 27 representative offices in 6 different cities and recruit 3 member firms, 2 associate firms, and a joint venture firm each. Firms are reporting fast growth and more work than they can handle. This is hardly surprising when you consider that 1.2 billion people live in China and there are only 57,772 practicing Chinese CPAs (a further 65,925 are in industry) tackling the workload created by a previously closed economy opening up to market forces.

Firm growth in China is evolving from such a low base that development of both accounting practices and the accounting profession as a whole still has a very long way to go. At present, all Western firms are limited to one area of work; advising multinational clients and Chinese enterprises trying to raise capital by listing on the stock exchange. Corporate finance is the fastest growth area because of the increasing numbers of state enterprises being privatized. The Big Six normally handles accounting, auditing, tax, management and investment consultancy, assets appraisal, personnel training, and consultancy for large domestic enterprises engaged in overseas investment and foreign trade. With advantages in personnel and technology, they act as financial, tax, and investment consultants for international companies who have operations in China. They also perform assets clarification for large Sino-foreign cooperative projects. They have intermediary services for Chinese enterprises with overseas listings and B-share issuance. Although the number of joint ventures with the Big Six accounts for less than 0.1 percent of the total number of accounting firms in China, they have acquired 10 percent of the market share.

Ernst & Young expects to increase staff by up to 50 percent in 1999, but Grant Thornton plans the most rapid expansion, hoping to almost triple its practice this year by adding at least 40 staff members to its 27-strong team. Moore Stephens almost doubled its staff in 1998, from 50 to 98; unusually, only three of them are expatriates. The firm plans to recruit another 50 employees in 1999. Coopers & Lybrand claimed to spend more money on training than any other accountancy firm in China. Indeed, the future development of international firms will depend mainly on training Chinese auditing professionals.

Making a profit in China is tough, however. On the one hand, China's infant accountancy profession needs big international accountancy firms. The secrets of double entry bookkeeping, auditing principles, professional standards, and modern IT need to be taught to a whole army of Chinese accountants so they can audit the growing number of listed companies. On the other hand, operating costs are very high and the market seems unable to bear the usual Big Six fees. At this stage, accounting firms often need to keep reinvesting in different locations because local clients are geographically dispersed. Furthermore, firms often remain unpaid for work on Chinese companies seeking a listing. For various reasons, many never actually make it to market, which makes the money firms pour in likely to go down the drain.

Competition is intense as well. The fierce competition is in fact not for multinational clients (which tend to stay with the parent company auditor) but to win over Chinese enterprises. Price Waterhouse, for instance, has lost clients in which it has invested when other firms have come in with lower fees. Chinese companies often take advantage of the situation when international accounting firms are competing against each other using a low-cost strategy. This competition is likely to be even harsher in the future when these firms start to compete directly against local accounting firms. Pressed by the aggressive expansion of foreign firms, the China Institute of Certified Public Accountants plans to take measures to support the growth and development of domestic accounting firms.

Nevertheless, given that there are still few qualified CPAs available for this huge market, accounting, auditing, and consulting services are still promising sectors for international firms. China is planning to further open its accounting industry to foreign firms. For instance, it encourages foreign firms to participate in the nation's certified public accountant qualification tests. Qualified overseas accountants will be allowed to practice in China.

There is a growing demand market for training by foreign accounting, consulting, or law firms. For instance, when the East Gate Consulting Co. entered China in 1993, the market for foreign company training was virtually absent of competitors. Now, training providers in China are numerous enough – and the demands of foreign-invested enterprises (FIEs) sufficiently complex – to have sparked the emergence of new forms of training-cum-consulting options. Areas of human resource consulting that are increasingly in demand among FIEs include compensation advice to help FIEs link reward systems with business goals and development of internal communication systems.

Legal Services

China's legal service sector has opened widely, although gradually. China's first tentative efforts to open its legal sector to overseas firms began in 1992. Firms wishing to open branches in China must obtain approval from the Ministry of Justice. There are now a total of 105 foreign law firms in China, including 26 from Hong Kong. Another 91 overseas law firms have submitted applications to set up offices in China. The Chinese branches of foreign law firms have played an important role in providing legal advice on trade, real estate, technology transfer, intellectual property rights, and bonds and securities.

Foreign law firms can now open offices in Tianjin and Qingdao in addition to Beijing, Shanghai, Guangzhou, Shenzhen, Haikou and Suzhou. The number of lawyers in China rose to more than 110,000 in 1997 from only 40,000 in 1993 when comprehensive reform began. Law firms numbered 8,300 in 1998, more than double the 1993 figure.

There are now three types of law firms in China, whereas only State-funded ones were allowed before the reform. According to China's Ministry of Justice, about 70 percent of law firms are State-funded, 10 percent are cooperatives and 20 percent are partnerships. In the past five years, Chinese lawyers have handled more than 2 million criminal cases, 1.21 million civil cases, 1.5 million economic cases, and 2.06 million cases not resulting in legal action. They also served as legal consultants to 250,000 government bodies or enterprises. Chinese lawyers have provided legal services in bidding and tendering for some major projects in China, such as the Three Gorges Project on the Yangtze River, the Xiaolangdi Water-Control Project on the Yellow River, the Daya Bay nuclear power station, and the Shanghai subway.

Neither Chinese nor foreign legal professionals would paint a completely rosy picture of their recent cooperative efforts, which have featured hope, frustration, conflict and compromise. In fact, problems have routinely cropped up since 1992, when the Ministry of Justice issued provisional regulations allowing foreign law firms to practice in China. The regulation has become the target of criticism by foreign law firms, who complain that some provisions have put a straight-jacket on their activities. According to the regulation, foreign law firms entering China are prohibited both from opening more than one branch and hiring licensed Chinese lawyers. Foreign lawyers are also not permitted to practice or give advice on China's laws, which means they cannot appear in Chinese courts. In practice, however, almost all foreign law firms have managed to bypass these restrictions in one way or another. Some have hired Chinese lawyers willing to give up their licences in favor of higher pay. Some have employed local lawyers to act on their behalf in court. And some law firms have set up more than one branch using legitimate disguises.

An increasing number of foreign law firms, such as Britain's Linklaters and the U.S.'s White & Case, are establishing themselves in Shanghai, which is becoming a financial center. The Chinese government does not want to see a concentration of foreign firms in Beijing. White & Case originally applied for an office in Beijing, but was refused. Nevertheless, firms continue to apply for Beijing offices in order to be closer to the national authorities. Law firms find it easier to obtain the texts of new laws and regulations, if they are in the capital city because governmental materials are not usually published throughout China. It is also helpful to remain in Beijing when following big projects because all deals over U.S.$30 million must be approved by the central administration.

Continous arrival of new firms in the legal service industry increases competition among foreigners, but the relations between foreign and local firms are more cooperative because foreign firms cannot practice PRC law. Furthermore, foreign lawyers need to cooperate with domestic ones in order to remain up-to-date as the legal system changes. They also need assistance in dealing with the administration, which continues to implement foreign investment law. At the same time, Chinese lawyers need help from foreign firms because, although they are professional, experienced Chinese lawyers, there are still too few of them. In the past, Chinese law firms were state-owned. Now there are cooperative firms and even private partnerships. Many large state-owned law firms are closing because young people are not willing to work there. Chinese lawyers are resigning to create their own partnerships. Chinese professionals returning from studying overseas are likely to become the backbone of the legal profession in China as they have excellent English skills, international understanding, Chinese experience, and connections with foreign firms.

4.7 Advertising Services

China's advertisers did $6.48 billion worth of business in 1998, a 17 percent increase over 1997, in spite of the Asian financial meltdown. China has become the second largest advertising market after Japan in the Asian and Pacific region. There were 61,730 advertising agencies across China with 578,876 employees by the end of 1998, an increase of 8.25 and 6.06 percent, respectively, over 1997. There were only 10 agencies engaged in advertising before 1979. In 1982, advertising firms had a sales volume of only $14.5 million.

Foreign advertising companies have been squeezing into the Chinese market. By the end of 1998, there were about 500 Sino-foreign joint ventures in the industry, with a business volume reaching $4.44 billion. Saatchi & Saatchi, one of the top agencies, ranks China as a very important market hub. Its blue-chip clients in China include Procter & Gamble, Johnson & Johnson and Kodak. Another top agency, the Japan-based Dentsu, has been cooperating with the China International Advertising Corporation, a commercial affiliate of the Ministry of Foreign Trade and Economic Cooperation. Their joint venture, Beijing Dentsu Advertising Corp., is 51 percent owned by Dentsu.

Severely restricted since the Communist takeover of China in 1949, advertising was totally banned during the cultural revolution. Better days for advertising activities were ushered in after the death of Chairman Mao and with the economic reorientation introduced by Deng Xiaoping in 1979. Indeed, although starting from a small base, advertising activity has grown in leap and bounds after 1980, boasting an annual growth rate of about 35 percent.

In order to protect consumers and other interested parties, governmental authorities have provided guidelines for the emerging advertising industry. In 1982, the first set of regulations was enacted, requiring that advertising be clear and truthful and prohibiting messages that deceive end-users and consumers. In addition, advertisers are banned from using obscene or crude language or pictures as well as having recourse to superstition or slander in their communications. For a government that has had a monopoly on public discourse for decades, political concerns are omnipresent and reflected in laws prohibiting any advertisement deemed reactionary, in contradiction with state policies, divulging state secrets, or harmful to the dignity of China's diverse ethnic nationalities.

Additional regulations enacted in 1986 target foreign advertisers. These rules hold both the advertiser and the publisher of an advertisement (media outlet) responsible for its contents. Buyers misled by false advertising and having suffered damages can seek redress under the law. In 1994, the State Administration for Industry and Commerce (SAIC) issued a set of new guidelines in an attempt to weed out fraudulent advertising, especially for medical and cosmetic products. In addition, a newly promulgated advertising law that took effect in February 1995 prohibits the direct advertising of some controlled substances, such as tobacco products. An ambiguous part of the law also requires that all advertisements correspond with the demands of socialism.

The content of advertising messages has changed drastically over the last decade. Consumer goods have replaced industrial products as the major object of advertising. Within the consumer goods category there has recently been a movement away from durables (appliances, furnishings, and home electronics), which were dominant in advertising even in the 1980s, to non-durable goods. The latter include in particular cosmetics, over-the-counter drugs, and food products, which have been heavily promoted in urban areas in the past few years. The advertising messages often associate the products with concepts of modernity and technology, which indicates a fascination with values considered 'Western'. The emotion-laden cues that are increasingly in use incorporate some typical Eastern as well as Western cultural values. Chinese advertising is thus emerging as a blend of cultural perspectives. For example, in a television commercial for Shanghai's VW Santana automobiles, a famous Chinese calligrapher is seen writing the character *qu* (fun) to describe the experience of driving the car. Foreign investors and exporters are well advised to refrain from reproducing their home advertising communications for the Chinese market. They should closely monitor the evolving cultural and social values in China and develop an advertising strategy that is responsive to the needs of the target population.

The possibilities for the dissemination of information have multiplied in China in recent years. New types of advertising vehicles are being introduced, while interest in more traditional media has not diminished. Newspapers, in particular, have high readership rates and constitute the country's most popular medium for advertisers. Magazines are another inexpensive advertising vehicle for foreign investors and exporters. Most of the magazines that accept advertising have national circulation. They address a variety of specialized interests, allowing advertisers to target specific segments of the market. Broadly, magazines can be categorized as professional, trade or consumer publications.

With the rapid increase in consumer purchasing power in China in recent years, the number of television sets owned by households has also risen dramatically. As a result, television viewership has expanded and advertisers have turned to television in increasing numbers, making it the second most popular medium in terms of advertising sales. The Chinese Central TV boasts 800 million viewers for its evening news. Television commercials are generally used to establish brand recognition or highlight the special characteristics of a product that sets it apart from its competition. The television campaign for Boeing is an example of brand recognition advertising. The commercials have helped the aircraft manufacturer gain a reputation for safety and comfort among Chinese viewers, most of whom probably have never flown. Television also offers the possibility for comparative advertising: similar products are often presented together and the superior qualities of the advertised product are often emphasized. Another possibility for advertisers is to sponsor a TV program. "Marlboro Sports World," for example, is aired every week under the sponsorship of Marlboro, Inc.

Often overlooked, radio remains an important and affordable medium capable of reaching a wide audience, including those for whom the printed press is inaccessible. Most radio advertising promotes consumer goods. An example of effective use of the medium is provided by the Coco Cola Co., which broadcasts a ten second message every morning before the 6:15 weather forecast on Shanghai Radio. It must be noted, however, that as other media have grown in importance in recent years, radio's percentage of total advertising revenue has dropped.

Alternatives to radio include not only the press and television, but also outdoor emplacements. Indeed, the heavy traffic and bustling crowds typical of most Chinese cities ensure large audiences for outdoor messages such as on billboard advertising. Their affordability, exposure, and long life (usually six months) make billboards the most popular mode of outdoor advertising. In addition, Plexiglass bus shelters, telephone cabins, and panels on the bodies of buses and trolleys are used for advertisements throughout China's large cities and coastal provinces. Pepsi Cola International says the placement of its advertisement on trolley front panels has drummed up customer awareness and hence sales of Pepsi and 7-Up.

Advertisers looking for flashier displays may want to consider neon signs, which have appeared in many Chinese cities over the last few years. As the number of skyscrapers in China's major cities increases, their roofs should provide an ideal location for neon signs, which can be seen for miles. It is important to emphasize that no single medium, regardless of its merit, could possibly satisfy all the complex demands of a comprehensive advertising campaign. A combination of media, selected judiciously, is likely to provide more timely and successful advertising strategies.

4.8 Telecommunications Services

Since economic reform began, the overall level of the national public communications network has improved remarkably. The telecommunications network in China has become one of the world's leading networks in terms of size and capacity. The Posts and Telecommunications (P&T) traffic volume has increased tremendously over the past ten years, as measured in terms of number of handsets per 100 people. Similar growth is being witnessed in the Chinese mobile telephone market. This is mainly because, with tariffs and connection fees falling all the time, people are beginning to view cellular phones as an instant and viable substitute for fixed line installations. In the mobile communications area, there were an estimated 18 million cellular subscribers across the country in 1998, up from around 6.8 million at the end of 1996 and 10 million at the end of 1997. The Chinese government predicted that by the year 2000 the country would have approximately 50 million cellular subscribers.

While the telephone and mobile communications networks grew rapidly, intelligence, supporting, data communications, and multimedia communications networks also registered fast growth. The port capacity for data communications reached 460,000, of which 160,000 was the total port capacity for the packet switched network, and 230,000 were the port capacity for the public data network. By 1997, all the provincial capitals were covered by the Internet (ChinaNet) and the construction of an intra-provincial access network had been completed in 22 provinces. Twenty-two cities were also interconnected with a public multimedia communications network, and 33 provincial capitals were linked by a digital synchronized network.

It should be noted that the market is protected by the government. Its concerns for national security mean that telecommunications in China are relatively insulated from the outside world. Foreign companies are only able to invest in Chinese telecommunication ventures via the *zhongzhong-wai* (China-China-foreign [CCF]) funding principle which allows them to participate through build-operate-transfer (BOT), complicated equipment leasing, management contracts and license royalty deals without actually making equity stakes. Regardless of the government's decision concerning CCFS, however, there is currently a huge demand for telecommunications services in China and the sector is growing at an unprecedented rate. Indeed, the nation's burgeoning telecommunications market has served as something of a life-saver for equipment suppliers such as Lucent, Ericsson, and Nokia. They all claim that the securing of contracts from China has helped soften the impact of lost business elsewhere in the region.

In 1993, the State Council issued regulations permitting other domestic companies to be licensed by the MPT to provide certain non-basic telecommunications services, such as radio paging and domestic VSAT communications services. The State Council also introduced limited competition into the telecommunications sector by approving the establishment of China Unicom. It was established to build and operate long distance, paging, value-added services and cellular networks nationwide in areas where public fixed line network coverage or capacity is limited or in areas authorized by the State Council and approved by the NTT.

In early 1994, the MPT was reshuffled following approval by the State Council. As part of this reorganization, the Directorate-

General of Telecommunications (DGT) was established as a state-owned enterprise with an accounting system independent from the MPT. On April 27, 1995, the DGT was registered with the State Administration of the Industry and Commerce as an enterprise with a legal personality. Its ratified names include the Directorate-General of Telecommunications, P&T, or China Telecom for short.

At the same time, the Department of Business, Department of Construction, Department of Network Operation and Maintenance, and the Department of International Affairs established organizational units affiliated with the MPT in order to optimize operational efficiency. The goal of the reorganization was to separate the roles between the MPT, as the industry regulator, and the DGT, as operator of the MPT system's telecommunications services. The new structure can better satisfy the growing demand for different levels and kinds of telecom services and strengthen the potential to accommodate changes in operation and management.

The primary responsibility of the DGT is the operation, maintenance, development and construction of the network as well as provision of universal telecommunications services for the country. China Telecom provides international and domestic telephone, telegraph, and facsimile services; lines and circuits for data communications; telecom equipment lease and maintenance services; issuing, printing, and selling telephone directories and telephone cards; investment in overseas telecom systems; satellite communications services; B-ISDN services; global personal communications services and various value-added telecom services. It develops telecom software; plans, designs, and implements telecom projects; supervises the manufacture and selling of telecom equipment; and offers consultancy in the field of technical and economic development of telecommunications. In the international communications field, China Telecom is responsible for taking part in international telecom organizations; concluding agreements on telecom service cooperation with overseas telecom operators; organizing international telecom and technical exchanges; and exercising account settlements and payment for bills which are realized through international telecom services.

Although the market is oligopolistic, the pace of telecommunication reform in the 1990s has successfully facilitated healthy competition between the two major telecommunications services providers, DGT (China Telecom) and China Unicom. In the area of wireless communications, in particular, the two competitors face head-to-head competition in major provinces, including Beijing, Fujian, Guangdong, Heilongjiang, Hunan, Jiangsu, Shaanxi, Shandong, Shanghai, Sichuan, Tianjin, and Zhejiang. It is expected that the introduction of orderly competition will have a positive impact on the market for telecommunications services in China by stimulating further network development, improvements in network quality, and customer service.

Under the new institutional reforms led by Premier Zhu Rongji, fifteen ministries and commissions were dissolved and four new bodies have been created. Key enterprises of various ministries and commissions have been spun off and regulatory functions of the government consolidated. The aim of such a restructuring is to downsize state bodies, shrink payroll, reduce the number of personnel, and economize on expenditures. On the telecommunications front, the long anticipated formation of a regulatory body to administer and regulate various aspects of the telecom and media industries has materialized. The Ministry of Information Industry (MII) was established in March 1998, based on the former Ministry of Posts and Telecommunications (MPT), Ministry of Electronics Industry (MEI) and the information and network administrative sectors of the Ministry of Radio, Film and TV (MFRT). The MII is responsible for invigorating the manufacture of information products and the telecommunications and software industries; formulating sectoral programs, policies, and laws codes; mapping out overall plans for telecommunications trunk networks (including local and long-distance telecommunications networks), broadcast, and television networks (including radio and cable television networks), and overseeing special-use telecommunications networks for military and other departments. MII manages sectors and allocation of resources, prevents project overlap and ensures information security. China Telecom and the governmental telecommunications regulatory framework are completely segregated, which reduces the monopolistic power of China Telecom.

There are six basic regulatory principles which the World Trade Organization agrees on for basic telecom services. These were not met by China's telecommunications market environment as of 1998. They are as follows:

1. Competition safeguards – Prevention of anti-competitive practices by a dominant player, which includes cross-subsidization and exploiting information obtained from competitors;
2. Interconnection – According to WTO regulatory principles, interconnection with a major supplier (China Telecom in this case) must be provided on nondiscriminatory terms, in a timely fashion, at cost-oriented rates, with sufficient unbundling so that competitors need not pay for network components of facilities they do not require;
3. Universal service – Telecommunications service operators must be administered in a transparent, nondiscriminatory, and competitively neutral manner;
4. Licensing criteria – The country must make publicly available all licensing criteria and the time period required for reaching a decision about an application for a license;
5. Independent regulators – Regulatory bodies should be separate from any supplier or service providers.
6. Resource allocation – Procedures for the allocation of resources such as telephone numbers and radio frequencies should be carried out in an objective, timely, transparent, and nondiscriminatory manner.

China Unicom has close connections with various ministries in the government (Ministry of Electronic Industry, Ministry of Railways and Ministry of Electric Power). For example, President Jiang Zemin was the Minister of Electronics in the mid-1980s before becoming the mayor of Shanghai and has always strongly advocated fast development of electronic and information technology. A former Premier and the current Chairman of the National People's Congress, Standing Committee are also deeply involved in the electronics and telecommunications arena. Therefore, althoug it is difficult for China to satisfy all six of WTO's regulatory principles, in order to gain entry to the World Trade Organization (WTO), Premier Zhu has implemented a list of reforms and has made a series of unprecedented concessions in the telecommunications industry. He has lifted the ban on foreign investment in telecom companies and will allow up to 35 percent equity investment in basic telephone services by 2005. Import tariffs on telecom equipment will be eliminated by 2005. Illegal foreign-controlled telecom ventures will be partially prohibited. The informal "buy local" order for telecom equipment will be repealed. Finally, CDMA technology will be used to expand domestic competition.

Although these reforms may not enable China to pass the WTO's entrance examination, the overall improved business climate will certainly be welcomed by foreign investors and countries building relationships with China. In fact, MII has drafted various plans for softening China Telecom monopolistic power in order to accelerate reform. The government has expressed the hope that as the country's telecommunications market opens wider, a more flexible fee system will come into being, allowing China to use telecommunications as a major lever in trade with other countries. However, privatization of the telecommunication sectors is going to take time and it is not going to be realized in the coming decade. The government should therefore provide an open market for the dominant firm model in the telecommunications sector.

5. Opportunities and Challenges in the Infrastructure and Agriculture Industries

Chapter Purpose

The Chinese government has attached paramount value to developing the infrastructure and agriculture industries over the past decade. The infrastructure sector is one of the key pillars supporting the growing economy, while agricultural development affects social stability and income disparity. The continuous growth of these sectors provides tremendous investment opportunities for MNCs with long haul objectives in the Chinese market. This chapter first highlights the general conditions of the infrastructure in China and then details the opportunities in the energy industry, describing the various choices and challenges pertaining to electrical energy, coal mining, oil and gas, and nuclear energy. The third section delineates the transportation infrastructure, including airports, ports, rails, and highways. The next section spells out the current conditions and future potential of the E-commerce infrastructure. It introduces relevant regulations, internet infrastructure, and opportunities for foreign companies. This chapter ends with a presentation of the Chinese agricultural sector and its business prospects for MNCs.

5.1 Infrastructure Overview

China has scored great achievements in the construction of energy and traffic infrastructural facilities over the past 20 years. Continued construction would maintain steady growth in the future. The construction of infrastructure provides a stable market for international investors, even during the Asian financial crisis.

Recently, the Chinese government made infrastructure, machinery, and high-tech industries the foci of investment at a time when oversupply is plaguing many sectors of China's economy. Since the economy soft-landed in 1996, it has entered a period of slower growth. GDP growth fell from 9.6 percent in 1996 to 8.8 percent in 1997 and 7.8 percent in 1998. Sluggish economic growth has worsened problems resulting from mired State-owned enterprises and a growing number of laid-off workers.

As a developing country, China needs to maintain high economic growth despite a surplus in the economy. In order to maintain 8 percent of China's GDP growth rate, its fixed asset investment rate should therefore reach about 35 percent in the next several years. In mid-1998, the Chinese Government issued 100 billion yuan (U.S.$12 billion) worth of State bonds used to expand investment in the infrastructure. Banks contributed another 100 billion yuan (U.S.$12 billion) in loans. China also continues to encourage foreign investment in the infrastructure despite easing of a bottleneck in the economy. The government has adopted preferential policies aimed at drawing foreign investment into the energy sector. In many power projects, the government promises the highest rates of return and minimum purchase levels. Now that the energy situation has improved, fixed return policies will be dropped. The energy and transportation sectors will continue to grow steadily, however.

5.2 Energy Industry

Overview

Although China is one of the world's largest producers of fuel, it consumes most of it itself. This is because it uses fuel very inefficiently. Geographic imbalances between the location of fuel reserves and the areas of demand are combined with an inadequate transport system. There is also an over-dependence on coal, despite its inefficiency as a fuel. The industrial output will have grown 400 percent between 1980 and 2000, while energy output will only have grown 200 percent in the same period. Energy efficiency must be enhanced. Major changes in energy use have to be organized.

China is in the midst of a major overhaul of its electric power generation network. According to the Ministry of the Power Industry, China will need to add 17 to 20 new power plants each year to reach its goal of 300 gigawatts of generating capacity by the year

2000. Central, provincial, and local authorities are actively seeking FDI in this sector. A second oil exchange was opened in Shanghai in 1994 as one move toward increased electrical power. The Three Gorges hydro-electric project on the Yangtze River also exemplifies China's search for alternative energy sources.

China will have probably the world's largest nuclear energy network by 2050, with a heavy reliance on power plants designed in the West. In its quest to feed a power hungry economy, China has taken some action to attract FDI to this sector as well. A shortage of capital, combined with the projected long term energy deficit, has forced China to seek the cheapest power it can buy. The BOT (build-operate-transfer) model is widely used for power plant investment. Foreign businesses may set up BOT projects by means of either equity or cooperative joint ventures with Chinese partners or as wholly foreign-owned ventures. Although no special laws or regulations pertain to BOT projects, procedures and approval are guided by prevailing policies concerning FDI.

Over the next century, China plans to develop the Shenfu and Dongsheng coalfields in Northwest China's Shaanxi Province and ease bottlenecks in coal transportation. It will also accelerate construction of hydroelectric power stations along major rivers and coal-fired plants near coal mines. The petroleum industry will prioritize oil and gas exploitation in western China and offshore areas. Major water-power production sites will be built on the upper Yellow River and middle and lower reaches of the Yangtze River. China's major oil supplies will come from Daqing in China's northeast province of Heilongjiang and Shengli in East China's province of Shandong. China will continue to rely on conventional energy resources, while making a greater effort to develop nuclear, geothermal, wind, solar, and tidal energy in order to optimize the structure of energy production.

Power Industry

Foreign capital is expected to continue to supplement the development of China's power industry for the foreseeable future, although China will mainly depend on domestic funds. BOT, Sino-foreign joint ventures, and leasing or buying existing power plants have been introduced as ways to woo foreign investment. Foreign investment is encouraged to exploit hydropower resources as well as develop pithead thermal plants and plants using clean coal. China is ready to utilize more foreign capital for electricity distribution and transmission projects. China seeks to import not only advanced power equipment but also the latest manufacturing technology from foreign investors.

The rapid growth of the country's power sector has benefited greatly from foreign cooperation. China's power industry already uses U.S.$11.65 billion in loans from international financial organizations and foreign governments. Loans from the World Bank, totalling U.S.$6.65 billion, have helped build six large and medium-sized hydropower stations, ten thermal power plants, three electricity transmission and distribution projects, and one urban grid upgrading project. The total installed capacity of these projects is 19.95 million kilowatts. The Asian Development Bank has provided U.S.$1.22 billion in loans for the construction of three hydropower stations, two thermal projects, and one transmission and distribution project, with total installed capacity of 3.37 million kilowatts. China has also borrowed 436.91 billion yen (U.S.$3.64 billion) from the Japanese government to fund the construction of six hydropower stations, six thermal projects, one transmission and distribution project, and one urban grid upgrading project, with total installed capacity of 9.62 million kilowatts. China has approved 36 foreign direct investment projects in the power sector, involving U.S.$2 billion in capital investment and U.S.$8 billion in overseas financing. By 1997, China had installed generating capacity of 254 million kilowatts, ranking second in the world.

Foreign investors are encouraged to provide about $17 billion of the $84 billion China plans to invest in the sector over the next 5 years. Under China's Ninth Five-Year Plan (1996-2000), the government aims to boost the country's power generation capacity at the rate of 15,000 MW to 20,000 MW annually by the year 2000. 100 percent ownership of power projects in China has already been permitted under BOT arrangements.

A typical independent power project in China brings together a number of different entities: the foreign investor supplies most of the equity; a local government or power bureau-owned partner contributes land use rights, some equity, relationships with the local authorities, and often operates the project plant; the local power bureau acts as electricity purchaser and perhaps fuel supplier; the provincial power bureau takes part in plant design, equipment procurement, construction, and commissioning; and the local government is the project's primary regulator.

The lack of *de facto* separation between different local governments combined with participation of many entities at all levels of project management and governance creates the impression of an 'open-book' project, that is, a situation where all interested parties have all the necessary information and participate in material decisions. This creates the risk that not only will the objective elements of the operations, maintenance, staffing, fuel supply, and so on be adjusted in the interest of local social and economic goals, but also that subjective elements, principally the amount and frequency of equity dividends, will be even more vulnerable to changes which satisfy the same goals, but which are detrimental to the foreign investor. The misalignment of interests is obvious and often gets in the way of a successful project. This is a function of both current conditions in China and the characteristics of power projects in general.

Under the above circumstances, finding an appropriate local partner is key to the success of power projects. A good partner can mitigate regulatory hazards, institutional volatility, and governmental interference. A local partner should be able to work successfully with its foreign partners, provide local resources, and assure separation between the joint venture and its regulators. Because of their ability to provide foreign investors with returns in excess of their proportional contributions to the venture's total registered capital, CJVs have been the vehicles of choice for BOT infrastructure projects.

On the other hand, 100 percent foreign ownership via a BOT can ensure that a foreign investor has control over the project and enjoys some autonomy from the government. This allows efficient decisions to be made at the project level. Interactions with the fuel supplier, off-taker, or regulator can take place at a true arms-length and between the relevant contracting (or regulating and regulated) parties themselves. A pattern of contract and regulation based behavior and therefore contractual and regulatory enforcement is thereby established. This pattern is fundamental to the rule of law in China, lowers the risk premium within the pricing of both debt and equity, and ultimately results in a greater amount of capacity at a lower per-unit price.

BOT is a guaranteed-fee method of cooperation by which an investor identifies a project in a host country, assumes sole responsibility for investing in the construction and operation of the project, and, after recovering its investment and obtaining some compensation, returns the project to a local organization in the host country. It is a relatively new means of international capital investment, applied usually to infrastructure projects which demand a huge investment and will take a great length of time. It is popular in developing countries short on capital and technology. The first BOT project, implemented in China on a trial basis, was the Beijing-Tongxian Expressway, built by Beijing civil construction departments and an American company. Construction started in September 1994, with 20 months as the projected time for completion. The approved term of the BOT is 20 years, after which the expressway will be returned to China.

Negotiation on one of the first BOT power projects was recently completed. According to officials in Southeastern Guangxi, the final contract for the Laibin B power plant will soon be signed with Electricite de France, Britain's National Power International, and Barclays Bank. Recently, China's State Planning Committee has ratified ten more BOT projects calling for foreign operations: (1) the Summer Palace light rail in Beijing; (2) the Zilanda hydropower plant; (3) the Tuoketro B power station in Inner Mongolia; (4) the State highway 104 in Shandong; (5) the Shenyang elevated expressway in Liaoning; (6) the Wuhan light rail line in Hubei; (7) the Yinglongshan power plant in Zhejiang; (8) the Second Nanjing Yangtse River Bridge in Jiangsu; (9) the Shenyang-Beijing Expressway in Liaoning; and (10) the Shenyang second ring road in Liaoning.

Coal

China is the world's largest producer and consumer of coal, which provides more than 70 percent of the country's energy needs. However, almost 81 percent of its coal firms operated in the red in 1998 by a total of 3.71 billion yuan ($447 million). To help make the money-losing industry turn a profit, the government is investing 10 billion yuan on technical upgrades at more than 70 mines. China has so far received $9.34 billion in contracted foreign capital for its coal industry, of which 4.18 billion dollars has already been used. It plans to absorb more foreign funds to speed up the development of new coal mines, particularly large surface mines, and modernization of existing ones. It will convert the existing state-owned assets of some selected coal enterprises into shares to upgrade the coal mines for better economic returns. Direct foreign investment will also be used to build coal slurry pipelines, tap coal-bed methane, build pit-head power plants, and develop clean coal technology. The government is particularly interested in attracting foreign investments to more than a dozen large-and medium-scale pit-head power plants in the Junggar Basin and other mining areas. In addition, the country will try to develop comprehensive coal utilization projects including coking plants, cement works, and mining machinery and refractory material factories.

Oil and Gas

China consumed 37 quadrillion BTU (quads) of energy in 1996, making it the fourth largest energy-consuming region on the planet. The world's largest energy consumers are the U.S. (93 quads), Western Europe (68 quads), and the FSU and Eastern Europe (EE) (50 quads). Natural gas plays a significant role, providing 23 quads (24 percent of primary energy consumption) in the U.S., 13 quads (19 percent) in Western Europe, and 20 quads (40 percent) in the FSU-EE region. Yet in China natural gas provides less than 2 percent of primary energy consumption.

Although natural gas currently accounts for less than 2 percent of Chinese primary energy consumption, the country stands on the brink of dramatically increasing use of the fuel. Gas consumption, currently around 22 billion cubic meters (bcm)/year, is projected to triple by 2010 to 60 bcm/year and rise to over 110 bcm/year by 2015. A combination of technological, economic, political, and environmental drivers could raise these figures much higher.

China's long-dormant natural gas sector is awakening in response to governmental initiatives on opening markets and improving air quality. The ninth five-year plan proclaimed that China will consume 6-7 tcf/year by 2010. However, for the industry to grow in an economically efficient manner, regulatory reform is needed to ensure that the industry becomes more sensitive to market realities rather than being run by government fiat.

For many years, natural gas was a relatively unimportant part of China's energy mix, considered by central planners as too valuable to burn and in short supply. In a country with over 1.2 billion mouths to feed, natural gas was essentially earmarked for fertilizer production. In 1998, over 45 percent of Sichuan province's 244 bcf of marketed production was used to produce fertilizers, while most of the remainder was used by the petrochemical industry. Only a small fraction, 31 bcf, was used for residential heating and cooking, while no gas was used for power generation.

China currently produces approximately 653 bcf/year of natural gas from four regions: the Sichuan province, Shan-Gan-Ning (Ordos basin), the Xinjiang Uygur autonomous region (Tarim, Chungeer, and Caidamu basins), and Nanhai West in the South China Sea. The Sichuan province is the largest gas producing area, providing 303 bcf/year of natural gas. The South China Sea is the second largest, providing about 113 bcf/year to Hong Kong and the Hainan province. There is reason to be optimistic about China's natural gas potential, given its underexplored status.

China will probably import natural gas from Russia and the Caspian states.

The Eastern Siberia basins of Irkutsk, Krasnoyarsk, and Sakha contain perhaps as much as 50 to 60 quads of reserves within feasible transmission distance of China. To China's west, Kazakhstan's giant Karachaganak gas field and Turkmenistan's Dauletabad field have over 90 quads between them. Farther west and north of China, the Western Siberian gas fields contain over 2,000 quads of mainly untapped gas resources. Over the next 10 years, most imports of foreign gas are likely to come from Turkmenistan and Russia's giant Kovyktinskoye field in the Irkutsk basin.

There are plans to build a 4,600-km pipeline from Turkmenistan to West China that could also serve as the basis of a main artery for China's domestic pipeline system. The pipeline would most likely have a capacity of 2 bcfd and carry about 600 bcf/year. Another pipeline on the drawing board, with a capacity of 2 bcfd, would bring natural gas from Russia's Irkutsk basin south to Beijing.

China's natural gas industry has suffered from rationing and price ceilings that bear little resemblance to China's true productive capability and costs. Consequently, gas consumption and production have remained stunted at little more than 500-600 bcf/year for the past 20 years. Meanwhile, China's proven gas resources are estimated at almost 60 tcf, with recoverable reserves of over 37 tcf, sufficient to last 74-120 years at current consumption rates. By comparison, North America possesses 10-11 years of gas reserves and produces 26 tcf/year; Western Europe, a major gas importer, has 17 years of reserves and produces 14 tcf/year; and Eastern Europe and the former Soviet Union (FSU) together possess 83 years of reserves, producing 23 tcf/year.

The Chinese gas industry is vertically integrated and exhibits monopolistic characteristics. The government regulates the industry by establishing ceilings on wellhead prices, transmission tariffs, and consumer prices. However, as with the natural gas industry in the U.S. during the 1960s and 1970s, low price ceilings inhibited exploration and infrastructure upgrades and development of new markets for gas. This has had a deleterious effect on the industry, resulting in infrastructural decay and stagnant production. Recently, the provincial and national pricing bureaus have increased price ceilings in response to rising costs, but complete price and allocation liberalization awaits major economic reform. Immediately evident is the extraordinarily low price that fertilizer manufacturers pay for natural gas compared with other sectors. This pricing complied with China's policy of promoting fertilizer production to enhance agriculture. However, it also means that fertilizer manufacturers account for 55 percent of the gas industry's gross revenue from gas sales, while other industry provides 28 percent, and the residential sector provides only 15 percent.

Despite low price ceilings, and even though China produces little gas compared with other fuels, the natural gas market is paradoxically in oversupply. This situation has resulted from government rationing that has kept consumption artificially low, drying up of demand in some areas, and the failure of the market to develop as anticipated. Most of China's current natural gas production is located in the southwest and the west, while the areas that are experiencing the most economic growth are in the east and southeast. A top priority for China's planners is to construct long-haul natural gas pipelines to serve the energy needs of these growing areas. Currently, China's pipeline system is regionally segmented and only connects productive fields to nearby consumers.

There are still many impediments to developing natural gas in China. Some of them are applicable to industrial development in general, while others are more specific to the natural gas industry. We assume in this discussion that China will continue on the road of economic liberalization and privatization and that the state will gradually wind down its involvement in the day-to-day running of industry. In general, the problems center on: the legal-regulatory framework and property rights, restructuring of state-owned enterprises, development of competitive markets, and development of regulatory bodies with clear responsibilities. China's government appears to be actively working to resolve many of these issues, although the pace of change is erratic as it struggles to balance necessary changes with social welfare during the transition from command-and-control to a free-market economy.

Presently, China's gas transmission sector is in its infancy, with the exception of an 860-km pipeline that runs east from the Ordos basin to Beijing. However, even this pipeline runs well below capacity due to the lack of a viable gas market in Beijing. Before the gas industry can expand efficiently, China must restructure its national companies and liberalize the current pricing and gas allocation system.

China is seeking more foreign investment to explore and develop its rich offshore oil and gas resources. China's offshore oil resources reach about 25 billion tons and natural gas 14,000 billion cubic meters. Explored reserves make up only 5 percent of the total expected reserves. Foreign petroleum companies have already shown great enthusiasm in jointly developing offshore oil resources. The China Offshore Petroleum Company has concluded contracts and agreements for over 130 petroleum exploration programs with over 70 companies in 18 countries and regions, involving nearly U.S.$7 billion in foreign investment. Through such joint efforts, China has sunk more than 400 exploratory wells and verified more than 100 oil and gas-bearing structures. China is planning to develop more oil and gas blocks in the South China Sea, East China Sea, and Yellow Sea through Sino-foreign cooperation.

In the Bohai and Yingge seas and the Beibu Bay there are 19 operational oilfields, with annual oil and gas output of 16 million tons and 4 billion cum, respectively. Very recently, Texaco Inc. signed a $500 million contract with the China United Coalbed Methane Corp. to recover an additional 500 million cubic m/year of methane from coal and gas fields in Anhui Province, which are thought to contain more than 60 bcm of methane reserves. ARCO is also actively engaged in studying coalbed methane and recently signed production-sharing contracts covering prospects in Shaanxi Province. Currently, China does not permit foreign countries to participate trading natural gas.

Nuclear Electric Power

China recently formed The China Nuclear Industrial Group (CNIG) to develop nuclear power and nuclear fuel, marking a new era for China's nuclear industry. Directly under the control of the central government, the CNIG will operate nuclear power stations, nuclear heat-supply reactors, scientific research reactors, radiation devices and other nuclear facilities and will also develop scientific research in fields related to the nuclear industry.

Currently, China has two nuclear power plants in service and four under construction. The two in operation are the Qinshan Nuclear Power Station in East China's Zhejiang Province and the Daya Bay Nuclear Power Station in South China's Guangdong Province, generating 12 billion and 50 billion kilowatt-hours respectively. The Chinese expect to include 10 new nuclear plants in their next five-year plan and spend some $60 to $100 billion on nuclear energy over the next 25 years. Nuclear power is expected to contribute about 3 percent of China's total power output by 2006, 2 percent more than at present.

France has been China's major foreign partner in nuclear power construction, with the Framatome Group being a key player. It has already installed four generators in the Daya Bay Nuclear Power Plant and Ling'ao Nuclear Power Plant, both are in South China's Guangdong Province. Their cooperation with Chinese partners over the past decade has enabled them to accumulate precious experience.

In order to ensure transfer of advanced technologies, China is encouraging firms from the United States and Japan to compete against French companies. Competition has been rising since the Clinton administration lifted the United States embargo on the sale of nuclear material to China in early 1998. The Westinghouse Electric Co. has recently organized an international consortium with Mitsubishi Heavy Industries from Japan and the Sepi Nuclear Group from Spain to tap the Chinese nuclear power market. This group is expected to become a powerful competitor because it combines financing from three countries. Westinghouse has already transferred steam-generation technology to the Shanghai Boiler Works for the second phase of construction of the Qinshan Nuclear Power Plant in Zhejiang Province. U.S. companies such as Westinghouse and General Electric have become more active in the Chinese market after President Jiang Zemin's visit to the United States in 1997 which brought about the implementation of the

Sino-U.S. nuclear cooperation agreement originally signed in 1985. Westinghouse has also signed an exchange agreement for nuclear reactor technology with the Shanghai Nuclear Project Research Institution.

Technological transfer is a key prerequisite for selection of future foreign partners for constructing new nuclear power plants. As a young industry in China, the nuclear power sector is short of qualified engineers and manufacturers. In addition, China will no longer import complete sets of nuclear power equipment in the next round of nuclear power planning. This decision highlights the importance of localization in developing the nuclear power sector, as China is determined to become self-reliant in designing, operating, and managing power plants. Foreign companies eager to enter the Chinese market are required to submit localization plans. They must share advanced technical information and design software and sell hardware and key manufacturing technology to China, as well as provide financing.

5.3 Transportation Infrastructure

Overview

China's transportation industry has continued its steady growth in recent years. The nation's combined transport services carried 13.3 billion passengers and 13.7 billion tons of freight in 1998, up 3.4 and 3 percent, respectively from 1997. By the end of 1998, the number of auto travelers increased by 5 percent more than 1997's 11.4 billion. The amount of freight transported on China's highways and roads grew by 4 percent over 1997's figure. The number of air travelers increased by between 5 and 10 percent over 1997's 56.3 million. However, China's sea forwarding and shipping industry has shown a slight decline.

By 1998, there were more than 5,000 kilometers of expressways open throughout China, allowing passenger and freight vehicles to travel faster. China's transportation industry will have more opportunity to expand in the next century as economic growth and social development boost passenger transport volume to 15.5 billion by the year 2000, an annual increase of 8 percent.

By the end of 1997, China had approved the establishment of roughly 50 subsidiaries of 16 foreign shipping companies and more than 120 Sino-foreign joint ventures involving international and domestic shipping.

China intends to invest 500 billion yuan (U.S.$60.5 billion) between 1998 and 2000 to extend highway routes by 74 thousand kilometers. China is seeking preferential loans, investment from overseas, and domestic funding to expand the transport infrastructure. The $17.4 billion in foreign loans and funding made available since 1979 have provided much-needed support for ambitious expansion of road and water transportation routes. Loans from international financial institutions and foreign governments account for 60 percent of total investment. However, foreign direct investment in the form of joint ventures, overseas stock flotations, project financing and leasing have also been on the increase since 1992, now amounting to U.S.$7 billion. In the future, preferential loans will be directed mainly towards national trunk highway projects in central and western China and waterway projects with significant economic benefits. Meanwhile, foreign direct investment is to be channelled largely towards projects for coastal ports and highways in the east of the country. Foreign capital will be concentrated in BOT and joint financing.

Airport

Pressure on the aviation sector has been high because the availability of top-quality airports and aircraft are insufficient to match the growth momentum. By the end of 1996, for example, China's 32 airliners had only 442 transport airplanes operating in 142 airports. CAAC, the Civil Aviation Administration of China, imported 48 airplanes in 1997 to bolster China's fleet and placed orders for another 97 aircraft. During the 1996-97 period, investment in aircraft purchases reached 110 billion yuan (U.S.$13.25 billion).

China's civil aviation business skyrocketed 20.5 percent annually for 16 consecutive years, 3.6 times higher than the average figure of member countries of the International Aviation Transport Organization. By the end of 1997, about 800 million yuan (U.S.$96.38 million) was channeled to build or upgrade airports and support facilities, and 200 million yuan (U.S.$24 million) was poured into key technological renovation projects. An additional 6 billion yuan (U.S.$722 million) raised by localities was also invested in airports. The diversion of massive funds into the civil aviation sector and opening of more international air routes in recent years enhances the operational safety and efficiency of the aviation industry and helped the sector achieve its goal of flying 61 million passengers in 1998.

Recent infrastructure projects include extending the Beijing Capital International Airport and construction of the Shanghai Pudong, Guangzhou New Baiyun, and Hangzhou Xiaoshan airports. Traffic to airports at Zhengzhou, Guiyang, Nanjing, Fuzhou, Yinchuan, Hefei, Nanning, Huhhot, Xuzhou, and Zhoushan was also completed. China also increased air freight turnover by 9.6 percent in 1998, reaching 9.5 billion ton-kilometers. Meanwhile, the total number of passengers traveling by air was about 61 million, exceeding 1997's 56.3 million. The number of international air routes increased from 106 to 124.

CAAC plans to build and upgrade 41 airports by the end of the year 2000. Combined handling capacity will account for 95 percent of the country's total, catering to soaring demand expected in the coming century. The airports are expected to be scattered over 40 different municipalities, provincial and regional capitals, economic showcase regions and tourist sites.

China's air transportation industry will maintain an annual growth rate of 8.1 percent over the next 20 years, much higher than the world's 4.9 percent annual growth rate. It is estimated that China will purchase 1,800 jet planes, total value of U.S.$125 billion. This will make China the second largest civil aviation market in the world. The main parts of 3,100 Boeing planes that are flying around the world are manufactured by Chinese enterprises. In addition, domestic aviation enterprises recently participated in the design and manufacturing of the tail of the 737 plane, bringing China's aviation manufacturing industry to a higher level of expertise.

CAAC is further opening the aviation sector to foreign investors to enhance the competitiveness of domestic airlines. The ratio of foreign investment in domestic airlines is going to be from 35 to 40 percent. The Tianhe Airport of Wuhan, capital of the Hubei Province, has been selected as a pilot venture implementing Sino-foreign joint management. Foreign investment will not be permitted to exceed 49 percent of registered capital in any aviation enterprise, however. China recently allowed foreign retailers to operate duty-free airport shops for the first time in the new Pudong International Airport. Previously, foreign investment had been restricted to the construction of terminal areas, ground services, aircraft maintenance, and affiliated hotels.

Port

Foreign companies can now invest in the management of joint venture wharves and ports. They are also permitted to set up wholly foreign owned enterprises to build and operate special-purpose wharves and waterways. Foreign loans from Japan's Overseas Economic Cooperation Fund, the World Bank, and the Asian Development Bank have been obtained by the Chinese government for port and berth construction at Qinghuandao, Dalian, Tianjing, Shijiazhung, Shanghai, Ningbo, Lianyungang, Xiamem, and Guanzhou. In recent years, 90 percent of foreign investment has gone toward container wharf projects. A number of foreign companies that have invested in real estate development, power plants, and manufacturing projects have also been permitted to build special-purpose wharves to cater to main-line shipping needs.

China plans to spend over $6 billion developing ports and waterways between 1994 and 2000. Ports in China generally have locational advantages. They are usually near major centers of population, industry, and economic development. Clusters of ports are evolving in three of China's most developed regions: Southern China, the Bohai Sea Rim in the north, and the Yangtze Delta in the east. Dalian, in the Liaoning province, has the largest shipyard in China. Shanghai, in cooperation with the Rotterdam harbor of the Netherlands, has built harbor systems in Shanghai and plans to implement more within the next few years. Container handling improvements for the future are concentrated in Lianyungang (Jiangsu province), Tianjing, Dalian, and Shanghai.

All major international shipping companies have agencies in several of the most important harbors of China: Shanghai, Tianjin, Guangzhou, Dalian, Qindao, Ningbo, Xiamen, and Qinhuangdao. The two largest Chinese shippers include the China Ocean Shipping Corporation (COSCO), which is state-owned and represents one of the biggest shipping companies in the world, and the China National Foreign Transportation Corporation (Sinotrans). Their businesses include transport by water, air, and land, handling of cargo from railway stations and harbors, storage, customs clearance, inspections, and the like. Although foreign companies are officially permitted to handle these operations, in practice a lot of resistance comes from governmental bureaucrats.

Shanghai: The Chinese government recently spent 8.46 billion yuan (U.S.$1.02 billion) expanding Shanghai port's docks and berths, which can now handle 930,000 tons of goods. Since 1984, the port has handled more than 100 million tons of goods annually. Shanghai port has forged business ties with more than 400 ports and 600 shipping companies in over 160 foreign countries and regions. With its new information network, the amount of time required to handle vessels has been cut drastically. Vessels had to stay in the port an average of 9.5 days some 20 years ago, but that time has now been shortened to 1.9 days.

With last year's container handling volume topping 2.5 million TEUs (twenty feet equivalent units), the entry port of Shanghai now ranks twelfth in the world. It is the largest port in China. The port's sustainable annual growth rate averaged 25 percent in recent years. Shanghai's fast-growing economy and its role as China's largest commercial and manufacturing center have been the major reasons for the port's dramatic expansion. It now handles one quarter of the country's international cargo shipping and a third of container shipping. Shanghai has nearly 20 shipping routes, accommodating 281 docking monthly, to more than 50 countries and regions in the world.

The Shanghai Shipping Trade Center was set up in November 1996 to standardize Shanghai's port transportation. It finished with 36 million tons of cargo trade by the end of October, 1997. China plans to upgrade container ports in east China's Jiangsu and Zhejiang provinces to make them part of an international container shipping hub. Construction will be centered on Shanghai through an administrative institute set up there. Other projects include rebuilding three container berths and massive dredge work in the deep water lane at the Yangtze River mouth. Moreover, the headquarters of the China Ocean Shipping Corp., one of the four largest shipping groups in the world, has recently moved to Shanghai.

Tianjin: The Port of Tianjin is the largest man-made port in China and Beijing's gateway to the sea. The port mainly handles import and export goods for Beijing and Tianjin as well as other provinces and cities in North and Northwest China. At present, the port has fixed assets of 6.63 billion yuan (U.S.$798.7 million), ranking first in the country. Its handling capacity reached 68 million tons in 1997 and it earned a profit of 2.2 billion yuan (U.S.$265 million). In the past 10 years, Tianjin has invested more than 4.2 billion yuan to add a production capacity of 10.58 million tons. Its fixed assets in 1995 were nearly 600 percent greater than in 1985. Tianjin has built and updated 19 deep water berths with a capacity of over 10,000 tons.

While improving port capacity, the port authority has enlarged its business scope. It has set up more than 90 new industries involving cargo shipment, trade, industrial enterprises, real estate, and financial securities. Moreover, it has also set up foreign-funded enterprises with total investment valued at U.S.$150 million. It has established business relations with more than 300 ports in more than 160 countries and regions, and is one of the busiest ports in the country.

Nearly 3 billion yuan was invested in infrastructure construction of the Tianjin Port during 1995-1998, including establishment of five new berths and renovation of eight berths. The main channel will be expanded from the present 80 meters to 180 meters. Two international passenger docks and a new container dock will also be built. By 2010, the port handling capacity will surpass 100 million tons and a 100,000-ton deep-water channel and several berths will have been completed.

Dalian: Dalian has completed renovation a 100,000 ton crude oil dock and construction of a 300,000 ton crude oil dock and a 200,000 ton ore dock. In 1998, the Dalian Port Authority and PSA Co. Ltd. of Singapore signed a contract to jointly rebuild the eastern part of the Dalian Port. This is the second time the partners have cooperated, having earlier collaborated in the construction of a container berth near Dayao Bay in Dalian. According to the contract, the two partners will invest a total of $2.8 million in Dalian Marine Ltd. The Dalian Port Authority is also cooperating with the Australian Humusly Mine Company in jointly constructing a 200,000 quay for ore in Dalian Port. This deep-water quay will be the largest in North China, able to berth 200,000 ton ships. Its yearly handling capacity will be ten million tons. A recent project of a 60,000-km class chemical terminal with 35 tanks has just commenced full operation. This project was established as a Japan-Europe-China joint venture by Mitsui & Co. (10 percent),

Storli ASA (44 percent), Dalian Port Authorities (36 percent) and Van Ommeren Tank Terminals (Asia) B.V. (10 percent). In order to establish a foothold in Europe, the Dalian port launched a new container shipping route direct to Europe at the end of 1998. The French shipping company, CMADALIAN, will operate nine container ships on a regular weekly basis. The route also links Dalian with several ports in China and with Malta, Mersin, Kawasaki, Kobe, Hatata, and Inchon. It substantially shortens the freight time and distance between northern China and Europe.

Qingdao: Qingdao port's handling capacity reached 84 million tons in 1998, with 1.21 million containers, up 17.4 percent over 1997. It is the second ranking seaside port in China. Its handling capacity for standard containers ranks first in the country. This port has opened three special trains and achieved automatic transfer of railway freight and shipments to enhance its handling capacity. It also opened 10 lines in 1998. Its new ore dock, now under construction, will have an expected annual capacity of 16 million tons. It will be the largest in Asia and the second largest in the world. It will make the Qingdao Port capable of handling 100 million tons of cargo a year. The Qingdao port has 14 docks and 70 berths and trade relations with more than 400 ports in 130 countries and regions. The port is the largest ore depot in northern China, the largest crude oil depot, the second largest container shipping port in terms of actual volume it transported, and the fifth largest coal port in the whole of China.

Ningbo: Though the third largest harbor in China, with an annual handling capacity of 82 million tons, Ningbo Port has limited cargo sources for container shipping and its deep-water potential has yet to be explored. Ningbo Harbor, composed of Beilun, Zhenhai, and Ningbo dock areas, is a comprehensive facility with docks located along the river, river mouth, and sea shore. It is one of four international terminals given priority for development by the central government. It currently has 60 docks each with a capacity to handle at least 500 tons. Twenty-three can harbor 10,000-ton ships. In 1996, Ningbo Port handled 76.38 million tons of cargo, ranking third after Shanghai and Qinhuangdao on the Chinese mainland. The average water depth of more than 30 meters in the Beilun harbor can allow ships of up to 200,000 tons to dock. Ships of up to 300,000 tons are now handled during flood tide.

Development of manufacturing in the Yangtze River Delta favors growth of the Ningbo Port. It now supplements Shanghai and other cities in the region as large ships carrying iron ore and crude oil are unloaded to smaller ones in Ningbo for other destinations around the country. Ningbo Port plans to expand its annual handling capacity to 100 million tons by the year 2000, when its container handling capacity is expected to reach 1 million TEUs. Apart from building facilities for handling coal, oil, iron ore, and liquid chemicals, Ningbo will concentrate on developing container shipping.

Guangzhou: Guangzhou is the largest foreign trade outlet in fast-developing South China. It handled a total of 78.6 million tons of cargo and 850,000 TEU of containers in 1998. It has an annual 24 percent growth rate. Its total business volume ranked third in the nation following Shanghai and Ningbo. The city has responded to intense competition by expanding cooperation with railway and ocean shipping departments and adding several container railway routes to inland areas and direct shipping routes to ports along the eastern Chinese coasts and to Japan, Australia, and Thailand. The port is also constructing a new project to expand a 58.6-kilometer section of its 115-kilometer navigation channels leading ships from the port at the mouth of the Pearl River out to the open sea. After completion, this section will be widened to 160 meters and deepened to 11.5 meters, enabling passage of 35,000-ton ships around the clock and 50,000-ton ships when the tide is high. As a result, the handling capacity of the port will be raised to 90 million tons.

Xiamen: The Xiamen port now has 81 berths. It is China's tenth largest in handling capacity. The port is linked with more than 50 other ports in China and around the world. It handled 17.54 million tons of cargo in 1997. Construction work on 7 berths with a total handling capacity of 2.1 million tons has begun. The project includes three 20,000-ton berths for general use and one 5,000-ton sundry goods berth. The project will cost 788.38 million yuan (U.S.$94.98 million), including U.S.$47 million in loans from the Asian Development Bank. It is expected to be completed in the year 2002.

Qinhuangdao: Located in northeastern Hebei Province, 281 kilometers from Beijing, Qinhuangdao port is of particular importance in transporting natural resources such as coal from northern China to the south. It is the world's largest coal port; it handled a total of 83.12 million tons of cargo (including 65 million tons of coal and 11 million tons of crude oil) in 1996 and almost 100 million tons of cargo, including 20 million tons of coal exports, in 1999. The port has launched a number of joint ventures in container transportation, edible oil, cement manufacturing, and tourism with Japan, Singapore, Belgium and other countries. The port now ranks second in terms of its handling capacity among China's coastal ports.

On June 10, 1898, the Qing (1644-1911) government proclaimed it an open port. The event was historic in that it was then the first port opened by the government, since all the other ports were opened by force or under the coercion of foreign powers.The Beidaihe summer resort nearby also enjoys special political significance. Since 1949, it has been a favorite place for State and Party leaders to work and relax.

Railway

The railway sector, one of the last bastions of the country's planned economy, has had a monopoly for decades. It was the prime mode of travel for most Chinese people in the past. Rapid development of the highway system now rivals the railway sector. A buyer's market offers more choices for both shippers and passengers. It has become necessary for railway departments to alter outdated modes of thinking and improve both efficiency and services. This benefits passengers, enhances services, reduces costs, and improves the industry's image. China has decided to reduce employment in the railway sector by 1.4 million people by 2000, including 300,000 workers from railway transport departments. The sector posted losses of 2.8 billion yuan in 1998, the fifth consecutive year it has been in the red.

China's transport system is still mainly based on rail system, however. China's railways carry 70 percent of the nation's cargo and 60 percent of its passengers. The total length of its railway tracks is about 54,500 kilometers, which is still short given the size of China. Approximately U.S.$48 billion has been invested in railways for the period between 1994 and 2000. Half of the funds provides for the construction of new lines and the other half is reserved to create double tracks and electrification on existing railways.

China's railway sector has recently mapped out plans for in-depth reform, centering on increasing transport volume and profit income while improving the safety of operations. Focus will be maintained on developing faster train services. An improved, high-quality transportation service is the major target for the sector in the coming years. With computerized services nationwide, it will be able to provide passengers with more convenient service.

China is opening its State-owned rail sector to foreign investors, importing a huge amount of technology and equipment. China plans to use at least 16.6 billion yuan (U.S.$2 billion) in foreign capital over the next five years as it continues opening this sector. Preferential policies regarding the import of railway technology and equipment have already been established. About 180 joint ventures or cooperative enterprises have been created. The government ensures market availability for such ventures. China is also planning to use other fund-raising methods such as commercial credit, issuing bonds overseas, or listing some railway enterprises overseas.

Highway

China plans to invest 180 billion yuan (U.S.$21.6 billion) in the construction of highways in 1999 to link more cities and promote local economic development. Investment in this field is to continue at the same planned growth rate of past years. One hundred and ten billion yuan (U.S.$13.2 billion) is expected to be poured into 279 major projects, adding a total length of 27,900 kilometers to the highway system. Of these, 15,784 kilometers will be first-class highways. Meanwhile, the country is investing 50 billion yuan (U.S. $6.02 billion) in upgrading the highway network and 20 billion yuan (U.S.$2.4 billion) in speeding up construction of roads which connect rural counties and villages. Upgrading quality control of highway construction and supervising highway projects by restructuring the highway management system are recent foci. Among 48 key projects, only 16 projects adopted the quality responsibility system. Many local transportation departments at provincial or city levels have misallocated state funding and engaged in fraud. Despite these problems, China is trying hard to speed up highway construction to stimulate the country's economic development. By the end of 1998, actual investment reached 211.8 billion yuan (U.S.$25.5 billion).

China will have 9,000 kilometers of expressway by the year 2000, concentrating on completing north-to-south and east-to-west highways, and 21,600 kilometers by 2020. Major problems have, however, arisen in acquiring the land required for building the roads. These problems have been compounded by prolonged flooding in certain areas of the country since June 1998. Floods have damaged 46 state and 483 provincial highways and 2,393 county roads to varying degrees. The damage has disrupted traffic and seriously affected construction work in the sector. Some 29,000 kilometers of roads have been damaged, about 2.5 percent of the country's total. As a remedy, China plans to beef up investment in highways and railways to sustain economic growth. The government has earmarked 60 million yuan (U.S.$7.23 million) for repairs to damaged roads.

There will be a need for at least $1 billion in annual private investment in new highway projects over the next 5 to 10 years. Although foreign investment is specifically encouraged in highway construction and operation, the national highway law promulgated in July 1997 provides only a sparse legal framework guiding highway projects. The Law fails to address the problems faced by foreign-invested infrastructure projects. For instance, a locality's pricing bureau has final say over an increase in user fees (e.g., tolls or tariffs). While the highway law could eventually provide a more secure framework for investors, in the short-term the model by which China and foreign entities jointly invest in highway development companies will likely hold up best. In addition, BOT is sure to become popular.

5.4 E-Commerce Infrastructure

Overview

The number of Internet users in China has increased by more than six times, from 620,000 as of October 1997 to 4 million at the end of June 1999 and 8.9 million at the end of 1999. China's Internet domain names increased from 1,003 in January 1997 to 18,396 in December 1998. By the end of June 1999, computers connected to the network reached 1.46 million. There are 29,045 CN domains and 9,906 websites. While domain names are about evenly distributed among sectors, commercial domain names (com.cn) dominate at 76 percent of domain-name registration.

The Chinese leadership has allowed the Internet to grow rapidly because it is viewed as an essential tool for economic prosperity, the harbinger of a knowledge economy in which information transfer replaces industrial processes as the basis for the economy. Over the past ten years, many sectors, such as telecommunications, have been growing at annual rates of 30 to 50 percent. Each year, about 10 million phone lines are added to the public network. However, China remains an agricultural society; only the eastern provinces are heavily industrialized. China's leaders hope to skip some of the classic intermediate stages of economic development by encouraging information technology.

Since 1995, when the use of the Internet began to spread through many sectors of Chinese society, the country's leaders have been deciding how to control it. They hope the Internet will lead to economic gain without destabilizing the country. Even though the technology allows decentralized coordination, the leadership has thus chosen to implement a hierarchy for managing its growth. Various ministries of the Chinese central government coordinate decisions while leaving room for private-sector investment and initiatives. This intergovernmental coordination, which continues to evolve, has given China's Internet its special local character. The government therefore has allowed some competition to develop between domestic ISPs while making sure the infrastructure itself stays securely under its control. The key to this Internet strategy is to restrict the number of organizations that can connect with the global Internet. These restrictions have so far not seemed to limit deployment of Internet infrastructure. Instead, China's state-coordinated infrastructure is becoming rapidly integrated throughout Chinese society. There are four interconnecting networks: two commercial ones (ChinaNet and China Golden Bridge Network – ChinaGBN) and two academic ones (China Education and Research Network – CERNet – and China Science and Technology Network – CSTNet). ISPs operate as branches of these networks or are independent of them. Officially, foreigners are not permitted to operate the services directly, although there are some exceptions.

The rapidly increasing number of Internet users in China has paved the way for introduction of electronic commerce. ISPs, regulators, and governments are working together to break down few existing barriers in the interests of allowing e-commerce to contribute significantly to the country's economic development. Firms are getting used to doing business via the Internet. The "China Market" website launched in 1998 by China's Ministry of Foreign Trade and Economic Cooperation (MOFTEC) displays nearly 20,000 commodities produced by more than 5,000 small and medium-sized Chinese companies. Over the past year, over 70 percent of these firms have reached agreements to cooperate with foreign customers and more than 20 percent have exported their goods.

Foreign Participation

China is the fastest-growing Internet market in Asia and is poised to become one of the world's leading markets in the next five years. Each new user that comes online creates new opportunities for Internet-related business, enabling companies to leverage their technology in one of the world's most exciting markets. This is good news for foreign companies specializing in Internet-related hardware and software. Firms such as Sun Microsystems Inc. (servers), Cisco Systems, Inc. (routers), Microsoft (web browser/server software), and Netscape (web browser/server software) currently dominate the sector worldwide and will continue to supply virtually all hardware and software, including routers, servers, and modems as well as web-related software.

Foreign involvement in China's Internet services is nonetheless limited to investing in an existing Chinese company or providing consulting services under the guise of systems sales or joint venture agreements. Foreign companies are otherwise prohibited from operating or managing value-added telecommunications networks. They are unlikely to be allowed greater entry into service provision any time soon.

It is safe to predict, however, that China's need for Internet related equipment will be significant. The Ministry of Posts and Telecommunications (MPT) launched commercial Internet services in Beijing and Shanghai in 1995 with help from U.S. firms. MPT offers full point-to-point protocol (PPP) accounts that allow world-wide web browsing, along with standard services like e-mail, telnet, and newsgroup access. Electronic business activities such as on-line ticketing, shopping, banking, and securities trading, as well as declaration of imported goods, are gaining popularity among Chinese commercial circles and ordinary residents. The value of this sector will exceed 160 million dollars in 1999.

Regulations

The Internet sector is highly regulated by the central government. It recently enacted the "Interim Regulations on International Interconnection of Computer Information Networks in the PRC," granting the State Council's former Steering Committee on National Information Infrastructure primary regulatory responsibility for China's Internet. The Committee defined the rights, obligations, and liabilities of international interconnection service providers, interconnecting organizations, accessing organizations, and users. Absorption of the Steering Committee into the newly formed Ministry of Information Industry in March 1998 gave the new Ministry full regulatory control over China's Internet.

Internet networks are often divided into two major categories: interconnecting networks and access networks. The former networks are directly linked to the global Internet through international leased lines. No one else is allowed to operate interconnecting networks without approval from the State Council. The four networks listed above are the only services granted by the State council so far. The Chinese access networks are the equivalent of ISPs in the Western world, providing access and content services, but no direct global interconnection. Any Chinese corporation, after meeting certain safety, legal, technological, and financial requirements, can be licensed as an ISP.

The Chinese government forbids transmission of information considered harmful to state security or 'public order'. In the long run, however, such efforts will be difficult to enforce. The Internet is a worldwide, borderless network beyond the control of any one government. Censorship and regulations are treated as damage to be bypassed.

The Internet is also protected by its sheer size. Millions of messages, web sites, and newsgroups cannot be consistently or cheaply monitored. The wide use of encryption also makes governmental control virtually impossible to enforce.

Internet Infrastructure

China's public telecommunications system was a China Telecom monopoly until 1994. A second carrier, China Unicom, was then licensed. It has successfully launched mobile telephone service in many cities, challenging the China Telecom monopoly. However, China Unicom's long-distance network and local wireline networks are still very immature. China's Internet is built mainly on China Telecom's physical networks.

In recent years, China Telecom has significantly upgraded its infrastructure with fiber-optic lines. The fiber-optic backbone of the long-distance network, completed in 1998, consists of eight horizontal and eight vertical trunk lines. It has nodes in all the provincial capitals and 70 percent of all other cities. All trunk lines now use either 622Mbps or 2.4Gbps synchronous digital hierarchy (SDH) technology, with capacity expansion readily available by adding wavelength-division multiplexing (WDM) technology. A national satellite network with 38 major earth stations and a microwave network covering remote and difficult-to-reach territories supplements this network.

The local access network is dominated by copperwire local loops. By the end of 1998, the phone penetration rate had reached 10 percent nationally, though it is as high as 27 percent in the cities. Trials on cable modem and digital subscriber line services are ongoing. Based on these physical transmission facilities, China Telecom developed three value-added data networks designed specifically for data communications: ChinaPAC, ChinaDDN, and China Frame Relay.

5.5 Agriculture

Since agricultural reform began in 1978, China has experienced impressive growth in agriculture, achieving an annual agricultural growth rate of 6.7 percent. However, the share of agriculture in current-price GDP has shrunk from 31.2 percent in 1979 to around 20 percent in 1995. With such a massive population, sufficient grain production is key to sustained economic growth. In addition, China's agricultural reform may also be important to the rest of the world, as unless China can improve the efficient use of agricultural inputs (especially water) and slow the diversion of land to other uses, it will not reach its goal of self-sufficiency and its reliance on imports may become so excessive that world prices may be driven up.

Agricultural Policy and Economic Growth
(1) Protectionism

Japan and South Korea's economy went on to achieve rapid industrialization and modernization after introducing protection to their agricultural sectors at a stage of economic development that China is now at. If there were a correlation, one would argue China should also pursue a protectionist policy. However, there is evidence that whilst those countries achieved economic success, their agricultural protection policy, in fact, largely failed and instead caused problems such as a heavy budget burden, stagnation in agricultural productivity, and source of trade conflict with its major trading partners which in turn caused difficulties in expanding their export markets.

Therefore, there is no evidence that such a policy would assist economic development, and in addition there seems little reason for China to pursue it. China has shown it can earn the foreign exchange required if it had to rely on the international food market to satisfy their consumption, so why should it be concerned about maintaining self-sufficiency thinking that necessary for social and economic stability? Also, imports may rise, but possibly not to the extent that it would pose a serious threat to world prices.

Indeed, the World Bank has urged China to abandon its 95 percent grain self-sufficiency policy and economists have shown that increasing self-sufficiency in food by ignoring an economy's comparative advantage is not effective. Artificially raising prices encourages inefficient allocation of resources which cause efficiency losses and prevents exercising any comparative advantage. Instead, by participating more deeply in the international division of labor (liberalization), an economy can increase its income and improve its welfare.

(2) Liberalization

Liberalization helps raise domestic productivity and promote income growth. Internationalizing the market will present serious readjustment problems for farmers. The agricultural industry in

China employed 67 percent of total of 490.35m rural employed persons in 1996 which itself represent 71.2 percent of a total of 688.5m employed. In other words, as many as 48 percent of the economically active population were still officially engaged in agriculture after nearly 20 years of the reform era. Following the world trend, the adjustment will have to be made at some time. Despite the recent warnings that the Asian economic crisis brought for taking a cautious approach to reform, this adjustment should be made earlier before the gap between domestic and international prices widens. In any case, the problems may not be that serious as the history of China's rural development after 1985 shows a series of successful adjustment and economic growth where farmers' income has grown due to the relocation of capital, labor and other resources from agricultural to nonagricultural activities; and adjustments can be accommodated smoothly in a dynamic and rapidly growing economy like China's.

Liberalization of agricultural trade will also indicate China's belief in free trade to the international community and help it join multilateral trade organizations such as WTO. The WTO in turn can help China's economic growth as a conduit to integration into the world economy. This will assist the growth of China's exports (in particular its labor-intensive exports – where its comparative advantage lies) in a stable and expanding international market. Increased exports will in turn produce more employment opportunities to absorb surplus farmers. Whilst China's agricultural policy remains inward looking, other economies will be reluctant to accommodate it within international institutions. A realistic move is to have China join WTO as a developing country with a commitment to a reform agenda such as the lifting of restrictions on imports of agricultural commodities within a finite period. The emergence of conglomerates that fill niche markets on a national or local basis will help discourage the provincial protectionism that has survive hitherto. In support of this, and to help development of the sector, the government has placed agricultural investment as one of 18 sectors where foreign direct investment (FDI) is encouraged.

Governmental Policy and Foreign Investment

The governments concern is to stabilize and reinforce the agricultural sector. Accordingly, the focus is on promoting agricultural and rural work and achieving a better regional balance of growth (previously disproportionately concentrated along the eastern seaboard of the country – where most FDI is). This will be done by implementing the policies adopted by the third plenum of the 15th CPC central committee; ensuring that the Party's basic rural polices remain stable, thus raising farmers' incomes and alleviating their burdens and generally ensuring the stability of rural areas and expanding domestic demand. Agricultural infrastructure linked to key water-control projects will be improved in an effort to make China able to fend off natural disasters. Efforts will be made to readjust and make maximum use of rural industrial structure and the mixture of products; the efficiency of management in the agricultural sector will be improved, township-enterprises developed; agricultural capital project construction accelerated, reforms in the grain marketing systems accelerated and sales of farm produce boosted; and the optimization of agriculture and the rural economic structure through science and technology will be optimized.

China also wants to reduce government losses for grain purchases by launching nationwide reform of the grain marketing system. Restructuring the grain distribution system represents a major aspect of the central government's reform agenda for this year, and is a main task for national economic development. Premier Zhu Rongji has repeatedly stressed the importance and urgency for reform of the grain marketing system. At present the state grain companies play a dual role in storage and marketing and official statistics show that state grain companies have lost more than 100 billion yuan ($12 billion) over the past seven years due to poor performance and mismanagement. The central government has responded by adopting a series of measures to reverse the trend. For example, state grain companies with sole rights to purchase grain directly from farmers are now required to purchase surplus grain at protected prices. The CADB (China Agricultural Development Bank) has also granted loans totalling 2.3 billion yuan ($277 million) during the first 10 months of this year for constructing temporary granaries.

Individual farmers lack the land and the capital to invest in cash crops, value-added food processing (which raises the potential value of agricultural products – a potato transformed into French fries multiplies its value by a factor of 10) or marketing. That, in addition to providing jobs and soaking up the rural employment, is where large companies can play a role. They, unlike most local firms and farmers, can provide inputs like capital, technology and managerial skills to increase productivity. This is where the government wants FDI to help develop these industries.

Foreign investment has brought such changes to food processing and now the government wants it to see it in the production stages. Today, only 2 percent of foreign investment goes to agriculture, but hopefully opportunities will grow with the government's renewed focus on developing the sector. This sector is on Premier Zhu Rongji's 1998 list of the 18 industries where foreign investment is to be encouraged. Encouragement includes duty exemption on capital equipment imports to be restored in these sectors, low tax (5 percent income-tax) and tax exemption for the first five years for former wasteland converted to productive use, and low interest rates from the bank. In addition, returns from agriculture investments are quite high and stable because agriculture is a basic part of GDP growth and can be regarded as a forever business. Agriculture is an area where investment has lagged yet demand remains high, particularly for value-added products. All these attributes present a good investment opportunity that should be capitalised on by foreign ventures.

Firms doing as such include the Jindi Group. They have invested 20 million RMB ($2.4 million) in land for farming in northern Heilongjiang province. Part of the land is being used to raise cattle, and part to grow corn and soya beans. Moving up the value-added ladder, Jindi merged with a pharmaceutical factory to process its corn crop into starch protein powder and citric acid – most of which is exported. SOEs plagued by overcapacity are also turning to agriculture as are foreign companies. Thailand's CP Pokphand has operations in more than 80 cities in China selling chicken feed and operated on a profit margin around 13%, Chemicals giant Du Pont has seen its fertilizer business double in the past two to three years, and U.S. feed mix company Contifeed has increased its sales tonnage more than 2000% since it entered the market in 1991.

For FDI however, problems still abound such as lack of infrastructure and inefficient and low-quality storage and distribution infrastructure. One Shanghai-based joint venture found the only way to beat the problem was to buy its own fleet of refrigerated vans to transport its beef products around the country.

In closing, returning the responsibility for production decisions to farmers is now regarded as one of the most successful moves made during China's whole reform process. By 1978 the government had recognized that solving managerial problems within the production team system in agriculture was the key to improving productivity by raising farmers' incentives. However, the government has recognized further reforms are needed to improve the growth of this sector. FDI is currently encouraged and other improvements are being made to increase yields. But in addition, China now needs to consider what direction they wish to continue reforms – a protectionist road or liberalization. The policy the government eventually adopts will depend to an extent on which decision maximizes its probability of remaining in power. As consumers and farmers currently do not support protectionism, it is likely that China will further liberalize this sector.

6. Analyzing Structural Dynamics and Selecting a Foreign Investment

Chapter Purpose

As industrial structure is partially exogenous, industry selection and investment strategy has a strong impact on international expansion performance. It determines the industrial environment and market demand that an MNC faces in China, which in turn affects its operational and financial outcomes. This chapter elaborates the importance of industry selection to MNCs entering China and presents an integrated analytical framework on how to choose an appropriate Chinese industry. In this framework, we illuminate four aspects of industrial dynamics, namely structural dimensions (uncertainty, complexity, and deterrence), structural forces (e.g., competitor, government, distributor, supplier, and buyer), structural attributes (e.g., profitability, sales growth, concentration, asset intensity, and technological intensity), and structural evolution (embryonic, growth, shakeout, maturity, and decline). Collectively, these factors are the core of an analytical framework for industry selection and investment strategy during international expansion.

6.1 Introduction

Globalization has become a permanent and irreversible part of economic life. It provides firms with both tremendous opportunities and daunting challenges. International expansion has become a pervasive and prominent strategic response to global economic dynamics for a large array of companies. The need to simultaneously balance the dynamic tension among multiple forces (geographic, product, market, and technological) has resulted in firms extending their presence all over the globe for a multitude of purposes and through a multitude of forms. Correspondingly, international expansion decisions and strategies have acquired increasing strategic significance.

FDI and MNC theories have shed some light on the importance of industry selection and investment strategy during internationalization. The existence of differences in industrial and market structures between countries influences an MNC's profitability. Particular industries are more attractive to the degree that they contain structural impediments to competition, thus allowing participating firms to sustain competitive advantages once their positions in the industry are obtained. MNCs can achieve higher performance than firms which only operate domestically because they benefit from the structural variance of industries between host and home countries. When the industrial structure of a host country is imperfect and entry barriers are low, FDI will flow in as a direct response. Structural imperfection in a foreign market constitutes a dominant factor which not only makes FDI preferable to trade or licensing but also determines the relative attractiveness of one host country over another. Firms in oligopolistic industries enjoy the advantages of economies of scale and other characteristics that give them market power. This power allows them to overcome the disadvantages of being foreign, and therefore, to compete with local rivals. Focusing on competition and life cycle stages, Porter (1991) also asserts that competition is a major driving force underlying international expansion. Firms in a harsh, competitive, domestic sector may expand overseas to regions where competition is low, an industry is at the growing or shakeout stage, or a competitive position would be more readily attained and sustained.

As in other host countries, MNCs in China seek economic benefits gained from both country-specific advantages (e.g., resources and pent-up market demand) and firm-specific advantages (e.g., ownership and internalization advantages). The extent to which an MNC can achieve these advantages largely depends upon industry selection. Selecting the right industry enables a foreign firm to benefit from both cost and revenue related advantages, as it affects the extent to which the firm can take advantage of factor endowments and market demand. Home country conditions may also influence this decision by offering a frame of reference by which MNCs judge and evaluate industrial dynamics. More importantly, strategic choices and outcomes of globalization are significantly determined by industrial conditions manifested in such areas as market, cost, competition, and governmental policy. These conditions vary in strength from industry to industry. The desired industry may not necessarily be the same as the firm's core domestic business. Both related (vertical or horizontal) and unrelated FDI diversifications can engender abnormal rates of return if the selected industry presents distinct preemptive opportunities and industrial dynamics aligned properly with a firm's competencies.

A major challenge for MNCs in China and beyond is how to become competent and attain sustained superior performance. International expansion through foreign direct investment tends to involve market conduct that extends the recognition of mutual market dependence – the essence of oligopoly – beyond national boundaries. Likewise, it tends to broadly equalize the rate of return on capital (equity) throughout a given industry in all the countries where production actually takes place. This common profit rate, however, may exceed a normal or competitive one since a persistent oligopoly, nation- or world-wide, is marked by barriers to entry of new firms and, perforce, to the inflow of capital. International competition and expansion reduces structural imperfections in a host country such as China. In practice, however, this effect differs according to industry and country. The structure of some Chinese industries is certainly more exogenous than others, as reflected by higher entry barriers, more governmental regulations, and greater asset intensity.

Like many other developing countries, China's industries are characterized by structural imperfections which partially result from a paradox wherein governments aim to alleviate structural distortions by injecting more competition and assimilating more foreign capital yet simultaneously impose policies which present new obstacles to the mitigation of imperfection. Some policies may increase rather than reduce structural distortions such as when a government attaches a high value to social stability, infant sector protection, and pillar industry subsidies. In sum, structural dynamics in China are complex, exogenous, and often heterogeneous across industries. The analysis of such dynamics should reveal not only structural dimensions such as complexity and uncertainty but also the impact of structural forces (e.g., suppliers and buyers), attributes (e.g., sales growth and asset intensity), and evolution (i.e., life cycle), as detailed below.

6.2 Analyzing Structural Dimensions

Structural dimensions include structural uncertainty, complexity, and deterrence. These dimensions may affect an MNC's profitability, stability, and sustainability in the Chinese market. International managers need to diagnose these dimensions in order to opt for an appropriate Chinese industry and develop a strategy that will enable the maximization of economic benefits without imposing uncontrollable hostilities and risks.

Structural Uncertainty

Strictly speaking, uncertainty means unpredictable variability whereas dynamism is comprised of both predictable and unpredictable elements. Both dynamism and uncertainty in an industry carry opportunities and challenges. Uncertainty may arise due to market force fluctuations or changes in industrial policies by the Chinese government. Structural uncertainty often results from high fluctuations in prices, sales, and material supplies. Under these circumstances, foreign companies confront more operational risks. If they intend to avoid these risks, they should reduce their reliance on local settings. In an effort to do this, foreign investors can decrease local sourcing and marketing while increasing exports. Many MNCs investing in Asia such as NEC of Japan, HP of the United States, and Siemens of Germany have used this strategy to respond to the financial chaos which recently occurred in the region. Generally, MNCs interested in entering an industry characterized by structural uncertainty should consider whether their ability to offset risks is sufficient to enable them to realize their international expansion goals. For instance, General Electric recently engaged in producing aircraft parts in China. Its diverse product portfolio in the country enables the company to offset possible risks from the high uncertainty of the Chinese airplane manufacturing sector.

Structural Complexity

Structural complexity refers to the diversity and heterogeneity of environmental factors (e.g., competitors, customers, and suppliers), while structural diversity is a measure of the different factors and issues that a firm must face, and structural heterogeneity refers to the characteristic differences among those factors and issues. High complexity in an industry reinforces the difficulty of using standardization and cost efficiency strategies. It also increases an MNC's operational uncertainties and production instabilities. As a strategic response to structural complexity, strategic and operational flexibility is imperative. A more focused strategy with respect to the scope of both products and markets appears to be the proper solution in this environment for those firms with little host country-specific experience or with only a short presence in the market. When a foreign firm has gained more diverse experience in dealing with competitors, customers, and suppliers, and has thus reduced the liabilities of foreignness, the firm may consider extending its line of business in order to explore more opportunities.

In deciding on a product portfolio for a complex foreign industry, using related diversification in the area of a firm's core competency seems a better choice than an unrelated strategy. For instance, Irdeto Access, a wholly-owned subsidiary of Holland Mindort, recently marched into China. Given limited experience about China, Irdeto Access chose to invest in its core business, namely cable TV in China. It plans to apply its advanced cable TV technology to the Chinese domestic cable satellite TV market. All these efforts are aimed to dominate the global cable TV market. Nevertheless, an investing firm's length of operations, the diversity of its host country experience, and the contribution of its local partner (if in a joint venture) may affect its industry selection and participation strategies. For instance, Legato Systems, which owns the world's first network storing management software, Net WorforuNix, recently entered China. In order to formally present in China's complex software sector, the company took three evolutionary steps: it developed an appropriate strategy; it established a department in charge of supporting the new market; and it found the best Chinese partners.

Structural Deterrence

Structural deterrence refers to the availability of resources from a specific industry and its support industries. An industry in China may not be complex or uncertain, but still be hostile. In this situation, the foreign business will be constrained in implementing its business- and operational-level strategies, deploying internal resources contributed to local operations, and participating in indigenous markets. For instance, the American Ai'erkang Pharmaceutical Co., which has a 50-year history and maintains the leading position in the sales of its contact lens protection products in Europe and North American, had not considered the Chinese market until recently in 1998. An important reason is that the ophthalmological products sector in China, although not complex nor volatile, were short of needed resources (e.g., skilled laborers and infrastructure) from supporting industries or markets.

Resource munificence, on the other hand, helps firms achieve operational and financial synergies from the interactions between internal resources (competitive advantages) and external resources (comparative advantages). Reliance on external resources comes from either the firm's strategic needs or the Chinese government's requirement that product components must be localized. In general, structural resources include: (i) natural resources, raw materials, parts, and components; (ii) investment infrastructure such as power supplies, telecommunications, and transportation; (iii) product factors such as land, capital, labor, information, technology, and management; and (iv) governmental treatment, assistance, and efficiency. MNCs need to ensure that all of these resources are available in the industry within which they will operate as well as in related or support industries. If not available or economical, then firms should calculate if it is worthwhile and capable of having them developed by themselves. For instance, Dell did not rely on retail buyers in China, who accounted for approximately 10 percent of Dell's China sales only. Instead, Dell made large inroads by selling directly to corporations. That way, Dell avoided going head to head against entrenched local market leaders like Legend. Established American PC makers in China such as HP, IBM, and Compaq, depend largely on resellers. Because of the cost savings derived from cutting out the middleman, Dell sells computers at lower prices than its competitors, thus attaining a larger proportion of market share. At the end of 1998, Dell's market share tripled to 1.2 percent while Compaq's fell from 3.5 percent to 2.7 percent.

6.3 Appraising Structural Forces

Relevant structural forces in most Chinese industries are composed of new entrants, suppliers, buyers, rivals, substitutes, distributors, and government authorities. These forces individually and jointly affect the level of competitive threat and bargaining pressure facing an MNC in the Chinese market. They determine an industry's competitive pattern, which influences a firm's competitive position, market power, financial returns, and growth potential. International managers need to identify the strength of each of these seven forces in a target market and choose an industry in which an MNC will confront the fewest competitive threats so it can maintain a superior competitive position.

Although Michael Porter's five forces model was designed for domestic settings, it can be revised to apply to industry selection in a foreign context such as China. Selecting the right industry overseas largely determines an MNC's profitability and competitive position in the host country market. The intensity of industrial competition and profit potential is a function of five competitive forces, whether in a domestic or host market: threat of new entrants, suppliers, buyers, product substitutes, and intensity of rivalry among competitors. A foreign company should analyze each of these five forces, identify possible opportunities or threats generated by each, and then select an industry and an investment strategy in the target country that best fits its organizational competencies and strategic goals.

In recent years, global industrial boundaries have become blurred. As a result, competition is no longer viewed as limited to direct business rivals. Instead, it is seen as coming from all avenues by which customers seek value. Porter argues that the stronger each of these forces, the more limited the ability of established companies to raise prices and earn greater profits. A strong competitive force is regarded as a threat since it depresses financial returns. A weak competitive force is viewed as an opportunity, for it allows a firm to earn more profit. Firms that constitute a competitive force include local companies as well as foreign investors or marketers that may influence each of the five forces.

It is also important to recognize the industrial evolution and dynamism of each force. When operating in China, an MNC often confronts operational uncertainty and risks derived from the industrial or macro-national environment. The strength and source of each of the five forces can change through time. For instance, suppliers could become competitors by integrating forward, as could buyers by integrating backward. The task facing international managers is to choose the industry that will allow them to seize opportunities while overcoming threats from these forces.

MNCs need to verify the threat of new entrants, whether local or foreign, to their subsequent operations. New competitors can threaten existing businesses by bringing in additional production capacity. Unless product demand is also increasing, the additional capacity will push consumer costs down, resulting in less sales revenue and lower returns for all firms in the industry. The likelihood that firms will enter an industry is a function of two factors: barriers to entry and the expected retaliation from incumbents. Entry barriers clearly exist if firms find that entry into a new industry is difficult or puts them at a competitive disadvantage. Normally, incumbents develop such barriers so that potential entrants will seek other markets where entry barriers are relatively insignificant. The absence of high entry barriers increases the probability that a new entrant facing relatively less barriers in comparison with other entrants will be able to operate profitably, at the expense of incumbent profits. Therefore, competent MNCs should opt for industries where entry barriers are reasonably high in order to keep out competitors.

International expansion often necessitates an extension of the value chain and reliance on external resources. The relationship with local suppliers affects an MNC's processes and quality of production, which in turn influences operational success. Increasing prices and reducing product quality are means by which suppliers can exert power over firms competing within an industry. If unable to recover cost increases through its pricing structure, a firm's profitability will be reduced. The likelihood of forward integration is enhanced when suppliers have substantial resources and provide the industry's firms with highly differentiated products. In the process of internationalization, MNCs should choose industries in which the bargaining power of suppliers is relatively low or does not have a critical effect on firm operations.

The prominent objective of most MNCs in expanding into China is to enhance their overall market power while improving their competitive position in the target market. The relationship with local buyers plays a large part in determining organizational reputation, customer loyalty, and gross profit margin. In general, buyers (customers of the focal industry or firm) prefer to purchase products at the lowest possible price, which means the industry earns the lowest acceptable rate of return on its invested capital. Buyers bargain for higher quality, greater levels of service, and lower prices by encouraging competitive battles amongst firms in an industry. When MNCs invest in China where they have greater bargaining power than the buyers, they can manipulate transactions and increase sales prices. Product differentiation and customer responsiveness in coping with demand changes and utility functions of segmented markets are important levers for enhancing MNC bargaining power over customers.

As a result of rapid technological change and reduction of entry barriers across borders, MNCs face increasingly greater competitive pressure from substitutes. The ongoing development of information technology is creating more and more new industries over time, further reinforcing threats of substitution. Substitute products are different goods or services that can perform similar or the same functions as the focal product. Functional substitutes place an upper limit on the prices firms can charge. In general, the threat of substitute products is strong when customers face few, if any, switching costs and when the substitute product's price is lower and/or its quality and performance capabilities are equal to or greater than established products. To reduce the attractiveness of substitution, firms must differentiate their offerings along dimensions that are important to their customers (e.g., price, product quality, delivery, after-sale service, and customer responsiveness). In selecting a target industry abroad, MNCs should assess the possible threat from substitute products manufactured by local firms or other foreign companies. The risk of substitutes directly influences the sustainability of a firm's competitive advantages and consequently, its competitive position in the foreign market. If MNCs have to choose an industry involving high risks of substitutes, the firm must at least maintain production and operation flexibility.

The vigor of competition among existing firms in an industry is undoubtedly the foremost factor to be considered. Competition has the most direct impact on a firm's entry, operations, marketing, and investment success. In many industries, firms compete actively with one another to achieve strategic competitiveness and earn above-average returns. To analyze the intensity of existing rivalry, MNCs may use such indicators as concentration, entry barriers, capital commitment, and minimum economy of scale. Competition among rivals is further stimulated when one or more firms identify an opportunity to improve their market position, which is usually by differentiating products/services or reducing costs/prices. Competitive pressure is particularly strong when an MNC is a late entrant into a foreign market. In this situation, the organizational capabilities of the firm are extremely crucial in determining whether or not it will survive. Strategic responses and adaptability to changes in the external environment are also important in heightening its competitive position. While it is natural that MNCs prefer less competitive industries in China, ceteris paribus, this choice is strongly influenced by strategic goals. For instance, if an MNC pursues cost minimization or exploits product factor advantages in the host country via production-export or global vertical integration, fierce competition in the host market will not constitute a major threat to the firm.

The competitive threat or munificence from distributors is another important force in international expansion. The supportiveness of indigenous distributors influences an MNC's profit margin, delivery efficiency, and customer responsiveness. As it is costly to establish a firm's own distribution system and less effective to use such a system to market products, MNCs often have to rely upon local distributors such as wholesalers, large retailers, exclusive agents, distribution centers, and even some host government-instituted distribution channels. Establishing a distribution network can be such a long process that foreign companies may be unable to seize market opportunities or align with contextual changes in a timely fashion. Building distribution networks in China can also be a complicated social investment. If the interpersonal or interorganizational relationship is constructed inappropriately, such networks will be unreliable. To overcome this liability of foreignness, MNCs therefore should verify that they will be able to collaborate with appropriate local distributors. Although a well-established distributor may possess greater bargaining power over the foreign company, its networks are essential for MNCs seeking market share and long-term profitability in the host country. Arranging long-term distribution agreements is advisable for MNCs that wish to mitigate possible threats from distributor bargaining power while benefiting from distributor competencies.

China's central and provincial governments are a critical structural force that MNCs must not overlook. Structural interference by the local government is generally based on two types of governmental policies, one related to industrial regulations and the other to FDI. Typical industrial policies used by the Chinese government include: (i) classification of industries as prohibited, restricted, permitted, or encouraged. Each category is treated differently in terms of taxation, financing, land rent, infrastructure access, and the like; (ii) ratification of projects in certain industries. In general, these industries are state monopolies or controlled; and (iii) preferential treatment for those MNCs which bring in more advanced technology, managerial skills, foreign exchange via export, or which substitute imported products. Discriminatory treatment is often designed by a government to rationalize its industrial structure, alleviate resource or price distortions across industries, create foreign exchange earnings, and modernize pillar industries.

In general, most developed countries provide foreign investors with national treatment, meaning that foreign companies enjoy the same treatment as local enterprises. The Chinese government, however, treats local and foreign investments differently, which is manifested in the following areas: (i) entry mode control, meaning that MNCs are allowed to enter into certain industries only through certain entry modes (e.g., joint ventures, co-production, technology transfers via international licensing or franchising, or build-operate-transfer). Generally, the host country government requires at least one state-owned enterprise to participate in the venture or collaboration; (ii) equity control, meaning that foreign investors are restricted from holding a certain percentage of equity in the joint venture. For instance, MNCs entering Chinese auto assembly industries can only maintain up to 49 percent of equity in the venture; (iii) location control, meaning that the government requires MNCs to locate projects in certain geographical regions. This requirement is expected to help boost regional economies by launching heavy investment in certain industries as planned by the central government. Projects in different locations are also taxed differently. Even within the same city, ventures in different locations can be subject to different treatment. The Chinese Economic and Technological Development Zones (ETDZs) provide more tax breaks than non-ETDZs within the same city or county; (iv) duration control, meaning that each FDI project should specify a term (number of years) in its joint venture contract. Although this term can be renewed, such renewal is not automatic but usually subject to a new round of approval by relevant governmental authorities;

(v) partner control, meaning that certain big projects must include local firms assigned by the government. These firms may or may not have a previous cooperative history with the foreign investors; (vi) timing control, meaning that the Chinese government may delay the approval of certain FDI projects for certain periods of time. This often occurs when the government and its agencies have over-approved new projects, surpassing the actual need for economic development. Major FDI policies may also be changed for a variety of economic and political reasons; (vii) project orientation control, meaning that each project must be identified in its application and confirmed by the government as belonging to one orientation category: export, technologically advanced, infrastructure, import-substitution, or local market. Each of these orientations is offered different treatment and support by the government. In general, the first three enjoy preferential treatment, including lower income tax and tariff rates, refund of value-added taxes, lower financing costs, better infrastructure access, governmental support, and cheaper land rent; and (viii) size control, meaning that projects with different investment sizes have to be ratified by different levels of the government. The greater the size, the higher the rank of the authority in charge. When plans change to increase a project's investment size, approval usually has to be obtained by the same authority that initially ratified the project.

Xerox in Shanghai is an illustrative example for the above discussions. It took Xerox four years (1983-1987) to negotiate a joint venture with China. Several local governments were eager for Xerox to select their region as the location site for the new company. Xerox ultimately chose Shanghai, primarily due to the presence of numerous component suppliers and skilled labor in the area.

During negotiations, the Chinese expressed a desire to export a large percentage of the products produced. However, Xerox encouraged the Chinese to initially focus on the needs of the domestic market. Since many companies in China were in the infancy stage, the decision was made to produce low-end to mid-level copiers which would meet domestic needs. Thus, the Xerox Shanghai facilities were designed to produce these products initially, but accommodate production of high-end products at a later date.

Xerox Shanghai did not wait for demand pressure to encourage development of high quality products or stimulate innovation. Instead, Xerox Shanghai substituted pressure from external forces with pressures from internal forces. The parent company, Xerox, practices a corporate quality control culture which is enforced in Xerox worldwide. Xerox also subjects supplied components to quality control standards. Further, Xerox Shanghai formed a customer satisfaction review board to ensure that product quality was upheld. As a result, Xerox Shanghai gained a very favorable reputation for reliable, quality products. By 1989, Xerox Shanghai had attained number one status in a market that was previously dominated by Japanese products. Thus, although the limited domestic demand did not create the pressure necessary to gain a competitive advantage, Xerox was able to create a more competitive atmosphere by creating internal pressures. This moved the demand conditions component of Porter's diamond in a more favorable direction.

As a compromise for gearing production towards domestic sales, the Chinese negotiated that 70 percent of the components used in production would be purchased from local vendors by the end of 1992. Although Xerox agreed, this would prove to be a very difficult task as none of the local vendors possessed the technical expertise or equipment to produce components at the quality level expected by Xerox Shanghai.

Both basic and advanced elements of factor endowments affect a location's competitive advantages. Basic factors are an inherent part of the nation including natural resources, climate, location, and demographics. On the other hand, advanced factors must be developed. Investing in general and higher education and training of individuals can facilitate the development of advanced factors which include communications infrastructure, sophisticated and skilled labor, research facilities, and technological know-how. Shanghai possessed the basic factors but lacked sufficient advanced factors. Nevertheless, Xerox selected Shanghai due to the availability of skilled workers and abundant component suppliers, even though the suppliers could not produce quality components. To resolve this situation, Xerox engaged in vendor development. Xerox's goal was to develop local suppliers by providing technology, equipment, and training in operational functions such as materials management, handling and accounting. This moved factor endowments in a more favorable direction.

Despite Xerox Shanghai's enormous investment in improving the quality of supplied parts, suppliers have still not attained economies of scale. Thus, the costs of locally sourced components continue to be higher than imported components. This results in higher price tags on the end product. Ultimately, the high end prices do not allow Xerox Shanghai to be competitive with other countries. Therefore, China's unfavorable condition in supporting industries inhibits Xerox Shanghai from exporting their products to other countries.

Government policies that directly affected the demand conditions in China included restrictions on the purchase of goods. The government policy affected the demand for copiers as customers experienced difficulty obtaining government purchase approvals. However, the Chinese government seemed inclined to grant approvals for customers purchasing products that were domestically produced. Thus, since Xerox Shanghai sourced most of their products locally, they eventually benefitted from the new law.

In conclusion, Xerox viewed China as a source of strengths that complemented their business of producing and selling copier machines and products. The strengths China possessed included low labor and design costs and a growing market for copier machines and products. Therefore, Xerox was determined to develop an environment in China that was conducive to success.

6.4 Assessing Structural Attributes

Structural attributes that are particularly important in China include industry profitability, sales growth, concentration level, asset intensity, growth of number of firms in an industry, capital requirements, and technological intensity. Within an industry, each attribute may have a different influence on firm operations. For instance, a growing industry may show sales growth but not necessarily profitability growth because of the heavy burden of classified or accumulated corporate income taxes in China. The important task of international managers, therefore, is to select a foreign industry that has structural characteristics best matched to the firm's strategic goals for expansion. Each individual attribute may have a different effect on the various aspects of international expansion success.

Interindustrial variance in profitability has been an enduring characteristic of most Chinese industries. In high profit industries, although competitive entry from both domestic and foreign firms can gradually erode supra-normal profits on invested capital, continued government involvement in the structural adjustment process can result in appreciable barriers to entry which enable established firms to maintain market power and competitive position for some time. Eastman Kodak, for instance, recently unveiled its $1 billion investment scheme in China under which three of China's seven enterprises in the photographic industry formed two joint ventures with Kodak, and another three received compensation funds to pledge not to cooperate with a third partner before December 31, 2001. Kodak expects that this aggressive approach will payoff as the company will be able to maintain its dominant position in this promising industry by that time. Giving permission only to Kodak, the government will not approve any other similar cooperative project with other foreign companies. These new joint ventures are now creating payoffs. For instance, in just four months after the start of production, the joint venture in Xiamen has generated 128 million yuan in income tax, exceeding the former state enterprise's total over the past 14 years.

Similarly, industry sales growth is a key component of market attractiveness for both local firms and foreign businesses. Growth serves as an indicator of disequilibrium (a condition favorably associated with entry) and as an indicator of industrial evolution. When an industry's sales growth is high, many new firms will enter the industry unless start-up costs or other non-government instituted entry barriers are extremely high. LG Chemical of Korea, for instance, recently jumped into China's plyvinyl chloride (PVC) sector and pooled $86 million for a Tianjin project and $70 million for another in Ningbo. The sector's sales growth has been over 60 percent annually. China, however, can only supply less than 50 percent of its demand for synthetic resins. Therefore foreign firms such as LG and American Xtal Technology, Inc. have entered the market in a very proactive way.

The concentration level of a target industry implies the degree of competition or monopoly that an MNC will face. If an MNC is able to invest and operate in a highly concentrated industry, it will more likely be able to achieve abnormal profits. If an MNC can sustain itself in a highly concentrated industry, it is likely to become one of the few oligopolists or monopolists in the industry, as characterized by holding a dominant market share and power. Because high concentration prevents free competition, the Chinese government has been wary of entry by Western MNCs into already concentrated local industries. Therefore, MNCs in these industries are likely to encounter high governmental intervention. In order to avoid such interference, MNCs should attain governmental support during entry and maintain good relationships with governmental authorities during operations. For instance, despite all of China's problems today, GM believes the country is still bound to be the world's largest car market in the future. They believe that losers will be those firms that came in halfway or not at all. The automobile industry in China is highly concentrated, providing participating firms an opportunity for oligopolistic advantages. Thus, GM has committed enormously to both the project in Shanghai and its relationship with the government. With government support, GM finished the factory in a lightning-fast 18 months. This project is GM's only fully integrated manufacturing and assembly plant outside its Saturn division. Early demand for its Buicks has exceeded expectations, and the plant easily hit its target of 20,000 cars in 1999.

However, the degree of inequality of firm shares in an industry does not necessarily reflect the vigor of competition. Governmental intervention and the existence of publically owned lead firms also have an influence. While the concentration ratio indicates an existing pattern of competition intensity, growth in the number of firms in an industry implies *ex post* patterns of competition that will eventually occur, depending upon the average length of time needed for a firm to reach full operation after entry in an industry. Therefore, this growth measure can be used as an important proxy for assessing the degree of competition in an industry. When a new industry emerges or the government deregulates or opens up an industry with pent-up demand, the number of firms, whether local or foreign, is expected to grow drastically as long as entry barriers are not too high. Over time, however, the increase in the number of firms in the industry is likely to boost competition, decrease disparities in profitability, and slow down local sales growth rates. For instance, Hawaii-based Bush Corp. established a 50-50 joint venture with Xinhua Financial Corp. in Beijing to offer financial consulting services to foreign investors and Chinese enterprises. Financial consulting has emerged as one of the fastest-growth industries in China, with the number of firms in the industry, mostly small, increasing over 30 percent annually. Fredy Bush, founder of Bush Corp., realizes that it is now the golden period for investing in this industry, and early movers will benefit more from the industrial prosperity than late entrants.

An industry's capital requirements affect an MNC's international expansion because it determines investment commitment, capital structure, and currency mix. While asset intensity has implications for levels of start-up and exit costs, capital requirements determine the level of dynamic commitment and economic exposure an MNC faces. In contrast to operations in a domestic setting, international investment often requires financing in local currencies from local commercial banks or other financial institutions. Local financing in China, however, faces more barriers and bears higher costs. This further impacts the MNC's capital structure, creating more difficulties for optimizing the capital structure of geographically dispersed businesses. On the other hand, full reliance on international financing may increase exchange risks if MNCs are focused on indigenous markets. It can reduce strategic flexibility if MNCs cannot diversify their sourcing and marketing activities. In recent years, many MNCs have chosen joint ventures to enter China in order to share the capital requirement with local partners. Risk and cost sharing is becoming increasingly necessary in rapidly changing industries. IBM, Siemens, and Toshiba each have financial strengths, yet still they formed alliances with Chinese partners to reduce their costs and risks. By keeping the levels of risk commensurate with each party, a joint venture tends to be more stable and has a more cooperative culture. BP-Amoco recently formed a $200 million acetic acid joint venture plant with China Petrochemical Corporation (Sinopec). As this project is its largest single investment in China, BP-Amoco was concerned about both capital requirements and local financing risks. Sinopec is certainly an ideal partner for this purpose because it is the largest state-owned, quasi-governmentally-run business in China.

Finally, an industry's technological intensity also influences an MNC's entry decision and operational outcomes. Competitive, innovative MNCs often prefer technologically intensive industries when entering China as it can help them overcome disadvantages of newness and foreignness. However, selecting this type of industry requires contributions of distinctive knowledge and technological skills. The payoff from such contributions can be highly uncertain in a Chinese industry because MNCs confront greater risks of imitation by local firms. The challenges of protecting uncompensated leakage of strategic assets are daunting. It is generally more difficult to maintain organizational control over international operations than over domestic ones. When international joint ventures are used as a vehicle for expansion into China's technologically intensive industry, this difficulty is magnified. MNCs thus need to make sure they are capable of achieving maximum payoffs from technological commitments in the course of choosing an industry. For instance, Merck Sharp & Dohme, one of the world's largest pharmaceuticals companies, is a highly innovative company which, in 1998, invested $1.8 billion for research and development worldwide. The company's technological skills have made the company become one of the most successful foreign investors in China's pharmaceuticals industry. The quality of its products such as antibiotic and vaccine is among the best in the market. To date, the company has established nine representative offices in China, including Beijing, Shanghai, Nanjing, Wuhan, Shenyang, and Hong Kong.

6.5 Diagnosing Structural Evolution

In selecting a target industry, an MNC should also identify the stage of its life cycle. This will provide insight into the demand side of the industry. Over time, most industries pass through a series of phases, from growth, through maturity, and eventually decline. The strength and nature of structural forces and attributes typically change as an industry evolves. This is particularly evident when analyzing existing and potential competition. International managers must be able to identify the current stage of a candidate industry and anticipate how long the industry will remain at that stage before moving to the next phase. The industry life cycle model is used by international managers to assess whether the company is able to take advantage of opportunities and counter emerging threats in light of its strategic goals. In general, the life cycle has a greater impact on those MNCs pursuing long term market power and a competitive position in the Chinese market than those seeking short term profits or using China as a manufacturing platform for worldwide export.

Five industrial environments can be identified in China, each linked to a distinct stage of an industry's life cycle: (1) embryonic; (2) growth; (3) shakeout; (4) mature; and (5) declining. An embryonic industry is one that is just beginning to develop (e.g., financial consulting in early 1990s). Growth is slow because of such factors as consumer unfamiliarity with the industry's product, high prices due to the inability of companies to reap any significant economies of scale, and less developed distribution channels. MNCs investing at this stage are generally recognized as first movers or early entrants who face many tradeoffs between preemptive opportunities and financial or operational risks. If opting for an embryonic industry, an MNC needs to assess whether it should, and can, capitalize on such opportunities while countering emerging threats. Ericsson plunged into the Chinese telecom market in early 1980s when most of its products were in the embryonic stage. By proactively utilizing its core technologies and carefully adapting to market changes in China, Ericsson is now one of the market leaders. The company has 3,700 employees, 23 agencies, and 9 joint ventures in China. China's telecom market became Ericsson's largest market in 1998.

Once market demand for the product begins to take off, a growth industry develops. First-time demand expands rapidly as many new consumers enter the market. In the internationalization process, investing in a growing industry in a target country is generally an ideal choice. A growth stage can be readily identified by evaluating growth of sales, profitability, output, and capital investments. This information is usually available from the statistical yearbooks or other periodicals. The length of the growth stage differs from industry to industry because it depends on such factors as entry barriers, capital requirements, economies of scale, technological requirements, risk and cost factors, and the openness of the industry to new local and foreign entrants. MNCs often encounter daunting challenges when taking the plunge into a growth industry because the Chinese government is likely to impose more entry or operational barriers on their fastest growing sectors. This is done in order to protect domestic firms or control the speed and pattern of foreign investment. The U.S.'s Allied Signal Inc. entered China in 1986 and now produces a variety of energy-efficient products like non-crystal power distribution transformers. Most of these products are in the growth stage in the industry. In order to avoid governmental interference, the company has provided millions of dollars worth of scholarships to Beijing's Qinghua University, Shanghai's Fudan, and five other top universities. It has funded 13 joint ventures and wholly-owned enterprises in China.

During the shakeout stage, market demand approaches saturation. Foreign companies may consider entering a shakeout industry if they aim to exploit short term profitability or establish a presence in the market for exploring product, market, or technological niches in China. This stage can be identified by looking at changes in the growth pattern over time. In general, if entry barriers are low to both local and foreign firms, the shakeout stage will not last very long. It is critical for foreign companies to find a market niche or new opportunities from product differentiation when they plunge into a shakeout industry. DSM, which also owns Gist-Brocades, recently established a second joint venture in China to produce APA, an intermediate for semisynthetic penicillin. While China's pharmaceutical industry is now moving toward the shakeout stage, semisynthetic penicillin is a promising niche resting in the growing phase with 15 percent annual growth.

An industry enters the mature stage as the shakeout stage ends. Although investing in a mature industry is generally inadvisable, some MNCs may choose to enter anyway if their objective is to shift home manufacturing sites to China where production factors cost much less. In other words, when an MNC's foreign operations are not designed to explore the economic benefits of pent-up demand, the impact of an industry's life cycle stage is minimal. In fact, MNCs with this orientation may be able to acquire more benefits from a mature industry by taking advantage of greater bargaining power with suppliers. Rockwell, an international electronic controls and communications company, recently opened three new facilities in China with a total investment of $30 million. The industry was approximately forty years old in China, yet Rockwell still benefited because of the low production costs. China was used by the company as the critical production center to expand its market presence in other international markets. Its elevated bargaining power over a large array of local suppliers during this stage allowed Rockwell to further decrease the purchase price.

An industry enters the decline stage when growth becomes negative for various reasons, including demographical changes, technological substitution, and international competition. Although there is no economic logic for local market-oriented MNCs to enter a declining industry in a host country, MNCs focused on minimizing costs may still benefit from starting production at a host site as a platform for export or vertical integration. Medium and small MNCs may use such sites for export to neighboring countries, its home country market, or other countries. As a result of increasing regionalization and gradual removal of trade barriers worldwide, this strategy will enable medium and small international firms to maximize benefits from their competencies in international distribution, strategic flexibility, and entrepreneurial orientation. Many Asian MNCs have successfully operated in China using this strategy. For instance, the impact of structural evolution is small on Nike's investments and operations in China. Nike maintains a very flexible market orientation by integrating its production in China with the rest of its global network. When the life cycle of certain products in the industry becomes mature in China, the company will focus more on other foreign markets and simply use China as the export platform.

It is generally advisable for MNCs to select a growth industry when expanding into a target country. This is particularly true for MNCs seeking long term market shares and a strong competitive position in the local industry. Today, most Western MNCs use this orientation when investing in China. An embryonic industry appears to be an appropriate choice if an MNC wants to pursue first mover advantages. It is critical for MNCs to know the industry life cycle stages of both home and China's industries. A mature industry at home may be embryonic or growing in China. MNCs pursuing market power should be able to preempt first mover advantages not only in a home industry but also in embryonic industries in the Chinese market. Firms that aim at cost minimization, transnational distribution, local market niches, or vertical integration within a global network may consider entering mature or declining industries where they can still benefit from cheaper production factors or comparative advantages in the host country. The market orientation (local market vs. export market), strategic goals (profit vs. market share), distinctive competencies, rival behavior, and host country government policies are all important factors in making a life cycle analysis before selecting an industry.

6.6 An Integrated Decision Framework

Each set of industrial dynamics presented above, namely structural dimensions, forces, attributes, and evolution, is useful for analyzing and selecting a Chinese industry. Each set as well reveals a different focus that is idiosyncratic yet complementary to the other sets of industrial dynamics. Collectively, they serve as the foundation of an industry selection framework. In this core, the structural dimension perspective (structural uncertainty, complexity, and deterrence) mirrors the nature of the target industry, while consideration of structural forces (supplier, buyer, potential or existing rival, distributor, substitute, and government) uncovers the competitive situation of the industry. Meanwhile, the structural attributes analysis (profitability, sales growth, concentration, asset intensity, growth of number of firms, capital requirements, and technological intensity) reveals industrial traits and the structural profile, and the diagnosis of structural evolution (embryonic, growth, shakeout, maturity, and decline) displays a Chinese industry's life cycle stage and corresponding characteristics of each phase.

The above four perspectives interact with one another. Structural dimensions are associated with all other structural dynamics. Industrial uncertainty, complexity, and deterrence contain the dynamics of each of the structural forces and in combination. For instance, if structural forces are munificent, structural deterrence will be low. Some structural attributes, such as concentration and growth of number of firms, are interrelated with structural complexity and deterrence. Structural evolution reflects the longitudinality of every structural dimension. In addition, structural forces and structural attributes are linked because the former provide conditions which nourish the latter. For example, favorable conditions in terms of existing rivalry, new entrants, buyer, and government segments may spur industrial growth in profit and sales. Moreover, structural attributes such as sales growth and concentration change over time along with the life cycle of an industry. These attributes are generally more favorable in early stages of structural evolution. Lastly, the competitive pattern of structural forces alters as structural phases evolve. For instance, the threat of potential rivalry is certainly more fierce in a growth stage than in a decline stage.

Given this complementarity, MNCs should identify and verify structural dynamics in an integrated fashion to assess specific overseas industries. For example, all three sets of structural dynamics were relevant to Motorola's decision to enter the Chinese telecommunications industry. Analysis of structural forces showed that the degree of existing and potential rivalries from both local and foreign firms were low, as was the threat of substitutes. Buyer and supplier bargaining power in the early years after entry was also relatively weak. The life cycle stage of the industry was embryonic in the early 1980s, and Motorola knew that the pent-up demand for its products could create tremendous market opportunities. Finally, although uncertainty was expected to be high, the industry's sales and profitability growth were also high. Moreover, the high asset intensity of the industry decreased the threat of new entrants and increased the company's bargaining power with the local government. By allocating most of its FDI projects to the east coast of China and to major municipalities such as Tianjin and Shanghai, Motorola largely mitigated the risks of structural deterrence.

Longitudinal and Comparative Pattern

Once the above four sets of industrial dynamics are cohesively and simultaneously examined, it is crucial for MNCs to analyze the industry and its opportunities and threats both longitudinally and comparatively. Structural dimensions, forces, attributes, and life cycle stages of an industry in China are generally different from those at home. In other words, MNCs are often unfamiliar with industrial dynamics in the Chinese context unless they have already operated there long enough. As most MNCs seek long-term economic benefits in China, MNCs need to scan, analyze, and interpret structural dimensions, forces, attributes, and the life cycle based on longitudinal information as a prerequisite for analyzing target markets where fluctuations frequently occur. This *ex ante* longitudinal assessment of structural dynamics, as well as opportunities and threats identified from such dynamics, solidifies an understanding of industrial characteristics and reduces the likelihood of negative consequences arising from information asymmetry. This longitudinal appraisal improves bounded rationality of a Chinese industry's dynamics, thus reducing transaction costs incurred during international expansion. Robert Bosch GMBH of Germany has formed six joint ventures in China, four of which produce automotive equipment and parts while other two are in the consumer goods sector. The company did not participate in this industry in China until late 1989, after a longitudinal study of the industry. Although the political environment was unfavorable at the time when it entered the country, the company believed that the market demand for auto parts and equipments was noticeably high. Bosch is now one of the market leaders in the auto part sector, and recently formed Bosch (China) Investment Holding Ltd. in Beijing, an umbrella company coordinating its nationwide businesses in the country.

In addition, MNCs need to compare the target industry's structural dynamics with those of home and other foreign countries. In recent years there has been an increasing tendency for industrial changes in one country to partially correlate with those in others as the result of technological advancement, international competition, capital flow, and reduction of entry barriers. Therefore, a firm should use a home or third country as a benchmark for assessing structural dynamics as well as opportunities and threats in a target Chinese industry. This comparison helps an MNC find an appropriate industrial setting which will provide maximum economic returns. As seizing opportunities and mitigating threats in a foreign industry depends upon an MNC's distinctive abilities and competitive strategies, this comparison also helps the firm to best match its competence-opportunity configuration and align the strategy-environment relationship. The ultimate leaders in the global marketplace are normally those firms which establish such configurations and alignments. AMP, Australia's largest life insurance company, launched a big housing project in Shanghai. The project costed a total of $60 million and acted as a springboard for the insurer to enter the real estate markets in other large Chinese cities. Despite the fact that the Chinese real estate market has passed its most prosperous period, the industry remains much more attractive compared to that in Australia. Further, housing is still in serious shortage in many smaller cities in China. The segmented nature of the industry offers AMP tremendous opportunities in the dozens of cities with a population of at least one million. AMP has also put $600 million worth of investment into China's transportation and telecom sectors in Beijing, Nanjing, Dalian, Xiamen and several other cities since it entered China in 1997.

Capability, Objective and Competitor Behavior

Evaluating whether or not the firm has the ability to seize opportunities and counter threats is important. This match often determines the financial and operational outcomes of international expansion in a dynamic, complex market. Misallocation of distinctive resources will waste not only internal resources but also external opportunities. The ability of an MNC to survive and succeed in today's turbulent international environment largely depends on its dynamic capabilities during international expansion. Dynamic capabilities refer to a firm's ability to diffuse, deploy, and use tacit, organizationally embedded resources in order to attain a sustained competitive advantage. Capability exploration (rent generation) and capability building (organizational learning) are two critical aspects of the dynamic capabilities needed during international expansion. Rent-generation, or firm-specific, strategic resources are critical to both gaining a competitive advantage and determining firm-level strategies which can exploit such advantages. Without such firm-specific capabilities (financial, technological, operational, and organizational), it is difficult for an MNC to explore and exploit preemptive, rent-yielding opportunities in a targeted foreign industry.

Dynamic learning capabilities are also critical. They ensure the evolutionary development of sustainable advantages and generate new bundles of resources. International expansion always calls for organizational learning to overcome the liability of foreignness. On the one hand, international expansion provides learning opportunities through exposure to new markets, internalization of new concepts, ideas from new cultures, access to new resources, and exposure to new competitors and terms of competition. On the other hand, learning does not take place in a vacuum, but rather results from coping with specific industrial environments. While rent-generating resources are necessary for MNCs exploring market opportunities, learning capabilities are imperative for trying to reduce vulnerability to contextual variabilities. Combining capabilities by integrating and synthesizing internal resources and external learning and applying them to the competitive environment, is vital to an MNC's survival and growth in a foreign industry.

Volkswagen is a good example illustrating the importance of an appropriate alignment between industry participation and firm capability. The firm has two joint ventures, namely Shanghai Volkswagen, which was established in 1985 with Shanghai Automotive Industry Corp., and FAW-Volkswagen, established in 1991 with First Auto Works in northern Changchun city. The two together maintain 60 percent of the market share of the passenger car sector. Its experience, adaptability, and proactive orientation helped the company successfully establish its presence in the Chinese auto industry in the 1980s. In order to keep its leading position and amid rising competition in this biggest potential market for passenger cars in the world, Volkswagen has set up a world-class research and development center in Shanghai. Shanghai Volkswagen alone already had more than 500 research and development staff. Its highly developed sales and service network as well as its strong ties with local industries boost the company's dominant competitive position. Volkswagen will further invest $1.6 billion in the next few years to capture the lucrative middle-to-upper segment of China's demand while solidifying the compact cars business for China's lower-income consumers.

Another match lies between a firm's objectives and the emergence of opportunities or threats in the Chinese market. Needless to say, every foreign market has opportunities that MNCs can explore or exploit. However, it is not realistic for an MNC to plunge into every market because its distinctive resources and competitive edge are limited. Therefore, an MNC's industry selection should be linked to its strategic goals. These goals include not only its objectives in operating in China (e.g., local market share, risk reduction, financial returns) but also its goals for overall global expansion. For example, if an MNC seeks horizontal FDI (i.e., FDI in the same industry abroad as in firm operations at home) or forward vertical FDI (i.e., FDI in a Chinese industry that sells the output of a firm's domestic production processes), the firm should opt for a fast-growing, low risk, less competitive industry. By contrast, if an MNC seeks backward vertical FDI (i.e., FDI in an industry abroad that provides input for production at a firm's domestic or other foreign subunits), it should attach more value to the comparative advantages of production factors of the host country. In principle, this decision should be made in such a way that the company can optimize goal fulfillment while using limited resources.

Let us take a look at the case of Otis Elevator, a wholly owned subsidiary of United Technologies Corporation and the world's largest manufacturer and servicer of elevators, escalators, moving walkways, and shuttle systems. These products are now all profitable in China, the world's largest elevator market. Otis Elevator has captured a notable 25 percent of this market. Otis's presence in the market is so predominant that its two most threatening competitors, Schindler and Mitsubishi, together share only 25 percent, making the market oligopolistic. Otis's strategic objective underlying entering China is very clear: long-term market share and corresponding returns. Otis predicted when it entered the market that China's total building projects would take up nearly one-fourth of the world's total. Indeed, since the 1980s, the flourishing of hotel and office buildings has created a high-rise rush in China. In Beijing, there are already eight high-rises over 100 meters high. Shopping mall, hotel, and office building construction creates a huge market for high-quality, high-speed elevators and escalators. To achieve its strategic ends, Otis took the plunge as the first mover into the Chinese elevator industry, which was uncharted water to most foreign companies in the early 1980s.

When promising opportunities emerge, other MNCs are expected to move in as well. If a firm enters a promising industry overseas, it will face competition from local businesses and other foreign rivals. Thus, before making the final decision on industry selection, an MNC should analyze the behavior of its major rivals. This means that it should ask such questions as whether the firm should go if its rival does, and when and how. If an MNC enters a target industry as a first mover, managers need to make sure that the first mover advantages outweigh the disadvantages. It should be able to seize first-mover opportunities in products, markets, and technologies, and sustain the first-mover position by driving out late competitors. If an MNC will enter the target industry as a follower or late mover, managers should probe whether it can earn risk-adjusted net profits from the industrial environment, achieve benefits from the first mover's experience and learning curve, and develop competitive advantages in the industry against other rivals.

Johnson & Johnson entered the Chinese pharmaceuticals industry as the first mover and recently enjoyed annual sales growth in excess of 40 percent. Before moving into the market, the company knew that other competitors like Squibb were to enter the industry as well. In order to obtain a head-start effect, Johnson & Johnson quickly set up a joint venture in Xi'an, which became the pioneer foreign firm in China's pharmaceuticals sector. By the end of 1995, there were more than 1,500 foreign-invested enterprises and another 3,000 state factories producing local brands that cost 30-50 percent less. As the first foreign mover, Johnson & Johnson is now benefiting from superior customer loyalty, organizational reputation, a strong relationship with the business community, and technological leadership.

6.7 Conclusion

The selection of a Chinese industry and a direct investment is a system project in which the firm must analyze structural dimensions, forces, attributes, and evolution, employ an interactive and integrated approach to appraising all structural dynamics, and identify opportunities and threats longitudinally and comparatively. Moreover, the industry selection decision should be coupled with the firm's strategic objectives, organizational capabilities and analysis of competitor behavior. International managers need to ensure that the firm has the ability to successfully enter the target industry, efficiently explore market opportunities and overcome threats, and compete against major rivals in the industry. If these are probable, then the firm's goals will most likely be accomplished.

MNCs should configure their market and strategic orientations as well as other entry strategies such as entry mode, timing, location, and partner selection with structural dynamics of a Chinese industry. Market orientation choices include local, export, and dual market foci. In principle, an MNC's orientation should be structured such that it can not only achieve its goals but also keep a certain degree of flexibility in responding to structural changes in a host industry and beyond. Similarly, strategic orientation (prospector, analyzer, defender, and reactor) must be arranged in a way that an MNC will be innovative enough to maximize benefits from structural dynamics without assuming risks it cannot control. Entry mode should be arranged to facilitate rent-yielding from industrial dynamics. When a host industry is undergoing growth, the wholly-owned entry mode seems a better choice than the joint venture. Because timing of entry always involves trade-offs between economic returns and investment risks, whether an MNC should pursue early-mover advantages by entering an embryonic industry or seek niche benefits as a late mover depends on the firm's experience, competency, and strategic goals behind internationalization. As China is economically and socio-culturally diverse, different locations may present heterogeneous structural dynamics. Therefore, industry selection and location selection decisions should be coupled properly so as to maximize risk-adjusted net wealth from international expansion. Further, partnering with a competent local firm can assist an MNC in accessing an ideal industry, escalating its competitive edge, and alleviating operational uncertainties and financial risks. Thus, industry selection should align with decisions such as whether to collaborate with a local partner and what organizational attributes the partner firm should possess.

Cases

1 SIEMENS IN CHINA

Company Introduction

Corporate History

Siemens AG was founded 150 years ago in Germany by Werner von Siemens, whose business skills made him a pioneer in electrical engineering and a world class entrepreneur. His brother, Wilhelm, had filed a patent in England for a gold electroplating method. Sale of patent rights provided the two brothers with enough income for Werner Siemens to work on his own research on the telegraph, which he believed would be the technology of the future. Siemens decided to go into business with a skilled mechanical engineer, Johann Georg Halske. They formed a company, Telegraphen-BauAnstalt von Siemens & Halske, in Berlin in October 1847.

In the early 1850s, the company was already successful enough to set up branch offices in London and St. Petersburg. In 1866, Siemens discovered the dynamo-electric principle and invented the dynamo-machine. The invention marked the dawn of the age of electrical engineering. The German term for the field of applied electricity, Elektrotechnik, was coined by Siemens. Siemens aimed the company towards electrical drives, lighting, and power engineering. By the time he retired from managing the company in 1890, its work force had grown to 5,500.

After his death two years later, his sons took over the company. Siemens went public in 1897 as a stock corporation under the name Siemens & Halske AG. In 1903, it merged with Elektrizitats-AG vorm. Schuckert & Co. to form Siemens-Schuckertwerke GmbH. Then, Siemens and AEG together founded Telefunken, which took the lead in radio and, later, television. By 1913, Siemens has sales reaching 400 million marks and a work force of 63,000.

In 1914, the company had subsidiaries in 10 countries and had set up 168 branch offices, but the first world war hit the company hard. All of its foreign assets were lost. Under the management of Carl Friedrich, Werner von Siemens' third son, the company made a big turn around. Over the next two decades he rebuilt the company. In 1925, Siemens took over a company called Reiniger, Gebbert & Schall, which specialized in electro-medical equipment, to form Siemens-Reiniger-Werke AG. By 1929, the Siemens work force has risen to 138,000. Then the Great Depression forced the company to lay off 60,000 workers. Nevertheless, by 1939 the work force has risen again to over 183,000. Sales likewise fluctuated, rising from 315 million marks in 1924 to 820 million marks in 1929 and dropping to 330 million in 1933. By 1939, sales hit one billion marks for the first time. Siemens was then the world's largest electrical company. It was hit hard by World War Two, however, losing 80 percent of its assets by the end of the war.

Siemens slowly rebuilt again. It became Germany's largest employer, with a work force of 200,000 in 1960, 300,000 in 1972. Company sales increased from 1 billion marks in 1951 to over 5 billion in 1962 and then to 11 billion in 1970. During the early 1950s, Siemens concentrated on consumer goods manufacturing at Siemens-Electrogerate AG. In 1966, Siemens merged Siemens & Halske AG, Siemens Schuckertwerke AG, and Siemens-Reiniger-Werke AG to form Siemens AG, Berlin und Munchen. Household appliances passed to a joint venture, Bosch-Siemens-Hausgerate GmbH, in 1967. In 1969, Siemens and AEG formed the Kraftwerk Union (KWU) to become the leading energy company. In 1977, KWU passed fully into Siemens' hands and has been part of the Power Generation Group since 1987. In 1978, Siemens took full control of Osram GmbH, a company it had co-founded in 1919 with AEG and Auer Gesellschaft. Today, Siemens AG is based in Munich, Germany under the management of Dr. Heinrich v. Pierer, President and Chief Executive Officer.

Siemens' Seven Principles

Besides being a great inventor, Siemens was a pioneer in the field of social policy. He believed that motivated employees were the basis for any company's success. He introduced benefits such as pension plans, nine-hour work days, and profit-sharing to his employees. His legacy remains encoded in the seven principles upheld by Siemens throughout its worldwide operations today.

i) Customers shape action: A top priority at Siemens is providing outstanding value to its customers; company success depends on customer satisfaction.

ii) Innovation shapes the future: Siemens encourages experimenting and imagination in its employees. Employees both promote and draw upon one another's ideas.

iii) Business success means profits: Siemens works to achieve profits while striving for industry leadership and a steady increase in the addition of economic value for the company.

iv) Excellent leadership fosters top results: All managers at Siemens are expected to set clear, ambitious, and inspiring goals.

v) Learning is the key to continuous improvement: Siemens measures itself against its competitors. Siemens' employees welcome and offer open feedback and learn from their mistakes.

vi) Cooperation has no limits: Cooperation is characterized by personal integrity, mutual respect, and open communication.

vii) Corporate citizenship is our global commitment: Siemens safeguards its people's future through ongoing training and education. It also believes that cultural differences enrich the organization.

Major Businesses

Over 150 years of innovation has made Siemens AG a market leader in technology and electronics. Siemens has been moving gradually from electrical engineering towards electronics, especially information technology and semiconductors. In 1989, the company reorganized to adopt a new structure built around 17 groups that better suit its current activities. In 1990, Siemens bought Nixdorf Computer AG, thereby becoming the largest PC maker in Europe.

Siemens' business segments and products include the following:

Energy – Siemens produces turbines and electric generators.

Industry – Siemens provides manufacturing and process industry products such as integrated automation and drive systems.

Information and Communications – Siemens designs and installs operator and business telephone networks.

Health Care – Siemens produces technologically advanced medical electronics.

Components – Siemens is one of the top three leading providers of semiconductor components.

Transportation – Siemens designs and builds high-speed trains and all-purpose locomotives, vehicle locking systems, and passenger protection systems.

Lighting – Siemens produces general-purpose and automotive lights for both the private and public sectors. It recently invented Plannon, the world's first mercury-free flat lamp that is as thin as a tile.

Financial Services – Siemens does counter-trade financing, administrates pension funds for institutional investors, and leases equipment.

Household Appliances – Siemens has invented such useful appliances as the washing machine and dryer.

Siemens AG is represented at 500 production sites in 50 countries throughout Europe, America, Asia, Africa, and the Pacific. Siemens generates 70 percent of its sales and employs more than half of its employees outside of Germany.

Siemens In China

Siemens began doing business in China in the late 1800s, when it supplied the nation with its first pointer telegraph and installed its first electrical generator, used to light up the Shanghai harbor. After China was opened up in 1979, Siemens opened its first representative office in Beijing in 1982. In 1985, a memorandum was signed between Siemens and China's mechanical engineering, electrical, and electronics industries. Between 1996 and 1998, Siemens was able to obtain contracts for approximately 45 percent of the SDH trunk lines for the whole China Backbone Network, which runs from Harbin in northern China to Guangzhou in the south and across the country from Qingdao in the east to Urumqi and Lhasa in the west.

Siemens Ltd. China was founded in Beijing in 1994 as a holding company to support Siemens' 45 local joint ventures with investment and help in sales and marketing, services, personnel management, purchasing, and financial and currency related matters. Approximately 27,000 people are employed by Siemens China and its local joint ventures. Sales exceeded DM 3.5 billion in 1998.

Siemens saw that it was wise to expand in China because so many regions there did not yet have the services and products Siemens could provide. Related and support industries for Siemens are all tied together, since Siemens not only provides products but also the raw materials and power for constructing them.

China was a non-competitive market when Siemens first turned its attention there. Governmental policies also influenced its choice. China was going through some major changes that made it more attractive to foreign corporations, including providing incentives such as tax credits for companies operating in specific high-tech sectors. The growing income in China also attracted Siemens.

External Environment

Siemens mainly serves the government in the energy and transportation sectors. Siemens has established a power generation committee which is responsible for maintaining plants and systems that produce electricity from fossil, nuclear, and regenerative sources. It also oversees instrumentation and other equipment used in fuel assemblies and nuclear synthesis processes.

After producing energy, Siemens is still responsible for transporting it to users. It established a power transmission and distribution committee to control the equipment and components used by turnkey power systems. In the transportation sector, Siemens produces rail signaling, safety, control, and turnkey systems and mass transit and main-line rolling stocks. Siemens also manufactures electronics systems and components for automotive companies operated by the government.

These capabilities are crucial to its success in China. China's rapid economic growth calls for foreign capital and technology which will boost its energy industry. By the turn of the century, China will require U.S.$20 billion in foreign investment to meet its goals, which include a total installed capacity of 300 MW of electrical power, Siemens' short-term goals in China include satisfying increasing energy and transportation demands by improving efficiency through continual technological innovation, as well as protecting the environment for the common good.

Siemens has already established 13 operating companies in China for the production of switching gears, transformers, power cables, and other related equipment. Siemens is involved in 9 coal-fired power plant projects which together have a total capacity to produce about 8,820 megawatts of energy. This puts Siemens first among the international power-plant suppliers in the Chinese market. Siemens was also awarded the first contract to construct a nuclear power plant in China. The Siemens Power Generation Group (KWU) has planned and supplied almost the entire instrumentation and control (I&C) equipment for the Lianyungang plant, valued at about DM300 million. Teamed up with Voith and GE, Siemens is also participating in the world's largest hydro-electric power plant, the Three Gorges Project.

In the transportation sector, Siemens offers all forms of mass rail transportation systems, ranging from underground lines, light railways, and long distance commuter trains to ICE systems as will be used in the proposed Beijing-Shanghai Line. Siemens heads a German consortium responsible for a subway project in Shanghai worth DM550 million. Siemens is responsible for the overall management of Guangzhou Metro Construction in addition to the delivery of safe and sophisticated electrical, mechanical, and electronic systems to the project. Siemens has also built an electronic interlocking system for rail safety in North Fuyang and automated China's postal system.

Siemens provides information and communications systems, medical technology, and electronic components to various businesses. The information and communications sector is aimed at ordinary businesses which need technological improvement. Siemens provides mobile phones, Internet services, electronic commerce, local and wide area networks, database design and administration, web site design and hosting, and other such services. It creates complete packages aimed at companies in China which have abundant financial resources but lack technology.

Another major customer base for Siemens includes hospitals and research centers. Siemens provides a wide spectrum of medical technologies, including x-ray, angiography, therapy, CT, MR, ultrasound, and electro-medical equipment, nuclear medicines, and imaging workstations. Its medical equipment is highly accurate in assisting doctors in improving the quality of life for their patients. Siemens is transferring state-of-the-art medical technology to China through joint ventures. September 1992 saw the foundation of Siemens Shanghai Medical Equipment Ltd. (SSME), a joint venture handling the manufacture and sales of computer tomography systems. It is the first Siemens manufacturing factory producing such equipment outside Germany.

Siemens provides semiconductor ICs and devices, passive components, electron tubes, and VAC products to manufacturers in China. Siemens is the only European company involved in future-oriented chip technology and the development of 64- and 256-megabite chips. The company has adopted the highest quality standards of chip production. Its high-tech, cost-efficient components play an important role in information technology such as telecommunications systems, computers, mobile phones, transportation systems, and manufacturing control systems. It also produces the relays and connectors, hybrids, fiber-optic components, and ferrite necessary for these industries.

Targeting household customers is a relatively new direction for Siemens. Siemens has established three joint ventures in this sector in China. BSW Household Appliances Co., Ltd. has already become one of the leading Chinese manufacturers of washing machines conforming to Asian design requirements. BSW Kitchen Electrical Appliances Co., Ltd. produces extractor hoods, gas cookers, and many other appliances for the kitchen. BSY Cooling Appliances Co., Ltd. produces freezers. Siemens has imported advanced technology from Germany enabling it to produce CFC-free refrigerators, making a contribution to environmental protection in China.

Siemens also produces lighting appliances through OSRAM. OSRAM is one of the three leading lamp manufacturers in the world, with sales of DM5.7 billion in the 1995-1996 fiscal year. Since 1995, OSRAM has expanded and setup offices and a factory in China. The OSRAM Foshan Lighting Co. Ltd. joint venture was established in 1995 by OSRAM, PLC (a lamp vendor in Hong Kong), and FELCO, all top lighting manufacturers. OSRAM holds 85 percent of the share in this company, PLC 10 percent and FELCO 5 percent. The total investment in the factory in Foshan will be in excess of U.S.$50 million. Over the past two years, OSRAM Foshan has introduced advanced German lighting technology to China. It manufactures T8 fluorescent lamps, compact fluorescent lamps, high pressure discharge lamps and automotive and motorcycle lamps. In order to better serve its customers, OSRAM has set up offices in Beijing, Shanghai, Chengdu, and Guangzhou.

With 99 GSM mobile telephone networks in 57 countries, Siemens is one of the world's leaders in digital mobile communications. The company has built 47 GSM networks in Asia alone. It is estimated that every third GSM phone call worldwide uses a Siemens system.

Siemens landed two major orders for mobile phone networks. Siemens' Information & Communication Networks Group has signed a contract with Anhui PTA to expand its global system network for mobile communication in the Anhui Province. This order alone is worth over DM240 million. Siemens will provide ten switching systems and more than 500 base stations to boost the Anhui PTA's network capacity from its current 300,000 subscribers to over 1.1 million subscribers by the end of the year. Siemens also received an order worth some DM120 million from the Shanghai PTA to expand its mobile phone network. Siemens technology will be used to nearly double the system's capacity, adding 400,000 subscribers to the current half million.

Although Siemens is a powerful company, it has still been suffering a loss and shrinking over the past few years. Existing competitors and new entrants have taken advantage of this situation and started an attack on Siemens' market share. Siemens continues to lose customers in most sectors other than energy and transportation. These two sectors remain stable because they require high technology and large scale facilities which are difficult to compete with. Siemens lost the largest piece of the cake in the household and individual sectors. Its main competitors are Changhong, Shanghai Bell Telephone, Rainbow, and Mahushita CPT.

Siemens has established many entry barriers against new entrants. Its level of technology is difficult for other companies to acquire. It has also set up good distribution channels by forming strong relationships with suppliers and buyers. This also leads to a lot of government contracts, such as for the nuclear power plant in China. Siemens also acquired the last portion of the limited network backbone in China. Therefore, it has partial monopolistic control over the industry. Siemens also makes use of its long history and demonstrable record of expertise to exploit the experience curve and compete effectively. Furthermore, because of its size, it can always use economies of scale and scope to lower production costs and stabilize the environment in the production line. For all these reasons, existing competitors and new entrants hit a brick wall when they try to take market share from Siemens.

Siemens' many accomplishments in China cannot be ignored. It already fills a large part of China's energy and transportation needs. Doing business in China can be complicated, however. Periodic political instability can affect the source of suppliers and international demand. Distribution channels are difficult to set up. Relationships are key to doing any business in China. Bribery and corruption are illegal, but happen everywhere. At the least, companies operating in China must expect to take people out to dinner regularly. Governmental policies have also restricted the markets to which foreign investors have access. Four industries are considered pillar industries by the government, however, including electronics, energy, construction and transportation. Fortunately, Siemens' businesses fall within all of these industries, enabling it to receive favorite treatment by the government.

The major features of the electronics industry in China can be summarized according to a few characteristics. Competition is tougher than in other parts of the world and brand awareness is more important. Products made in China are comparable to imported ones, but often come with lower prices. Investment in local manufacturing is usually profitable. Traditional electronics exports amounted to U.S.$1.28 billion in 1996, 6.8 percent of the total. This was a decrease of 27 percent over the previous year. Value-added export processing increased by 39 percent, amounting to U.S.$17.37 billion, or 91.4 percent of total export. Three electronics categories make up 63.6 percent of total imports to China: communications products (U.S.$4.8 billion), computers and parts (U.S.$2.7 billion), and IC and micro components (U.S.$2.42 billion). Growth rates for the industry differ by geographical location. They are increasing in Beijing, Tianjin, Hebei, Jilin, Liaoning, Fujian, Shandong, Guangdong, Hunan, Henan, Sichuan, and Shanxi. The output value for 1996 was greater than 10 billion Yuan in each of the following areas: Guangdong, Jiangsu, Shanghai, Beijing, Tianjin, Shandong, Zhejiang, Fujian, Sichuan, Shaanxi, and Liaoning. Together, these accounted for more than 80 percent of the total output value in 1996. The following lists show Siemens' major competitors in China (page 248).

The economic situation has not been good in China recently. The State Statistical Bureau blames the Asian financial crisis and summer floods for the decline in growth. Millions of workers have

Top Ten Electronics Companies by Sales (Million Yuan) in 1996

Rank	Name	Sales	Main Products	Location
1	Changhong	10,745	CTV, components	Sichuan
2	Legend	7,744	computer software	Beijing
3	Rainbow	6,300	CTV tube, CTV	Xian
4	Konka	6,025	CTV, HiFi	Shenzhen
5	Stone	5,726	computer software	Beijing
6	Panda	5,451	CTV, telecom, HiFi	Nanjing
7	Shanghai Broadcast TV	5,110	CTV, CTV tube	Shanghai
8	Shanghai Bell Telephone	4,575	Telecom switchins	Shanghai
9	TCL	4,547	Telephone, CTV	Huizhou
10	Shenzhen Huaqiang	4,408	CTV, VCR, CD, HiFi	Shenzhen

been laid off by state-owned enterprises. Nevertheless, although China has experienced decreases in domestic demand, exports, and foreign investment, its economy has still been better than that of its neighbors. China's government has spent massive amounts on public works such as railways, highways, power grids, and water conservation projects, hoping to stimulate the economy. It has had to slow down its efforts to restructure state-owned companies, however, because of rising unemployment and the threat to social stability. Meanwhile, its state-owned banks are plagued by bad loans. Growing job insecurity has also led to decreasing consumer demand and subsequent rising inventories.

As the wounds of the Asian financial crisis slowly heal, it will be time for Siemens to exploit China's low wages and inexpensive resources. Since Siemens is already a target for governmental spending on the infrastructure, Siemens should be able to weather these hard times.

At the international level, Siemens must continue to face competitors such as Cisco, AT&T, Hitachi, GTE, 3Com, and Motorola. These companies have also made substantial investments in China. Their great strength and high technological abilities will enable them to overcome the entry barriers Siemens has set up.

Internal Environment

Financial

Sales in Germany are decreasing recently, while in other parts of Europe, the Americas, and the Asia-Pacific region, sales are increasing. This means that Siemens' overseas investments are very strong. Siemens has been facing decreasing profitability ratios, however. Its gross profit margin dropped from 28.34 percent to 27.52 percent in 1998, while the return on equity dropped from 9.18 percent to 3.03 percent. These ratios probably decreased because Siemens started a new Ten Point Program mid-1998 in an effort to improve sales and management. It used many resources implementing the program, resulting in loss of profit.

The leverage ratios (debt-to-asset and debt-to-equity) increased in 1998, while activity ratios (inventory and fixed-asset turnovers) did not change much. These ratios indicate that Siemens is still stable.

Siemens' lowest stock prices increased from 70.80 to 90.30 and the highest from 130.00 to 138.60. Its stocks are traded on the Frankfurt market. In future, Siemens is planning to list shares on the New York exchange. Although Siemens had negative income last year, it distributed the same amount of dividends on each of its five-mark shares. Siemens transferred 1.082 billion from retained earnings to cover this dividend distribution.

Operational

Siemens China maintains good relationships with both its customers and local partners. Siemens China closely cooperates with local partners to increase transfer of expert knowledge to China while remaining open to differing opinions. It is eager to help customers when they have questions. Siemens has hotline phone and fax numbers and is connected to its headquarters in Germany and hotline centers in the United States and Singapore. It also provides training programs for customers. Its instructors are trained in Germany but speak Chinese. These programs teach customers about new products, technology, and services provided by Siemens.

Siemens sets prices based on demand and supply. During the economic crisis in Asia, demand decreased and prices came down. Increased supply of memory chips also drove prices down, explaining decreasing profits in the semi-conductor segment mentioned above.

Siemens China has its own promotional webpage that presents different kinds of information such as about new technology and services. Stockholders, customers, and anyone else who is interested can access the page and send back comments through the Internet. Siemens China also sends out brochures and newsletters informing the public about its services and products. Most of Siemens China's sales and promotion take place in large cities such as Shanghai and Beijing in the north, Shenzhen and Guangzhou in the south, and Zhengzhou and Wuhan in central China. Siemens is also developing markets in nine provinces such as Tianjin and Jiangsu.

Technological

The high pace of innovation of logical components and memory chips demands that a large amount of resources be taken up with research and development. Siemens spent DM9.1 billion in 1998 on research and development alone, an increase of 12 percent over the previous year. Siemens spent DM3.3 billion on research and development on its Information and Communications segment and DM1.6 billion on the Components segment. Increased outlays for Public Communication Networks and Private Communication Systems were primarily channeled into the mobile radio network and mobile phone sectors.

The Siemens Management Institute (SMI) helps build a qualified local work force and management team in China. In addition, the Siemens Technical and Management Training Company Ltd., Beijing (STMT) was designed to provide training to customers and suppliers so as to transfer the latest technological know-how and management expertise.

Organizational

Each of Siemens' different segments and locations has its own department head. The present president of Siemens China is Ernst Behrens. Siemens provides many educational programs for its employees. The new Siemens Management Learning Program is being offered all over the world. Managers from different segments and countries work together in teams that cross national and business borders. Using concrete tasks and real business case studies, participants learn to confront problems and find solutions as a team. The Siemens Technical Academies are located in Munich, Erlangen, and Berlin. These programs for young trainees focus strongly on engineering tasks. Another program is the German Academic Exchange Services-Siemens Scholarship Program ASIA 21st. This joint project finances continued studies for high-potential junior engineers from various Asian countries. Nurturing highly-qualified, internationally-oriented engineers helps ensure Siemens' global competitiveness.

Corporate-Level Strategy

Related Diversification

When Siemens started investing in China, it used a related diversification strategy so it could operate in several different businesses, industries, or markets at the same time. All of these businesses are fundamentally related, however, allowing Siemens to leverage a distinctive competence in one market in order to strengthen its competitiveness in others. Each of its operations is linked to the others via the Siemens name and logo.

Related diversification has several advantages. First, Siemens does not rely on a single product or service, which makes it less vulnerable to economic threats. For example, if Siemens faces increased competition in the electrical components sector, its electrical power division can offset potential decline. Second, having related businesses and a powerful image makes it more difficult for outsiders to compete with Siemens. For example, other electrical components manufacturers have trouble selling components in competition against a well-known name like Siemens. Furthermore, they must buy advertising at commercial rates, while Siemens inexpensively promotes its new components to households who receive their electrical bills from Siemens or commuters who travel on its mass transit systems.

Related diversification also generates economies of scale. For example, Siemens can take advantage of its vast size to buy parts or materials at favorable prices from Asian manufacturers and then divide the purchases among its subsidiaries. Related diversification also allows a firm to use technology or expertise developed in one market to enter a second market more cheaply and easily. For example, Siemens used its expertise in producing electrical products and cables to become China's telecommunications giant and its knowledge in the steel and energy industry to become a major mass transit provider. Such synergies are a major advantage of the related diversification strategy.

Unrelated Diversification

Siemens also pursues unrelated diversification as part of its corporate strategy. It operates in several unrelated industries and markets, yielding further benefits. First, the corporate parent is able to raise capital more easily to support these industries than any of its independent units would be able to do alone. The parent can then allocate capital to the most profitable opportunities available among its subsidiaries. Second, overall riskiness can be reduced because the company is less subject to business cycle fluctuations. When one industry is in decline, losses can be offset by profits from unrelated industries. Siemens also is less vulnerable to competition, since any given threat is likely to affect only a portion of its total operations. Fourth, Siemens can easily shed unprofitable businesses because they operate independently. It also can buy new operations without worrying about how to integrate them into existing businesses.

The creation of conglomerates through an unrelated diversification strategy is out of favor today, primarily because of lack of potential synergy across unrelated businesses. Since Siemens uses both unrelated and related diversification, it does not need to worry about any one operation proving unsustainable or failing to enhance others. It may also be easier for its staff at corporate headquarters to effectively manage diverse businesses because they understand a very wide array of businesses and markets. This enhances performance monitoring of individual operations.

Business-Level Strategy

Whereas corporate strategy deals with overall organization, business strategies focus on specific businesses, subsidiaries, or operating units within the firm. The products and services of each of Siemens' strategic business units (SBUs) are dissimilar. These relatively unrelated SBUs include: Energy, Industry, Healthcare, Transportation, Household Appliances, Lighting, and Telecommunications.

Competitive Strategy

Once Siemens selects a business strategy for an SBU, it typically uses that strategy in all of the geographical markets that SBU serves. Its differentiation strategy is the most commonly used one at the business level. Siemens differentiates products in terms of quality so it can charge higher prices for products that have limited sales agreements with only a few dealers. For example it only sells its hospital equipment to certain dealers.

An overall cost leadership strategy is used by Siemens to focus on achieving highly efficient operation procedures so that its costs will be lower than those of its competitors. This allows it to sell its goods or services for lower prices. This strategy may result in lower per unit profitability due to lower prices but higher total profitability due to increased sales. For example, Siemens produces a lot of cables and then uses them in many of its organizations. High volume production and a worldwide distribution network have allowed Siemens to flourish.

A focus strategy is used by Siemens to target customer groups or regions for specific types of products. Geographical region and ethnicity differentiate these groups.

Siemens succeeds thanks to a comprehensive range of services and products, including consultation, engineering, and training. It realizes that in a global market, attention to customers counts as much as top-of-the-line technology. The ability to solve problems jointly with customers and be a reliable partner with local businesses plays a vital role in continued success.

Siemens displays superior efficiency because it owns related and supporting industries. Siemens is able to use existing materials, products, services, and power that it produces and thus are always at its disposal. It constantly innovates in the transfer of knowledge between the many industries in which it operates. Siemens maintains superior quality because it knows that every one of its components and products has been tested for durability and reliability. Siemens also exhibits superior customer responsiveness by putting a top priority on providing outstanding value. All of these qualities give Siemens a competitive advantage over other organizations.

Entry Strategy

Siemens had some early experience with China from having supplied it with a pointer telegraph in 1872 and set up its first representative office in Beijing in 1982 after China adopted the open door policy in 1979. A representative office is a quick, flexible, and relatively simple way to become familiarized with the Chinese market. The office allowed Siemens to establish contacts with key industrial ministries and build its reputation in China. There are other advantages to this entry mode. Unlike an equity joint venture or wholly foreign-owned enterprise, the representative office gave Siemens a formal presence in China without the complications of an unfamiliar local partner or strong financial commitment. A representative office has no minimum registered capital requirements. Representatives offices do not face as many restrictions, such as what fields of business the company can pursue. For example, the government discourages foreign participation in media communications, except for through representative offices. Moreover, closing down a representative office is relatively easy. Finally, representative offices can hire talented Chinese college graduates or managers who see employment there as a way to gain exposure to the world of international business or as a springboard to working at the head office in the future.

This entry mode has several disadvantages, however. Regulatory and start-up costs makes them quite expensive to maintain. Also, representative offices must usually pay high rent because they tend to be located in major cities where office space is in short supply. The first Siemens representative office was located in Shanghai. Representative offices also have to pay duties as high as 100 percent on all imported office equipment.

Much later, Siemens changed entry modes by starting a joint venture in order to avoid paying transfer taxes on imported equipment. Its first joint venture in the telecommunications industry was the Beijing International Switching Systems Corporation

(BISC), established in 1991 to serve the domestic public communications network sector.

One benefit of joint ventures is the learning effect. Siemens can learn the marketing skills appropriate to the local culture, gain distribution channels, and improve its relationships in China by having a Chinese partner. In addition, by sharing skills and resources, joint ventures have large economies of scale. Technology transfer is another advantage. The Chinese government normally favors equity joint ventures (EJVs) because they often involve significant technological transfers to Chinese firms. Since Siemens and its local partners have slightly different goals, their resources tend to be complementary. Lastly, Siemens can share risks with other parties by being involved in EJVs.

Siemens currently has 45 joint ventures in China, including 9 in telecommunication, 6 in energy, 4 in transportation, 3 in health care, 10 in electronics, 13 in other industries.

EJVs are hard to sustain, however, because China is vast and varied, its culture and traditions are profoundly different from those of the West, and its social, governmental, and economic systems are particularly complex.

The growing complexity of operations by many multinational corporations in China and the need to more closely coordinate its numerous joint ventures led Siemens to changing entry modes once again. In 1994, it founded Siemens Ltd. China as a holding company, also known as an investment or umbrella company. A holding company is able to unite existing investments under one umbrella company, combining sales, procurement, manufacturing, and maintenance for greater efficiency. It can also help balance foreign exchange reserves between joint ventures, act as a clearinghouse for intra-group RMB financing, and smooth the establishment of new investments.

Timing and Location

Siemens supplied the first pointer telegraph to China in 1872 and reestablished its foothold there in 1982 after China opened its door to the outside world. Therefore, it can be considered as an early mover in telecommunications industry. As a pioneering firm, Siemens has had several advantages because it has been able to invest strategically in facilities, distribution channels, product positioning, patentable technology, natural resources, and so forth. As a first mover, the firm has been able to take advantage of new market opportunities and, in so doing, grasp market power and erect entry barriers against followers. It has also had the benefit of low competition and the ability to pre-empt scarce resources at cheaper prices than its followers had to pay. Moreover, as an early mover, Siemens may benefit from the first-in advantages of holding technical leadership and creating buyer-switching costs. Finally, the early mover pre-empts marketing and distribution channels, gains sustained pioneering information, and enjoys long-term brand recognition.

Many of Siemens' joint ventures are located in major cities. Out of 45 joint ventures, 11 are in Shanghai, and 9 in Beijing. The density of telephone and other communications systems are much higher than the national average in these cities. They also have good infrastructures and strong industrial power. FIEs in Shanghai are also entitled to some preferential treatment. For example, they are exempt from tariffs and value-added taxes for equipment and materials imported for production and from value-added tax on export of their products.

Industry Selection

China needs advanced technology and international management experience to further its economic goals. Siemens not only offers equipment and services, but also transfers technological know-how and provides training courses which will enable China to meet its most urgent needs for a developed infrastructure.

Telecommunications is already one of Siemens' areas of expertise. It chose to operate in this industry in China because it is also one of the industries that foreigners are allowed to invest directly in.

Siemens also entered the energy industry in China. China is one of the world's largest producers of fuel, but also one of its largest consumers. China's energy problems are combined with geographic imbalances between the location of fuel reserves and the areas of demand and an inadequate transport system. There is also an over-dependence on coal as the major source of energy. Siemens can help China achieve more efficient and cleaner production of energy.

Efficient, reliable, low-cost transportation is crucial to the economy of a country the size of China. Lack of an adequate transportation infrastructure hinders the country's development. The demand for various forms of mass rail transportation is almost insatiable. For decades, Siemens has been at the cutting edge of innovative rail technology. It can offer an entire rail system from a single source, providing all the key subsystems necessary to build a modern transportation system. Siemens is a market leader in signaling systems with the greatest reliability and highest safety standards. The Siemens interlocking-system supplied to the Beijing-Kowloon line, for example, is the world's most advanced, fully electronic interlocking system. Reliable power supply systems are a precondition for effective, powerful, efficient and economic transportation. Siemens has also supplied power components for the first Chinese high-speed line from Guangzhou to Shenzhen, the Beijing-Zhengzhou line, and also for the metro systems in Shanghai and Guangzhou. Finally, Siemens has a worldwide reputation for its advanced rolling stock, whether used on mass transit vehicles, electrical multiple units, or electrical and diesel electric locomotives.

The electronics industry is among the fastest growing sectors in China. There are several reasons for the boom in China's internationally competitive electronic industry. First, export aspirations have made producers spend more on research and quality control to meet international standards. Second, local production of parts and components greatly drives down costs. Third, MNEs from the Greater China region (i.e., Hong Kong, Taiwan, and Singapore) have brought in many innovative ideas, technological skills, capital resources, international channels, and managerial expertise, further facilitating the competitive edge of the Chinese electronics industry in the global market. This has been greatly attractive to Western investors, including Siemens.

Cooperative Strategies

Partner Selection

In choosing partners for each of its 45 joint ventures in China, Siemens has evaluated the objectives of each to identify whether or not they are compatible with its own. The situation that holds the most promise for compatibility is one in which the strategic goals of their partners converge with their own, while their competitive goals diverge. Siemens also looks into the potential for cooperation with its partner. This significantly influences mutual trust, which affects venture success. Having complementary skills, including management styles, is also important. Both partners should also take on a commensurate level of risk if the international joint venture is to hold together. If nothing is at risk, there is less of an incentive to stay together.

The success of an international joint venture largely depends upon the local partner's absorptive capability, that is, its ability to acquire, assimilate, integrate, and exploit knowledge and skills. The firm's ability to process and deploy an inflow of new knowledge and skills depends on how closely these skills are related to those it has already established. Siemens therefore chooses partners who have demonstrated the ability to work in the same industry the joint venture will be operating within. Their absorptive capability contributes to the venture's profitability and sales growth.

Sharing Arrangement

Sharing arrangements are tied to a firm's core competency contributions, control over subsidiaries, bargaining power with local partners, globally integrated synergy, and parent-subsidiary relations. For example, Siemens set up a joint venture for locomotives and drive components in China with two local partners. Siemens holds a 51 percent stake in the new company, called Siemens Traction Equipment Ltd. The remaining 49 percent is shared by the two partners; Zhuzhou Electric Locomotive Works (ZELW), the biggest locomotive plant in China, holds 33 percent and Zhuzhou Electric Locomotive Research Institute (ZELRI), China's largest producer of electronic and electrical components for rolling stock, has a 16 percent stake.

We might think about why Siemens holds this percentage and other two local partners hold that percentage. Actually, there is relationship between sharing arrangement and EJV performance. First, the majority and split status of sharing arrangement have a significant influence on EJV's overall performance. However, these two different sharing arrangements have different univariate effects on the multidimensional EJV performance. While the split-arrangement has a significantly positive impact on accounting return and asset efficiency, the majority-arrangement has a non-significant effect on these efficiency measures. Second, the majority status of sharing arrangement is not significantly related to operational risks. Although the majority status of sharing arrangement enables Siemens to have greater power to control the EJV, operational uncertainties resulting from the contextual settings may outweigh those arising from contractual factors. Alternatively, the split status of sharing arrangement is significantly and positively related to ROI, asset turnover, and domestic sales growth. Lastly, the relationship between sharing arrangement and EJV performance is significantly moderated by project-type selection. The majority status positively interacts with technologically-advanced projects, and this interaction has a significant effect on EJV performance. This implies that advanced-technology represents an essential competency which can increase the competitive power and hence result in larger market share or high market growth.

Conclusion

The founder of Siemens AG, Werner von Siemens, was an extraordinary man. His great vision and ambition created a foundation which has made Siemens one of the most successful companies in the global market today. Siemens serves governments and a large portion of businesses.

Although the economic crisis has reduced growth throughout Asia, Siemens has still been able to benefit in China because of the government's increased spending on the infrastructure. Nevertheless, according to our internal analysis, Siemens is experiencing a downturn in business. At the same time, it is clear that Siemens is developing a stronger business by cooperating with partners and bringing better services to its customers.

Siemens has adopted a powerful strategy of diversification in both related and unrelated industries. This means that Siemens is relatively invulnerable to competitive or economic threats. Diversification enables Siemens to enjoy steady demand, achieve lower costs, and become more competitive. Its related diversification strategy also allows the company to exploit low costs and thus charge lower prices for its products than its competitors can afford.

Simultaneously, Siemens focuses on certain hot products, like mobile phones, so as not to miss promising investment opportunities. It is likely that Siemens will eventually eliminate its unrelated businesses, however, since they lack the benefits of synergy.

As an early mover in China, Siemens enjoyed technological leadership, an environment without competition, preemption of scarce resources, high local demand, and brand recognition. Eventually it was able to gain market power and set up high barriers against followers.

Most of Siemens' business is located in Beijing and Shanghai, focusing on basic infrastructure industries that are hardly likely to fail. These industries provide high demand for Siemens products and services. Even if the Chinese economy shrinks, it will still need strong energy, telecommunications, and transportation industries. In conclusion, although Siemens is suffering a loss due to the Asian crisis, its investment lies in pillar industries which means that Siemens can easily weather this downturn. Siemens is expected to be profitable again within the next five years.

2. TOYOTA IN CHINA

Company Introduction

The Toyota Motor Corporation (TMC or Toyota for short) was founded in 1937 by Kiichiro Toyoda. Kiichiro Toyoda started in his father's company, the Toyoda Automatic Loom Works, in the Automobile Manufacturing Division, where he worked on building a prototype passenger car. At that time, the Japanese government decided to exclude foreign-made cars which then dominated the Japanese market. The new Toyota company became the first licensed Japanese motor vehicle manufacturing company, producing military trucks for the war effort. Toyota continued secretly to develop and improve cars, resulting in the production of the Toyopet Crown.

Toyota rejected a partnership offer from the Ford motor company since it was convinced of its ability to produce cars independently, but nearly went bankrupt in 1950 during an economic depression. Toyota survived management crises, labor disputes, and the depression to make a comeback during the Korean War, a time of increased demand. In 1953, Eiji Toyoda, Kiichiro's cousin, became chairman of the board.

In the 1960s, TMC began turning out cheap, dependable cars using the Kanban ('Just In Time' inventory) and Total Quality Control systems. In the 1970s, OPEC slashed production of oil and Japan's fuel-efficient rode a wave of demand into garages across America. Meanwhile, Eiji Toyoda fought all attempts of U.S. auto manufacturers to gain market access to Japan. By 1980, the Toyota Motor Corporation ranked second worldwide only to General Motors in total number of cars produced. By the beginning of the 1990s, it commanded an overwhelming 43 percent of the Japanese car market and sold more than one million cars and trucks in the U.S.

Aside from these two mainstay markets, TMC began solidifying its global operations, particularly in Southeast Asia and Latin America. A global economic downturn brought prolific growth to

TMC's overseas earnings. The Toyota Motor Corporation is today the third largest automotive company in the world and the number one company in Japan.

The Japanese recession and a strong yen battered TMC's overseas earnings in the early 1990s. In 1993, TMC lost nearly four percent of market share. In order to survive, TMC began to restructure the company by installing new and younger managers up and down its chain of command. TMC is still changing its structure in order to maximize corporate resources and create an organization that can respond flexibly and efficiently to advanced globalization and the emergence of new businesses.

Mission

TMC's main priorities are to anticipate and respond quickly to demand, refocus research and development on issues of concern to its customers (safety, the environment, and energy conservation), integrate global operations by region, mobilize marketing resources in Japan to bolster market share, develop nonautomotive products and services, and increase shareholder value. TMC has always been committed to providing people with the best possible products. At the same time, it is trying to build a global network of vehicle and parts plants which can supply products efficiently around the world and maximize its economic and industrial contributions in each market. Its business plan includes greater regional localization by increasing local production capacity and exports and procuring local parts and materials.

To accomplish its goals, TMC is guided by a few specific principles: be a company of the world; serve people through attention to safety and the environment, assert technological leadership and give customers satisfaction; contribute to the communities of every nation; foster a corporate culture that honors individuality while promoting teamwork; pursue continuing growth through efficient, global management; and build lasting relationships with business partners around the world.

Major Businesses

In the early stages, Toyota primarily focused on manufacturing small cars and producing auto parts. After World War II, it started piecing together usable parts from wrecked or worn-out trucks in order to build recycled vehicles. Currently, it builds car, truck, and bus bodies, complete motor vehicles, and vehicular parts and accessories. The company introduced 13 model changes and new vehicles in 1995. It plans to export its Prius hybrid-powered (gas and electric) sedan to Europe and North America in the year 2000.

TMC has been diversifying into non-automotive businesses such as telecommunications, prefabricated housing, industrial equipment and vehicles, and financial services, but its core products remain passenger cars, trucks, and vans. Its line of passenger vehicles varies from the sporty Supra to the classy Avalon and the Camry. The Camry was the best-selling non-luxury car in the United States in 1997. TMC also created the new automotive category known as the minivan.

International Markets

TMC operates in eight international regions: North America, Europe, East and Southeast Asia, the Middle East and Southwest Asia, Latin America, Oceania, Africa, and Others. TMC makes about 30 percent of its cars in 25 countries outside of Japan. About 60 percent of the 2.5 million vehicles TMC sold abroad last year were made overseas.

In February 1984, TMC established a joint venture with GM called New United Motor Manufacturing, Inc. (NUMMI). Production at its plant in Fremont, California began in December 1984 with an annual output of 300,000 vehicles. In 1986, TMC set up a plant in Georgetown, Kentucky as Toyota Manufacturing U.S.A, Inc. (TMMU). TMMU production started in 1988 at the rate of 200,000 Camry cars a year aimed at the U.S. market. The Georgetown plant also produces engines and axles. In September 1989, TMC launched its 4.0 liter luxury-class car, the Lexus (known as the Celsior in Japan), in the U.S. In Canada, TMC built a car plant in Ontario with an annual capacity of 65,000 units. In British Columbia in 1985 it set up a wheel-making plant. Production throughout North America is today running at around 730,000 vehicles annually and is set to rise to over 1.2 million by the end of this year.

In Europe, TMC began producing cars jointly with Volkswagen in 1989. It then opened two plants (one for cars, one for engines) in the U.K. in 1992.

Before 1949, TMC entered China at first when it established an assembly plant and a body plant in Tianjin. Around the mid to late 1980s, it set up mechanic training centers in Shanghai, Beijing, Guangzhou, Shenyang and Tiajin. By 1991 it had established production at the Shenyang Jinbei Passenger Vehicle Manu Co., Ltd. In 1994 it started a marketing office in Hong Kong. That was soon followed by the Toyota Motor Technical Center Co., Ltd. which adds to the current functions of the China Support Center by carrying out local vehicle compatibility surveys, expanding production support operations, and transplanting technologies. The Tianjin Automotive Industrial (Group) Co., Ltd. was set up to manufacture minicars. Toyota Group member companies and Toyota-related parts makers currently operate twenty-eight companies throughout China via joint ventures and other partnerships. Sixteen of these firms, including four affiliated with TMC, are located in Tianjin City. Tianjin Toyota Motor Engine Co., Ltd. produces 1.3 liter 8A-FE gasoline engines which will be installed in the Charade manufactured by Tianjin Automobile. Tianjin Fengjin Auto Parts Co., Ltd., the only wholly-owned subsidiary, produces forged parts.

External Environment

TMC's major competitors within China's automotive industry include six passenger car manufactures (First Auto Works, Second Auto Works, Shanghai-Volkswagen Automotive Company, Peking Jeep Company, Tianjin Automotive Industry Corporation, and Guangzhou Peugeot Automobile Company) and two minicar production ventures (North China Industries Corporation and Guizhou Aviation Industry Corporation). The First Auto Works and Second Auto Works together hold the majority share of the market.

The First Auto Works, also know as Jiefang Consolidated Automobile Industry Corporation, has numerous enterprises within the provinces of Liaoning and Jilin. It produces Jiefang trucks, Hongqi coaches, and Red Flag limousines. In 1988, it set up an agreement with Volkswagen and initiated production of the Audi 100 at Changchun. A second joint venture with Volkswagen allows it to produce approximately 150,000 Golfs and Jettas.

The Second Auto Works was established in 1981 in Shiyan (Hubei province). Its production line includes Dongfeng trucks, special vehicles, and buses. In collaboration with Nissan Motors, it built a new factory in Xiangfang to produce bus chassis and truck axles. It next set up the Dongfeng Citroen Automobile Company as a joint venture to produce 150,000 Citroen ZX at a new production plant in Wuhan (capital of Hubei).

The Shanghai–Volkswagen Automotive Company is the largest car manufacturer in China. Shanghai-Volkswagen formed a twenty-five year agreement starting in 1984 in which Volkswagen holds a 50 percent share, Shanghai United Automobile & Tractor Industries (SATIC) has 25 percent, 15 percent is owned by the Bank of China, and 10 percent by the China National Automotive Industry Corporation. By 1993, Shanghai-Volkswagen was producing an annual output level of 100,000 cars. Shanghai-Volkswagen's Santana parts plant is producing components with a local content of 82 percent, which allows the company to apply for a reduction in import tariffs.

The Beijing Light Vehicle Company is a state owned company formed in March 1983 by Chrysler (with 42 percent ownership and an option to increase to 49 percent) and Beijing Auto Works. The company produces the Chinese version of the Jeep Cherokee called the BJ 213. The company has an estimated production of 100,000 units per year.

The Tianjin Automotive Industry Corporation is cooperating with Daihatsu to produce the TJ 135 pickup, the Hijet commercial vehicle, and the Charade passenger car. In 1992, Tianjin produced 34,000 Charades and 22,000 Hijets.

Guangzhou Peugeot in collaboration with its partners established GPAC in 1985 with a goal of producing 15,000 pickups per year. The production of the Peugeot 504 began at Huangpu with a production capacity level of 30,000 pickups per year and plans to increase to 150,000 per year. GPAC wants to begin producing high-end pickup models as well.

The Suzuki Minicar venture was established in 1993 through a JV with China North Industries Corporation. It has manufacturing plants in Chongqing, Wangjiang, Xinan, Beijing, Shuiding, and Baotou. Its minicar production was estimated at 50,000 cars per year in 1996. In a 1998 agreement with Mercedes, Suzuki began producing trucks at its Baotou factories. Its plant in Beijing has been producing four-wheel drive and pickup versions of the Suzuki Carry since 1996. It plans to produce more than 150,000 vehicles annually.

Subaru Rex minicars are produced by the Guizhou Aviation Industry Corporation with an annual production rate of 10,000 vehicles as of 1994.

In 1994, the EIU predicted that sales of passenger cars in China would increase at a faster rate than those of commercial vehicles. By the year 2000, passenger vehicles were expected to account for 45 percent of all vehicles sold. In 1996, however, the demand for new cars declined by 6 percent, attributed to low consumer purchasing power. Nevertheless, as China becomes more economically stable, experts believe that automobile sales will increase and automobile firms will be able to operate in the black.

Since a large number of companies are involved in the making of an automobile, the industry is inherently structurally uncertain. Relationships with suppliers and buyers are especially important. TMC maintains close relationships with its subcontractors and tries to make them dependent on it without itself becoming reliant solely on one supplier or distributor. Like other Japanese automobile manufacturers, it does this through collaboration with a *keiretsu*, a group of manufacturers and suppliers. TMC's *keiretsu* supplies it with all the necessary parts for production of vehicles. As of 1997, TMC did not have any parts made in China, but along with its *keiretsu* has made numerous strategic moves to penetrate the Chinese market. For example, Nippondenso plans to produce car starters and alternators, Toyota Gosei wants to make brake hoses, Arco produces car seats, and Aisin Seiki manufactures gearboxes. The establishment of a *keiretsu* in China will lower TMC's costs and make it competitive in the Chinese auto industry.

China's market is highly attractive to automobile manufacturers around the world. Within just twenty years the market has been saturated with different models. Toyota faces an almost unlimited number of competing substitutes. For example within the passenger car market, there are vehicles such as the Golfs and Jettas from Volkswagen and the Citroen ZX from the Second Auto Works corporation. Within the mini-vehicles market, substitutes include Suzuki and the Subaru Rex.

The newest entrant to China's automobile industry is Korea's

Daewoo which joined with three Chinese partners in a $946 million dollar venture to make auto parts in Shandong. The plant is expected to produce 300,000 auto parts annually.

Although firms in China's automobile industry are constantly trying to establish joint ventures all over the country, the two latest joint ventures that could impact TMC sales are Nissan's venture in Zhengzhou and Lemforder Metallwerke in Shanghai. Nissan will produce 50,000 trucks annually. Lemforder Metallwerke will be supplying auto makers with alternative auto parts.

China's policie regarding the automobile industry represents the largest barrier to entry. The duty on imported automobiles can add up to 240 percent. Automobile firms therefore find it more profitable to engage in joint ventures since prices of Chinese-made vehicles are substantially lower than imports. Unfortunately for TMC, however, governmental protectionism has a negative effect since TMC does not produce vehicles locally but rather imports kits from Japan.

The government has instituted other policies to protect its automobile industry. From 1994 to 1997, auto manufacturing joint ventures were prohibited. Credit policies, elimination of tax exemptions for purchase of foreign vehicles by foreign-funded firms, and the anti-corruption campaign have made it nearly impossible for government officials to acquire luxury foreign cars. This had a negative impact on Toyota's revenue, which decreased from 70 billion yen in 1994 to only 16 billion yen a year later.

Protectionism has hindered the advancement of China's automotive industry by creating a vicious cycle in which the high costs of sub-scale production result in high prices that put automobiles out of reach of most Chinese consumers. Local plants are thus prevented from expanding output. The immediate future of China's automotive industry seems dim. Although the government is aiming to produce two million cars annually by the year 2000, sales are unlikely to reach the same level.

Internal Environment

Technological advancements allow TMC to achieve product differentiation and boost revenues. In 1997, TMC debuted technologically advanced, environmentally friendly, and economically sound vehicles. Prius, the world's first hybrid electrical vehicle, can be mass-produced for the ecologically concerned market segment. TMC's modification of the MR2 to the much lighter MR S sports car, with 25 percent fewer parts, will make its production process more economical. This simplification means the sports car will more attractive to developing markets as in China.

Toyota founded the Just in Time system, also known as JIT or Toyotaism. JIT is not only a tool to reduce inventory. It is a continuous process aimed at eliminating waste and solving problems throughout the supply chain. One of the key factors in Toyota's success is that it pulls most of its materials, parts, and subassemblies from suppliers close to its assembly plants. Localizing supplies allows TMC to develop a closed-loop distribution network that is able to deliver parts from suppliers to the plant as soon as it needs it. Another component of Toyota's JIT success is that it can coordinate the quality control program with suppliers. This reduces waste and, therefore, cost.

TMC's organizational and corporate structure can be viewed as both a weakness and a strength for the firm. Its conservative corporate structure saved TMC from many of the problems GM experienced in Northeast China. This same conservatism sometimes also prevents it from seizing opportunities. For example, TMC's reluctance to provide Chinese auto makers with the technical support they wanted proved costly over the long-run since it failed to establish a joint venture and achieve market penetration prior to the economic boom of the mid-1980s. TMC's centralized and bureaucratic corporate culture prohibits it from adapting quickly to changing expectations of its sometimes fickle Chinese partners or alterations of governmental policies.

During the fiscal year ending 1998, TMC had a 0.67 quick ratio and 1.42 current ratio. Nissan's quick and current ratios were 0.53 and 0.54, respectively, and Honda's were 0.41 and 1.08 respectively. Higher ratios means that Toyota is liquid and more attractive to short-term creditors, although it can also mean that it is making inefficient use of cash.

TMC's debt to equity ratio at the end of fiscal year 1998 was 0.46, lower than both Nissan and Honda's debt to equity ratios of 1.45 and 0.61 respectively. TMC's profit margin of 0.04 is about the same as Nissan's and Honda's (0.01 and 0.04 respectively).

Corporate-Level Strategy

Some of TMC's diversified products are horizontally related. Besides producing cars, TMC has finance, high-technology, and software businesses. It finances installment sales and facility leasing for TMC dealers and affiliated companies. High technology businesses include research and development of factory automation, development and manufacture of measurement-control systems, and press mold design. In the software business, TMC develops and sells computer systems related to automobile development. Through these businesses TMC takes advantage of economies of scope by transferring capabilities in these businesses to its dominant business of producing cars. Other advantages of using the related diversification strategy are market power, customer loyalty, and operational stability.

TMC decided to enter China based on factors analyzable through the diamond model. Although the most obvious reason for any organization to enter China is to take advantage of the low cost of labor, probably the main reason TMC did so was demand. China currently has approximately 7 million vehicles, of which only 500,000 are privately owned. China's current market capacity is only 400,000-500,000 cars annually, but China has a population of more than one billion people. The China National Automotive Industry Corporation estimates that by the year 2010, annual demand for cars and trucks will reach 5.5 million. This would make it the third-largest automotive market in the 21st century.

Government policies also play a significant role in the decision to enter China. China's sixth five-year-plan opened the door to foreign investment. There is no limit to the share a foreign investor can own in a joint venture or the duration of joint venture contracts. Foreign investors do not have to pay customs duty or consolidated industrial and commercial taxes on equipment. They also enjoy fairly long periods of tax reduction and exemption under the new tax law.

Although infrastructure remains a problem, China is emphasizing modernization of agricultural, power, transportation, telecommunications, and electronics industries and increasing its technological knowledge. China's roadways should soon be able to accommodate the expected growth of private car use.

One problem that TMC may encounter in China is meeting raw and intermediate material needs. Producing components can require raw materials such as bauxite, iron ore, oil, gas, coal, and copper ore. Intermediate materials include aluminum, iron, sheet steel, resins, and wire. These materials are turned into body panels, wheels, engine blocks, and motors. China has an abundance of bauxite reserves, but still relies heavily on aluminum import. Iron ore reserves are estimated at six percent of the world's reserves and iron production in China accounts for one-quarter of total global production. The quality of Chinese iron ore is low, however, so many Chinese firms are forced to import iron ore from overseas. Unless China can provide a reliable supply of high quality, competitively priced raw materials, foreign auto manufacturers will not be successful. China must improve its processing technology.

Japan and China share some cultural values such as harmony, collectivism, respect for age, hierarchy, preservation of face, and the importance of relationships. These commonalties give TMC an edge over American business people in creating good relations in China

Business-Level Strategy

TMC continuously researches and develops features that customers value and that differentiates its cars from those of its competitors. It sets the standard in productivity, efficiency, and quality in manufacturing and product development.

TMC achieves efficiency through its JIT system. While other car makers see TMC's JIT system as a concept to be copied, TMC sees it as a process that can be continuously improved. Each plant uses JIT principles in a slightly different way. This has led to some problems, however. TMC has not been able to duplicate the same level of efficiency outside of Japan. Its U.S. plants still takes 30 to 50 percent longer to assemble a car than in Japan. This may be in part due to lack of well-trained local managers. In Japan, managers may have twenty years experience and work with people who have the same cultural background. Overseas managers may have no experience at all and must work with people who do not share their cultural background or speak the same language.

TMC gains a competitive edge in quality by staying in step with consumer wants and concerns. In reaction to society's growing concern over the environment, TMC has developed an environmentally safe car. The Prius uses an electric motor, gets sixty-six miles to the gallon, and produces only half the normal amount of carbon dioxide as waste. TMC also has strong after-sales services. In 1989, three months after its introduction, minor defects were found in the Lexus LS4000 model. TMC recalled about 8,500 units. Each owner was personally called and given the option to either bring in the car to be fixed on the spot or have it be picked up and returned the next day. Each car was also washed inside and out and had its tank filled. Those which could not be fixed easily were replaced at no cost. One customer was so thrilled with the unexpected service that he bought another car.

Quality is also maintained amongst TMC employees. Assembly line workers are expected not only to use their trained skills, but also common sense in producing cars in the best condition possible. Quality circles were established to look for ways to improve products and production processes. These generated 860,000 employee suggestions, 94 percent of which were ultimately adopted, resulting in over $30 million in savings per year for TMC.

TMC's style of management is highly innovative. TMC believes that there is an inverse relationship between efficiency and worker frustration. If production processes are efficient, the job is less frustrating. Employees are expected to master simple, standardized tasks before more tasks are added. Managers are expected to help workers understand the nature and value of their jobs. This structure is upside down to that of most companies in that management is at the bottom of the pyramid supporting employees, instead of at the top. Trust, communication, and training are all valued in the relations between management and other personnel. TMC guarantees lifetime employment, bases pay on seniority, and provides bonus payments tied to company profit. Employees in turn can initiate improvements instead of just responding to problems and agree to flexible work assignments.

Entry Strategies

Entry Mode Selection

TMC entered China very early when it set up a repair factory in 1937 in Shanghai and an assembly plant and body plant in Tientsin in 1940. These later merged with the Motor Vehicle Department of the Northern China Transportation Co., Ltd. to become the North China Motor Vehicle Co., Ltd. which engaged in repair. Following World War II and establishment of the new government in China, Toyota only had a few offices and training centers. It then tried to set up a wholly-owned assembly plant, but failed. Finally, it began entering China through joint ventures.

TMC has taken a step-by-step approach to building automotive operations in China through joint ventures, starting with training and technology transfer. The Mechanic Training Center at Shenyang, also known as the Chinese National Automobile Industry Toyota Gold Cup Skilled Worker Training Center, was established in September of 1990 by the China National Automobile Industry Corporation and the Shenyang's Gold Cup Automobile Corporation Ltd. in cooperation with Toyota. It was set up to develop the skills of Chinese mechanics.

The Toyota Technical Center was established by companies in the Toyota group in April 1995. Its goal is also to develop China's automobile and auto parts industries through greater localization of auto parts. In February 1998, the Toyota Motor Technical Center became incorporated. It carries out vehicle compatibility surveys, expands support operations, transplants technologies and acts as the base for jointly developing vehicles.

TMC has agreed to engage in joint ventures with Tianjin-affiliated auto parts makers to produce steering wheels and other parts. Currently, seven TMC affiliates have established eight joint ventures with local partners to produce crucial automobile components and systems. Toyota Group members and Toyota related parts makers currently operate 28 companies in China, producing automobile parts through joint ventures and other partnerships.

The joint venture mode makes sense for TMC since its strategic objective is to grow in the long run even at the risk of less than optimal short run results. The firm already has a lot of experience making foreign direct investments that it could apply to the Chinese situation. Its local Chinese partners, primarily the Tianjin group, have strong customer loyalty that can help TMC establish itself more directly in China.

Despite these advantages, it has not been easy for TMC to implement joint ventures in China. The Chinese government places restrictions on joint ventures with foreign companies, requiring them to use high local content in their products. This enables

China to have more control over outside companies and gives Chinese people a larger job market. A two year ban on joint ventures involving foreign car parts was implemented in April 1994, forcing TMC to put its ventures on hold. Even after the ban was lifted, TMC has had to contend with competition from other top international automobile companies which already had joint venture agreements with the top Chinese firms. It took almost two years for TMC to negotiate the first joint venture with Tianjin. The expected annual output of 150,000 engines from this venture has yet to be achieved.

Timing and Location

Since Toyota was one of the first companies to export automobiles to China, it has already achieved popular brand name recognition. Toyota was a follower rather than a leader, however, when it comes to manufacturing automobiles in China. Originally it was wary of taking risks and slow to make investments in the country. It is still building parts and engines rather than whole cars. It has become bolder in recent years and is aiming to grasp more of the market share.

One benefit of being a late mover is that the country's infrastructure is better developed. Another benefit is that TMC is not subject to incumbent inertia. The biggest detriment has been lack of variety of partners, plants, and so on from which to select.

The majority of TMC's recent joint ventures have been made with the Tianjin Group in Tianjin, northeast of Beijing. Tianjin is the largest industrial and commercial city in Northern China with a strong transportation infrastructure including large trading ports, rivers, and the Bohai bay. Tianjin is also rich in natural resources and has a good climate.

Cooperative Strategies

Partnering companies rarely have identical goals but may have ones which are compatible. For example, China wants to export more goods and TMC wants to increase its overseas output. TMC and the partners in its numerous joint ventures all share the common desire to improve China's automobile industry. TMC hopes to assist in industrial growth because it would like to increase its business in China, while its partners are looking to expand their businesses. In addition, TMC and its suppliers and subcontractors have strong relationships that allow for the low cost JIT system to be implemented. Many of TMC's affiliates are located in the same area where the majority of it's joint ventures are located. Although the Tianjin firms have not dealt with other foreign joint ventures, its growing presence and the fact that other major Chinese companies are involved in joint ventures with TMC's competitors makes the Tianjin group a good investment. Additionally, because the Tianjin group is in competition with other local firms, there is less chance of leakage risks. TMC provides expert knowledge of automobile processes to its partners while benefiting from their market knowledge.

A well publicized indication of TMC's commitment to Asia as a whole is that it won an award as "The World's Most Admired Automotive Company" in both 1997 and 1998 due to long term strategies of continued localization of business operations, production of vehicles on a global scale which incorporating local designs and style, and its seven-platform world-wide system for streamlining production.

TMC has proven its commitment to China by working directly with the government and investing heavily in the country. Many of TMC's joint ventures involve a thirty year contract. This is quite long since the average joint venture only lasts five to fifteen years.

TMC generally takes greater risks by investing more capital in each venture than its partners do. This is because Chinese firms do not have as much to offer in terms of procedures or technology. TMC is willing to do this because its main aim is to gain a stronger position in the Chinese market.

TMC already has experience dealing with different cultures and building cooperation through its global network of technical and design centers. Unlike many rather secretive Japanese companies, TMC President Okuda prefers to address problems and solutions in public and behave in an open manner with employees. He has also increased the number of foreigners with power and responsibility at TMC because he knows the Japanese can learn from their creativity and originality. The company is decreasing the number of levels of hierarchy to simplify decision making and spread responsibility.

In China, TMC fosters a cooperative culture by training some of its Chinese employees in Japan. TMC is also strictly following governmental policies and guidelines.

TMC sought partners that had the resources to produce and assemble automobile parts and had repair facilities. It also looked for signs of innovation and creativity amongst key people in each firm.

TMC tends towards an analyzer orientation. That is, it is innovative yet concerned with cost. It is taking more risks than before and seeks partners with a similar orientation. Partnering with Chinese companies that have extensive market knowledge and power is critical to TMC's success because it is the quickest way to expand in the local market.

TMC has been raising its stakes in China to offset the government's skepticism about its willingness to make a commitment. It contributes a wide range of equity in different ventures in order to gain more market power and have more control. For example, TMC paid $325 million to raise its stake in the Daihatsu Motor Company Ltd. from 16.8 percent to 33.1 percent in 1995. Daihatsu is a TMC affiliate that has been building automobiles and engines on consignment since 1967. Daihatsu is one of the few manufacturers authorized to make automobiles in China. Raising its equity share gives TMC an entry point into China.

One joint venture with Tianjin Automobile and Tianjin Auto Chassis Parts General Factory is the Tianjin Fengjin Auto Parts Co. Ltd. which makes and assembles constant velocity universal joints. In this joint venture TMC is the majority stake holder, with more than 75 percent of contributed equity. This gives it more control over operations.

Global Integration

TMC is using a global strategy in which standardized products are offered across country markets and competitive strategies are dictated by the home office. This does not mean TMC is operating in a single world market or treating the world as a single, homogeneous marketplace. TMC uses its global strategy to bring its entire worldwide resources to bear when competing in any market. This strategy implies that: the world is viewed as sets of country markets; homogenous market segments are sought across country market sets; and standardization of the marketing mix is sought wherever possible but adapted locally when necessary.

Benefits of the global strategy include creation of economies of scale in production and marketing, a uniform global image, and high control and coordination of operations. There are also disadvantages since it is difficult to coordinate decisions and activities across country borders or respond quickly and effectively to local preferences.

Before the Asian financial crisis, TMC's global strategy called for factories to produce primarily for local markets. Toyota learned a lesson from the Asian economic crisis, however, and is forging a new strategy to protect itself. Demand for cars in the Philippines and Thailand plunged in 1997 with the onset of the currency crisis; Toyota sales dropped more than 50 percent in one month. TMC responded by closing its Bangkok factories for retooling and turning them into export bases. TMC is continuing to redesign other plants so that it can quickly shift to exporting to strong markets when necessary. It wants to match its factories in one part of the world with markets in other parts of the world where demand exceeds supply. It calls this strategy 'global complementation'.

For example, Toyota makes a Corolla model in Brazil and another version in Canada and the U.S. While the outward appearances of the cars differ somewhat from country to country, their platforms and power trains are the same. If sales in South America slow substantially, TMC could quickly retool the body-stamping operations and produce Corollas in Brazil for export to North America. TMC's global complementation strategy will enable the company to effectively move capacity around the globe. It remains to be seen whether this new strategy will be sufficient to insulate Toyota from the worldwide economic slump.

In Japan, TMC uses a functional operational strategy with a bureaucratic structure characterized by standardization, functional departments, and centralization. Internationally, it uses a divisional operational strategy characterized by standardization, divisional departments, and moderate decentralization. This operational strategy pushes decision making downward one or two hierarchical layers so that vice presidents and their immediate subordinates share in the process of digesting information and making key decisions. This strategy is also more flexible than the functional structure. Each division can react to issues concerning their own products, regions, or client groups without disturbing the operations of other divisions. The limited degree of independence afforded each international division means that one division could stop doing business without seriously interrupting the operations of other divisions.

Currently, TMC is seriously looking at more efficient ways to run its international divisions. It is considering adopting a matrix operational strategy which incorporates both functional and divisional departments while making mutual adjustments at the top of the organization to coordinate the upper layers of the matrix. Decision making would become decentralized among matrix managers or divisions. This would provide even greater flexibility.

Conclusion

The Toyota Motor Corporation has always been committed to providing people with the best possible products. In that spirit it has grown into a corporation that serves customers in nearly every corner of the globe and contributes to the economic vitality of many nations. Toyota needs to structure a product line that can be more readily adapted to the needs of different markets, however. It should optimize its research, production, and purchasing with an eye to maximizing efficiency and competitiveness in a global context.

Although TMC makes about 30 percent of its cars overseas, none of its operations work as well as the ones in Japan. It has not been able to duplicate its efficient processes outside Toyota City. Indeed, its large, unique system is hard to duplicate. Overseas plants do not have the advantage of having parts delivered eight times a day; they still take 50 to 70 percent more time to assemble each vehicle. TMC has to change its production procedures in order to attain greater efficiency. It must create better ways to incorporate foreign employees into its system and train overseas plant managers to implement the JIT system so that it will work efficiently in each plant. In other words, TMC needs to avoid remaining Japan-centric.

For TMC to succeed in the Chinese automobile industry, it must become less adverse to risk and more flexible and quick to respond to market shifts. A conservative attitude is not the best way to enter markets where competition is fierce. Its competitors have already gained the first entrant benefits of market share and customer loyalty. It is critical for a company to establish and maintain a good reputation if it wants repeat purchases and loyal customers. TMC therefore should tailor its automobiles and provide exceptional products and services that suit the needs of the Chinese people.

Its early conservatism and unwillingness to make large investments has disappointed the Chinese government once. TMC must also work harder to create long term relationships with governmental agencies and successful Chinese companies if it wants to increase its market share in China. Joint cooperative efforts in technical education and the automobile and automobile parts industries will help bring success to Toyota.

At the same time, TMC should avoid creating the impression that it wants to take too much control of joint ventures. Chinese companies may feel that TMC does not trust them, which can lead to bad relations. The firms TMC is associated with do not have its level of experience; it should give its Chinese partners enough autonomy to learn on their own.

TMC has already achieved a strong position as the world's third largest auto manufacturer. By using a product differentiation strategy and engaging in continuous research and development to bring greater value to its customers, TMC can continue to set the standard in productivity, efficiency, and quality.

3. LUCENT TECHNOLOGY IN CHINA

Company Introduction

Lucent Technologies was originally created by AT&T. AT&T took over American Bell in 1899, and then set up Bell Labs in 1925 along with Western Electric, while maintaining a controlling equity position. AT&T separated into three corporations in 1996, forming Lucent Technologies and NCR. AT&T felt the splitting the company would help each core business unit focus on its particular target market. Lucent went public in April of 1996, providing the largest initial public offering in American history with 3 billion dollars of capital raised. Lucent Technologies became a Fortune 40 company overnight. Lucent Technologies provides the hardware and software that run global communications networks. It builds business telephone systems, local networks, and consumer telephones that can access global networks. The company also manufactures microchips and related components to run a host of systems and products.

The company's mission is to provide customers with the world's best and most innovative communication systems, products, technologies, and customer support. Powered by excellent people and technology, Lucent Technologies will strive to be a customer-driven, high performance company that delivers superior, sustained shareholder value. We make the things that make communications work.

Lucent Technologies has established offices or distributors in more than 90 countries or territories in their efforts to design and build a whole world of communications solutions. Twenty percent of the company's employees work outside of the continental United States. Lucent's goal is to continue its expansion as the leader in communications systems across the globe.

Lucent has acclimated well to the dynamic, uncertain Chinese market conditions, while facing little competition due to relatively high entry barriers. It now readies itself to adapt to increasing competition expected in the future. Lucent Technologies sought ways of entering the Chinese market in the early 1980s, a time when foreign direct investment was beginning to pour into China. China posed a tremendous market as the most populous country in the world with expanding technological and telecommunications needs. Lucent had already established markets for its products in other Third World countries, but had maintained its production facilities in the West. Moving into China was regarded as an important step for exploring ways to share in the market. Lucent's international strategy is summed up as aggressive but selective globalization.

Lucent, like many other high-technology companies, faces the challenges of global expansion combined with seeking growth opportunities in competition with new entrants. This case outlines an environmental analysis of Lucent Technology's Chinese operations, discussing past strategies for entering the market and their current results. We conclude with recommendations to executives interested in making a transition into the Chinese market.

External and Internal Environment

China generally has very low materials and labor costs, which provides opportunities to manufacture and operate relatively inexpensively. Low costs open up opportunities to export, assuming licensing rights can be worked out with the Chinese government. This is an environmental opportunity many FFEs (foreign-funded enterprises) are pursuing in China.

China's emerging economy supports opportunities for long-term market growth, as well as an expanding market. As part of this growth, China added twenty million new phones in 1997, a favorable circumstance for companies such as Lucent. In general, by contributing their distinctive resources to local capital/tech intensive industries, FFEs manifest their long-term commitment to indigenous production and host market expansion. Whenever a host industry appears to be highly competitive as a result of an increase in the number of firms in the industry, FFEs are likely to shift from local market development to production factor exploitation. This strategic shift towards cost-minimization and globally-integrated network utilization is expected to result in high export sales for the FFEs.

One major structural headache for FFEs in China lies in the government's need to control the ownership of state firm assets while allowing them to be acquired or merged with domestic or foreign investors. Higher asset intensity industries are thus subject to greater government interference. Clearly, the political involvement of the Chinese government provides considerable risk and uncertainty to foreign companies.

Another threat to FFEs comes from the economic risks from changes in foreign currency exchange and interest rates. Such variability can have a strong impact on operation results and financial conditions. A common problem for Lucent and most other MNEs is the cultural differences in management practices between the host country and the expatriate company. Chinese people are said to hold a collectivist philosophy, whereas Lucent's American management is generally considered individualistic.

At the industrial level, the first and most important source of competition comes from competing sellers. This is the strongest of five types of competitive forces. It results in ongoing jockeying for position amongst rival firms. In China, Lucent is fortunate in having been a 'first mover' in the telecommunications industry, which mitigates against this kind of competition. Political intervention in China has kept the number of competitors to a minimum. Increasing demand has also afforded Lucent competitive space.

The competition from new entrants is still only moderate. Companies that have recently entered the Chinese market are less experienced and pose only a small threat. The enormous investment required for entry into high-tech industries has discouraged new entrants. The only newcomers causing concern are those exporting to China from the Pacific Rim. These competitors operate at lower costs, but lack a competitive technical advantage. China's bureaucratic policies also tend to be open mainly to those foreign companies engaged in equity joint ventures, further making it difficult for new entrants to gain a foothold.

The third competitive force comes from substitute products. Often firms in one industry can provide ample substitutes for products in another, but this is not the case with Lucent. Lucent manufactures extremely high-tech equipment from radar and communications to security and defense systems. The vast majority of these products are custom tailored and produced in bulk. Because few substitutes can be accepted when it comes to issues of national security, the competitive force of substitute products is moderate at worst.

The power of buyers strengthens the more bargaining leverage they have over price, quality, service or other terms of sale. The buyers of Lucent products are primarily governments and large corporations. Their purchasing behavior is characterized by few, but large, contracts. As noted in Lucent's annual report, historically, Lucent has relied on a limited number of customers for a substantial portion of its total revenues. Lucent is seeking to diversify its customer base, nevertheless, Lucent expects that a significant portion of its future revenues will continue to be generated by a limited number of customers. This tendency contributes to the variability of Lucent's performance. The bargaining power of Lucent customers therefore tends to be quite strong.

The power of suppliers is always more powerful when the suppliers can produce components more cheaply than the corporation using them can make them itself. Right now the uncertainty of the future causes Lucent to outsource materials from inexpensive Chinese suppliers. Until entry barriers are lowered (i.e. become less financially demanding) this is the most competitive of the five forces facing Lucent. Even then, the suppliers will wield plenty of leverage, at least until the number of suppliers increases.

A checklist for performance strengths and weaknesses has been constructed for examining Lucent's internal capabilities. Included is Lucent's relative strategic emphasis according to the head of Lucent's Chinese division. Lucent's strengths include company name recognition and reputation, effective innovations, financial position, and technical skills. Lucent received 809 patents in 1997, providing evidence to its investors that Lucent is still growing and innovating.

Lucent's current weaknesses in China are human resource-related. Employee performance and efficiency is generally low. The costs of hiring and training have hurt Lucent as there remains a small pool of qualified workers who can be promoted. The ability to produce on time has been another problem for Lucent in China. Problems range from frequent power outages to the human resource problems mentioned above. These difficulties are not unique to Lucent, however; they are common problems for its Chinese competitors as well. Since both parties often wait, for good reason, until the goods are in production in the transferor's factory (the transferor wishes to be sure of the technology to be transferred, and the recipient wishes to assess the value of the technology by reference to the finished article), the product is almost by definition obsolete by the time the recipient is in a position to export.

The quality of service has suffered as Lucent and their Chinese partners have remained unclear about the licensing agreement. Lucent was pushing for a so-called 'dry' license in which its Chinese partners would have to provide service, while the Chinese, naturally, wanted a 'wet' license requiring Lucent servicing. This contrasts with technology transfers, such as between the U.S. and Germany, where both countries are at roughly the same level of development. In such cases, 'dry' licensing is appropriate. In China, generally speaking only 'wet' licensing is likely to work, although it is less advantageous to the company providing the technology transfer. The lack of decisive negotiations on this issue has had a negative affect on quality.

Entry Strategies

There are many possible forms of investment in China. A Chinese Marketing Unit was established by Lucent in 1981. Three major forms of international cooperation strategies were proposed and discussed by this unit. These included either setting up an equity joint venture, licensing, or the hybrid co-production form. A wholly foreign-owned enterprise was not seriously considered, although it would have allowed Lucent to exercise full control over the business. Such enterprises lack the local counterpart Lucent considered necessary for assistance in dealing with the Chinese bureaucracy. Wholly foreign-owned enterprises can also meet with hostility from anti-foreign elements of the local society.

The manufacturing equity joint venture (MEJV) is generally the Chinese favorite because both foreign and local partners take higher risks and share any profits and losses; this forces them to put more effort and planning into ensuring future growth. In the MEJV, the foreign partner would own 25-50% of the venture. Lucent would have to successfully transfer management techniques as well as technology to its Chinese counterpart.

Lucent initially favored the MEJV, but was concerned about problems in China such as lack of infrastructure, inadequate telecommunications facilities, insufficient management autonomy and capabilities, poor Chinese products, and untrained workers. Joint ventures are also difficult to manage, especially in developing countries like China.

Another concern was the convertibility of foreign exchange in China. Equipment and production relied heavily on imports in the 1980s. The Chinese government needed foreign currencies to pay for its imports. Even when foreign companies profited from their investments, it was difficult to convert the Chinese Renminbi to home currencies because of government barriers to exchange.

Licensing was an alternative which focused on technology transfer. 'Wet' was preferred over 'dry' licensing, since Lucent and its potential counterpart were not at the same level of development. A 'dry' license focuses on the transfer of documentation, prints, and intellectual property rights. 'Wet' licensing focuses on technology transfer, and includes staff training and hiring. A 'wet' license allows risks to be divided and associated services to be negotiated if China is not able to absorb new technology. The Chinese government, however, felt that a wet license did not sufficiently and legally commit foreign partners to unlimited, open ended support in achieving the project.

Co-production is a short-term contractual agreement which mixes 'wet' licensing and an MEJV structure. Co-production appealed to Lucent because it was a flexible form of business that divided the risks between the partners but made Lucent responsible, within reasonable limits, for the absorption of the technology by the recipient. Because of short-term obligations, partners lowered their risks and responsibilities. If the project turned out unsuccessful, neither party would be obligated to continue once the contract had expired. The foreign partner does not contribute equity capital, nor shares the responsibility for management of the factory. A number of high-technology transfer projects were already running in China in co-production form, since manufacturing in China was a concern.

There were barriers to setting up co-production. Many foreign investors wanted to benefit from the low labor costs in China in order to export products at competitive prices. The Chinese government and local authorities did not fully support this type of business. From the government's point of view, co-production mainly assisted the foreign partner in export marketing without contributing to the long-term interests of China. In addition, the scope and objective of co-production projects tend to be limited. All high-tech production requires training and continuous innovation and reinvestment. If a contract only lasts for a couple of years, production will only be kept to a small scale, leaving future expansion uncertain.

At last, Lucent decided to begin with a co-production project. Under the negotiated terms, Lucent promised to transfer technology successfully. Its local partner, the Xin Hua Factory, would be responsible for production and guaranteed payments to Lucent in return. Although the time set for co-production was only five years, Lucent regarded this venture as its first step in making an ongoing commitment in China. The key issue to Lucent was how it could turn its first experience into a long-term advantage.

There are several environment factors affecting entry mode selection. When Lucent entered the market, the Chinese government had recently implemented an open door policy, creating a favorable business environment for foreign investors. This policy began in the late 1970s and then picked up pace in the mid-1980s. China found itself far behind western countries economically. The new policy brought about enormous economic reformation. The government allowed more imports and encouraged direct foreign investment and technology transfer. In China, as in many developing countries, the demand for capital, equipment, and technology was very high. At the same time, the government wanted to increase its exports to pay for these imports.

As China became more open, Chinese business people encountered entirely new business concepts and production procedures from the West. Chinese partners were concerned with whether or not they would be able to absorb new technology. As production methods became more complicated, Chinese partners were not always able to handle and adapt to these changes. For foreign investors and first movers, it was important not only to transfer technology but also provide sufficient technical and managerial training to offset these problems.

Lucent agreed to set up production in a factory conveniently situated in central China. The advantages to this location were that it was a heavily populated area, having close links with the target industry, and conveniently connected to other major cities and provinces in China which facilitated import and export. The selection of a convenient location not only established a distribution channel for Lucent but also provided expansion opportunities for the future.

The technological industry in China is very competitive because of the government's support, open door policy, and high market demand. As the technology becomes more advanced, the life cycle of high-tech products are progressively shortened, which also goads competition. If companies in high-tech industries do not invest in innovation, research, and development, they are quickly left behind.

Lucent is a leading company in telecommunications and networking. Its first investment in China was a high-technology transfer project on a co-production basis. Before Lucent entered the market, there were already a number of similar projects running in China, all of which concentrated on manufacturing. These products were intended to serve the demands of the domestic market.

Cooperative Strategies

Period 1: 1981-1988

As discussed above, Lucent made its first step toward long-term development and commitment to the Chinese market in co-production mode. This decision was a sound strategy. Resource-based theory suggests that different firms benefit from different types of resources which can be used to achieve cooperative and strategic advantages as well as competitive and financial benefits. Sharing highly specialized, complementary resources between partners allows each to obtain these benefits from increasing economies of scale, the learning effect, risk reduction, and global integration synergies.

Partner selection became easier for Lucent choosing the co-production strategy. The Xin Hua Factory was selected in consultation with the electronics ministry, and after visits to several factories. Negotiation between Lucent and Xin Hua started in 1982; a 5 year contract was signed in 1984.

The early stages of negotiation were difficult and proceeded slowly. Both sides were experimenting in an unfamiliar culture. The necessity of using interpreters more than doubled negotiation time. During later negotiations, disagreements focused on the value of intellectual property rights, since China was unwilling to pay for initial R&D, documentation, and training. The need to justify prices of components and sub-assemblies also surfaced. These problems were due to the fact that Xin Hua was used to being run by the state; it saw costs only in terms of labor and materials. Lucent was concerned with overhead and other factors. The initial price requested by the Chinese was 30% below Lucent's offer, but was vigorously negotiated by Lucent to within 5% of its original proposal.

Final terms for technological transfer and payment schedules were agreed upon. Initially, the transfer of technology came first. Then, the establishment of a production line took precedence. Supply of CBU, SKD, CKD and other components were expected to follow next. Training in Lucent's home factory and the Chinese factory were to be continuously supported. The introduction of new products in 1986 proved easy to arrange.

Lucent considered both production and development technology as transferable. The former, used to manufacture the product, was crucial to the short term economic success of the project and was absorbed easily through repeated use. The latter was not able to be practiced regularly as it was part of the invention process. It was transferred only in theoretical form and was not successfully absorbed.

Lucent aimed to reduce costs and increase reliability by reducing direct labor and utilizing automatic equipment. This strategy actually led to greater overall costs because more money had to be invested in equipment and training, while less advantage was taken of low Chinese labor economies. The growing sophistication of production methods worsened the situation. Learning by doing is most likely to achieve success, but the process is slow and costly in terms of foreign personnel.

The contract was generally successful. Lucent and Xin Hua each made a reasonable profit and increased their experience. However, even though Xin Hua's production was satisfactory, it lacked the marketing ability and dynamic qualities suitable to partnership in any future EJV. The likelihood that the Xin Hua team would actively develop a Chinese market for the product remained in doubt. The Chinese bureaucracy further showed itself to be incapable of turning the Lucent/Xin Hua venture into a national point of excellence by protecting the new product line against unbridled imports of similar goods produced overseas. This illustrates the problems of developing countries trying to break into foreign markets. The pace of technological change often hampers these efforts when product life cycles are likely to be shorter than the time required to negotiate a contract, set up an overseas production line, and fully train production workers.

Period 2: 1989 to Present

Lucent and the Chinese authorities had different expectations and concerns when the original agreement was renegotiated in 1989. Lucent wanted to have more opportunity to penetrate the domestic market, and increase savings on foreign exchange through import substitution. Lucent was worried that Chinese components being introduced into the product would reduce quality. Moreover, the company expected to broaden the range of products being produced in China by introducing designs tailored to Chinese export requirements. Meanwhile, Lucent's extensive search for Chinese countertrade products was unsuccessful.

Chinese Authorities, on the other hand, pressed for exports from the project. They also stressed that ventures involving foreigners should meet their foreign exchange requirements without concessions from the government. Therefore, they would not accept import substitution as a valid exchange.

The biggest decision that faced Lucent at this time was whether to become involved in an MEJV in the electronics field or continue with co-production. Those who were against the MEJV stated that a joint venture should only be pursued if it was able to be self-financed in foreign exchange. Besides, they argued, there was no evidence that a strong EJV could be built with Xin Hua using the items produced so far, because the volume of each product was small and the domestic market was static. The possibility of successful exporting seemed unlikely. Opponents to the MEJV further stated that Lucent should not become involved in a business likely to experience a loss until answers had been found for the many potential problems. The company should instead plan for the long term, spending resources only to achieve profitable business, rather than on goodwill gestures.

Other executives felt that enough had been learned about Lucent's partner and doing business in China to make this a viable option. They argued that better relationships and stronger commitments in China should be established as soon as possible since the number of other EJVs was growing quickly and might squeeze Lucent out over the long term. After evaluating the current business environment and competition in China, Lucent decided to go ahead with a joint venture.

In 1990, Lucent Technologies of Shanghai was established. One of its partners is the Ministry of Posts & Telecommunications. This venture builds urban, provincial, rural, and long-distance telecommunications networks for about 50 government customers. Out of 350 employees in their Shanghai facility, only 2 are expatriates. The JV has had little trouble attracting the best and brightest Chinese personnel for its local workforce. Today, Lucent holds roughly 30% of the Chinese market for optical fiber transmission equipment. This JV is ranked as the company's largest overseas optical fiber plant.

In 1993, another JV, Lucent Technologies Qingdao Telecommunications System (LTQTS), was established. It is gearing up to become a key switch supplier for the country. It produces 5ESS switches, which industry experts describe as the world's most advanced digital program-controlled switch. China has 5ESS switches operating on 6.5 million telephone lines. LTQTS received orders for 1.5 million more 5ESS switches in 1997. The market potential for the 5ESS is great. If only 30% of the Chinese households get telephones, the country would need a switching system with a 600 million line capacity. China's present switching system can only handle about 100 million lines.

Lucent also set up a Bell Lab in Shanghai as its scientific arm, providing technological support to its JVs in China. With strong technological backing from the Bell Lab and LTQTS, and an annual investment of $7 million in technological research, LTQTS maintains 5ESS's technological advantage.

In 1993, Lucent signed a contract with the State Planning Commission in Beijing to commit U.S.$150 – $200 million in investment in China. By 1995, Lucent was listed among the country's top 500 enterprises, ranking first in telecommunications. In 1996, Lucent passed the $100 million mark for annual sales, and its total investment in the country reached U.S.$150 million. In addition to the Shanghai Bell Lab, Lucent set up another Bell Lab in Beijing. Lucent's technology transfer is being carried out in 3 stages. First, via breakthroughs at its Bell Labs; second, by tailoring technological achievements to the specific needs of Chinese customers; and, third, by manufacturing products incorporating these technologies at its JVs in China. Also in 1996, Lucent opened its first wholly owned subsidiary in Qingdao, China. Its objective was to invest and expand continuously into the Chinese market, while becoming a major supplier for telecommunications power systems products throughout the Asia Pacific Region.

Today, Lucent has one headquarters, six regional offices, seven joint ventures and two wholly-owned subsidiaries in China. It has a work force of more than 1,800 employees and has developed a network of offices and ventures to serve the entire Chinese market. China continues to occupy a significant position in Lucent Technologies' international strategy because its telecommunications are developing more quickly and on a larger scale than any other investment area in the world.

Global Integration

Much of the world is still isolated from modern communications networks. The worldwide demand for telecommunications equipment and infrastructure is growing at a rate of 10 percent annually; in some areas demand is growing even faster. As barriers fall around the world, opening up new markets, Lucent aims to be a key player in providing service. Lucent already has sales and manufacturing locations in Asia, Australia, Europe, North America and South America. Lucent has set up country headquarters and regional offices in each of the countries where it conducts business.

A multi-domestic strategy best describes Lucent's current global operations. This strategy focuses on competition within each country in which the firm operates. Such a strategy assumes markets differ and are segmented by national boundaries. Decision making is decentralized to each strategic business unit in order to tailor products to the specific needs and preferences of local customers.

Lucent adopted a multi-divisional structure in its organization. This structure is characteristically composed of different operating divisions, where each division represents a separate business or profit center, and the top corporate officers delegate responsibilities for day-to-day operations and business-unit strategies to division managers.

Lucent Technologies is composed of four operating units and a research and development division. Each operating unit has established its own sales and manufacturing locations or joint ventures around the globe. Lucent's five core business units are: Consumer Products, Business Communication Systems, Microelectronics, Network Systems, and Bell Laboratories.

1. Consumer Products sells, services and leases telephones and other telecommunications devices through retailers, representing 17,000 point-of sale locations.
2. Business Communications Systems designs, manufactures, installs, and services business telecommunications systems, including private branch exchanges, key systems, structured cabling and voice processing systems.
3. Microelectronics produces high-performance integrated circuits, power systems and microelectronics component for Lucent Technologies and other leading communications and computer manufacturers.
4. Network Systems supplies network telecommunications systems, software, and services to telephone companies around the world, the U.S. government, private communications network operators, cable companies, and wireless service providers.
5. Bell Laboratories focuses on several core technologies: software, digital signal processing, telecommunications networking technologies, micro-electronics and photonics.

Bell Labs is the research and development arm of the firm, contributing all the research, technologies, and innovations necessary to support the development of the operating units in the global market. Bell Labs has set up a network of laboratories in various different countries.

Lucent's two Bell Labs Research and Development facilities in China extend to China world-renowned R&D expertise in telecommunications technologies and systems software. Bell Labs are renowned for their ability to bring leading-edge technology research into innovative product development. Bell Labs will work closely with Chinese universities to establish joint programs promoting the exchange of knowledge, while complementing Lucent's manufacturing presence with local R&D.

Given Lucent's decentralized multi-domestic strategy and multidivisional organizational structure, we can expect that Lucent's global integration in its operating units is low and local responsiveness is high. Strong local responsiveness enables Lucent's subsidiaries and joint venture establishments to respond quickly to changes in the social, economic, and political environments of different markets. By catering to local markets, however, Lucent fails to benefit from economies of scale in its global production. Bell Laboratories, however, provides a highly integrated R&D facilities network that allows each operating unit to share innovative technologies, providing the key to success in the global telecommunications equipment marketplace.

At the corporate level, Lucent's structure enables the officers to more accurately monitor the performance of each business unit, which simplifies the problem of control and also facilitates comparisons between divisions. This improves the resource allocation process. Furthermore, it stimulates managers of poorly performing divisions to look for ways to improve. Lucent has also appointed key personnel at management positions in order to impose its corporate goals on the joint ventures.

Conclusion

In order to form successful joint ventures, it was necessary for Lucent Technologies to show a long term interest in doing business in China. It is very important for the Chinese to feel that they are negotiating with a company that wants to contribute to the prosperity of China. A foreign company must be prepared to share technology on an ongoing basis. Most JVs in China fail after a couple of years because foreign companies are not always prepared to continue to invest in new technology, which causes disappointment to their Chinese partners. Therefore, it is not only important to invest heavily in R&D (16.3% of Lucent's sales in 1997), but also to share technology with the Chinese joint-venture partner.

Other factors also complicate the business environment. It is hard to figure out how profitable China really is for foreign firms. Many international companies complain that they are not operating as well as they had expected in China. Profits and benefits can be offset by problems such as capricious changes in the laws governing foreign investments, as well as corruption, murky intellectual property rights, and other issues. Transfer pricing and other complexities obscure evaluation of real profits to the corporations.

High asset intensity discouraged initial competition when Lucent Technologies first entered China. However, high asset industries are more highly regulated by the government than less asset intense industries. The likelihood that Chinese officials will lower industrial entry barriers through regulation, combined with the attractiveness of the market to other international communications companies, makes increased competition inevitable for Lucent in China.

Lucent will need to shift away from local responsiveness to production factor exploitation as competition intensifies in China. The company should also consider consolidating its production facilities in central China to help achieve better economies of scale. Lucent also needs to diversify its customer base. This would help reduce financial uncertainties in its China operations as new entrants attack its current market.

The Chinese government is opening up the economy and trying to attract foreign investment. To be successful, Lucent must continue to prove that they have a long-term interest in doing business in China. The development of technological innovation requires heavy investments, and transfer of technology may take many years to accomplish. Knowing this, the government remains concerned about whether foreign companies are really committing themselves. The government and local authorities will be more willing to show their support if the projects are aimed at long-term partnerships, and investors are clearly intending to contribute to the prosperity of China. Co-production was successful at first, as it is related to intense competition in a high-tech industry. But it is not sufficient when the contract only lasts for a short period of time, and this is not indication that both the foreign and local partners intend to invest for the future. Such forms of production find it difficult to achieve economies of scale. Furthermore, if a company fails to maintain a technological edge, it will find it hard to survive in China and compete with its many rivals. Limited objectives therefore cause problems for companies entering China.

4. DUPONT IN CHINA

Company Introduction

DuPont is currently the fifteenth largest company in the United States. Its goal is to become the world's most successful chemistry-based company by creating high quality, innovative products that make people's lives better. DuPont now operates in over seventy countries worldwide. DuPont is a global chemical and energy company offering high-performance products based on chemicals, polymers, fibers, and petroleum. The company maintains its position as the world's largest chemical company through research and technology dedicated towards improving quality of life and enhancing the vitality of the communities in which it operates.

DuPont is one of the oldest continuously operating industrial enterprises in the world. It was established in 1802 by a French immigrant, Eleuthere Irenee du Pont de Nemours, who set up the company to produce gunpowder. His product ignited reliably which was greatly appreciated by citizens of the fledgling U.S. republic. Thomas Jefferson wrote thanking du Pont for the quality of his powder.

DuPont's corporate headquarters are now in Wilmington, Delaware. Charles O. Holliday, Jr. is current president, chairman, and CEO. According to Fortune 500, in 1997 DuPont was the fifteenth largest U.S. industrial/service corporation, with revenues of $45 billion and a net income of $2.4 billion. Its exports amounted to nearly $4.0 billion, 48 percent of its total sales, making the company one of the largest U.S. exporters. DuPont operates in 70 countries worldwide, with 165 manufacturing and processing facilities. A third of the company's 97,000 employees work abroad. It has established major markets in North America and Europe and is expanding its presence to the Asia Pacific and South American regions.

DuPont does business in areas related to the aerospace, agricultural, apparel, automotive, construction, electronics, packaging, refining, safety, and transportation industries. DuPont products carry major brand names such as Lycra (spandex fiber), Teflon (fluoropolymer resins), Stainmaster (flooring systems), Kevlar (aramid fiber), Silverstone (non-stick finishes), Tyvek (spunbonded olefin), and Corian (solid surface material). Its chemical segment includes White Pigments and Mineral Products which use titanium dioxide, Specialty Chemicals which produce a range of chemical intermediates, and Fluorochemicals which produce refrigerants. Its fiber businesses include Nylon, Lycra, Dacron, Nonwovens, and Advanced Fiber Systems. A diversified mix of specialty fibers is produced to serve end uses ranging from protective apparel, active sportswear, home fabrics, carpeting, and packaging to high-strength composites used by the aerospace industry. The polymers businesses include Packaging and Industrial Polymers, Automotive, Corian Engineering Polymers, Fluoropolymers, and DuPont Dow Elastomers. Its life sciences businesses consist of Agricultural Products, with a focus on crop protection chemicals and biotechnology, and Pharmaceuticals. Finally, it has a diversified group of businesses consisting of Polyester Films, Polyester Resins and Intermediates, Photopolymer and Electronic Materials, and Printing and Graphics Products.

Since 1992, DuPont has been going through a major reorganization. Administration was reduced by 80 percent, senior management cut by 40 percent and the general DuPont population was reduced by 25 percent. This was achieved through generous early retirement incentives, including cash payments, and through attrition. During this period it has also reorganized around self-contained strategic business units to speed its involvement with its customers. For example, old fiber department has been replaced by a series of SBUs such as Dacron, Lycra, and Nylon which have more autonomy and responsibility to meet profit objectives. The SBU structure has eliminated one whole level of management, the executive vice presidents and their staff that previously headed its major departments.

DuPont has set up eight joint ventures in China, mostly located in Shanghai, Guangdong, Jiangsu, Shandong, and Liaoning. Its first wholly-owned investment in China was made in 1989 in Shenzhen which produces Riston photopolymer film, x-ray film, and Tyvek spunbonded olefin. It recently broke ground in Shenzhen again when it set up two additional wholly-owned facilities to manufacture Delrin, an acetal resin and Tynex, a nylon monofilament. DuPont's chairman has affirmed a commitment to increasing the company's presence in China by tripling its $300 million investment by the year 2000.

Some of DuPont's recent acquisitions are a joint venture with BASF to manufacture and sell Nylon intermediates in Asia. Another joint venture was with the Thai Container Group which will enable it to print corrugated packaging with high quality halftone process work as well as improve the overall level of print quality.

External Environment

The potential for new competitors in the chemical industry is relatively low due to the tremendous amount of capital investment needed to set up a chemicals company. But as more companies break up into smaller units, speed and service have become increasingly essential. To stay ahead of this trend, DuPont has begun concentrating on stabilizing prices and using state of the art technology and resources.

In the U.S., the top four chemical companies are DuPont, the Bayer Group, Dow Chemical, and 3M. In 1997, DuPont led the pack with $12.4 billion in U.S. sales, followed by the Bayer Group with $9 billion, Dow Chemical with $8.8 billion, and 3M with 6.7 billion. Major rivalry with established Chinese companies includes Shanghai Hua Yi Group, which is the biggest chemical and pharmaceutical group in China.

Buyer bargaining power is minimal for new products since many of DuPont's products cannot be obtained from any other company. More mature products lead to moderate bargaining power for buyers who can turn to other companies for similar products. Relationship building is important to DuPont since it promises highly innovative quality products to buyers in order to retain their loyalty.

Supplier bargaining power is also minimal since DuPont manufactures most of its own products. DuPont runs its own research and development laboratories and agricultural facilities in various locations around the world.

The threat of substitute products has become an increasing concern for DuPont as licensing and partnerships have distributed proprietary knowledge to other companies. DuPont therefore continues to focus on product innovation in order to maintain a strong market share.

DuPont products range from being in the embryonic to the decline stages of their life cycles. In the United States, products like Teflon resins, Lycra brand spandex fiber, and Stainmaster stain-resistant carpets are reaching maturity. Titanium dioxide products and advanced fibers are in the growth stage. Products in the embryonic stage include much of the company's agricultural and biological technologies. In China, most of its products are in the embryonic, introductory, or growth stages due to China's expanding economy and relatively recent openness to foreign investment.

Chemical industry sales in the U.S. approach $372 billion a year. This accounts for almost 24 percent of the world's total chemical output. By the year 2000, sales are expected to reach $430 billion. This growth is in part because the industry is not constrained by labor unions or the kinds of conservative business practices found in other countries.

Major acquisitions have also altered the balance of the global chemical industry to favor U.S. operations. Many companies in the industry have been downsizing or reengineering in order to remain profitable and efficient. The number of U.S. firms has increased due to the breaking up of large firms into smaller ones which can better serve customers and use resources more efficiently.

The availability of loans has been high thanks to a strong U.S. economy which has seen little or no recession in recent years. Interest rates and inflation are low, and savings rates are high. By contrast, in China the cost of investment is substantially higher. This has prevented growth in the number of new firms there.

All business dealings in China are based on the development of strong relationships between partners. This can be a complex process involving many more luncheon and dinner banquets and office and factory visits than is usual amongst Western companies. Western managers may feel that little work is getting done, but the relationships that are being built will be very valuable in the future. An important attribute of good relationships is flexibility, which is required for the alignment of partner goals.

Having set up its first office in China 80 years ago, DuPont has been reaping the benefits of long term relationships. It has learned to manage a culturally diverse work force and understand the issues that motivate its Chinese employees. Patience has been key in building successful joint ventures in China. Negotiations in China take longer and require a lot more resources than in other countries.

In the U.S., governmental policies are minimal and most chemical product categories are not highly regulated. Foreign companies producing or selling chemical products in China are facing tougher laws. China's chemical industrial plan stresses technological transfer as a condition for foreign investment, places heavy emphasis on mergers and acquisitions, favors technical renovation rather than new construction, and espouses adherence to international environmental standards. China's rapidly developing legal infrastructure and its shift from administrative to judicial enforcement of laws and regulations will hopefully reduce local protectionism and the previous lack of willingness to enforce existing laws.

Under the new law, chemicals brought into China from early 1998 will have to undergo risk assessment by local environmental protection agencies. Imported chemical products will also undergo a rigorous registration process by Chinese authorities that will require payment to secure product registration for a specific period of time. For toxic chemicals, the fee is $10,000 for two years. This brand new legislation remains somewhat ambiguous, however. By working with the Chinese authorities, companies have been able to ensure fair implementation of the laws.

Chemical technology has become more readily available because of increased availability of licensing. Processes are becoming more simplified but also quickly become outdated. Companies must invest tremendous amounts of capital on research and development if they wish to remain competitive.

The skill level of employees varies greatly because of broad product diversity and the size of the firms in the industry. For instance, line workers require minimal skill levels, while product developers and engineers require a great deal of know-how. As technology increases, the skill level of employees must also increase.

Internal Environment

Financial

DuPont's sales rose 3 percent to $45.1 billion in 1997. Tax avoidance in this industry is difficult. However, there is a low petroleum excise tax. The petroleum segment sales were $21.0 billion, 4 percent over the previous year. Sales for the combined chemicals and specialties segments were up 2% to $24.1 billion. Outside of the United States, sales made up 46 percent of the total worldwide chemicals and specialties. DuPont's cash as provided by operations as a percent of total debt is 58 percent. Its total debt as a percent of total capitalization is 50 percent. The return on average investors capital is 12.3 percent.

In 1997, DuPont strengthened the company's position in the chemicals, energy, specialties, and life sciences markets through four strategic acquisitions. The first was when DuPont's Conoco division spent $0.9 billion to purchase the Lobo natural gas properties in South Texas. Next, the company purchased a 20 percent interest in Pioneer Hi-Bred International for $1.7 billion. It then acquired ICI's global polyester intermediates and resins businesses for $1.2 billion and the Protein Technologies International business from Ralston Purina for 22.5 million shares of DuPont stock, valued at $1.3 billion.

DuPont routinely uses forward exchange contracts in order to maintain a balance with its foreign currencies so that exchange gains and losses are minimized. It also uses forward exchange contracts to establish the U.S. dollar amount of future firm commitments denominated in a foreign currency. The decision to hedge is made on a case by case basis taking into consideration the amount and duration of exposure, market volatility, and economic trends.

Technological

DuPont has achieved its position as the nation's fifteenth largest company through its continuous effort to be at the forefront of technology. It is constantly transforming itself and finding ways to stay ahead of the competition. DuPont is now becoming a world leader in pharmaceuticals and biotechnology. It runs more than forty research and development labs in the U.S. alone, with thirty-five labs in eleven other countries. New product sales account for about $1 billion in sales each year. The company holds approximately 2000 trademarks and brands.

In its agricultural segment, researchers are trying to alter the genetic makeup of wheat, soybeans, and corn to make these crops more resistant to disease and insects and more nutritious. They are planning to use a gene found in spiders to create a new artificial silk that would be stronger than steel. The pharmaceuticals segment of the company has developed some promising new drugs such as Cozaar, the fastest growing hypertension drug. Its Conoco venture focuses on advances in deep water petroleum production technology.

Organizational

DuPont employs about 98,000 people, 35 percent of whom work outside the United States. The characteristics it seeks in its employees include global experience, a strong external focus, creativity, enthusiasm, devotion to customer satisfaction, and a team orientation. It carefully selects and trains employees who it feels will help the company maintain leadership and enable it to expand into new areas. It treats its employees as valued resources and makes safety, health, and the environment top priorities.

Recently, the company's costs were exceeding revenue growth, forcing DuPont to raise prices, which resulted in a decrease in customers. To counter this problem, DuPont reduced administration by eighty percent, senior management by forty percent, and its general employee population by twenty-five percent. This major restructuring enabled it to reduce costs by about $3 billion.

At the same time, it broke departments down into Strategic Business Unit, or SBUs, which allowed the company to increase its speed of service and customer responsiveness by providing each unit with greater autonomy and responsibility. SBU leaders report directly to the Office of the Chief Executive, which includes the president and CEO of DuPont, the president and CEO of Conoco, the chairman of DuPont Europe, the chairman of DuPont Asia Pacific, and the Chief Financial Officer. With fewer layers of management, the employees at DuPont have more freedom to make direct contributions to the company.

Operational

DuPont's main businesses are broadly grouped into three main types. It has been most heavily investing in the Life Sciences, including agricultural products, pharmaceuticals, and biotechnology, in its bid to achieve long term growth. Its most stable areas are the Differentiated businesses, including Lycra brand spandex, automotive products, titanium dioxide, advanced fibers, and Tyvek spunbonded olefin. It is already a market leader in these areas. The company was founded on technology which produced nylon, polyester, and engineering polymers, which are grouped under the Foundation heading. These products continue to provide DuPont with the necessary cash flow and growth so that it can explore other areas.

DuPont promotes it products mainly through television commercials, radio advertisements, and the newspaper. Some of its more successful advertising campaigns have been "Comfort Begins Inside," and "Better Things for Better Living." Last year, it came out with a new corporate campaign promoting some of its best-known brands according to the personal benefit they provide. For example, Lycra Power helps with an athlete's endurance, and CoolMax takes moisture away from the skin. DuPont it trying to promote specific products rather than an overall image. The company also began running ads on television and radio and in major newspapers and farming publications that focus on farming issues. The goal of the "Voice of the American Farmer" campaign is to provide a platform for farmers to help the non-farming public understand and appreciate contributions agriculture makes to small communities, the nation, and the world.

Due to its recent restructuring efforts, DuPont has been able to contain costs and stabilize worldwide selling prices. In the United States, its prices were down less than 1 percent but outside the United States, prices averaged 7 percent below 1996. For its mature products, it uses a competitive pricing strategy. For new products it uses a high price strategy.

DuPont also licenses its process technologies to achieve revenues which offset research and development costs while establishing new alliances and joint ventures. It aims to generate $10 million a year in licensing revenues and add ten licenses annually to its current fifty. By 2005, it expects licensing revenues to reach $100 million.

Corporate-Level Strategies

DuPont has chosen to enter China for several reasons. China has the fastest growing economy in the world. Its GNP has grown at a rate of 10 percent annually since 1980, while the world average is less than 3 percent. Per capita income for living expenses in urban households has increased by 3.3 percent. Hong Kong, recently reunited with China, has the most open economy in the world. Exports represent about 200 percent of GDP and its GDP growth averages about 7 percent annually.

China is the world's most rapidly growing consumer nation. The urban coastal provinces are flourishing. China's chemical industry has been growing at a rate of 9 percent each year for the last seven years, a rate expected to continue through the year 2000. DuPont usually knows what products are most likely to be in demand in China, but is hampered in cashing in on its own forecasts by the length of time it takes to set up new plants and by competition from Chinese state-run enterprises which often come out with similar products at lower prices.

Continuing improvement of China's infrastructure and distribution system allows multinational companies to invest in world-scale projects rather than small regional facilities that would be less competitive in the marketplace. DuPont has the ability to invest huge amounts of capital into projects in China without worrying too much about short term profit. The total amount it has invested so far is about $300 million; it plans to triple that figure by the year 2000. Its sales in China grew 40 percent last year; they are expected to grow at least 30 percent annually.

Although China is predominantly a rural society, its urban population is increasing as people migrate from the countryside to coastal provinces to find work. Despite the problem of lack of education amongst these workers, cheap labor has made China attractive to DuPont. China's labor costs are an astounding one-tenth of Western wages.

One problem DuPont faces is lack of health and safety guidelines in the Chinese workplace and ignorance on the part of Chinese workers concerning basic safety measures. According to China's Ministry of Labor, about 70 percent of all accidents are related in part to insufficient training, particularly in the handling of chemicals. Zhen Lihua, a physician in the burns unit at Shenzhen Red Cross Hospital, notes that about one-third of his patients are victims of industrial accidents. While accidents at foreign-invested operations make up only a small percentage of the total, there has been a substantial increase over previous years. DuPont is trying to curb this problem by providing close supervision and more frequent visits to its chemical plants, including hiring independent auditors to keep an eye on implementation of safety protocols.

Another problem that manufacturers transferring technology to China must take under consideration is the large-scale copying of such technologies, particularly in the pharmaceutical and agrochemical sectors. Products made from pirated technologies then compete with foreign products at lower prices. The Chinese government has been making strides in rectifying its intellectual property rights system, however.

Progress on large petrochemical joint ventures has been slowed by the limitations imposed by the Chinese government on foreign investment. A formal joint venture plan and feasibility study must first be prepared for approval by several organizations: the Industry Ministry, Provincial Government, and the Ministry of Foreign Trade and Economic Cooperation.

There are tax benefits available to many foreign invested enterprises, including reduced income taxes, tax holidays, and refunds. The standard 33 percent tax rate, which includes federal and local tax, can be reduced in a number of ways. The 3 percent local tax rate can be waived by the local government. A 24 percent federal rate is available to manufacturing entities established in Economic and Technological Development Zones (ETDZ), Coastal Open Economic Zones (COEZ), or other designated zones. A 15 percent federal tax rate is available to entities established in Special Economic Zones (SEZ) or in designated industries within the ETDZ or COEZ areas. Tax holidays are available to foreign investment enterprises which have been in operation for more than ten years, when 50 percent or more of their revenues come from production or processing activities. Tax holidays can be extended for qualifying export or high technology enterprises. When a foreign enterprise reinvests profit into the business for at least five years, 40 to 100 percent of the profit reinvested may also be refunded.

Business-Level Strategy

President and CEO Holliday says that the organization is aligned so that its chemicals and specialties businesses can aggressively implement differentiated strategies with a focus on long term growth. Product diversification is key to this strategy. Many different products are sold directly to the consumer market, but DuPont also makes many intermediary products.

The company's central business managers provide freedom to local employees to make critical decisions, so long as these are compatible with the company's global strategy. They are also expected to adjust production levels to meet the demands of the marketplace at both the global and local levels.

In order to maintain its position in the industry, DuPont formed an alliance with two major firms to handle its information technology needs. These are the Computer Sciences Corporation (CSC) and Andersen Consulting. CSC manages DuPont's global mainframe, midrange and personal computer infrastructure, and global telecommunications network. It will also handle business and staff function computer applications in Europe, Canada, and the United States. Andersen Consulting is a global management and technology consulting organization that helps its clients change to stay ahead in their respective industries. It provides chemical and energy business solutions designed to improve DuPont's manufacturing, marketing, distribution, and customer service.

Entry Strategies

Entry Mode Selection

DuPont first invested in a wholly-owned facility in China in 1989. Chinese regulations stipulate that wholly-owned enterprises should contribute to the development of the nation's economy, use advanced technology and equipment, and export all or a large portion of their products. DuPont's strategic objectives were to use its technological strengths to meet China's industrial needs, develop a better understanding about Chinese business practices, and create a broad base of local people who could operate its plants in the future. At the same time, DuPont chose the wholly-owned mode because it distrusted the Chinese property rights system. It felt that entering through joint ventures would increase the risk of proprietary knowledge (such as chemical patents) being stolen by future competitors.

Next, DuPont wanted to increase its investments by establishing joint ventures. In 1991, DuPont formed its first joint venture with the Asia Pacific Chemical Group Company to produce Londax rice herbicide. Since then, DuPont has continued to set up new joint ventures, including a photomask joint venture with the Shanghai Photomask Precision Company and a Lycra spandex fiber manufacturing joint venture with China Worldbest Development Corporation. It has also formed joint ventures with other foreign companies in China, including BASF Akitengesellschaft and Foshan Hongii Plastic Packaging Materials Company Ltd. Today, DuPont has twenty joint ventures in China.

Owning its own facility allowed DuPont to maintain the service and quality it required initially in a foreign country, but it then wanted to be able to compete in China by meeting market demand. This was accomplished by setting up many joint ventures which could produce different products in response to demand. DuPont's strategic move to use joint ventures was also aimed at garnering greater customer loyalty amongst the Chinese people. Furthermore, joint ventures allowed DuPont to overcome trade barriers and gain access to distribution channels.

Lastly, participating in joint ventures helped reduce the culture clash related to differences in business practices between China and the United States.

Entry Timing

DuPont can be considered an early entrant to the chemical and energy industries in China. As an early entrant, it was able to establish strong market power and create entry barriers for followers. It faced little competition because there were only a few companies in China that participated in the same industry. DuPont also had the advantage of making use of some of China's raw materials before any other company. DuPont took advantage of these factors to build a strong foundation for itself while increasing its presence in China, gain technological leadership, and establish its brand name.

It also faced some operational risks as an early entrant. Because China is still shifting to a market based economy, it has sometimes been difficult for DuPont to keep up with rapid market trends and economic changes in the country. In addition, China's infrastructure and distribution system did not allow DuPont to make the kinds of investments in world-scale technological plants to which it is accustomed. It has instead had to focus on smaller regional facilities.

DuPont also had to deal with high anti-imitation costs since the government demanded that foreign investors share their know-how as a condition for doing business in the country. Since patents were unprotected, in 1991 a local entrepreneur took one of DuPont's fiber formulas and started up a rival firm to produce the same product. It was not until 1993 that new laws were introduced to supplement and strengthen China's patent regulations, extending patent protection from ten to twenty years and requiring patents to be registered in China.

Location Selection

DuPont chose China for its low labor costs, high demand, and abundant raw materials. DuPont selected areas such as Shenzhen, Shanghai, Guangdong, and Beijing which are Special Economic Zones (SEZs) with low tax rates. Shenzhen and Guangdong, for example, are coastal city SEZs enjoying increased economic activity while offering tax rates of only 15 percent to investors. Shenzhen was the site of DuPont's first investment in China. The Guangdong region is China's largest exporter and leader in attracting foreign investment.

Shanghai was chosen because it is a major industrial and financial center. Shanghai accounts for a little over 1 percent of China's population, 8 percent of GDP, and 20 percent of total foreign investment. Shanghai and other eastern coastal provinces such as Jiangsu and Zhejiang form the heart of China's chemical industry. A new chemical industrial zone is being built on the outskirts of Shanghai at Caojing on Hangzhou Bay to solve the problem of Shanghai having reached its limit in room of expansion of chemical plants. The new twenty square kilometer zone will be equipped with ten wharves which can accommodate large ships, have ample storage facilities, and are able to handle specialized chemicals. DuPont formed Agricultural Chemicals Ltd., a joint venture with China Worldbest Development Corporation. It has another joint venture with Shanghai Pacific Chemicals.

Cooperative Strategies

DuPont believes that partnerships are supported by the willingness to make long-term commitments. DuPont has therefore formed several joint ventures that are expected to last up to 50 years. DuPont's main goal in the formation of joint ventures within China is to align itself with local industrial leaders that can help the company settle in places where it has not previously done business and provide new distribution channels for its products. One example is Shanghai Hua Yi, a holding company formed from a merger of Shanghai Chemical Industry Holding (formerly Shanghai Chemical Industry Bureau) and the Shanghai Pharmaceutical Industry Bureau. Shanghai Hua Yi has seven production sites in China and holds assets of over $3.7 billion. It is comprised of five large companies, each with different specialties in the chemical industry. Hua Yi is coordinating the Caojing project, the new chemical in dustrial zone mentioned earlier. It also already has formed a number of joint ventures with overseas partners such as DuPont. Partnering with Hua Yi will enable DuPont's agrochemical joint venture to make the transition from five years of struggle to becoming a profitable operation.

Another big player in the chemical industry that DuPont aligned itself with is the Asia Pacific Agricultural Chemical Company (APACC). APACC is one of the largest agrochemical enterprises in China with foreign trade autonomy. The APACC group consists of the Shanghai Pesticide Factory, the Shanghai Union Chemical Factory, the Shanghai Dongfeng Pesticide Factory, and the Shanghai Pesticide Research Institute. The company specializes in the production and marketing of pesticides, insecticides, chemicals, and chemical intermediates. Its production capacity is an impressive annual 15,000+ tons.

DuPont's partner selection is partially based on its having complementary skills in marketing, technology, and manufacturing. For example, DuPont chose the China Worldbest Development Corporation because of its innovativeness and strengths in the sciences.

Capability is another important characteristic in good partners. DuPont seeks partners that have already been successful in China over the years. DuPont formed a joint venture with the Shanghai Chemical Holding Company because it is the largest chemical company in China. It has also had time to develop a business culture similar to DuPont's.

An Equity Joint Venture (EJV) is the most commonly used joint venture operation in China. It is favored by Chinese companies and the government. EJV partners in China have limited liability and must own at least 25 percent of the venture. There is a limit of a 2:1 Debt to Equity ratio for EJVs with over $30 million in equity. DuPont prefers a dominant share of equity and control, so it usually has more than a 50 percent stake in any joint venture. For instance, it has a 90 percent stake in its joint venture with the China Worldbest Development Company and an 80 percent stake in the joint venture with the Shanghai Asia Pacific Chemical Group. It is less concerned with maintaining control when it chooses other foreign companies in China as partners, however. For example, BASF and DuPont share their joint venture equally.

DuPont uses a global strategy in its international operations. Each product unit in various countries is controlled by corporate headquarters. DuPont standardizes all it products for a variety of markets. Each product market has its own strategic business units in which individual business unit leaders report directly to the CEO. Each product division is responsible for its own international business relations and is internationally diversified. DuPont therefore makes use of product divisions as its international business structure.

5. AT&T IN CHINA

Company Introduction

AT&T was the first telephone service provider. Until 1984 it was also the largest corporation in the world, with $155 billion in assets and a net income of $7.1 billion. AT&T has undergone major restructuring following an antitrust settlement in 1984 and divestiture in 1997. It continues to hold onto its core mission of bringing people together. It has placed a major focus on developing international markets and now has joint ventures and alliances in over 30 countries. Its Chinese operations began with one representative office in Beijing in 1985, but now include five manufacturing joint ventures and several partnership agreements and strategic alliances with the Chinese Telecommunications Administration.

AT&T's founding father, Alexander Graham Bell, invented the telephone in 1876. With the help of several financial backers, he formed the Bell Telephone Company in 1877. American Telephone and Telegraph was established in 1885 as a long distance subsidiary. AT&T had a monopoly on the telephone until 1894, when its patents expired. AT&T enjoyed a position as a government regulated monopoly for many years. In 1974, however, MCI Communications filed an antitrust lawsuit against AT&T and won. AT&T was split into the seven regional 'baby bell' companies in the settlement. Nevertheless, until 1984, AT&T was the largest corporation in the world and set industrial standards worldwide.

More recently, AT&T has been split into three different companies: AT&T, which provides communications services; Lucent Technologies, which focuses on systems and technology; and NCR, which specializes in transaction intensive computing. In addition to this trivestiture, AT&T was internally restructured with a change in CEOs in 1997. The new CEO, C. Michael Armstrong, is described as decisive and unorthodox. He is trying to transform AT&T from a monopoly-oriented company into a global competitor concentrating on the Internet and data transfer. He negotiated the purchase of cable giant TCI for $48 billion in stock. He plans to provide extensive services to rural areas with telephone, video, and data transfer all part of the same infrastructure. Under his guidance, AT&T has also formed a joint venture with British Telecom to combine international telephone operations. AT&T has purchased the Teleport Communications Group, a telephone company that serves big businesses in city centers. AT&T has also sold its credit-card services. Finally, it has negotiated long-term service contracts with CITI and Banc One to provide them with communications networks.

AT&T chose to enter China due to the vast potential of the Chinese consumer market. AT&T was a first mover in China. One of its most successful strategies has been developing long-term relationships with the Chinese government.

Major Businesses

AT&T's mission is to give people easy access to one another by providing the information and services people need while building shareholder value. AT&T is the largest telecommunications company in the United States. It has begun shifting from simple long distance communications into full range telecommunications and information services, including use of the wireless and Internet.

AT&T provides long distance service to every country and territory in the world. It is a major presence in Latin America, the Caribbean, Europe, the Middle East, Africa, the Asia Pacific region, and North America, with operations in over thirty countries. Its foreign investments totaled more than $5 billion over the past five years.

External Environment

The Chinese economy is an attractive emerging market to many multinational companies. It offers the largest consumer market in the world with a potential 1.2 billion consumers. Many firms are able to take advantage of its relatively cheap labor force. China is the fastest growing economy in the world today, with a GDP growth rate at 9.3 percent in 1997. Its consumer price inflation rate fell to about 4 percent the same year.

China's economic growth has been hampered by lack of the fundamental elements of an infrastructure such as electricity, telecommunications networks, and transportation. Developing the energy industry is China's top priority. It currently has the world's fastest growing electrical power industry. As much as $80 billion will be invested in the near future in power generation projects. The Chinese government also plans to build six new railways, four major subway systems, and better municipal transportation systems. The government has also taken steps to implement changes in laws concerning commercial and central banking, insurance, and securities in order to encourage and support foreign investment. It has taken steps to align itself with international standards with regard to trademark registration and patent protection.

China has two different types of import tariffs. These remain high overall despite gradual reductions. They can be as little as 3 percent for those import goods which are being promoted (i.e. new technology) or up to 150 percent for imports which are being discouraged (e.g. automobiles). China also has a complex system of licensing that acts as an effective non-tariff import trade barrier. China has a 17 percent value added tax on many goods.

AT&T's major rivals are MCI WorldCom and Sprint. MCI is in the number two position, with $7.3 billion in revenues for 1997. MCI provides local and long distance phone services, international telecommunications, and cellular and paging services. It owns American Sky Broadcasting and offers internet access over fiber optic cable. MCI is AT&T's largest threat because its annual sales growth increase is phenomenal (63.9 percent compared to AT&T's 1.7 percent). Sprint is the number three U.S. long distance telephone service provider, although it holds the second position for local telephone service. Sprint earned revenues of $14 billion in 1997 and had a single year sales growth increase of 5.9 percent.

There is a high potential for new rivals to enter the telecommunications industry because of its rapidly changing technology. The Telecommunications Act of 1996 broke the barrier between local telephone and long distance carriers and cellular, digital, video, and cable providers. Telecommunications systems now transfer voice, video, and digital data over a variety of wired and wireless systems, allowing existing companies to move rapidly into new territories. Many firms are establishing alliances and mergers to position themselves for more intense competition.

Since AT&T has its own manufacturing plants, supplier bargaining power is usually not an issue. The bargaining power of the buyer is very high, however. Aggressive price competition places a lot of pressure on telecommunications firms to continuously lower their prices. Many of AT&T's service contracts were renegotiated at lower prices as customers shifted into more favorable calling plans. Competition has forced AT&T to offer even greater discounts to high volume users.

At this time, it is impossible to predict which multimedia and interactive products will dominate the marketplace. Due to rapidly changing telecommunications technology, there is great potential for substitute services and products including wireless and cellular phone systems, VSAT, cable, and satellite access.

The traditional long distance telephone industry is in a decline characterized by great change. There is a profusion of new technologies, services, and competitors. The resulting new telecommunications industry is therefore still in an embryonic stage. Key product developments include widened bandwidth usage, optical transmission and switching, VSAT, satellite technology, distributed databases, wireless communications, digital technology, and various Internet protocols.

Internal Environment

AT&T has very strong financial capabilities. Its 1997 cash flow was $8.4 billion, an increase of 7.1 percent over the previous year. Increased cash flow has primarily resulted from nationwide improvements in customer cash collection methods and the collection of employee benefits receivables. AT&T has the highest gross and net profit margin in the industry at 42.6 percent and 9 percent, respectively. Its 20.5 percent return on equity is two times that of MCI's. AT&T has also reduced its outstanding long-term debts from $11.6 billion in 1995 to $6.8 billion by the end of 1997.

Future financing will be accomplished by issuing commercial paper long-term debt and equity, with the timing of issue, principal amount, and form depending on the company's needs and prevailing market and economic conditions.

CEO Armstrong has set up a strict cost cutting strategy and a new corporate culture in which, for example, executives are expected to drive themselves to work. He has cut 1.6 billion in cost and laid off 20,000 employees, with more layoffs expected in the future. The message from the new CEO is operational efficiency, moving AT&T away from a stagnant monopolistic approach into innovative and aggressive strategies.

In 1997, AT&T spent $829 million on research and development of new products. It has also filed at least 8,000 patent applications, including ones for the dual-tone multi-frequency signal transfer protocol, call screening, a voice-directed telephone directory, and a method for selecting wireless communications providers in a multi-service provider environment.

Corporate-Level Strategy

AT&T chose China as one of the most significant markets of the future. AT&T had already invested about $2 billion in China before 1996. With its telecommunications sector growing at an annual rate of over 50 percent, China is expected to become one of the world's top telecommunications markets by the year 2020. As of 1997, China had 406 telecommunications related manufacturing plants, 51 of which were foreign-funded and 188 state-owned, altogether employing 94,000 people. Chinese suppliers are beginning to take a larger portion of the market, with the foreign share expected to decrease from 35 to 30 percent. At the same time, a 20 percent increase is expected in the overall market.

China's telecommunications sector was worth $16 billion in 1996, a 34.5 percent increase over 1995. 1996 showed a 15.5 million increase in telephone subscribers over 1995, bringing the total to 61.8 million. The waiting period for phone service was also shortened to a month. Nevertheless, in 1996 China's phone coverage was still only about 6.3 percent for the whole nation (22 percent in urban areas). There were a total of 93.2 million office phone exchanges in 1996. Cellular phone subscribers increased by 3.2 million to 6.9 million, with digital cell phone subscribers at 1.6 million. 8 million more people began using pagers, bringing the 1996 total to 25.4 million. Email users went up to 9,888 and internet users (on ChinaNet) went up to 33,634. China is investing approximately U.S.$12 billion annually, planning to double its phone capacity to 170 million lines with 123 million subscribers by the year 2000. Cellular phone subscribers are also expected to increase to about 18 million. Even with these increases, however, the national coverage will only be about 10 percent (30 percent in the cities).

All of AT&T's investments in China are related to its primary industry, telecommunications. AT&T's related diversification strategy allows the company to generate stable profits with lower risks. By 1995, AT&T had nine joint ventures in China producing related products and providing a wide range of services including switching and transmission systems, international long distance communications services such as calling cards, international toll-free calling, fax, mail, data interchange, computer products, networking systems (e.g. fiber optic cable networks and Internet access) and home appliances.

In 1994, AT&T and S. Megga Telecommunication Company announced a joint venture partnership with the Post and Telecommunication Industrial Corporation of China to produce and sell AT&T brand products such as corded and cordless phones, digital answering machines, videophones, and fax machines. In 1995, AT&T signed a contract worth more than U.S.$150 million with the Guangdong Province Post and Telecommunications Administrative Bureau (GPTB) to supply advanced telecommunications equipment to Guangdong Province in Southern China. This contract is the first phase of a U.S.$500 million cooperation and purchase agreement. In 1997, AT&T, China Telecom, and eight other carriers signed a contract to build the first fiber optic undersea cable directly between China and the United States. The whole project will cost about 1.4 billion and is expected to be completed by the year 2000.

Business-Level Strategy

The telecommunications market in China is highly competitive. Every global telecommunications company in the world is trying to get a piece of China's market, including AT&T, MCI, IBM, Motorola, Nortel, Sprint, British Telecom, and Ericsson. AT&T has developed a competitive strategy of product differentiation and specialized focus on China's market. Its R&D laboratories are running 24 hours a day in order to provide China with high-quality voice and information transmission and easy-to-use products and services. In November 1997, AT&T signed a contract with China

Telecom to introduce T45, the fastest Internet access in China. It offers a transmission speed of approximately 45 megabits per second. China Telecom predicts there will be three to four million Internet users in China by the year 2000. Another service, AT&T Solution, helps corporations or governmental departments set up internal or external networks and solve communications problems.

AT&T's investment strategy further supports its competitive strategies. Investment depends on the stage of the industrial life cycle and the strength of the company's competitive position in the industry. The telecommunications industry in China is in the embryonic and growth stage, with great opportunities to gain high profits. AT&T already has a strong competitive position due to early entrance, leadership, advanced technology, and a good relationship with Chinese government. In the past decade, many of the AT&T's top executives have visited China and met with some of its top officials. Setting up joint ventures with local and other companies is essential to maintain and increase market power. By 1995, AT&T already had nine joint venture projects in China and expected to add more.

One of AT&T's commitment is to offer high quality services and products to the Chinese customers. It has transferred a great deal of technology and experience to China, including training Chinese engineers and telecommunications network managers. In 1993, it sponsored a forty-day program on management style for thirty-four Chinese executives and senior managers from China. In 1995, AT&T signed a joint venture contract with the Chinese government which promises that it will transfer technologies for processing and designing large scale integration devices to Huajing Electronics Corporation Group. With the help of new technology and experience, high quality products can be produced efficiently at a lower defect rate.

AT&T is the leader in developing new technology for the industry. AT&T Labs and the Chinese Academy of Sciences have joined together to develop an English-Chinese speech translation system containing several thousand words. This will allow business travelers and tourists to communicate in their respective languages in commonly encountered situations. It should be completed by the year 2003.

AT&T's R&D department responds quickly to customer demands. For example, the new undersea fiber-optic cable project was implemented to meet China's future telecommunications needs. Other than that, some of AT&T's services are monitored 24 hours a day to ensure high quality service. Furthermore, in 1995, AT&T offered a special plan for Chinese people to call their relatives in the U.S. during the Chinese New Year. Not only was the plan 50 percent cheaper than usual, AT&T had Mandarin-speaking operators in the United States assist Chinese callers.

Entry Strategies

Entry Mode Selection

AT&T first entered China in 1985 when it opened a representative office. This signaled its intent to establish a presence in China. Ten years later, it formed the AT&T China Co., a wholly owned subsidiary which gave it more control over its operations. The subsidiary implemented various Memorandum of Understanding with the Chinese government for different projects. It also offered more flexibility in responding to variables in the economic, social, and political environments. Finally, it allowed AT&T to expand its resources as needed.

It is difficult to establish a strong presence in China. China's industries are strictly regulated. Establishing good relations with the Chinese government means patient cultivation of relationships with Chinese officials and compliance with the governmental plan to improve the telecommunications infrastructure by 2020. For example, in 1994 AT&T was asked to invest an $150 million over the next three years and establish two switching joint ventures. Joint ventures are encouraged by the government because they transfer technology and know-how to China. They allow AT&T to take advantage of the existing facilities and distribution networks of local partners as well as low labor costs while its partners take advantage of its global market power, technological and financial resources, and brand image. Joint ventures also signal to the government that AT&T intends to make a long-term commitment to improving China's telecommunications infrastructure. The bulk of AT&T's business in China has therefore been done through manufacturing joint ventures and cooperative partnership agreements.

Currently, AT&T has five manufacturing joint ventures: AT&T of Shanghai Ltd.; AT&T of Beijing Fiber Optic Cable Co. Ltd.;

AT&T of Shanghai Fiber Optic Company Ltd.; AT&T of China Ltd.; and AT&T Consumer Telecommunications Products, Beijing Ltd. The manufacturing joint ventures were established to produce fiber optic cable networks, digital transmission equipment, and subscriber loop carrier systems. Besides these, AT&T has also formed several cooperative joint ventures and partnership agreements with administrations of China's national telecommunications industry to do large projects and provide services. Its partners include the Guangdong Post and Telecommunications Administration, the Ministry of Railways, Shanghai Post and Telecommunications Authority, and China Telecom. These agreements and joint ventures have doubled AT&T's revenue to more than $500 million in sales.

Timing and Location

Between the late 1970s and early 1980s, China started welcoming foreign investors, opening a window of opportunity for major companies to capitalize on one of the largest markets in the world. AT&T decided to enter China in 1985 with the goal of building a strong market position, strengthening its presence in the Asia-Pacific region, and becoming a major player in the global telecommunications industry

There have been several advantages to being a first mover. AT&T has built a good reputation and powerful brand image, key attributes that are even more important than quality in China. It also has a good relationship with China's national telecommunications industry and has thus built high entry barriers against its competitors. Being the first entrant gave AT&T the opportunity to capitalize on local resources and manpower and establish a strong customer base.

AT&T's headquarters are located in Beijing, the capital of China and home to most of the multi-national companies operating there. Two of its main offices are in Shanghai and Guangzhou. Shanghai is the center of the consumer boom sweeping China. It hosts over 9000 industrial enterprises and 2000 foreign joint ventures. It also accounts for $17 million in imports and $14 million in exports and is expected to dominate business activity in China in the next century.

Guangzhou, the capital of Guangdong province, is also a bustling city. The Guangdong Posts and Telecommunications Administration has spurred its technological growth. Being near Hong Kong has kept its economy strong, with a 13 percent annual GDP growth rate. It accounts for approximately 27,000 million in exports and 19,900 million in imports. It is a huge market, with 66 million Chinese residents, and has links to various flourishing southern regions in China.

Cooperative Strategies

The joint venture AT&T Consumer Telecommunications Products, Beijing Ltd., formed in 1994 is a good example illustrating partner selection. Its partners include AT&T, S. Megga Telecommunications Ltd. of HK (Megga), and the Post and Telecommunications Industrial Corporation of China (PTIC). AT&T brand name products including corded and cordless phones, digital answering machines, video phones, and fax machines are sold through the venture. PTIC distributes these products while AT&T supplies the technology. Megga manufactures the products and provides facilities. Each partner thus has clear-cut responsibilities and receives specific benefits, encouraging commitment and cooperation.

PTIC is a division of the Ministry of Post and Telecommunications (MPT). State-owned corporations such as PTIC often enjoy far greater advantages than private corporations in terms of market power, industrial experience, access to capital and resources, and good relationships with other governmental authorities. This means that PTIC has better bargaining power among suppliers and buyers, a vast network of marketing and distribution channels, and faces fewer political risks. These advantages provide stability to the joint venture. PTIC benefits from the joint venture by adopting AT&T's technological capabilities and know-how. PTIC is likely to pursue the goals of the industry and be fully supported by the national government. Therefore, it is more likely to have a high absorptive capacity. The degree to which it can learn AT&T's knowledge and skills determines the venture's rate of growth.

On the other hand, state-owned firms are known for being bureaucratic and slow to change. Their managers are often unmotivated, compared to those in private companies, and lack decision-making autonomy. The organizational leadership of PTIC is uncertain since the real power lies with the government and not the corporation. AT&T has little reason to fear, however, because the Chinese government has placed such a high priority on the telecommunications sector that PTIC will certainly obtain the necessary financial and administrative support.

At 53 percent, AT&T has the largest share of this joint venture. Since it supplies technology and a brand name, it has more of a stake in the venture. A larger share means that it has more control over operations and distribution of its technology. On the downside, it risks more if the joint venture fails.

PTIC has a 30 percent share so it faces less risk. Thirty is still considered a large percentage of ownership, signifying the monopolistic control of PTIC over the industry. As the manufacturer, Megga has the smallest share of only 17 percent.

Global Integration

AT&T employs a global integrated transnational strategy such that it offers high-technology products and services to multiple nations. Since each country has different market demands, AT&T also employs a multi-domestic strategy. Making a wide-range of telecommunications products and services available is necessary to gain advantage over competitors. AT&T also has the ability to network with local firms and governments. This is important since most countries have strict policies regarding foreign investment.

AT&T's business structure is based on a global matrix of divisions. AT&T has operations, joint ventures, and alliances in at least thirty different countries. Its global operations are categorized by region: Latin America and the Caribbean, Europe, the Middle East, Africa, and the Asia-Pacific, with headquarters in Hong Kong, Canada, and the United States.

Due to the different market demands of each country, AT&T's marketing strategies are country specific. For example, it offers direct international calling services and individual as well as corporate calling cards in all regions, but only offers long distance and wireless services to selected markets. Advertising is also oriented towards each country's special market, incorporating local cultural values and languages. AT&T also builds its reputation through sponsorships and community services. For example, it sponsored the Chinese team during the 1996 Olympic Games in Atlanta. When natural disaster strikes one of the countries within which it operates, AT&T donates money and resources. It also established the AT&T Global Distance Learning Project, now offered in sixty universities in twenty-six countries, including China. This project enables students and teachers to use communications technology in teaching, curriculum development, and educational research.

The organization is supported by two main business units: AT&T Network and Computing Services and AT&T Labs. AT&T Network and Computing Services is responsible for designing, operating, and expanding the capabilities of the company. AT&T Labs is responsible for creating new technologies, products, and services to support the company's customers.

Within these two main units, AT&T is further divided into five product and service divisions that address specific market needs. The Consumer Market Division provides service to residential customers while the Business Market Division provides service to small and medium sized businesses, and large corporations. AT&T Solutions provides consulting and networking services to multi-national companies. The AT&T Wireless Services Division manages wireless communications products. Finally, there is the AT&T Universal Credit Card Services Division.

Conclusion

The telecommunications industry as a whole is experiencing tremendous change driven by technological advancement and industrial deregulation. In response to these changes, AT&T needs to focus on operational efficiency and relationship marketing with consumers. Another key area to focus on is research and development. By owning the patent rights to new technology, AT&T will remain the market leader because it can provide better quality services at lower costs.

China is a key region in AT&T's goal to become the global leader in the telecommunications Industry. AT&T's strategy of making a long-term commitment and establishing deep relationships with the Chinese government has led to many large contracts and success in China.

6. AVON IN CHINA

Company Introduction

Avon is one of the largest direct sellers of beauty related products and cosmetics. Its core product lines consist of skin care, cosmetics, fragrances, and toiletries. It first entered China in 1990 through a joint venture with the Guangzhou Cosmetics Factory. Avon supplied cosmetics formulas, technical expertise, and sales and marketing equipment. Guangzhou Cosmetics simply supplied the location. Avon invested approximately one million U.S. dollars in this business arrangement. This joint venture was initially very successful. Avon met its six-month sales projections within the first two months of operations. Then, in April 1998, China imposed a ban on all direct sales operations. Two months later, Avon China was allowed to resume operations as a wholesaler. It remains to be seen whether or not the company will adapt to this new approach to doing business.

Avon has a very long history. Founded in 1886 by David H. McConnell, it soon became the world's largest direct seller of beauty and related products. Women were selling Avon products for 34 years before they won the right to vote. Mrs. Albee of New Hampshire was the first woman to explore the opportunity to earn additional income and gain financial independence as an 'Avon Lady'.

Avon aims to be the best at understanding women and satisfying their needs. Its key operating principles are a 100% money-back guarantee and provision of prestigious beauty products at affordable prices. Its skin care line consists of brand names such as Anew and Skin-So-Soft. The cosmetics line includes the Avon Color and Color Trend brands. Millenia, Natori, and Starring are a few examples from the fragrance line. It also produces toiletries, fashion jewelry, apparel, gifts, collectibles, and family entertainment products.

In 1997, Avon reported $5.1 billion in annual revenues and held the 308th rank on the Fortune 500 list of America's largest companies. This tremendous growth has only come after a period of struggle and restructuring. Avon lost its great public image during the 1970s and 1980s due to a combination of factors including more women entering the work place and an upsurge in new beauty products companies. Although Avon has the experience of time and brand name familiarity on its side, it has had very stiff competition. It has combated this by devising growth based on four distinct goals. The first goal is to continue supplying customers with outstanding beauty products worldwide. The second goal involves improving its brand and beauty image on a global scale. At the same time it is improving its direct sales by expanding access and increasing convenience. It is also committed to entering new markets.

In order to achieve these goals, Avon has set up a business process redesign program which will make additional funds available for investment in an increased customer base. The program focuses on global marketing, that is, coordinating product development on a global level and expanding access, advertising, and image-building. The supply chain is being analyzed and improved to allow for global sourcing opportunities, accelerated cycles, more accurate sales forecasts, and more reliable product availability. Order management, including product delivery and order entry, now incorporates a more efficient inventory system. Automated transaction processing, upgraded information systems, and reorganized administrative functions support core business activities, reduce costs, and make operations more efficient. All of these changes are part of Avon's increased global focus.

Avon products are now available in 131 countries. Avon has made direct investments in 42 of these countries, which are divided into two markets, developing and established. The developing markets include the Americas (e.g. Bolivia, Venezuela), Europe (e.g. Russia, Ireland), the Pacific (China and Indonesia), and South Africa. The established markets include the United States, Canada, and several locations in Europe and the Pacific. Avon products are available in the remaining 89 countries through Avon representatives, local distributors, or licensees. Avon is currently considering Bulgaria, Romania, the Ukraine, and Vietnam as possible future markets.

Avon initially attempted to enter China in Beijing, but after five years of negotiations within an extremely bureaucratic environment had still failed to reach an agreement. It then successfully set up a joint venture with the Guangzhou Cosmetics Factory in

1990. Avon's initial investment was approximately U.S.$1 million and it controlled 60 percent of the venture. In July 1997, Avon China was considered the company's largest growth investment. In April 1998, however, China imposed a ban on direct sales. Two months later, Avon received approval to resume operations in China as a wholesale and retail business. The following discussion will address Avon's operations before the ban and some projections for its continued success in China.

External Environment

Avon operates in somewhat unpredictable industrial and national environments in China. Avon's biggest challenge is to locate a position within the Chinese cosmetics industry in which it can favorably influence competitive threats and the bargaining power of suppliers and buyers. So far, it has been successful in these regards and has made above average returns.

Avon was one of the first foreign cosmetics companies authorized to manufacture in China and the first company, either domestic or foreign, allowed to sell directly to Chinese consumers. There was no existing rivalry at that point, but it now competes with Amway and Mary Kay. Despite high start-up costs, the cosmetics industry is wide open to competition from other foreign companies because Chinese cosmetics factories tend to lack advanced technology and have a low production capacity. Foreign companies such as Avon face stringent currency restrictions, however. For example, Avon has to use its profits from China to purchase Chinese products for its promotional campaigns.

China is a unique market due to a huge population, unsophisticated consumers, and low per capita income. There are more than 500 million women in China, more than the U.S. and Europe combined, yet these women have little or no experience in applying makeup or skin care products. Avon's direct sales approach, in which Avon ladies also serve as beauty consultants, proved very successful in China although it was already outdated in the U.S. and other developed countries. Avon also adopted a pricing strategy unique to the Chinese market, that is, charging lower prices there than what it charges for the same products in the U.S. This made its products affordable to Chinese women.

In larger cities such as Beijing, Shanghai, and Guangzhou, Avon has begun to lose its appeal. More affluent consumers prefer famous name brands such as Chanel, YSL, Estee Lauder, Christian Dior, and so on. They perceive Avon products as cheap, lacking glamour, and associated with an unsophisticated, rural lifestyle. Products from Taiwan and Hong Kong are also a threat to Avon's market share. Avon needs to reinvent itself as a more posh company in order to combat this tendency.

The cosmetics market in China is in a growth stage due to increasing discretionary income amongst Chinese women. After tremendous growth in the early 1990s, Avon still enjoyed an amazing growth rate of 70% in 1996, although this dropped sharply to 16% in 1997. The ban on direct sales in China in 1998 devastated Avon's earnings. Whether Avon can bounce back depends on its ability to convert a wholesale and retail operation. It has had to let a lot of its sales promoters go and re-evaluate its representation policy. Some remote sales offices have had to be closed because of loss of sales.

Internal Environment

Avon is a very successful company. Since 1989, its sales have grown at a compounded annual rate of 7 percent; earnings from continued operations have increased at a rate of 16 percent. It has maintained a high gross profit margin of about 60 percent from 1995 through 1997. Its net profit margin of 5.71 percent in 1995 increased to 6.67 percent in 1997. Its return on assets increased from 24.7 percent in 1995 to 25.4 percent in 1997. Its return on equity, however, decreased from 1.3 to 1.2 over the same years.

Avon's current ratio remained at about .98, indicating that Avon's short-term creditors are pretty much covered by its short-term assets. Its quick ratio, however, ranged around .6, indicating it may need to sell its inventory in order to pay off short-term obligations.

Avon is highly leveraged. Its debt-to-asset ratio ranged from about 88 to 91 percent. Its debt-to-equity ratios were at an amazingly high level of 9.7 in 1995, down to 7.0 in 1997. Its long-term debt-to-equity ratios were also relatively high, at 3.2 in 1995 to 2.2 in 1998.

Avon has a relatively low inventory turnover rate of 3.63, or every 100.51 days in 1997. It average collection period is short, approximately 11 days. This is due to the way Avon traditionally operates. Typically, a customer places an order with an Avon lady, who picks up the merchandise and delivers it to the customer. The customer then pays in cash or with a check when she receives the goods. There is no accounts receivable with this direct sales method.

Avon shows remarkable growth in international sales. More than 65 percent of its sales come from the international market. Sales in China increased from $39 million in 1995 to an impressive $75 million in 1997. Interestingly, Avon does not use derivative financial instruments to offset foreign exchange and interest rates. Instead, it uses interest rate swaps and caps to hedge portions of interest payable on debt.

Avon invested heavily in China. Its capital expenditures increased from $104 million in 1996 to $169 million in 1997. It recently opened a $40 million manufacturing plant in the Taiping Industrial Development Zone in Guangdong.

Avon was the first direct sales company in China. Its success was due to its unique pricing strategy and successful recruitment of professional women as Avon ladies. By April 1998, it had 68 subsidiaries and 150,000 Avon ladies in China. It also used decentralized branches and satellite stores to serve China's many markets. It now faces distribution and marketing challenges since the direct sales ban began.

Avon's youthful, innovative management team was appointed in 1997. Its new president is 38 year old Andrea Jung. The new team is introducing new products and marketing strategies in order to capture younger consumers. It has also opened retail stores and an Internet shopping network to adapt to changing consumer tastes and demographics.

Corporate-Level Strategies

Avon's combination of resources has enabled it to diversify across business areas. One area of diversification has been geographic. As a global company, Avon markets its products through approximately 2.6 million independent sales representatives. It currently places emphasis on expansion into countries with emerging or developing economies. China represents its number one growth opportunity. Until Avon arrived, most Chinese cosmetics were sold in government-owned stores which offered few choices, little inventory, and sloppy service.

Avon's direct sales approach initially proved very successful in China. Avon recruited doctors, engineers, teachers, economists, and computer scientists to its entrepreneurial, incentive-based system. Most of its dealers in China hold full-time jobs and sell Avon products on the side to boost their incomes.

Lack of a retail infrastructure in China is also beneficial for Avon. Its Chinese ventures operate from branch depots. Registered representatives buy products there and then deliver them personally to their customers. Franchise dealers have also done very well, earning commissions of up to 30 percent of sales. Dealers can supplement their own sales efforts by appointing Avon ladies, consequently an additional 30 percent cut from the sales made by these representatives. Some of the top franchise dealers earn up to $3,000 in commissions a month; this is a sizable amount considering that the average per capita income is around $400 a year.

Avon is a related-diversified firm. That is, more than 30 percent of its sales volume comes from businesses different from but related to its dominant business. Avon has succeeded as a related-diversified company because it enters similar businesses instead of diverging too greatly from its core. Its product lines fall into four main categories: 1) cosmetics, fragrances, and toiletries; 2) apparel; 3) fashion jewelry and accessories; and 4) gifts and decorative products.

Avon has strong assets and competencies that are applicable to these various business areas. One of these resources is its brand name. The Avon name is associated with high quality products. Avon products are thus readily accepted in new markets. Avon uses a global brand strategy that enhances its image while improving its manufacturing and marketing efficiency. Its global brand products share five main characteristics. Each 1) is in the mass or mass-prestige consumer segment; 2) has the potential to be among the top three brands in its market; 3) is sold in at least six of Avon's major markets; 4) has the potential to generate more than $75 million in annual sales; and 5) enhances the company's beauty image. Its global brand products are expected to account for 70 percent of its cosmetics, fragrances, and toiletries sales by the year 2000.

Through the development and support of global products, Avon can continue to improve its prestige and image, the consistency of its products and packaging, and the efficiency of its manufacturing and marketing. Avon currently boasts eleven global brands including its Avon Color makeup line, the Far Away, Rare Gold, Natori, and Josie fragrances, Anew (the world's first alpha-hydroxy acid skin care product; one jar costs $41), and Avon Skin Care products. The Avon Skin Care products are its top sellers in China.

Business-Level Strategy

Avon has a focused differentiation competitive strategy in that its products are designed to meet the needs of a particular consumer segment. As expressed in its mission statement, this segment is the global female consumer.

Avon is committed to increasing shareholder value. It has enjoyed nine consecutive years of sales and earnings growth and eight consecutive years of dividend increases. Its current annual dividend rate is at $1.36 and it had a two-for-one stock split in 1996. It also had a three-year share repurchase program that ended in February 1997. 12.7 million shares were bought for $424 million. It have since begun a new three-to-five-year $500 million share repurchase program.

Avon needs to communicate a compelling and consistent beauty image to its customers. To assist with this, Avon provides its marketers with a media kit, including photographs, product layouts, and advertising samples. It is also developing a global database of creative concepts that can be downloaded from the Internet. Finally, its Avon Image Center showcases global brands and offers beauty salon and spa services to women.

Direct sales accounts 98 percent of Avon sales. The company has also begun selling its products on the Internet and through mail order. Catalog sales generate an average order almost double that of direct sales through representatives.

Entry Strategies

Entry Mode Selection

Avon first experienced a failure in entering the Chinese market in the mid-1980s when it tried to set up as a wholly owned subsidiary in Beijing. After conferring with contacts in the Hong Kong area, executives decided to set up an equity joint venture instead in Guangzhou. Its partner is the Guangzhou Cosmetics Factory.

Avon pursued a joint venture for various country-specific reasons. After its failure in Beijing, Avon realized that the cultural distance was too great to try and go it alone. Having a partner with experience in the territory was critical. China remains a fairly closed society. Having an established local partner guide Avon's business practices has proven less risky and made integration into the market smoother. Although Avon has to share its profits with the Guangzhou Cosmetics Factory, the demand for cosmetics in China is so high that it is worth it. Having a local partner also means that the Chinese government is less stringent in applying policies which normally work against the benefit of foreign companies.

Avon has maintained primary control of the company, gained use of already existing buildings and avoided prohibitive import duties. The Guangzhou Cosmetics Factory had gained a top-selling cosmetics company as a partner which has enabled it to export high quality products.

Timing and Location

Avon initially decided to enter China in the mid-1980s, although it did not succeed in doing so until 1990. At that time, China had begun industrializing the country and taking a more free market approach to commerce. It also had a strong desire to increase its exportable goods. Demand was also extremely high. There were no other companies that offered the wide variety of products that women wanted. Avon's potential for meeting this great demand was high. Women at that time were also in need of more employment opportunities. The Chinese Avon Ladies were enthusiastic about earning greater income. Based on all of these reasons, Avon decided that the time was right to enter into the market. It was right; sales and profit have continued to exceed expectations from the beginning.

Although Avon initially wanted to start business in Beijing, it later chose the decentralized city of Guangzhou because it is faster growing and less controlled by the government. This allows Avon to concentrate on its business operations instead of dealing with the bureaucracy as much.

Cooperative Strategies

Avon chose the Guangzhou Cosmetics Factory for four main reasons. First, it was already well established and had the ability to produce Avon's product lines. Second, although both companies were in the same business, they are each responsible for different, complementary aspects of operation. Third, they share the same goals. Both want to produce quality beauty products for the Chinese people. Finally, the Guangzhou Cosmetics Factory is able to guide Avon in Chinese business practices.

Avon is the dominant partner, controlling 60 percent of the joint venture, while the Guangzhou Cosmetics Factory controls 35 percent, and Avon's Pacific Rim contact, David Li, holds the remaining 5 percent. Avon wanted to obtain dominant equity so it could control the board of directors and choose the CEO. This is important because its partner only supplies manufacturing facilities to the venture, but it is the Avon name and products that make the venture a success.

Global Integration

Avon's strategy for international operations has been identified as a multi-domestic strategy. In a multi-domestic strategy, units in various countries are independent. Each unit treats its market as distinct from all others, and corporate headquarters is simply another unit in the company.

Avon is headed by four operating business units. Each of these units has operating authority and profit/loss accountability. The four units are North America, Asia Pacific, Latin America, and Eastern Europe and Emerging Markets. China is included in the Asia Pacific unit. Avon China operates based on government regulations and specific consumer demands. Avon China has complied with all regulations set by the Chinese government, including the recent regulations regarding direct sales.

Avon is organized into international business divisions. This type of structure means that each international division is solely responsible for itself. Advantages of this structure include limited costs and a high degree of integration. A disadvantage is lack of flexibility in regulating international businesses.

Avon uses direct sales as its core business strategy worldwide.

Direct selling begins with sales campaigns that occur every two to three weeks. Avon customers receive brochures or catalogs from representatives. The representatives then take customer orders and send them to an Avon Distribution Center for processing. As the orders become ready, representatives deliver products to customers, who, in turn, pay the representatives. Avon receives payment from the representatives who in turn earn sales commissions averaging 30 to 40 percent of sales.

Conclusion

Avon China has enjoyed tremendous growth up until the recent ban on direct sales. It remains to be seen how well Avon China will adapt to becoming a wholesale/retail operation. Some implications can be drawn from its early experience in China, however. Successfully conducting business in China is strongly related to a healthy relationship with government officials. Avon already has this, as illustrated by its ability to resume operations within two months of the ban. The ban will also prevent other direct sales companies from entering China, which could be beneficial to Avon as it re-evaluates its current marketing and distribution strategies.

7. GILLETTE IN CHINA

Company Introduction

The Gillette Company was founded about a century ago. It started as a small company in Boston, Massachusetts, then developed into a global enterprise. Gillette is a leader in sales of razor blades, toiletries, batteries, and dental hygiene and stationery products. In 1980, Gillette began doing business in China. It has now developed a big market there thanks to assertive analysis and a strong diversification strategy.

The Gillette Company is a globally focused consumer products company that seeks competitive advantages in markets for quality, personal care products. It competes in three worldwide businesses: personal grooming, stationery, and small electrical appliances. Its goal is to achieve worldwide leadership in all core product categories. The company shares skills and resources among its business units to optimize performance. It is committed to sustained sales and profit growth plans that recognize and balance both short and long term objectives. Its long term objectives are continued double-digit annual growth, expansion into Asia, Russia, and Latin America, and increasing emphasis on new products. Gillette is already the world leader in male grooming products, a category that includes blades, razors, and shaving preparations.

The Gillette Company was founded in Boston by King C. Gillette in 1901. Two years later, it manufactured and received a patent for the first safety razor. In the early twentieth century, Gillette began operating abroad, establishing a sales office in London and manufacturing site in Paris. It supplied a large number of safety razors and blades to the armed forces during World War I.

During the mid-1900s, Gillette broadened its product portfolio with the acquisition of the Toni Company and its line of home permanents. It also began television advertising. Between the late 1950s and early 1990s, Gillette again diversified its product lines by acquiring the Paper Mate Pen Company, Braun AG (a West

German manufacturer and marketer of small electrical appliances), the Liquid Paper Corporation, Oral-B Laboratories (the leading manufacturer and marketer of toothbrushes in the United States), Waterman (French manufacturer of premium writing instruments), and the Parker Pen Company. Gillette then introduced the Braun Oral-B electric plaque remover. In 1994, Financial World Magazine ranked Gillette the ninth most valuable brand in the world. Two years later, Duracell International, the world's leading seller of alkaline batteries, merged with Gillette.

Gillette's global restructuring plan organizes the company into six core business categories, resulting in a projected $200 million year savings in marketing expenses by the year 2000. There will also be an 11 percent reduction in Gillette's 43,000 employees along with fourteen factory and twelve warehouse closings and about thirty office closings or consolidations.

Major Businesses

Gillette's sales in 1997 amounted to over ten billion dollars. Every day, at least 1.2 billion people around the world use one or more Gillette products. This is not surprising, since the company has a stable of powerful global brands organized into six major business segments: Blades & Razors, Toiletries, Stationery, Braun, Oral-B, and Duracell. These products include deodorants, electrical appliances, pens, liquid paper, oral hygiene products, and batteries.

In recent years, Gillette has introduced more than twenty new products annually. In 1997, a record 49 percent of the company's sales came from products introduced within the last previous years. This strong pace of new product development has continued.

Three of its most exciting new products are the Gillette MACH3 shaving system, the Duracell Ultra line of high-tech alkaline batteries, and the Braun Oral-B 3D plaque remover. Also recently introduced is the SATINfloss dental floss line and Cross-Action Toothbrush. Gillette predicts that revenues from its oral health products should double to about $2 billion by the year 2001, boosted by these premium-priced products.

Gillette has sixty-four manufacturing facilities in twenty-seven countries. Its products are distributed to over 200 countries and territories around the world.

External Environment

Gillette is ahead of the industry in terms of profitability. In 1998 Gillette had an 18 percent profit compared to the industrial average of about 12 percent. Its average over five years was about 20 percent, compared to the industrial average of 9 percent. Gillette has enjoyed high sales growth and economic expansion.

Companies in the household products/personal care industry often demonstrate a consistent ability to maintain solid financial instruments and natural hedging, strong margin expansion programs, positive pricing, geographic diversification, and produce less discretionary products. The industry in general has high earnings-per-share (EPS) and growth rates of around 14 percent.

When China opened its economy to foreign investment, domestic production of household and personal care products was extremely unsophisticated. The socialist government regarded brand name shampoo or soap as bourgeois. The state planning committee did not focus on developing these products. On the other hand, the government was less concerned with protecting these industries from foreign domination than it was of other industrial sectors such as steel or power. This enabled multinational companies with experience in developing markets to enter China. With businesses focused on fast-moving consumer goods, companies like Unilever, SC Johnson, and Gillette were ready to manage operations from supplies to delivery. They employed Chinese expatriates that understood China's infrastructural problems and were willing to take on the challenge of doing business there. By early 1996, foreign brands in major urban areas made up 78 percent of the soap market, 90 percent of the shampoo market, and 56 percent of the toothpaste market. Some of Gillette's major rivals are discussed in greater detail below.

Like Gillette, Colgate-Palmolive has developed strong businesses worldwide and continued expanding globally regardless of weak local currencies or international uncertainty. Colgate's productivity programs and global sourcing have enabled it to become a leader in oral care. Although Colgate is not Gillette's main competitor in China, it has a strong position in China's shampoo market.

Proctor & Gamble is the number one manufacturer of household products in the world. Like Gillette, P&G is undergoing a global restructuring program. With an improved cost structure and lower material commodity prices, P&G will also have continued gross and operating margin expansion. In China, P&G took control of two key local brands in the detergent market and has joint ventures with three leading manufacturers of China.

SC Johnson's biggest competitive advantage is in the household products market. The Shanghai Johnson joint venture is an efficient integrated manufacturing, sales, and distribution business. Although Shanghai Johnson competes with P&G, Unilever, and Colgate in the shampoo market, the company holds healthy shares of both local and international brands.

Unilever is an Anglo-Dutch company that has enjoyed great success in the Chinese soap market. Through selling key products such as Vaseline lotion, Pond's skin cream, and Lux soap, Unilever's strategy is to attain high growth nationwide. By setting up various joint ventures with Shanghai Soap, Shanghai Toothpaste, and Shanghai Detergent, Unilever has eliminated intra-partner competition and ensured that both Chinese and foreign are working toward the same goals. The company's success can be attributed to centralized marketing support and training.

In the case of Gillette entering the Chinese market, entry barriers were practically nonexistent because of Gillette's expertise in international business and superior technology. Competition was practically nonexistent once Gillette set up a joint venture with China's largest razor blade manufacturer, the Shanghai Razor Blade Factory (SRBF). There are high capital requirements for companies in the industry. Large manufacturing plants and production facilities are needed for operations. Products are produced in mass quantities and exported to hundreds of countries. The asset intensity of the industry is thus quite high and potential competitors find it difficult to compete with highly capitalized companies such as Gillette. New companies also need to be able to set up multiple production plants to compete with companies which already have an established global position. Gillette not only has the financial capacity to support sizable foreign investments, but is also a well-recognized brand image.

In China, four companies are considered potential competitors. The Tung Tit Razor Industrial Corporation is a razor blade manufacturing company that exports twin blade disposable razors to foreign markets. It thus competes with Gillette's core market. Shanghai Kok Yung Daily Articles Co. Ltd. specializes in manufacturing toothbrushes. The Shanghai Jahwa Company is the largest cosmetic enterprise in China. It is one of China's top 500 companies and has the largest production capability in the industry. In the 1950s, Shanghai Jahwa merged with five other enterprises to become both more customer and technologically oriented.

China's consumers are very price sensitive since the average per capita income in rural areas is only U.S.$200 and in urban areas U.S.$500. Since discretionary income is higher in cities, Gillette's market mainly lies in urban areas. The urban population is about 350 million, many of whom are young Chinese individuals living at home and thus enjoying higher discretionary income. In China, there are many individuals who budget and save extra income to afford their vision of the good life. They are often interested in purchasing luxury household goods as status symbols. According to research done by a securities firm, a person earning $250 annually can still afford Gillette razors.

By manufacturing in nearly 30 different countries, Gillette derives over 60 percent of its revenues from international operations. In its joint venture with the Shanghai Razor Blade Factory, Gillette has been able to gain both a market share and a well-established manufacturing company. Gillette Shanghai is the company's third largest plant in the world. Although Gillette has four production plants in China producing razor blades, electric razors, and toothbrushes, materials must still be imported in order to manufacture its products. To secure foreign exchange for steel imports, Gillette Shanghai exports blades to the Philippines, Hong Kong, and the South Pacific, and makes correcting fluid brushes for a Gillette company in the U.S. Nevertheless, a shortage of capital on the Chinese side has impeded Gillette's ability to grow as fast as expected. As a result, the supplier bargaining power is low.

In the household products/personal care industry, there are a wide variety of brands and product lines to select from. Consumers usually choose products according to criteria such as price, brand name, necessity, or usage. Gillette's partnerships in China have enabled it to capture roughly 90 percent of the domestic market. The joint venture with the Shanghai Razor Blade Company has helped Gillette attain brand recognition. Thus, the buyer propensity to substitute is moderate although the cost of switching to a less expensive brand is low.

The life cycle of a product allows company executives to determine when they should introduce, continue, or eliminate a product. In the U.S. and European markets, Gillette's blades and razors are in the mature stage. There has been an annual 18 percent earnings growth in the past five years. Revenues have been boosted by an expanded new product line and increased advertising.

In developing markets such as China, Poland, and India, Gillette's razors and blades are in the growth stage. Rapid global introduction of these products has contributed to an increase of consumer usage. Compared to five years ago, there are already twice as many users in these countries.

Analysis according to the market framework focuses on a company's market share versus market growth. The amount of market share is determined by sales relative to those of other competitors in the market. Market growth, on the other hand, is the industrial growth rate in constant dollars. In the United States, Gillette is a star performer. The company enjoys both a high market share and market growth. In China, Gillette is today considered a cash cow, but has moderate market growth. Over the last five years, Gillette's sales growth has been an average annual 9.5 percent, compared to the personal care industrial average of 7.8 percent.

In 1992, sales in China's thirty-five largest department stores soared by 31 percent. Imported cosmetics, cameras, and jewelry, all increased by 30 to 40 percent. Ten million retail enterprises have annual sales of $200 billion, which is expected to triple by the year 2000. According to research, growth in China's shaving market is not expected to exceed 5 percent per year. While this may seem like a low growth number, Gillette is planning for the long term. Given China's huge population, even a small growth rate can be profitable.

There has been a continued trend towards liberalization of the retail market in order to spur consumerism. The central government has allowed a gradual entry of foreign chain stores into the market. It is best to think of China as a group of regions rather than a single nation due to its size, diversity, and political organization. It can therefore be approached as a group of markets instead of as a single market. Although all the regions are linked to the central government, fierce competition amongst them has caused inefficiency and interference with the free flow of trade. Because of regional protectionism, for example, Johnson & Johnson is forced to send empty trucks back to its plant in Xian after delivering pharmaceuticals to major cities.

It took several months and dozens of trips to China for Gillette to set up operations there because of China's lack of experience with industrial joint ventures. Equity joint ventures established must be approved by the Chinese Government as legal entities and are subject to jurisdiction and protection under Chinese Law. The liability of each party to a joint venture is limited to the capital subscribed by it. The proportion of the foreign party's investment must be at least 25 percent registered capital. The joint venture must: use advanced technical equipment and scientific managerial methods; be technologically innovative so as to bring about quicker returns and bigger profits; help expand exports and increase foreign currency receipts; and train technical and managerial personnel. Gillette has adhered to all these requirements. In one instance it also invested nearly $15 million in updating SRBF facilities to avoid the need to seek special State Planning Commission approval. Other than this one time, Chinese governmental policies have rarely been a problem for Gillette's business operations.

By far the majority of the population is under 35 years old. Companies thus should orient their marketing towards the youthful segment of the population. Women are also a target market, especially those in the coastal or urban regions of China who are relatively modern, well-educated, and aware of various brands.

Facial hair is not a major concern for Chinese men, who begin shaving at a relatively late age if at all. The vast majority of women do not need to shave or are disinclined to do so. Encouraging Chinese people to take up shaving requires major advertising outlays. Parallels can be drawn with Proctor and Gamble's expensive campaign to convince Chinese people that dandruff is anti-social and unattractive. Gillette will have to attach the same stigma to facial hair while strengthening its brand equity to ensure that it is not simply making the pie bigger for its rivals. While so far Gillette is still trying to convince women in rural areas to shave, urban women have already begun adopting this habit. This is beneficial since urbanites are most likely to have discretionary income.

Many companies in the household products/personal care industry such as Avon, Colgate-Palmolive, P&G, and Gillette are restructuring their global programs to enhance margin and earnings growth. All of these companies have shown a consistent ability to withstand volatility. However, due to pervasive economic ad financial difficulties across multiple markets and problems for retailers in financing inventory levels, revenues have fallen. An ongoing global deflationary and recessionary environment have added pressure on sales at consumption.

Gillette has made great strides in expanding into fast-growing markets like Eastern Europe, Latin America, and the Pacific which have high population levels that stimulate demand for personal care products. Despite expanding overseas sales, however, the global economic crisis has undermined Gillette's earnings growth. Profit pressures from international markets will most likely offset strong sales of its newest shaver, the Mach3. Altogether, the company's international and diversified profits are expected to be down 25-30 percent.

Meanwhile, the United States still provides a strong market due to a high desire for health and fitness amongst consumers. Although Gillette's products are used by individuals ranging from fifteen to seventy years of age, its target market is the baby boomer generation. Shaving is considered part of daily personal hygiene in America, a habit greatly encouraged by Gillette's marketing plans. Women who shave continue to drive growth at Gillette.

Internal Environment

Financial

Gillette's Financial Ratios

Profitability	**1995**	**1996**	**1997**
Gross Profit Margin	1.0%	62.0%	62.1%
Net Profit Margin	14.0%	10.0%	12.1%
Return on Equity	27.2%	21.1%	27.6%
Liquidity			
Current Ratio	1.78	1.62	1.58
Quick Ratio	0.99	0.96	0.92
Leverage			
Debt-to-Asset ratio	0.15	0.18	0.16
Debt-to-equity ratio	0.28	0.34	0.28
Activity			
Inventory turnover	6.71	7.14	6.97
Average collection period	90.23	101.15	93.35

Due to the Duracell merger in 1996, financial ratios show an overall reduction. Special one-time charges such as transaction costs and integrated activities contribute to the effect. However, over the years, Gillette has maintained strong growth and superior performance. Its stock has continually outperformed the stock market and industrial averages.

Technological

Companies that built production facilities in China more than fifteen years ago have already become outdated in terms of efficiency and technology. Low technological capabilities have slowed growth for many firms. The floods of 1998 that damaged much of China's rural areas and manufacturing plants have at the same time encouraged companies to rebuild and update old equipment and buildings.

The Shanghai Gillette Factory requires major technological upgrading in order to achieve future growth. The factory is still too outdated to produce Gillette's best selling Sensor razors. Lack of advanced systems also results in inefficient and inappropriate distribution systems and raised costs. Although Gillette emphasizes research and development to enhance growth, R&D in China is not yet as advanced as in the United States. Gillette plans on increasing investment spending to improve production efficiency and launch new products.

Operational

Gillette expected to acquire a market share in China based on the somewhat risky presumption that Chinese people would prefer a more expensive shaver. Instead, China has proved to be a low growth, low value market for Gillette. The toughest task for its marketing staff has been convincing both men and women to shave. Gillette dispatches 'mobile propaganda units' to show movies and commercials that appeal to the Chinese audience and also teach them how to shave. Gillette also holds demonstrations on shaving and distributes free plastic razors. This enables local storekeepers to sell blades. Once consumers start shaving, Gillette introduces shaving cream. Through packaging blades to be sold individually or educating people about the joys of shaving, Gillette is pursuing a growth strategy. By 1992, nine years after the first production of Gillette's Rhino brand carbon blades and plastic disposable razors, double-edged blade consumption was up to seven per male per year in China.

Human resource problems also persist. Expatriate managers of one joint venture were miserable living in the grim industrial city of Shenyang. Gillette Shanghai experienced illegal trafficking problems. Gillette also had to invest considerable resources to build a sales force and develop an adequate distribution infrastructure.

Gillette had a problem with surplus work force, employing as many as 1,000 laborers that did not have the skills it needed. Deference to age was also a problem. Older workers would not listen to younger managers. That meant Gillette either had to get rid of the young managers or the workers. It was unable to lay off people at will, however, because of local worker councils. Nevertheless, Gillette insisted that job candidates be tested for skill level and ended up laying off more than 160 workers. Gaining permission to replace unskilled, older employees with younger, better-educated ones ended up becoming a year long process.

Organizational

Gillette uses a human assets approach in which the chief executive manages success through policies, people, and principles. Gillette also places emphasis on having experienced international managers since its future growth rate is directly related to its ability to distribute competent employees abroad.

In China, management differences arose because of differing goals amongst partners. Gillette has aimed at long-term goals, while its partners are mainly interested in short-term profit. Gillette has been unable to set up harmonious *guanxi* relationships. Cultural conflicts have resulted in inefficient operations and frustration on both sides.

Corporate-Level Strategy

Gillette began to globalize after WWI, opening factories in Europe, Latin America, Russia, the Middle East, South Africa, and India. Establishing itself in Asia has been more difficult. It opened its first branch office in Shanghai in 1919, but political hostility to foreign investment and foreign goods minimized its impact in China. From 1949 until 1979, Gillette was unable to do business there. Once word got out that China was interested in razor blade manufacturing, Mike Hawley from Australia and several other of Gillette's management team immediately went there and set up Gillette's first Chinese joint venture in 1980 in Shenyang in the Liaoning province.

Gillette selected production facilities based on factor endowments. Gillette often rents plants equipped with depreciated machinery shipped from elsewhere as an exploratory step before setting up manufacturing in a new country. The Shanghai Razor Blade Factory and the Shenyang Daily Use Razor Company both were considered fully depreciated companies, thereby lowering setup costs. Gillette usually starts operations using its worst technology and then upgrading as the market is penetrated. This allows it to make small initial investments in new regions of the world.

Gillette's first choice in China was to build a "greenfield" factory from the ground up, but it ended up with a "brownfield" factory, soon named the Shenyang Daily Use Metals Products Company. Factory equipment all had to be replaced, supplemented, or refurbished due to China's foreign exchange restrictions. Gillette's next joint venture in Shanghai, Pudong was also troublesome. The facilities had been built in 1947 and needed considerable upgrading.

Gillette met the financial challenges of doing business in China by hiring managers with a great deal of international business experience along with mainly local employees. Finding competent local managers was difficult. Chinese universities had stopped functioning during the Cultural Revolution. The Gillette team spent numerous hours teaching new managers about business taxes, distribution, hiring procedures, insurance, accounting, and other business functions that were very unfamiliar to the Chinese. All the mangers now employed at the Shenyang factory are Chinese except the Malaysian general manager and Filipino factory boss.

Despite such difficulties, Gillette made a profit in the first full year of operations at the Shenyang Daily Use Metals Products Co. Domestic sales of its Rhino blades soon strained production capacity. The quality of its Nacet and 7 O'clock blades have reached a standard permitting export. Seventy percent of its safety razor output is being exported. The factory is also gearing up to produce and export office product components. Gillette has thus been able to increase its foreign currency receipts and expand exports.

Gillette initially focused on razor blades in China because China had expressed interest in razor manufacture and the razor market in the U.S. had already matured. Gillette has since increased its production lines to include writing instruments, Oral B toothbrushes, and Braun products at its Shanghai facility.

Business-Level Strategy

Michael Hawley, the mastermind behind the joint ventures in China, developed the following rules to shape Gillette's success: start small; set limited goals feasible for the Chinese environment; establish long-range training programs; bring in seasoned expatriates with substantive shop floor experience; train Chinese personnel overseas; develop rapport and ongoing working relationships with the bureaucrats who administer rules for foreign investors; and begin early on import substitution and export development. These strategies have enabled Gillette to profit from its operations at both its Shenyang and Shanghai facilities.

Gillette stays competitive by keeping costs low. It sets different prices for products of varying quality. For example, the blades (e.g. the Rhino razor) produced in China are of lower quality than those (e.g. the Sensor) produced in the United States. The ability to manufacture a range of products also provides a buffer in case of recession and allows Gillette to appeal to different classes of consumers.

Gillette fulfills the guidelines of the four building blocks in the following ways. First, its razors are considered superior because they are more dependable than most other brands of razors in China. Second, it is working on a strategy to attract more of the Chinese market. Gillette discovered that although there is a huge population, the number of people who actually shave is not large. Third, Gillette has become more efficient. It has lowered its process spoilage rate from a nonviable 25 percent in 1983 to half that by 1986. Finally, its ability to penetrate the domestic market, implement import substitutions, and develop exports and expatriate profits has enabled it to dominate the Chinese razor blade market.

Entry Strategies

Entry Mode Selection

In the early eighties, Gillette saw other MNCs enter the Chinese market expecting large returns on their investments based solely on the sheer size of China's population. These MNCs soon had to pull out of China when these expectations were not realized. Gillette learned from these mistakes and decided to enter the Chinese market with modest expectations. It therefore started out with a small joint venture set up in the province of Shinmei in Shenyang. The terms of the contract stipulated 50/50 ownership, a time frame of 25 years, and a $2 million investment on the part of Gillette. The venture employs 100 people and produces local Rhino brand razors. Production has expanded on an average of six to eight percent annually since the venture was set up in 1983. It now produces more than eighty million blades a year. Aside from positive profit margins and overall growth, Gillette gained knowledge of the Chinese market unequaled by any other international razor blade manufacturer.

In 1992, Gillette started its second joint venture, this time with the highly regarded Shanghai Razor Blade Factory. This 70/30 joint venture controlled by Gillette is named Gillette Shanghai. It required an estimated $4 million by both parties as an initial investment, with an additional $20 million later invested by Gillette. This partnership enabled Gillette to increase its market share from 15 to 90 percent. It also gained a more prestigious public image.

Gillette's strategic objective in China is to maximize its razor blade market share. Having established a dominant market share, Gillette hopes to expand to other businesses. SRBF will also be a good partner in toothbrush and dental floss operations.

Gillette's international strategy involves recycling outdated technology. Since China's domestically made razor blades are extremely outdated by American standards, Gillette can bring in its worst technology and it is still years ahead of anything local companies possess. It then upgrades the market from there. Since most of the equipment used in international ventures is fully depreciated, the set up costs are extraordinarily low, allowing new operations to be profitable within an average of a year. Abandonment of these assets due to political upheaval would not prove a huge material loss.

Entry Timing and Location

Gillette enjoyed distinct advantages as an early investor and first mover in the Chinese market, including market power and creating entry barriers. Once Gillette solidified the joint venture with SRBF, it held a very large, almost monopolistic, share of market power. Coupled with the reliable brand advantage SRBF gave to Gillette, entry barriers became almost insurmountable.

As a first mover, Gillette ran the risk of dealing with macroeconomic uncertainty. While Gillette hopes that China's economy will grow, it cannot be sure that people will spend their discretionary income on razor blades. Another operational risk Gillette has to deal with is incumbent inertia. Despite having captured 90 percent of the razor blade market, Gillette has to continue to keep its customers happy by offering high quality and technologically advanced products.

Gillette has established four manufacturing sites in China. One of the first strategies Gillette employed in the micro-context was targeting a relatively small consumer constituency in Northern China, customers who were more likely to need razors because they grow heavier facial hair. Gillette's Shinmei Daily Use Products Ltd. in Shenyang is its northern manufacturing site.

At the macroeconomic level, Gillette targeted people with money, that is, those that live in urban areas. Gillette Shanghai in Pudong is its largest and most strategically placed site. Shanghai alone generated 12.5 percent of all of China's financial revenue in 1996. Shanghai also attracts over 20 percent of all tourists to China. Shanghai's average income per capita is over 41 percent higher than China's national average. Gillette's southern factory is in Dongguan. The fourth site is in Minhang.

Cooperative Strategies

Clearly, Gillette has made wise partnership choices. It has been able to claim more than 50 percent of the market in Shenyang, which has a population of 4.5 million. By partnering with the Shanghai Razor Blade Company, Gillette now controls over about 90 percent of China's $51 million razor-blade market.

Gillette chose the Shanghai Razor Blade Factory as a partner because it was the largest and most well respected razor blade company in China and therefore had the capabilities needed to succeed in Gillette's target market. It already controlled over 75 percent of China's razor blade market.

Apparently, SRBF would complement Gillette's financial, technological, and international strengths with a strong sales force, an established network of government contacts, and a respected, trusted, and easily recognized brand name. While SRBF did have the government connections Gillette sought, its sales network turned out to be insufficient. Gillette was surprised to find out that its prospective partner's sales division consisted of only thirteen people. Considerable resources have since been invested to build Gillette Shanghai's sales force to 140 personnel in order to develop an adequate distribution infrastructure.

Both companies seem to have compatible goals. Gillette saw SRBF as a way to get into the Chinese market with a firm that already had a huge market share. SRBF saw Gillette as a way to expand its reach into neighboring countries through exports while gaining access to Gillette's knowledge and superior technology.

Gillette runs the risk of disadvantages as well as to gain advantages because of its 70 percent stake in the joint venture with SRBF. One disadvantage is the risk it runs if the joint venture becomes unprofitable or fails. Gillette stands to lose much more financially than does its partner. Furthermore, the integrity of Gillette leadership would then be called into question, which could lead to a possible loss of respect throughout the international business community.

On the other hand, Gillette will profit substantially more than the Shanghai Razor Blade Factory if the venture is a success. Furthermore, Gillette as controlling partner has the final say concerning most business operations.

Global Integration

The Gillette Company uses a global strategy which maximizes economies of scale. It enforces highly centralized production and marketing standards. All units in various countries are under the control of corporate headquarters which focuses on producing standardized products suitable for a variety of markets while implementing a global marketing plan. One advantage of the global strategy is ease in making administrative decisions concerning manufacturing and marketing strategies at both the local and international levels. Another advantage is that regional managers do not need to provide much input. Centralization sometimes leads to less contact with regional consumers, however. When products are standardized, they do not always fit customer preferences. Nevertheless, some regional customization has been necessary. For example, the names of products are translated into different languages.

The company invests a large amount in promoting the same products worldwide. It spent $60 million marketing the Duracell Ultra battery globally. Its newest razor, the Mach3, is backed by a $300 million global marketing budget.

Four operating groups under Gillette headquarters are responsible for manufacturing, marketing, and research and development. These are the Gillette North Atlantic Group, the International Group, the Duracell North Atlantic Group, and the Diversified Group. Each group includes an executive vice president and other vice presidents in charge of different divisions.

The Gillette North Atlantic Group, created in 1988, includes the European Division and North American Division. It is responsible for manufacture, distribution, and materials management for blade, razor, and toiletry products in North America and Europe. The International Group covers Latin America, Africa, the Middle East, Eastern Europe, and the Asia-Pacific region. It produces and markets blades, razors, toiletries, stationery, and batteries throughout these areas. The Duracell North Atlantic Group is located in Bethel, Connecticut. It also contains European and American divisions. Each of them manufactures and markets the batteries for these regions. This group also includes Manufacturing and Technical Operations, New Products and Technology, and Commercial and Operations sections which manage product development and maintain technological supremacy.

Finally, the Diversified Group consists of three businesses divisions: Braun, Oral-B, and the North Atlantic Stationery Products Group. Braun and Oral-B are organized on a worldwide product line basis. Braun is responsible for manufacturing and promoting electric hair removal products and other small electrical personal care appliances. Oral-B produces and sells oral care products. The North Atlantic Stationery Products Group manufactures and markets stationery for North America and Europe. Other departments include the Board of Management, Business Management, Area Group Sales, and others which make sure operations and research and development for each product line runs smoothly.

As a global corporation, Gillette has to face cultural differences throughout the world. It therefore pursues ways to integrate its corporate culture with local business norms. It devotes some resources to studying diverse cultural backgrounds and measuring people's cultural values. Solving cultural differences is partly achieved by effective human resources management. For example, in China old workers do not listen to young managers. Age of employees therefore had to be taken into consideration during the hiring process. Gillette also had to learn how to establish *guanxi* with both the Chinese government and its own workers in order to maintain harmonious working relationships.

Gillette's marketing strategy includes using a mix of television, radio, print, billboard, and Internet advertisements. New products are first promoted in western countries before expanding globally. Gillette's central slogan is providing products that are "The best a man can get."

Conclusion

Gillette's success as a global corporation can be attributed to the beneficial acquisition of other companies and continuing commitment to innovation. It continually produces new products that show significant improvement over old ones.

Gillette could put more attention into its operations in China. It should increase its investment in advanced technology and manufacturing equipment that will raise its standards in China. Its managers also need to build better *guanxi* networks which can be achieved by studying more about cultural differences and sending more expatriates to China. Advertising should be extended to more regions until Gillette's ideas about personal hygiene are spread all over China and its products are in ever increasing demand.

8. NESTLÉ IN CHINA

Company Introduction

Henri Nestlé founded the Nestlé corporation in Vevey, Switzerland in the mid-1860s. Henri Nestlé was a trained pharmacist who experimented on developing an alternative source of infant nutrition for mothers who were unable to breast feed. His successful experiments resulted in condensed milk. This soon led to a fierce rivalry between Nestlé and the Anglo-Swiss Condensed Milk Company which lasted for nearly four decades before they merged in 1905.

The Nestlé company began producing chocolate candies after Henri Nestlé's neighbor, Daniel Peter, figured out how to combine milk and cocoa powder successfully. Nestlé merged in 1929 with Peter-Cailler-Kohler Chocolates Suisses. In 1947, Nestlé merged with the Alimentana company, due to Julius Maggi's creation of a food product that used legumes that were quick to prepare and easy to digest. By the end of World War One, Nestlé Company's world production had more than doubled. The demand for dairy products after the war initially helped Nestlé grow, but it suffered its first loss when consumers switched back to fresh milk as it became available again.

The end of World War Two forced Nestlé to transfer many of its offices to Connecticut in the United States to avoid disaster if neutral Switzerland were targetted for any reason. The expansion to other countries such as Latin America in addition to its existing factories in France, England, Australia, Germany, and Spain allowed Nestlé to acquire other foreign businesses.

Starting in the early 1970s, Nestlé began a dynamic period of mergers and acquisitions. It merged with Ursina-Franck in 1971 and acquired Carnation in 1985, Buitoni-Perugina and Rowntree in 1988, and Perrier in 1992, increasing its global presence further. The last major acquisitions occurred in 1998. These acquisitions have allowed Nestlé to survive despite economic difficulties in some parts of the world.

Today, Nestlé is Switzerland's largest industrial company. It is considered the world leader in the food industry, which it has accomplished through selling such globally important products as coffee and bottled water, as well as acquiring many other companies. Nestlé's core products include Beverages, Milk Products, Nutrition, Ice Cream, Prepared Dishes and Cooking Aids, Chocolate and Confectionery, and Pharmaceuticals. Nestlé markets its products in different fields under the following main brandnames: Taster's Choice soluble coffee products; mineral waters such as Calistoga; Coffee-mate coffee creamers; Alcon eye-care products; and L'Oreal cosmetics.

Nestlé currently has a total workforce of 225,808 employees working in 495 factories worldwide. It sells over 8,500 different products in more than 70 countries. Nestlé is traded publicly with the NESN ticker. The current Chairman of the Board is Helmut O. Maucher, who was also the Chief Executive Officer until 1997. The current CEO is Peter Brabeck-Letmathe, a fifty-four year old Austrian who was previously the executive vice-president in charge of marketing at Nestlé.

Nestlé's international markets include Africa, the Asia/Pacific region, Europe, Oceania, and North/South America. Its major markets in Europe are Spain, Germany, Switzerland, Sweden, England, France, and Italy. Australia and New Zealand are its most significant Oceania markets. The United States, Chile, Brazil, Ecuador, and Canada make up the North/South American region, while Japan, Taiwan, Hong Kong, Vietnam, the Philippines, and China are included in its Asia/Pacific markets.

Nestlé focuses mostly on long-range strategies while making sure that its short-term survival is not in jeopardy. Nestlé's long-term goal is to provide food and nutrition to an ever-growing global population, especially in the new millennium. Nestlé expects the population to double by the year 2100. Nestlé focuses on achieving its goal by intensifying research, striving for innovation, and improving product quality.

One curious facet of Nestlé's management is that the company does not have a mission statement. It seems that such a statement would be too general to apply throughout such a huge company with so many diverse employees or it would be too specific to be relevant to all the countries within which it does business. Thus, a mission statement that was appropriate to operating in China would be inapplicable in the United States. Instead of a mission statement, Nestlé has installed general guidelines.

Nestlé simultaneously enforces uniformity of principles, policies, rules of conduct, and strategies along with diversification into various areas of expertise. The company principles are flexibility and simplicity, especially when it comes to management style and responsibility. Although Nestlé respects the customs and beliefs of different nationalities, it applies its general principles to all of its employees, regardless of country of origin. These include having a positive attitude towards work and doing business pragmatically. Nestlé wants its employees to have a realistic and open-minded approach to their daily business activities. A personal style of management in an atmosphere of mutual trust and modesty is strongly encouraged.

Nestlé demonstrates a principle of decentralization by not considering its Swiss headquarters as the center of the Nestlé universe. Each of its headquarters in various countries is treated fairly, based on the local region's situation and resources. Nestlé regards its employees, people, and products as being of more importance than systems. It works to ensure that each of its products is convenient, of high quality, provides variety, and sells at a reasonable price. Its Research and Development departments look for ways to develop products that are both helpful for people and not harmful to the environment. Nestlé is a strong supporter of environmental protection.

Restructuring Issues

Nestlé's current restructuring plans do not include any major acquisitions. According to Mario Corti, Nestlé's Chief Financial Officer, there are no more interesting candidates of the size and potential to attract Nestlé's interest. Anti-trust legislation has also made such big deals more difficult, especially in Europe and the U.S. Instead, its long-term thinking and continuity help it focus on new opportunities. The Nestlé Company decided to restructure its food business in 1995. It abandoned canning and dropped many of its products from the Crosse & Blackwell brand, which include tomato ketchup, salad dressing, baked beans, pasta, and canned soups. The food division was then divided up under three managers: one for frozen food, one for chilled food, and another for ambient food. The whole purpose for this restructuring was to improve efficiency.

Another major restructuring event has to do with information technology. It plans to use ERP or Enterprise Resource Planning technology to link retailers with the company. This will enable Nestlé to respond more quickly and accurately to changing market demands and customer needs, to make appropriate promotions, and cut administration and inventory costs. For the first time in the history of the company, Nestlé's technology will play an important global role. As recently as 1992, Nestlé only had Email in its Swiss headquarters and major offices in the U.S. and U.K. Once ERP is implemented, the company expects to serve different regions in a more unified way, realizing economies of scale, and serving its international customers more effectively.

External Environment

The food industry is a perfectly competitive market. From this perspective, barriers to entry are virtually nonexistent. However, entry into the food industry at the level at which Nestlé operates is no easy task. Nestlé is a transnational corporation with manufacturing plants in every continent. The corporation has the ability to transport capital to any emerging market. Many customers and retailers are loyal to and familiar with the Nestlé brand, so access to distribution channels by new entrants can be difficult. For example, before China was classified as an emerging market, Nestlé had already been providing quality products (coffee and noodles) to it and the rest of Asia for nearly 100 years. This relationship with the consumer is a potential barrier to entry for new entrants.

Suppliers do not have strong bargaining power first of all because suppliers of raw materials (foodstuffs and commodities) are numerous and their market is perfectly competitive. For example, there are many wheat, milk, and cocoa producers in the world market. Second, Nestlé and other food manufacturers are significant customers of suppliers of raw materials, which means that the suppliers depend on them for their business. However, suppliers do have some leverage because their raw materials, which contribute to the final product, are critical to the food market. Conceivably, suppliers could integrate forward into the food product market, but in practice they lack the capital requirements (factories and machinery) and the ability to produce a highly differentiated product. Thus, realistically speaking, market suppliers have no power in this regard.

Buyers enjoy considerable bargaining power in the food market. This is because customers purchase a large share of the industry's output. Since consumers are critical to purchasing, they have the power to demand quality and reasonable prices. Again, this power is derived from a perfectly competitive industry and the fact that most products are fairly standardized. Standardization allows consumers to switch from Nestlé products such as Taster's Choice coffee to other brands such as Maxwell House without high switching costs.

Nestlé's products are vulnerable to substitution. Below are some of the substitutes that threaten Nestlé's products.

Nestlé Product	**Substitute**
Nestlé's Quik	Chocolate Milk
Nescafe & Taster's Choice Coffee	Lipton Tea
Libby's Fruit Juice	Soda
Perrier Bottled Water	Tap Water
Nestlé's Baby Milk	Natural Breast Milk
Nestlé's Crunch & Butterfinger Bars	Nabisco's Chips Cookies
Friskies Cat Food	Purina Cat Chow

On a global level, there are little, if any, competitors that rival Nestlé's extensive operations and its ability to enter emerging markets. On the local level, however, Nestlé is confronted with fierce competition. Nevertheless, Nestlé manages to earn above-average profits. Its global diversification strategy and integration of R&D and nutrition (a rarity in the food industry) are reasons for these high returns.

A transnational company such as Nestlé is faced with an abundance of opportunities. Anywhere there is a demand for fair priced, quality food represents an opportunity for Nestlé. The emerging markets of Asia and the nutritional needs of developing countries present Nestlé with opportunities to exploit cheap labor and raw materials. As Nestlé establishes factories and subsidiaries in different countries, it is faced with threats from the political, economic, socio-cultural, legal-regulatory, and technological arenas, however. Nestlé has converted these threats into opportunities by implementing the principle of decentralization. Again, although Nestlé is registered in Switzerland, it does not consider that country its only center of operations. It delegates operational responsibility to local firms by allowing many of the decisions regarding products and personnel to be made by local managers. As early as 1933, Nestlé entrusted the manufacturing of its products in Japan to an all-Japanese firm. Decentralization, empowerment of employees and executives, and an open-minded approach to the world has enabled the Nestlé company to overcome many of the threats that usually bedevil multinational corporations.

Internal Environment

Technological

Nestlé is unique in the food industry because it has an integrated R&D program that engages in applied and basic research in the fields of human physiology, health, nutrition, and raw materials. Its R&D centers have two main tasks: to create new products and manufacturing processes and to improve those that already exist. These centers play a key role in providing safe, quality products, protecting the environment, and conserving resources.

Environmental concerns are pertinent to any development process. The Nestlé R&D centers ensure that future commercial operations will meet environmentally sound standards. Adding value to industrial residues is one benefit that Nestlé provides. R&D centers also make environmental impact studies for new products and processes and provide decision-making information to management on whether or not to market a new product or introduce or modify a process. Based on the above information, Nestlé's technological capability is a strength.

Organizational

As mentioned earlier, a major feature of Nestlé's organizational structure is decentralization. With decentralization, authority flows horizontally as opposed to being concentrated at the top of the organization. The guidelines Nestlé disseminates (i.e., personal style of management, positive working attitude, atmosphere of mutual trust, open-minded approach to the world market) help maintain this decentralized structure. These minimal guidelines provide Nestlé with the flexibility and strength to adapt to cultural, political, and economic differences that it encounters internationally.

Nestlé actively recruits employees and executives who have talent and international experience. It actively seeks to empower employees by allowing decisions regarding personnel and products to be determined locally.

Financial

Profitability: Nestlé's overall financial environment is strong. Nestle's return on assets (7.3% in 1997) and net profit margin (5.7% in 1997) are well above the industrial averages of 5 percent and 2 percent, respectively. Between 1996 and 1997, Nestlé experienced 11 and 12 percent surges in its return on assets and net profit margins, respectively.

Liquidity: For a company that is financially strong, Nestlé's ability to meet its obligations (its current ratio) is below the industrial average, 1.2 as opposed to 1.8. Moreover, Nestlé's quick ratio indicates that it is heavily dependent on the sale of inventory to meet short-term obligations.

Leverage: In 1997, 55 percent of Nestlé's assets were in the form of debt. This percentage is in the moderate range, slightly below the industrial average of 59 percent. For every capital dollar contributed, Nestlé borrowed 19 cents. This is a moderate and acceptable mix in its capital structure.

For 1997, Nestlé's leverage ratios were as follows:

DOL (the responsiveness of EBIT to a change in sales) = 1.
DFL (the responsiveness of EPS to a change in EBIT) = 0.75
DCL (the responsiveness of EPS to a change in sales) = 0.75

Asset Management: Between 1996 and 1997, Nestlé increased its effective use of inventory by 12 percent, as indicated by its inventory turnover ratio. In 1997, it took Nestle 21 days to sell its finished goods, as opposed to 24 days in 1996. Moreover, the time it takes for Nestlé to move inventory out the door is above the industrial average of 32 days.

Nestlé has also been effective in utilizing its plants and equipment. Its fixed asset turnover ratio indicates that it is able to extract $2.41 in sales from every dollar invested in plants and equipment. This ratio is far superior to the industrial average of $1.50.

Corporate-Level Strategy

Why China?

Nestlé's primary objectives in this area are to achieve both a global presence and local responsiveness. When Nestlé selected China for operations, it would have considered the following factors:

Nestlé is very meticulous in selecting raw materials for its products. Most of the countries where Nestlé operates are rich in quality natural resources. Nestlé's products are mostly labor intensive. Many of the countries that Nestlé selects have large labor pools, which enables Nestlé to produce its products at lower costs than its competitors. Many host governments also support Nestlé's operations because of its principle of decentralization. China has these factor endowments available.

When a company selects a country in which to start operations, the issue of demand must be addressed. With the world's largest population and a universal need for quality food products, China is clearly an acceptable selection.

Due to Nestlé's principles of decentralization and entrustment of operations to local subsidiaries, the surrounding industries and institutions that develop management and science have to be strong. China's university system (Beijing University, China Europe International Business School, and other institutions) are adequate for producing managers and scientists to help Nestlé compete in China.

Nestlé's strategy of acquisition, its decentralized structure, and development of human resources generate a competitive advantage against rivals in the countries it selects. In China during 1997, Nestlé increased its participation in the Nestlé Dairy Farm from 51 to 100 percent and acquired one of its rivals, Shanghai Fuller Foods. Nestlé's decentralized structure enables local management to react swiftly to changes in trends, tastes, and prices of products in the Chinese market. A more rigid centralized structure is not capable of taking into account specific characteristics of each country's food market. Nestlé's excellent technical training program, favorable promotions, and development of long-term careers are further factors that attract quality employees to Nestlé, further increasing Nestlé's competitive advantage.

Product Diversification

Nestlé is practicing related product diversity as indicated by their eight SBUs: Beverages, Chocolates, Prepared dishes, Ice cream, Milk products, Bottled water, Instant coffee, and Performance nutrition. This diversity increases Nestlé's economies of scale by enabling it to produce different products using the same plants and equipment.

Nestlé's research has led to the introduction of new and improved products in the fields of infant and clinical nutrition. Nestlé was the first to introduce a dietary product (Nidal) designed for infants who experience slight regurgitation. In 1998, Nestlé introduced an oral supplement (Clinutren) for hospitalized patients, combining micro- and macro-nutrients to remedy or prevent malnutrition. In Europe, Nestlé introduced an innovative pizza (Findus) with a self-rising crust that mimics authentic pizzeria quality. In France, Nestlé introduced the first local fish specialty that can be prepared in the microwave.

Nestlé has had a presence in Asia since 1907 when it built warehouses in Singapore, Hong Kong, and Bombay to supply the rapidly growing Asian markets. Naturally, it was only a matter of time before Nestlé would begin production in Asia, although sales from the region only account for 2 percent of total sales. China was a reasonable choice because some of Nestlé's infrastructure was already in place and many of its brand names had been familiar to Chinese customers for nearly a century.

Entry Strategies

Entry Mode

Nestlé entered the Chinese market just after China started its unprecedented economic reform in the 1980s. In 1978, Nestlé saw the vast potential for growth offered by China's enormous market size. Nestlé had already opened in major international sites all over

Asia and Europe, but it found that opening up in China was a whole different process. Nestlé officials from Switzerland created plans and flew over to China several times to meet with the government of the Heilongjiang Province to negotiate a contract. It took over 12 years of hard work, dedication, and weathering rejections before the contract was finalized in 1987 and the first Nestlé factory began to be built.

By the 1990s, Nestlé was enjoying huge success in the country. To date, Nestlé has 7 joint ventures and 4 wholly owned enterprises in mainland China and 2 enterprises in Hong Kong. Nestlé produces milk, milk products, culinary liquids, confectionery, coffee products, and even ice cream in China. In 1990 alone, one of its factories produced 316 tons of powdered milk and infant formula. Nestlé budgeted $260 million in 1994 for investments in China over the next three years. Its average sales growth has been about 20 percent a year. Nestlé sells about $200 million worth of products annually in China and will hit the $700 million mark by 2000.

Nestlé (China) Ltd. is Nestlé's head office. It provides common managerial services to all Nestlé's operating factories and markets in China. Nestlé opened its first joint venture factory in China on July 7th, 1990. The venture, Nestlé Shuangcheng Ltd., involved a partnership with the Municipality of Shuangcheng (15.5 percent share) and the Chinese Society for Development and Investment in Beijing (20.5 percent share). Nestlé is the major shareholder with 64 percent. The five member board includes 2 people from the Chinese partners and 3 from Nestlé. Nestlé chooses the managing directors for all sectors of the company. Duration of the joint venture is initially for 15 years and continuation will be considered.

Timing and Location

Nestlé is considered one of the earliest Western investors in the milk product industry in China. It became dominant after all its contracts were settled and factories built. When it started negotiations in 1979, it was considered good timing because China wanted to gain Western technology and re-establish a balance of payments by exporting more products. China's drive to modernize was in part a response against the encroaching 'Asian Dragons' such as Japan. China also wanted Westerners to help boost milk production in the region. Nestlé's main goal was to expand and tap China's consumer base of over one billion people.

Nestlé did not have much of a choice in selecting the location of its new factories, since the Chinese government made most of these decisions. The first site that was chosen was Taikang, north of Harbin. However, the area was isolated and the climate bad for milk production. Therefore, Shuangcheng County, south of Harbin, was chosen because of its better climate, highway connections, and farmland.

Cooperative Strategies

The Chinese government chose Nestlé's joint venture partners, but the partnership has worked well because of complementary skills and capabilities and similar levels of commitment and compatible goals.

China wanted Nestlé's technological equipment in order to increase milk production and lengthen the quality and freshness of the milk produced. At that time, China did not have refrigerators or even ice boxes to preserve quality. Nestlé has the technology, the knowledge, and the know-how to make milk production run productively and efficiently. Nestlé's factories are very clean and workers and managers have good relations. In return, the Chinese government has the connections and the power to expand Nestlé throughout China.

All three partners are committed to the joint venture because they all want to achieve similar goals and benefit from the operation. Both Nestlé and the Chinese government believed that they could cooperate to build a milk factory which would allow them to improve production, expand throughout China, and export products to Asia.

The Chinese companies wanted new refrigerators to keep milk in. They therefore supplied the materials and tools so that Nestlé engineers could help them build refrigerators to put in selected towns and provinces to which milk was going to be delivered.

Nestlé invested the most in this joint venture, as noted above. Nestlé will therefore have the majority share of profit, but also must deal with a higher portion of expenses.

The Municipality of Shuangcheng, one of Nestlé's Chinese partners, was basically a large milk farm. The governmental partner, CSDI (Chinese Society for Development and Investment in Beijing), fixes the prices for all Nestlé factories, from the price of fresh milk to the prices of the finished products.

Operational Strategies

Nestlé and CSDI must establish three special funds during operations in China: a reserve fund, an enterprise expansion fund, and an incentive and welfare fund for personnel. Together, the funds total around 10 to 15 percent of profits. These are being saved for future emergencies and other developments.

Nestlé's philosophy in any country is to prepare local executives to take over from Nestlé's expatriate staff. Nestlé therefore gives appropriate professional training to ensure that its standards for quality are met at all levels.

Salaries are set depending on professional qualifications, years of experience, and degree of responsibility of Nestlé employees. The joint venture commonly pays its employees 20 percent higher salaries than they would get at state-run firms. Besides base salaries, they also have major benefits, including payment of 90 percent of medical costs, 80 percent of dental costs, and a 75 percent contribution to a pension fund for social security, education, retirement, and so on.

Since Nestlé does not know how the Chinese people respond to promotions or advertisements, marketing of Nestlé products is being done by Chinese specialists in each province.

Conclusions

Nestlé's global presence has certainly impacted many lives. Its strategic management style proves that geographic and product diversification are both vital to company growth. Its early goal of having a positive impact on the nutrition of mothers and infants has extended to benefit everyone through diversified products such as bottled water and eye solutions.

Nestlé's management style further allows the company to effectively and efficiently apply its general principles and guidelines across many international regions. The company also performs excellently by meticulously dealing with governmental and corporate entities.

Nestlé's growth will undoubtedly continue. Although the company may encounter economic hardship in one country, its corporate-level strategy of geographic and product diversity prevents it from huge suffering due to any economic crisis. Its business-level strategy of continuous innovation firmly solidifies its competitive strategy.

Bibliography

Anderson, C. R. and Zeithaml, C. P. (1984). Stages of the Product Life Cycle, Business Strategy, and Business Performance. *Academy of Management Journal*, Vol. 27, pp. 5-24.

Barney, J. (1997). *Gaining and sustaining competitive advantage*. New York: Addison-Wesley.

Bass, F. M., Cattin, P. and Wittink, D. R. (1978). Firm Effects and Industry Effects in the Analysis of Market Structure and Profitability. *Journal of Marketing Research*, Vol. 15, pp. 3-10.

Beamish, P. W. (1993). The Characteristics of Joint Ventures in the People's Republic of China. *Journal of International Marketing*, Vol. 1, pp. 29-48.

Bettis, R. A. (1981). Performance Differences in Related and Unrelated Diversified Firms. *Strategic Management Journal*, Vol. 2, pp. 379-393.

Brewer, T. L. (1993). Government Policies, Market Imperfections, and Foreign Direct Investment. *Journal of International Business Studies*, Vol. 24, 101-120.

Buckley, P. J. and Casson, M. (1985). *The Economic Theory of the Multinational Enterprise*. London: The MacMillan Press.

Buckley, P. J. and Casson, M. (1988). The Theory of Cooperation in International Business. In Contractor, F and Lorange, P. (eds.), *Cooperative Strategies in International Business*, pp. 31-34, Lexington, Mass.: Lexington Books.

Byrd, W. A. (1992). *Chinese Industrial Firms Under Reform*. Oxford: Oxford University Press.

Byrd, W. A. and Lin Q. (1989). *China's rural industry: structure, development, and reform*. New York: Oxford University Press.

Casson, M. and Zheng, R. (1991). 'Western Joint Ventures in China', *Journal of International Development*, vol. 3, pp. 293-323.

Caves, R. E. 1971. International corporation: The industrial economies of foreign investment. *Economica*, 38: 1-27.

Caves, R. E. and Mehra, K. (1986). Entry of Foreign Multinationals Into U.S. Manufacturing Industries. In Porter, M. E. (eds.), *Competition in Global Industries*, Harvard Business School Press, Boston, MA, 1986.

Child, J. (1994). *Management in China During the Age of Reform.* Cambridge, England: Cambridge University Press.

Contractor, F. J. and Lorange, P. (1988). The Strategy and Economic Basis for Cooperative Venture. In Contractor, F. and Lorange, P. (eds.), *Cooperative Strategies in International Business.* Lexington, Mass.: Lexington Books, 1988.

Davidson, W.H. (1987). 'Creating and Managing Joint Ventures in China', *California Management Review*, vol. 29, pp. 77-94.

Davidson, W. H. (1980). The Location of Foreign Direct Investment Activity: Country Characteristics and Experience Effects. *Journal of International Business Studies*, Vol. 12, pp. 9-22.

Doz, Y. L. and Prahalad, C. K. (1991). Managing DMNCs: A Search for a New Paradigm. *Strategic Management Journal*, Vol. 12, pp. 145-164.

Dunning, J. H. (1979). Explaining Changing Patterns of International Production: In Defense of the Eclectic Theory. *Oxford Bulletin of Economics and Statistics*, Vol. 41, pp. 269-296.

Geringer, J. M., Beamish, P. W. and da Costa, R. C. (1989). Diversification strategy and internationalization: Implications for MNE performance. *Strategic Management Journal*, 10: 109-119.

Ghoshal, S. (1987). Global Strategy: An Organizing Framework. *Strategic Management Journal*, Vol. 8, pp. 425-440.

Hall, M. and Weiss, L. (1967). Firm Size and Profitability. *The Review of Economics and Statistics*, Vol. 49, pp. 319-331.

Hofer, C. W. (1975). Towards a Contingency Theory of Business Strategy. *Academy of Management Journal*, Vol. 18, pp. 784-810.

Hymer, S. H. (1976). *The International Operations of National Firms: A Study of Direct Foreign Investment*, Cambridge, MA: MIT Press.

Jefferson, G. H., Rawski, T. G. and Zheng, Y. (1992). Growth, Efficiency and Convergence in China's State and Collective Industry. *Economic Development & Cultural Change*, Vol. 40, pp. 239-266.

Jefferson, G. H. and Rawski, T. G. (1993). *A Theory of Economic Reform*, University of Pittsburgh, Department of Economics, Working Paper No. 273.

Jenkins, R. (1991). The Impact of Foreign Investment on Less Developed Countries: Cross-Section Analysis Versus Industry Studies. In P. J. Buckley and J. Clegg (eds.), *Multinational Enterprises in Less Developed Countries*, pp. 111-130. MacMillian, London.

Jia, L. (1991). A Quantitative Analysis of Chinese Industrial Structure and Technological Change: Production Functions for Aggregate Industry, Sectorial Industries and Small Scale Industry. *Applied Economics*, Vol. 23, pp. 1733-1740.

Kelley, L. and Luo, Y. (1998). *China 2000: Emerging Business Issues*, Thousand Oaks, CA: Sage.

Kim, W. C., Hwang, P. and Burgers, W. P. (1993). Multinationals' diversification and the risk-return trade-off. *Strategic Management Journal*, 14: 275-286.

Lawrence, P. R. and Lorsch, J. (1967). *Organization and Environment.* Cambridge, MA: Harvard University Press.

Luo, Y. (2000). *Guanxi and business.* New York: World Scientific.

Luo, Y. (1999). *Entry and cooperative strategies in international business expansion.* Westport, CT: Quorum.

Luo, Y. (1999). Time-based experience and international expansion: The case of an emerging economy. *Journal of Management Studies*, 36(4): 505-534.

Luo, Y. (1999). Structure-performance relationships in the transitional economy context: An empirical study of the multinational alliances in the P. R. China. *Journal of Business Research*, 46(1): 15-30.

Luo, Y. (1998). Timing of investment and international expansion performance in China. *Journal of International Business Studies*, 29(2): 391-408.

Luo, Y. (1998). *International Investment Strategies in the People's Republic of China*, Aldershot, UK: Ashgate.

Luo, Y. (1998). Joint venture success in China: How should we select a good partner? *Journal of World Business*, 33(2):145-166.

Luo, Y. (1997). Partner selection and venturing success: The case of joint ventures in China. *Organization Science*, 8(6): 648-662.

Luo, Y. (1997). Pioneering in China: Risks and Benefits. *Long Range Planning*, 30(5): 768-776.

Luo, Y. (1997). Industry attractiveness, firm competence, and international investment performance in a transitional economy. *Bulletin of Economic Research*, 49(3): 1-10.

Luo, Y. (1995). Business Strategy, Market Structure, and Performance of International Joint Ventures: The Case of Joint Ventures in China. *Management International Review*, Vol. 35, pp. 241-264.

Luo, Y. and M. W. Peng. (1999). Learning to compete in a transition economy: Experience, environment, and performance. *Journal of International Business Studies*, 30(2): 269-296.

Luo, Y. and J. J. Tan. (1997). How much does industry structure matter on foreign direct investment in China. *International Business Review*, 6(2): 1-23.

Kogut, B. and Singh, H. (1988). Entering U.S. by Joint Venture: Competitive Rivalry and Industry Structure. In Contractor, F. and Lorange, P. (eds.), *Cooperative Strategies in International Business*. Lexington, Mass.: Lexington Books.

Mitchell, W., Shaver, J. M. and Yeung, B. (1993). Performance Following Changes of International Presence in Domestic and Transition Industries. *Journal of International Business Studies*, Vol. 24, pp. 647-669.

National Council For U.S.-China Trade, *Special Report on U.S. Investment in China*, Washington, D.C.: Department of Commerce, 1991.

Naughton, B. (1994). *Growing Out of the Plan: Chinese Economic Reform, 1878-1993*. New York: Cambridge University Press.

Nee, V. (1992). Organizational Dynamics of Market Transition: Hybrid Forms, Property Rights, and Mixed Economy in China. *Administrative Science Quarterly*, Vol. 37, pp. 1-27.

Nolan, P. (1996). Large Firms and Industrial Reforms in Former Planned Economies: The Case of China. *Cambridge Journal of Economics*, Vol. 20, pp. 1-29.

Osland, G.E. and Cavusgil, S.T. (1996). 'Performance Issues in U.S.-China Joint Ventures', *California Management Review*, vol. 38, pp. 106-130.

Perkins, D. (1994). Completing China's Move to the Market. *Journal of Economic Perspective*, Vol. 8, No. 2, pp. 23-46.

Phillips, A. (1976). A Critique of Empirical Studies of Relations Between Market Structure and Profitability. *Journal of Industrial Economics*, Vol. 24, pp. 241-249.

Porter, M. E. (1980). *Competitive Advantage*. New York: Free Press.

Porter, M. E. (1986). *Competition in Global Industries*. Boston, Mass.: Harvard Business School Press.

Porter, M. E. (1991). Towards a dynamic theory of strategy. *Strategic Management Journal*, 12: 95-117.

Prahalad, C. K. and Hamel, G. (1990). The Core Competence of the Corporation. *Harvard Business Review*, Vol. 90, pp. 79-91.

Rawski, T. G. (1994). Chinese Industrial Reform: Accomplishments, Prospects, and Implications. *American Economic Review*, Vol. 84, pp. 271-275.

Roman, Z. (1986). Competition and Industrial Organization in the Centrally Planned Economies. In J. Stiglitz and G. F. Mathewson, *New Developments in the Analysis of Market Structure*. MacMillan Press, London.

Rumelt, R. P. (1991). How much does industry matter?. *Strategic Management Journal*, 12: 167-185.

Scherer, F. M. and Ross, D. (1990). *Industrial Market Structure and Economic Performance*, Third Edition, Houghton Mifflin Company, Boston.

Shan, W. (1991). Environmental Risks and Joint Venture Sharing Arrangements. *Journal of International Business Studies*, Vol. 22, pp. 555-578.

Shaw, S. M. and Meier, J. (1993). 'Second Generation MNCs in China', *The McKinsey Quarterly*, vol. 4, pp. 3-16.

Shenkar, O. (1990). International Joint Ventures's Problems in China: Risks and Remedies. *Long Range Planning*, Vol. 23, pp. 82-90.

Su, N. (1993). China's Industrial Policy During Economic System Transformation. Paper delivered to an International Conference on Macroeconomic Management, Dalian China.

Tallman, S. and Li, J. (1996). Effects of international diversity and product diversity on the performance of multinational firms. *Academy of Management Journal*, 39: 179-196.

Teece, D. J. (1985). Multinational Enterprises, Internal Governance, and Industrial Organization. *American Economic Review, Papers and Proceedings*, Vol. 75, pp. 233-238.

Teece, D. J., Pisano, G. & Shuen, A. (1991). Dynamic capabilities and strategic management. Working paper, University of California at Berkeley.

World Bank (1998). *China 2020: China Engaged*, Washington, D.C.: The World Bank.

World Bank (1999). *Global Economic Prospects and the Developing Countries*, Washington, D.C.: The World Bank.

World Bank (1996). *The Chinese Economy: Fighting Inflation, Deepening Reforms*, Washington, D.C.: The World Bank.

World Bank (1995). *China: Reform of State-Owned Enterprises*, Washington, D.C.: China and Mongolia Department, World Bank.

Worm, V. (1997). *Vikings and Mandarins: Sino-Scandinavian Business Cooperation in Cross-Cultural Settings*. Copenhagen: Copenhagen Business School Press.

Willmore, L. (1994). Determinants of Industrial Structure: A Brazilian Case Study. In J. H. Dunning (eds.), *Transnational Corporations: Market Structure and Industrial Performance*. The United Nations Library on Transnational Corporations, Vol. 15, pp. 96-129.

Yang, D. L. (1995). From Command to Guidance: China's Turn to New Industrial Policies. *Journal of Asian Business*, Vol. 11(2), pp. 33-66.

Yip, G. S. (1995). *Total global strategy: Managing for worldwide competitive advantage*. Englewood Cliffs, NJ: Prentice Hall.

About the Author

Dr. Luo (Ph.D, Temple University) is Associate Professor of international business strategy and recipient of Distinguished Professorship Award at the Department of Management, University of Hawaii. As a Dennis Ching Teaching Excellence Award (1997) and CBA Teaching Excellence Award (1999) recipient, he teaches strategic management, multinational management, international business, Chinese business, among others, at the undergraduate and MBA levels. His research interests are in the area of global strategy, international expansion, and Chinese management. As the recipient of Regents' Medal for Excellence in Research at UH (1999), the first awardee ever in the history of CBA, Prof. Luo has published eight books (including those in press) and more than sixty journal articles. He is the author of *International Joint Ventures: Theory and Practice* (with A. Yan), *Entering China Today: Choices and Challenges*, *Strategy, Structure, and Performance of MNCs: Comparing Asian and Western Investors in China*, *Guanxi and Business*, *Partnering with Chinese Firms: Lessons for International Managers*, *Entry and Cooperative Strategies in International Business Expansion*, and *International Investment Strategies in the People's Republic of China*. His recent papers appeared in such journals as *Academy of Management Journal, Journal of International Business Studies, Organization Science, Journal of Management Studies, Journal of International Management, Journal of World Business, Journal of Business Research, Management International Review, International Business Review, Long Range Planning, Journal of Small Business Management, Asia-Pacific Journal of Management,* among others. Before coming to the United States, Dr. Luo served as a provincial official in China in charge of international business for six years. Dr. Luo is a consultant of several transnational corporations.

Index